RADICAL PERSPECTIVES ON THE RISE OF FASCISM IN GERMANY, 1919–1945

edited by

Michael N. Dobkov

Monthly Review Press
New York

Library of Congress Cataloging-in-Publication Data
Radical perspectives on the rise of Fascism in Germany, 1919 to 1945 /
    edited by Michael N. Dobkowski and Isidor Wallimann.
        p. cm.
    Bibliography: p.
    Includes index.
    ISBN 0-85345-757-3.   ISBN 0-85345-758-1 (pbk.)
    1. Germany—Politics and government—1918–1933.   2. Germany-
-Politics and government—1933–1945.   3. National socialism.
    I. Dobkowski, Michael N.   II. Wallimann, Isidor, 1944–
DD240.R25 1988
943.085—dc19   88-22506
                                                                                    CIP

Monthly Review Press
122 West 27th Street
New York, N.Y. 10001

Manufactured in the United States of America

10   9   8   7   6   5   4   3   2   1

To the Voices of Resistance

Contents

7

Acknowledgments

The two of us come to the study of German fascism from different disciplines and from different sides of the Atlantic Ocean. That we could produce this joint effort is a tribute to the respect we have for each other, both personally and professionally, and to our commitment to multidisciplinary work and interchange.

We wish to thank colleagues in our respective institutions and other friends and students who have provided an intellectual environment that was conducive to productive work. We are particularly grateful to the contributors for the prompt submission of their essays and the quality of their work. To those who offered editorial advice and assistance we give special thanks. We would also like to express our appreciation to Martha Baker for her excellent translation of Reinhard Kühnl's essay. We benefited from several anonymous reviewers whose comments helped make this a better book and from the encouragement received from colleagues in the field, particularly Renate Bridenthal. We are, of course, responsible for any errors that remain.

We would like to offer special thanks to Gary Thompson of the Hobart and William Smith Colleges Library staff for his assistance. A special acknowledgment goes to Susan Lowes, editor of Monthly Review Press, who gave us much support and to Karen Judd, the editor who nursed this project along in its final stages.

Credit for typing goes to Ann Hovey, Debbi Smith, and Pati Mattice.

As always, thanks to Karen Gabe Dobkowski for all her assistance and encouragement and to Jessica, Jonathan, and Tamar for the pleasures of childhood diversions.

Acronyms

ADGB	German Trade Union Federation
AFA	Anti-Fascist Action Committee
AVAVG	Employment Facilitation and Unemployment Insurance Law
BBB	Bavarian Peasant Association
BVP	Bavarian People's party
CNBLP	Christian National Peasants and Rural People's party
CDU	Christian Democratic Union
CSU	Christian Social Union
DDP	German Democratic party
DHP	German Hanoverian party
DNVP	German National People's party
DVP	German People's party
IKL	Patriotic National Movement
KPD	German Communist party
KPD(O)	Germany Communist party—Opposition
MSPD	Majority Social Democratic Party
NSBO	National Socialist Organization of Industrial Cells
NSDAP	National Socialist German Workers party
PSI	Italian Socialist party
RDI	League of German Industry
RLB	National Rural League
SA	Sturmabteilung
SAP	Socialist Workers' party
SED	Socialist Unity party
SPD	Social Democratic party of Germany
SS	Schutzstaffel
USPD	Independent Social Democratic party
VVN	Association of Persons Persecuted During the Nazi Regime
Zentrum	Catholic Center party

Introduction

Michael N. Dobkowski and Isidor Wallimann

The rise of National Socialism in Germany and the resulting Holocaust has proven to be one of the most engaging subjects of historical reflection. For the most part, scholars have focused on the more traditional questions of Hitler, political culture, the place of ideology and anti-Semitism, the strategy of dominating Europe, the Nazi movement, or the functioning of the regime itself, especially its bureaucratic mechanisms. In more recent years, scholars in both Europe and the United States have focused on Nazism's attitudes toward women and gender and argued that they were second only to racism in structuring the new German society and defining its enemies. These are of course important issues that require attention in order to explain the rise of German fascism and its genocidal project. However, they will at best render only partial explanations and possibly even distorted ones because they lack, we think, an adequate appreciation of the structural—that is, economic, class, and power—dimensions that largely led to' the collapse of the Weimar Republic and the successful rise to power of the Nazi party. It is this area and approach that we are highlighting in this volume. Rather than presenting the Weimar Republic as a failed democracy, flawed in both its political culture and its democratic institutional tradition, and undermined by an economic collapse, the emphasis here will be on seeing it as a developed capitalist society with distinct structural deficiencies and contradictions that weakened it from the outset.

There is, of course, a relatively small but important and growing number of scholars who are working in Marxist and/or other structural traditions in both Europe and North America in an effort to better understand the rise of German fascism, and we collected and introduced a number of their works in our 1983 volume *Towards the Holocaust: The Social and Economic Collapse of the Weimar Republic*. Several of the principal contributors to that volume, such as Dietmar Petzina, John Nagle, Reinhard Kühnl, Ulrike Hoerster-Phillips, and Richard Geary, described "a republic fatally flawed at the outset by a failure to effect structural changes which would have secured a democratic order—of a republic that consequently was undermined because the bourgeois elements which should have defended it would not do so, and the working-class and minority group elements which tried to defend it, could not do so."[1]

Previously and since the argument has been advanced by David Abraham's important book, *The Collapse of the Weimar Republic: Political Economy and Crisis,* which maintained that important segments of the economic and political elites of the Weimar period, in their search to overcome their own structural and economic and political problems, passed political and economic power to individuals who eventually helped doom the Weimar Republic by transferring power to the Nazis.[2] When it was first published, this book occasioned great controversy concerning both its thesis and its methodological scholarship. Abraham has admitted that in places the first edition contained errors in footnoting, translating, and paraphrasing. While he has apologized for these, and has corrected them in the second edition, he has also resolutely denied the accusations of fraud and fabrication.

The charges against Abraham, however, far transcend the alleged carelessness of an individual. Certainly the allegations and controversy, amounting virtually to a witch hunt, indicate that the very interpretation and approach utilized by Abraham touched some raw nerves among historians. Without engaging in the minutiae of the controversy, we think that its intensity and excess were motivated at least in part by an attempt on the part of some scholars who have a stake in a different picture of the German elite's relationship with the Nazis, to discredit a historical approach that had the temerity to suggest that there might be close structural links between German industrialists and Junkers and the rise of fascism. With the question of these links made even more urgent by recent signs of historical and political amnesia in Western Europe, it is an opportune moment to introduce additional material, interpretations, and authors that contribute to the further development of Marxist and other structural perspectives, and thus to the debate. Authors such as Kurt Gossweiler and Reinhard Kühnl, who either enrich or relativize the Abraham thesis, have not previously appeared in English (with the exception of Kühnl's essay in our 1983 volume), although their research and writing have been significant in Germany for many years.

The apparent amnesia about fascism and World War II in Europe has taken various forms, including the resurgency of right-wing apologists for Nazism; a passion for Hitler memorabilia, including the forged diaries purchased by *Stern* magazine; public apathy concerning unpunished war criminals; the controversial invitation by West German Chancellor Helmuth Kohl to President Ronald Reagan to visit the German military cemetery at Bitburg; the election of Kurt Waldheim as president of Austria and his subsequent audience with the pope; and perhaps most disturbingly, the tendency on the part of established and recognized scholars to write about the period in ways that would have been politically and morally unacceptable even several years ago.

In Germany today the actual scandal lies in playing down the Nazi period rather than in its outright denial. Some, like Joachim Fest, Hitler biographer, have attempted to incorporate Nazism into a universal notion of "totalitarianism." This is one side of a growing historical relativism that has been described as "helpless antifascism"—helpless because of its mental inertia and appeal to a passive morality that is grounded in neither fact nor morality.

Other scholars, such as Ernst Nolte and Andreas Hillgruber, have attempted to contextualize the Nazi Holocaust by arguing that Hitler had reason to fear the Jews (Nolte), or that German atrocities must be seen in the light of previous Soviet atrocities and political developments at that time (Hillgruber).[3] This revisionist tendency is part of a larger political and historiographical agenda that has as its basis the temptation "to forget," that seeks a unifying myth that might restore to Germans a measure of pride in their past and a sense of resoluteness against their "real" enemies, the Soviets. This reconstruction of the historical past cannot be fashioned without considerable sleight of hand. This volume is intended to expose the "magic" of some historical practitioners and offer a scholarly corrective.

Articles in the present volume accordingly fall into three categories: those that offer new insights into and/or empirical analyses of the class alliances that supported fascism; those that reexamine the ability of existing opposition forces to resist its rise; and those that look at current revisionist tendencies and the conditions that have fostered them.

Part I presents the contributions to the nature of the dominant alliance, set in the context of the national and world political economy. It is well known that in terms of industrial production Germany had a relatively "late" start compared with other industrializing countries. However, by 1914 industrial production had grown so rapidly as to place Germany among the very top in terms of its share in the total world industrial output. Other countries appear to have made the transition from a preindustrial to an industrial mode of production over a longer period of time, thus producing, so it could be concluded, less of a structural strain. Germany's rapid transition implies that despite its industrial might remnants of the preindustrial society lingered on, well into the twentieth century. It might also be argued that these remnants were stronger, able to exert significantly greater political power, than in countries where a longer period of time had essentially reduced feudal powers (such as the church and the aristocracy) to a "negligible quantity" by the time of the Nazi movement and its subsequent rule.

Observations of this kind have raised the question as to whether German fascism should be viewed as the outcome of irreconcilable structural conflicts resulting from a distinct pattern of industrial development, an independent force that was able to influence the course of capitalist development, or a syncretic combination of the two.

Both Geoff Eley and Derek Linton speak to this question and evaluate the merits of reasoning from which it springs. Kurt Gossweiler addresses the same problem, if only indirectly, when he suggests that Weimar democracy might have been saved through a broadly based coalition and an economic policy designed to weaken the Junkers' economic and political position through land reform.

All capitalist societies that thoroughly asserted themselves over feudal powers, however, subjected populations to incessant change, although of unequal magnitude or intensity. A number of prominent social scientists have suggested that it was the "middle class" particularly—threatened by processes of modernization or change and crises in capitalist production—that supported and thus was "responsible" for the Nazi rise to power. Eley rejects this view, suggesting instead that Nazism be seen as a larger movement responding to the society-wide insecurity produced by the speed and magnitude at which capitalist production had taken hold, uprooting millions and tearing apart the traditional social fabric of entire nations.

A phenomenon such as German fascism—not having been observed earlier—clearly is symbolic of a "new era," one most strikingly characterized by monopoly capitalism and imperialism. It is reasonable to ask, therefore, whether these developments, relatively recent in the history of world capitalism, had anything to do with the rise of German fascism. Further, is fascism to be observed in any nation that has reached the state of monopoly capital and imperialism, or does it rise only in specific—emergent capitalist—conditions? The "Bonapartist" perspective on fascism, examined by Linton, sheds a good deal of light on this question, as does the more recent work of Nicos Poulantzas, evaluated by Jane Caplan.

One aspect of Poulantzas' work on fascism was to examine economic and political dimensions of the societies in which it arose. Both Gossweiler and David Abraham attempt to determine the degree to which German fascism can be linked to specific economic interests and elites and the extent to which it emerged from political processes outside the realm of production. We have included a revised version of previously published work by Abraham because it represents a cohesive and powerful presentation of his very suggestive and important structural analysis of the rise of German fascism within a model of class differentiation.

Nazi rule was also initiated and made possible by the existing elites—economic, political, and military—as Gossweiler points out. He argues that those who were "victorious" in bringing about Nazi rule could have preserved the Weimar republic but chose not to because they were unwilling to accept the anticipated lower long-run rate of capital accumulation. Instead, important segments of these elites empowered a "new" political elite to manage the affairs of government by dictatorship.

Gossweiler's claim raises an interesting question: What is the process by which "new" elites, based in emergent political movements, are able to gain legitimacy with existing elites? How can "old" elites, particularly the capitalist ruling class, gain sufficient confidence in an emerging elite, not of its mold, to allow it to dictate its affairs in the realm of politics? John Nagle and Brian Peterson investigate these questions in Germany, showing how the National Socialists chose distinct tactics to make themselves acceptable to established elites and to generally legitimize itself with its voters—Nagle examining aggregate national politics, Peterson looking at regional elites and their relationship to the NSDAP. Together their work presents the often contradictory diversity of the Nazi movement and policy as well as the conflicts among existing elites.

In Part II a number of authors explore the specific weaknesses and divisions in the ideology and tactics of those who tried to oppose the fascists. Gunter Remmling analyzes the role of the German Communist party and the "legal" destruction of the left and the labor movement; Kurt Pätzold examines the function of Nazi terror and demagoguery in pacifying the opposition; and Ben Fowkes looks at the divisions within the Social Democratic party and the consequences for the ability to resist. Fowkes argues that the failure of a broad left coalition to curb the economic and political power of the Junkers was due in part to the fact that the left could not agree on such an aggressive stance. The major strategy of the noncommunist left, particularly the Social Democratic party, was to defend the existing democracy, not to further the material interests of the workers to challenge directly the power of the economic elites.

Articles in Part III take up the issue of historiography, in an effort to explain the movement away from an antifascist front to a posture that is increasingly apologetic of German fascism, its war and genocide. Looking at Dachau, the town with the first concentration camp built by the Nazi dictatorship, Tony Barta demonstrates how and by whom the antifascist front was defeated within months after the German capitulation and over the course of the American occupation. Addressing the same process from a national perspective, Reinhard Kühnl follows these patterns into the 1980s. He demonstrates the various ways in which the German right, having transferred power to the Nazis, has been engaged in relativizing, downplaying, and excusing the fascist dictatorship ever since the war. Academics have played no small part in this endeavor, too often accepting the political right's cold war ideology and its insistence that German fascism be viewed outside of social structure and its economic, class, and power relationships.

In 1959 Theodor W. Adorno warned that "we'll have come to terms with the past only when the causes that have led to it will be abolished."[4] Individual and national identity should not be awakened at the cost of repressed truths and false historical legitimations. Today the real danger seems to us to be not the few neo-Nazi organizations and active fascists, but the readiness to minimize the crimes of the past, to relativize and universalize them, or, as in the case of some historians, to try to put things "into perspective" by equating Nazi crimes with those committed by other nations, by suggesting dubious parallels, and by denying the singularity of what happened. It is our hope that the essays in this volume will help to illuminate the shadows of the past so that they will not again fall upon the future.

Notes

1. Michael Dobkowski and Isidor Wallimann, *Towards the Holocaust: The Social and Economic Collapse of the Weimar Republic* (Westport, CT: Greenwood Press, 1983), p. 15.
2. David Abraham, *The Collapse of the Weimar Republic: Political Economy and Crisis* (Princeton: Princeton University Press, 1981; 2nd. ed., New York: Holmes & Meier, 1985).

3. *"Historikerstreit": Die Dokumentation der Kontroverse um die Einzigartigkeit der nationasozialislischen Judenvernichtung* (Munich: Piper Verlag, 1987).
4. Theodor W. Adorno, "What Does Coming to Terms with the Past Mean?" in Geoffrey Hartman, ed., *Bitburg in Moral and Political Perspective* (Bloomington: Indiana University Press, 1986), p. 129.

Part I

Reclaiming the Past: History and Theory

State and Classes in Weimar Germany

David Abraham

Some forty years ago, Franz Neumann, though writing at a time hardly conducive to a generous reading of the political possiblities of the late Weimar Republic, observed that there had been several political alternatives to fascism, not just a socialist alternative. Much of the debate that has sought either to indict or exonerate capitalism (or capitalists) has taken the collapse of the bourgeois republic rather too much for granted. Similarly, the study of the political development and social origins of modern state forms has allowed the importance (and horror) of fascism as a "final outcome" to do considerable injury to the actual political possibilities of Weimar Germany. Finally, although recent discussion of organized capitalism and corporatism has cast valuable light on economic transformations during a period that included the Weimar era, the polyvalence of the political is frequently short-changed.[1]

In the following I will examine the different ways in which the social dominance of the various fractions of the capitalist elite might have been expressed politically within the political framework of the Weimar Republic: how the dominant fractions could have organized their own interests, incorporated or repressed the interests of at least some of the subordinate classes, and achieved some balance of those interests as a neutral, national interest. The inability of the dominant classes to organize their own interests posed a crucial stumbling block to winning mass support, while the limited mass support available became an intolerable burden on the accumulation process. As a result, stability was tenuous and expensive. Since the resulting breakdown was a state crisis, we begin with an examination of the relationship of the state to the economy and society.

State and Economy

The functions of the state vary from society to society, but every state, except one on the brink of collapse, performs one function above all others—and in a sense comprehending all others: it underwrites and maintains the principal social and economic relationships of its society. In a capitalist and industrial society such as Weimar Germany, the state provides cohesion for economic, political, and cultural processes and relations. Yet capitalism's economic relations are relatively independent of its political ones. Production in capitalism, in comparison to feudalism, for example, does not rely on political mechanisms to be set in motion. Thus, political relations can develop separately from economic relations, and the state in capitalist society may be relatively autonomous.[2] In the parliamentary democratic state, formally equal competition increases this autonomy. Within limits determined by the specific status or conjunctures of the economic, ideological, and political realms, state policy output is a product of recognized, rule-bound, institutionalized bargaining where the outcome in any given case cannot be determined beforehand.[3] But at a minimum, the state in a capitalist society must guarantee that capitalist production can take place and that the social relations of that production are reproduced.

The state is the regulating mechansim for the equilibrium of the entire society. Ultimately, it is through the agency of the state that the dominant social classes are organized, that is, elevated from the level of their selfish, individual interests to that of their collective, class interest. Alone, the private and competitive nature of the appropriation of surplus would tend to foster systemic disunity among capitalists. Similarly, it is through the state that the dominated social classes are disorganized, that is, kept from the level of their class interests and kept at the level of their interests as individuals, citizens, and members of the nation.[4] The Marxist expectation that the (increasingly) social nature of production in industrial capitalism would by itself engender working-class unity has not, on the whole, proven correct. To organize the interests of the capitalist class and its allies successfully and to turn these into "national interests," the state must stand at a distance from individual capitalists; it must not allow itself to become the creature of specific capitalist class members or interests.[5] The crisis of the last years of the Weimar Republic stemmed in large part from the inability of the state to organize the interests of the members of the ruling bloc in an autonomous fashion. The republic was unable to safeguard existing social relations not because of any revolutionary threat but rather because of the conflicts and contradictions within the bloc of dominant classes *together with* the expensive welfarist policies of the preceding years.

It can be argued that since the "Keynesian Revolution" the separation between state and economy has collapsed: civil society and state are joined. The state both reflects and acts upon prevailing social and economic relations. The government bureaucracy is responsible for the planning, direction, and control of economic undertakings whose costs and technological needs are too much even for large monopolies. The security of private property, of economic growth, and of crisis-free economic performance now require constant intervention by the state, an approach followed almost as closely by conservative governments as by social democratic ones.[6]

Although this interdependence was not yet fully the situation in Weimar Germany, there were substantial elements of such a development and demands for it.[7] The role of the Prussian-German state in nineteenth-century German industrialization, unprecedented at the time, provided the groundwork for later forms of organized intervention.[8] To the extent that there were government attempts to intervene in and alleviate the economic crisis after 1928, and to the extent that such interventions were expected by the great majority of the population, the economic crisis exacerbated the political crisis. There was increased conflict in the political realm precisely at those points when the state was called on to do more in the economic realm. Heinrich Brüning, with his limited, largely negative intervention, had trouble maintaining—and Franz von Papen and General Kurt von Schleicher, with their more active intervention, had trouble establishing—political legitimacy through mass loyalty partly because their economic interventions were unsuccessful.[9] The failures of their policies were not primarily due to any inherent lack of wisdom in the content of the policies. Indeed, some of the von Papen and Schleicher policies were quite promising and were adopted a short time later by the Nazi government. The conflicts of needs, interests, and ideologies within the bloc of ruling classes were largely responsible for the ineffectiveness of government policy, and it was only once these were resolved that a coherent state policy was possible. So long as the ruling bloc itself lacked clear and organizing leadership its members could not rise above the level of *sauve qui peut*.

That Germany was furthest down the road of organized capitalism did not alter the need for leadership within the social and economic elite. The development of the first constitutive elements of this system only increased the saliency of state-economy interaction. H. J. Puhle enumerates those elements, which developed even before World War I:

> the increased taxing prerogatives of the state, the growth of public works and services and insurance, the bureaucratization and organizational tendencies of large industry, especially the new strategic growth industries (electro-technical, chemical, motor and engineering) and the workers' movement . . . further that of political and public-oriented pressure groups which contributed decisively to changing the relationship between government, parliament and public, thereby lastingly altering both political landscape and style and binding the sectors of the private economy together with each other and with the agents of the state through their intervention in elections, in the press, in parliament and its committees and through the activities of their representatives in regional government and professional organizations.[10]

An indicator of the advanced role of the state is the percentage of the gross national product (GNP) devoted to public, state expenditures. Thus, in the United States the figures for 1900 and 1929 were 4 percent and 10 percent respectively; in Germany they were already 16 percent and 30.6 percent. But the increased interpenetration of state and economy did not "free" state activity from nonpolitical constraints, and it did not relieve the dominant social classes of the need to accomplish an internal ordering crowned by a hegemonic fraction. The patriarchal social commitment of the German bureaucracy augmented the state's autonomy but did not determine the nature and outcome of political practices and the form of society. Germany would be home to *organized* precapitalism, *organized* capitalism, and *organized* socialism.

Care must be taken to avoid reifying the concepts of autonomy and mass loyalty. While there were moments in late Weimar Germany when the state seemed to be functioning as the instrument of capital as a whole, or even of just one sector of it, there were other times when the state seemed "merely" to be sanctioning and protecting the rules and social relationships of the capitalist order. In these latter instances the state was probably functioning more independently. Yet it is exceedingly difficult to delineate the social mechanisms that account for one type of functioning or another. The number of contacts between industrial leaders and members of the government or the bureaucracy, for example, did not (and generally do not) vary a great deal. Linkages were both constant and institutionalized; there is no evidence of the state's "holding the rifle butt over the heads" of the Weimar capitalist class. Describing this autonomy as "relative" is, therefore, not enough. We shall have to analyze very carefully the individual policy formulations, outputs, and outcomes in order to relate the concept of autonomy to the conflicts within the ruling bloc. Similarly with the concept of mass loyalty: equal votes need not be of equal significance. The percentage of the German electorate that voted for the Nazi party in the autumn of 1932 (33 percent) was not substantially greater than that which voted SPD in 1928 (30 percent), but, these were different voters, and a qualitatively different mass loyalty emerged to replace the rather tenuous loyalty enjoyed by the republic.

The autonomy of the state is conditioned by the ways in which the economic realm is dependent on state activity. Broadly conceived we can locate five areas of such state activity. (1) The state guarantees the organizational and legal principles of the capitalist system (e.g., the inviolableness of contracts and freedom of labor).[11] (2) It establishes and constructs some of the material preconditions for production that are for the benefit of all economic actors but beyond the reach of any one of them (e.g., infrastructure and other external economies such as railroads and canals). Although this is an old area of activity, the increased dependence of industrial production on technological advance has enlarged the scope of these activities and further "socialized" the costs of production.[12] (3) The state occasionally and regularly participates and intervenes in the course of economic activity and growth, to secure growth and avoid and remedy crises (e.g., government contracts—especially military, fiscal, and monetary policies—and tariffs). Growing concentration and inflexibility (cartels, monopolies) render commodity production and exchange increasingly incapable of regulating themselves. (4) The state regulates conflicts between capital and labor so as to avoid constant social crises (mediation and even compulsory arbitration have been accepted by capital). Generally capital shares an interest in keeping these conflicts within limits so as to facilitate the final area of state activity. (5) The state maintains the legitimacy of, and mass loyalty to, the social system as a whole (e.g., distributive and social welfare measures, foreign successes).

Whereas activity in the first two areas is undertaken with the full cooperation of representatives of capital, activity in the last three areas is undertaken against the will of some, perhaps even a majority, of the representatives of capital. The state's successful execution of these activities brings to it increased legitimacy. Legitimation is, therefore, both an activity of the state and an outcome of its activities. The growth of the role of the state is part of a three-stage historical development: organization of the market to relieve the pressure of competition faced by individual capitalists (monopolies, self-financing); the institutionalization of technological progress to relieve the threat of crises faced by the economy as a whole (research and development, investment outlets); and state regulation of the entire system to relieve the pressure of social, political, and economic tensions.[13]

What the state needs in order to execute these activities limits the possible range of its action and policy outputs. The state needs financial resources, a capacity for technological rationality, an already existing legitimacy or mass loyalty, and the loyalty of the owners of the means of production. The Weimar Republic after 1929 was progressively deprived of these, and its ability to act diminished commensurately. The loyalty of capital was essential for a number of reasons. As Müller, Brüning, von Papen, and Schleicher all discovered, the state can only make offers or set limits in a process in which the owners of the means of production dispose of them as they see fit. Too much state pressure can precipitate investment and employers' strikes, a loss of cooperation, or a "crisis of confidence," thereby exacerbating the crisis instead of mitigating it. In order to be able to stabilize the economy the state needs mass support, which is forthcoming only when demonstrable economic successes are at hand; to obtain these, cooperation with the private sector is essential. The owners of the means of production abandoned the Weimar Republic in its attempts to achieve mass support in part because of the constraints placed upon it by the results of a parliamentary democracy where all citizens were entitled to press equal claims. The capacity for technological rationality, which the state also requires, is limited by the fact that the private sector is frequently the source of economic data and other information.[14] The financial needs of the state are met primarily through tax revenue. Although the state may set tax rates that attempt to reflect the interests of all of society, receipts from business remain particularly vulnerable; the growth of the economy as a whole presents itself as the only way out.[15]

Political and economic developments may dictate an increased and ongoing state role in the economy. The state may undertake economic planning so as to maintain, implement, replace, or compensate for particular economic processes. Curiously, however, the more the state needs to intervene in the economy, the more dependent it becomes on the owners of the means of production. This is true regardless of whether the need for intervention is episodic or organic; the need may even be purely a function of developments within the economy. Thus, with the onset of the depression the Weimar state became increasingly dependent on *die Wirtschaft*. The ideological hegemony of the bourgeoisie and its logic of accumulation limits the range of possible state policies by successfully characterizing some of them as "utopian."[16] The growing expectation of improvements in the standard of living also renders the state more dependent on the dominant economic powers. This is ironic since it is generally social-democratic parties and governments that encourage such expectation.[17] Once such expectations are rooted they are nearly impossible to reverse democratically, and their costs invariably seem to grow, during both normal and crisis periods.

Clearly such was the case in Weimar Germany. From Müller on, the state was cast in the role and burdened with the responsibility of economic coordination; it could not possibly succeed since economic decisions remained the private prerogatives of the industrialists and their leaders. It was in this context that the results of the predepression conflicts and decisions over the distribution of state revenue came to threaten the very ability to produce and accumulate surplus. Despite the institution of consumption and other regressive taxes, it was impossible to pass increased state costs completely on to wage earners and other taxpayers. So long as revenue sources remained domestic, the areas of state activity came into conflict with each other and further weakened the state. The functions of facilitating private accumulation and guaranteeing mass legitimacy could not be reconciled.[18]

This outline of state/economy relations under conditions of capitalist crisis merits elaboration. In a series of essays and lectures,[19] Knut Borchardt has offered an analysis of the specific structure and core problems of the Weimar political economy very much like that presented here and throughout my own work. In an important sense this is highly ironic, for although Professor Borchardt is generally understood as making a conservative argument, few scholars have made the central point as clearly as he has: in capitalist democracies capital rules, and it is *its* logic that enjoys hegemony.[20]

At the core of the "Borchardt thesis" lies the argument that political alternatives after 1930 were heavily constrained by economic necessity: in particular, Chancellor Brüning could do little to save the Weimar system because orgainzed labor's wage and social policy victories had paralyzed German capitalism. A strong labor movement extracted wage increases in excess of productivity growth, thereby squeezing profits, discouraging investment, and antagonizing capital. The entrepreneurial class could then only welcome the growth of a reserve army of the unemployed in order to weaken the bargaining position of labor and strengthen its own. To argue this is to say, in effect, that the vehement objections of Weimar capitalists to high and "political" wages were rationally founded, whatever the ideological functions of such objections. Weimar, in other words, suffered from an economic crisis that was, in good measure, a profit crisis engendered by a militant reformist labor movement. This circumstance left republican and socialist politicians with little room for maneuver, facilitated the growth of right radicalism, and eventually encouraged the migration of parts of business into the right-radical camp. For Borchardt, as for the analysis here, the system suffered from a structural problem that went well beyond the pressure of reparations and high interest rates.

Borchardt portrays the Weimar economy as nonfunctional and untenable (*"nicht funktionsfähige"*) and existing within a barely functional and tenable political system. I believe one can accept his judgment without inferring "anti-labor" conclusions. Borchardt finds a net social product per capita during Weimar that lay well below the long-term trend line (the 1913 level was not reattained until 1928); real net investment per capita (despite the wave of "industrial rationalization") about 12 percent less than in the immediate prewar years; personal consumption levels 16 percent higher and public expenditures 34 percent higher in 1928 than in 1913; and an unprecedentedly high share of national income (nearly 67 percent) going to wages. He links low investment levels to high levels of public borrowing and spending, disproportionately costly wages to a successful wages policy by labor and the state, and slowness in productivity growth to these and other factors. Due to the political strength of labor, high unemployment did not succeed in adjusting wages downward in time, and the rate of exploitation remained inadequate. The "relative powers of the combatants" Marx referred to in *Capital* seemed to weigh in favor of labor.

In other words, the Social Democratic party (SPD) and trade unions succeeded at much of what they had promised to do. Once they experienced defeat and abandoned efforts at revolutionary transformation after 1918–19, the SPD and the German Trade Union Federation (ADGB) militantly and successfully pursued redistributional struggles. These were often facilitated and even encouraged by political and legal mechanisms, such as binding compulsory arbitration by the state, as well as by elections. By the time of the SPD's successful 1928 election campaign, socialist theorists and representatives of capital alike had come to believe that the weekly wage was a political wage, dependent on the political representation of labor. Incremental social and wage gains lay at the center of labor's strategy—and capital's fears. Indeed, successful social democratic reformism appeared as more of a threat than communist agitation. As we shall see, wage and social-welfare policy became the *sina qua non* of left politics in Weimar. Indeed, to labor's ultimate grief, they were the litmus test applied to all governments—before and after 1932. Labor's approach worked for a while, but once it began to fail, there was no *Spielraum* and no simple escape route: the piper had to be paid. Domestic-oriented and heavy industries, partially on account of their greater labor-intensity and tighter markets, were the first to call the question and demand an end to the Weimar system. With little change in labor's posture, and with worsening world trade protectionism, the export and dynamic industries lost their relative preeminence within German capital and moved closer to the position of their more nationalist and conservative colleagues.

Social democratic scholars in particular respond with great unease to arguments affirming the reality of the "profit squeeze." They fear blaming (productive) labor, fear suggesting a shortage of investments and profits rather than of demand and jobs.[21] Actually, the thesis of labor-induced profit squeezes is not the intellectual property solely of conservatives and neoliberals or the policy property of business. Historically, there has been a left/right confluence on this question.[22] Analyses that stress the profit squeeze have understandably generated a great deal of discomfort among those German scholars who see such arguments as blaming labor for the severity of the depression, the collapse of Weimar, and worse.[23] From the perspective of the present, they seem also to justify the contemporary abuse of labor by Christian Democratic, Thatcherite, and Reagan-Republican governments while suggesting the sterility of any collective or demand-centered recovery strategy. Today, as in Weimar, the question can be asked: *Are there not enough jobs for people or not enough profits for investment?* And though investment there must be—capital strike and flight notwithstanding—can one assume that private capitalists do it better than socially-oriented public organs? Posed this way, Borchardt's argument appears to be intrinsically anti-labor, redolent of the desire of Weimar capitalists to *take advantage of* the economic crisis to weaken labor and its organizations and to undermine democracy.

Social-democratic power does not alter the core of capitalism. As we shall see, the Weimar labor movement's search for economic rationality, social justice, and political participation was inevitably and decisively constrained by the privileged status systematically accorded the logic of accumulation. It seems that the best that can be accomplished is the worst that can be done: paralyzing capitalism without being able to transform it. [24] The Weimar SPD and ADGB were highly effective but also terribly vulnerable. Having mistakenly assumed that democracy would overcome capitalism *within* the new system of capitalist democracy, they were at a complete loss to deal with the system in distress. Having persuaded most of their members that success was to be measured almost uniquely by wage and social welfare gains, the SPD and ADGB had virtually no idea what to do once capitalism ceased producing surplus they could skim. Rather than inferring from profit-squeeze analyses only the possibility of a "right turn" or retreat by labor, is it possible to posit the possibility of a turn away from economism and a politically-oriented turn to the left to escape the crisis? At least one of Borchardt's critics, Holtfrerich, citing arguments of the sort made here, has cautiously suggested something of this sort by stressing the availability, feasibility, and desirability of job-creation and pump-priming programs.[25]

Yet to stress the availability, feasibility, and desirability of job creation and other antideflationary measures is not enough to solve the riddle of state-economy relations in the Weimar capitalist democracy. There was no *economic* way because there was neither *political* will nor an alternative political economy. Chancellor Brüning, in his efforts to balance and further various capitalist interests while also retaining the tacit support of labor, could not abandon the imperative of accumulation. At least not unless he, as political entrepreneur, was forced to do so. For that to have happened would have required one of two inducements: either the pressure of a broader worker-salaried employee-popular constituency such as came into being in the 1960s but which was impossible in Weimar, or a rapprochement between the Socialist and Communist movements. Yet socialist complicity in and commitment to the system seems to have been too great to permit any undoing of the fatal decisions of 1918–19 that split the labor movement. And if, somehow, the SPD and German Communist party (KPD) had been able to join forces, the evidence suggests that the leftward pressure thereby exerted would have been directed to toppling Brüning. With that, political warfare would have replaced economic constraints.[26]

State and Society

The crisis of the Weimar state was not a social crisis of the sort anticipated by many communists: a "maturation" of class antagonisms that coincided with the "catastrophic development" of the capitalist economy.[27] The depression was indeed a catastrophe, and class antagonisms of all sorts were rife, but the impetus for the *state* crisis came from the determination of capitalist groups to make hay while the clouds shone. This, in turn, brought about the political crisis that led to the abandonment of and opposition to parliamentary government. Both capital and labor, but especially the former, now oriented their struggles toward a transformation of the internal organization of the state; their class struggle became *political* for the first time in a decade. The availability of a new mass base was then secured and a new form of government encouraged. The divergent interests of the various capitalist groups were organzied anew, and the new form of government could function as the new guarantor of cohesion for unchanged social relations. What were the bases of these various capitalist groups; how, and under whose leadership, were they formed into the "historical bloc of ruling classes"?

It is an axiom of Marxist analysis that the manner in which surplus value is extracted from the direct producer determines the social relations involved in production and ultimately the relationship of the rulers and the ruled.[28] Those involved in production are the carriers of the social relations engendered by the given mode of production. The capitalist mode of production allows for the separation of economic, political, and ideological relations because surplus is extracted solely within the economic realm, virtually unassisted by political or ideological mechanisms. In capitalism these carriers of social relations become classes through their activity—through their practice in the political realm.[29] An objective relationship to the means of production, being a carrier of certain social relations, is an insufficient base for a class in capitalism.[30] As indicated earlier, the state, when functioning coherently, helps organize the owners of the means of production into a class; this same function is performed for wage labor by political parties.[31] Unless so organized, wage laborers will appear in this dominant political sphere simply as individuals, as citizens seeking to achieve their selfish interests. Conversely, those in dominant classes will appear as spokespersons for the interests of the nation as a whole, and the actualization of their needs through the state will generally be consented to and accepted as legitimate.[32] This is one meaning of the term *hegemony.* Thus, to overstate the case somewhat, social relations become historical activity in their political embodiments.[33]

No society, including Weimar Germany, is characterized by just one mode of production with its attendant social relations. Although industrial capitalism was by far the dominant mode of production in Weimar Germany, other modes also existed: the family peasant, small commodity, and even feudal modes coexisted with industrial capitalism. The economic, political, and ideological practices of all these partially amalgamated "subsocieties" constituted the German social formation. A half century earlier Marx had remarked on the incompleteness of capitalist development in Germany. Even in the Weimar period it remained true that Germany suffered "not only from the development of capitalist production, but also from its incompleteness. Alongside of modern evils, a whole series of inherited evils oppress us, arising from the survival of antiquated modes of production. . . . We suffer not only from the living, but from the dead."[34] These "dead" were to play a crucial role in the resolution of conflicts within the historical bloc of ruling classes.

The ruling bloc

The East Elbian Junkers continued to occupy vital positions in the military, civil service, and judiciary and remained an important force within the ruling bloc. Although total agricultural production contributed under 15 percent to the GNP, and the agricultural portion of the population had slipped to 25 percent by 1925, the agricultural elite continued to enjoy vastly disproportionate influence. Up to 1918 industrial development, despite its rapidity, had taken place within a semi-feudal context, and the Junkers preserved a political and ideological supremacy greater than that of any other landed group in industrial Europe.[35] They continued as a class in charge of the state and as a ruling class. Gramsci characterizes them as

> the traditional intellectuals of the German industrialists who retained special privileges and a strong consciousness of being an independent social group, based on the fact that they held considerable economic power over agriculture. . . . The Junkers resemble a priestly-military caste, with a virtual monopoly of directive-organisational functions in political society, but possessing at the same time an economic base of its own and so not exclusively dependent on the liberality of the dominant economic group. . . . the Junkers constituted the officer class of a large standing army, which gave them solid organizational cadres favouring the preservation of an esprit de corps and of their political monopoly.[36]

In the Weimar period their political monopoly was broken, and they did become increasingly dependent on the liberality of the hegemonic industrial group, but per se the dominant economic group, the bourgeoisie, had never directly ruled in Germany. The earlier political and cultural monopoly of the nobility impeded the development of an extensive and independent bourgeois political personnel.[37] This lacuna had much to do with the continued parliamentary crises and the fragmentation of the liberal parties; in turn, the Catholic Zentrum and the SPD were aided in their prewar growth precisely by this fragmentation.[38] Bourgeois fragmentation continued throughout the Weimar period. The Gustav Stresemann circle constituted perhaps the only successful, representatively bourgeois political group of the entire era.[39] The bulk of industrialists greeted his death with a sigh of relief, anxious as most were to disavow him. Representatives of the agricultural elite, however, despite their even greater dissatisfaction with government policies, continued to fill posts and participate in the state apparatus at all levels down to the very end of the republic and beyond. Although it had partially merged into the bourgeoisie, the agricultural elite continued to constitute an autonomous class or fraction within the ruling bloc dominated by industry.

Viewed strictly in terms of their percentage contribution to the GNP or portion of the population, representatives of the agricultural sector ought to have been little more than junior allies or supporters of a ruling bloc. However, even after World War I the agricultural elite of estate owners continued to occupy vital positions in both political and civil society; all reaches of the military and civil service, for example, continued to bear their mark. An additional factor was at least equally important in preserving the status of the rural elite as members of the ruling bloc: the composition of the agricultural and industrial sectors was not symmetrical; the relationship of the peasant majority to the large landowners was very different from that of the worker majority toward the factory owners. Even when organized, peasants, unlike unionized workers, did not generally adopt an adversary posture toward their putative betters. Peasants simply did not hate the big estate owners the way workers hated the Herren of industry. The resolution of the economic and political conflicts between grain-growing estate owners and the body of dairy- and livestock-producing peasants enabled *Landwirtschaft* to appear as a solid front and buttressed the position of the agricultural elite both vis-à-vis industry and in society generally. In the final two years of the Republic, this solid front began to dissolve; many non-Catholic peasants voted for the Nazis, yet even this did not signify abandonment of the agricultural elite's core interests. Toward the end of the Republic, an attempt to reconcile estate-owner and peasant interests through the "Green Front" occurred, with demands crystallizing around autarky. Not only socialists but also important industrial and commercial groups tried unsuccessfully to exploit rural cleavages and break this agricultural front, which even in the 1920s operated to retard capitalist development.

The dominant element within the unity of dominant classes, what we can call the hegemonic class or fraction, did not remain the same throughout the Weimar years. Rather, largely cartelized and domestic-oriented heavy industry vied for hegemony with generally less cartelized dynamic and export industry. These two fractions of industrial capital entertained similar but far from identical interests. Their relations to their commercial, financial, and agricultural partners also varied, and rivalries between and among these fractions were always present.

Thanks to the cheap debt-retirement, bankruptcies, and lowered real wages resulting from the inflation and Ruhr occupation, most of German industry was able, with the assistance of American capital, to rebuild, modernize, and expand capacity quickly after 1923. An already cartelized industrial sector became even further dominated by grand monopolies and cartels. Both the labor unions and the workers' parties were demoralized by a series of defeats between 1919 and 1923, and the election results of 1924 embodied the new "economy-friendly" state of affairs. What various branches of German industry chose to do, or could do, with their plants was conditioned by a number of factors. Conflicts arose out of the divergent production desiderata, trade, and political needs of the various branches of German industry.

The first central cleavage during these years was between domestic-

and export-market-oriented industry. The domestic-market-oriented branch consisted mainly of heavy industry, led by iron, steel, and mining interests, especially those of the Ruhr. (Except for brief interludes such as the British coal strike of 1926, Germany's basic heavy industries were not exporters.)

After 1925 and certainly by 1927 heavy industry was burdened with substantial overcapacity, and it suffered from unsatisfactory shares in various international cartels (such as the International Raw Steel Community). In the prewar period income from German ferrous metals production was one quarter of the world total; by early 1929 it was down to one eighth. Only an expanded domestic market could absorb this sector's production at high prices. Almost all production and ownership units here were large and cartelized, and the burden of wages constituted a much greater share of total costs. The growing and prosperous export industries, by contrast, accepted high protective tariffs for domestic primary industry, so long as they received refunds from the primary producers equal to the difference between world and domestic prices for those quantities subsequently exported. Heavy industry was thus more hostile toward the gains of the organized working class in the realm of wages, hours, social-welfare legislation, and labor relations. Of all industries, mining had the highest percentage of total costs devoted to labor and social insurance. Despite increased production, its 1927 profit rate was only 4 percent; the iron-producing industry's an even lower 2.8 percent.

The other fraction of industry was export industry: the dynamic, technologically more advanced, and prosperous sector of industry. It was led by the machine, electric, and chemical industries but included a broad range of producers (including, somewhat anomalously, textiles) as well as commercial interests. Profit rates in this sector were sometimes more than triple those in heavy industry. In contrast to overcapacity in heavy industry, the net value of industrial exports nearly doubled between 1925 and 1929. By the latter date, nearly 35 percent of industrial production was for export. This dynamic fraction was behind the most-favored-nation trade treaties negotiated with a host of countries after 1925, and it supported Stresemann's foreign policy of international reintegration enthusiastically. Its primary markets lay in the developed countries of the west and north. Wage labor constituted a smaller share of total costs in these industries (lowest of all in chemicals) while contributing more of what the industrialists themselves called "added value." These industries were more prepared to work together with organized labor while regularly opposing the demands of organized agriculture.

By contrast, the internal-market strategy and greater opposition to the organized working class by heavy industry helped this fraction forge and maintain links to the agricultural sector and the policies it proposed. Lowering production costs was a central refrain for them both, as were protection of the borderlands and revision of Versailles.

Relations between the representatives of industry and agriculture did not follow any smooth pattern during the Weimar years, however. Although the industrial elite was in a position to set both the tone and the agenda for capitalists during the entire period, its willingness to make sacrifices on behalf of its rural partner varied. Viewed from the perspective of general economic policy, agriculture was increasingly shortchanged between 1924 and 1929. The year 1925 marked the beginning of a trend characterized by trade treaties unfavorable to agriculture, growing agricultural imports, disadvantaged access to capital, widening price scissors, and then, by 1928, the onset of the agricultural depression. Since the home market for heavy industry enjoyed only a brief spurt, agriculture was' left, until the end of the stabilization, as the only serious proponent of a semiautarkic "domestic-market" strategy. With the growing struggle over "costs of production" inside the last bourgeios/working-class coalition government (1928–30). However, relations between agrarian and industrial leaders improved. As was the case before World War I, organizations representing heavy industry moved toward the policies advocated by agriculture, while more dynamic and successful export industry groups called on agriculture to make itself more efficient, cut costs, and help itself. (Even socialists were no more critical of German agriculture and its elite than were the spokesmen for these dynamic industries.) If we use influence within the all-encompassing League of German Industry (RDI) as an indicator, we can conclude that heavy domestic industry was ascendant over other industries until 1925 and again after 1930. Patterns of trade and social legislation recommended by industry as a whole and the policies of the state bureaucracy reflected this predominance (although severe conflicts persisted throughout the Weimar years).

Other cleavages involved capital composition and ideology, factors that also contributed to divergent attitudes toward labor and toward agriculture. Within the League of German Industry (RDI), power was wrested after 1930 by the heavy-industry conservatives from the dynamic-export liberals who had held it since about 1925. The processing and smaller finishing industries then buckled under the menacing of heavy industry's vertical cartels and a political campaign against the system of export rebates. Beginning in the late 1920s, mining and steel organizations threatened to withdraw from the RDI and from other organs whose policies they deemed insufficiently conservative or overly attentive to export and parliamentary constraints. Industrial circles began to plan a trade strategy that abandoned the pacific market of northern and western Europe and overseas in favor of the "imperial" market of eastern and southern Europe. The relatively virgin markets of the East were presented simultaneously as an inducement to export circles and as a threat to agriculture to encourage their lining up behind heavy industry. The prospects of renewed profitability were thus ultimately tied to a changed social and political system at home and an imperial policy in central Europe presented as autarky.

Each hegemonic fraction attempted to make its own economic interests into political interests and to represent the common interests of the classes and fractions in the bloc.[40] In the Weimar context, each was charged with the primary responsibility for "getting us off the current socialist road and enabling industry to speak in the name of the economy and the nation, not just capitalism."[41] Taken as a whole, however, these classes were the power bloc in Weimar Germany.

The Mittelstand and the peasantry

Allied to the power bloc politically, albeit not wholeheartedly, and opposed to it economically, was the Mittelstand.[42] Composed of shopkeepers and commodity producers on one hand and salaried employees on the other, each constituting just under 20 percent of the population, the alliance proved frustrating for the Mittelstand. While the salaried employees found themselves profiting economically from a massive bourgeois-social-democratic collaboration (1924–29) in the realm of employee rights and *Sozialpolitik*, they found the value of their political patronage declining and withdrew their support from the bourgeois parties when the bourgeois parties hardened their positions on *Sozialpolitik*.[43] At the same time, their self-consciously separate status prevented them from moving left.

The shopkeepers and commodity producers defected even earlier. Not only did they suffer more from the inflation, but the costs of the bourgeois collaboration with social democracy were not offset by any redeeming benefits. Initially, they had nowhere else to go, but once the movement to the Nazi party began, it became a stampede.[45] Losers in the inflation and unable to penetrate the system of industry-labor collaboration, the Mittelstand could be mobilized politically against it.

Further support for the ruling bloc was provided by the bulk of the peasantry. Unlike the "allies," these "supporters" of the ruling bloc obtained little in exchange for their support. Certain half-truths propagated by ruling-bloc-ideology shored up this support: an identity of interests shared by all agriculturalists, big and small alike, and a fear of antiproperty, urban reds. Although peasant support was retained within the range of older bourgeois parties until 1930, it too seemed to disappear overnight (among Protestants at any rate) as soon as an uncompromising advocate presented itself. Once the republic appeared to announce itself to the peasantry only with the tax collector, the peasantry announced itself to the republic with the "Emperor."[46]

Class and Coalition Politics

There are two ways of looking at coalition politics, both actual and potential, in the Weimar period. The first is in terms of the social classes or forces represented by various political parties; the second is in terms of the political parties and electoral coalitions themselves. Let us examine first the actual and potential class blocs and then the electoral results. Several blocs or coalitions of classes were formed (or were possible) during the Weimar years. These blocs were unstable and shifting. In addition, at different moments, different fractions of a bloc were in a position to set the tone and agenda for a bloc as a whole. Economic and political bonds brought and kept bloc partners together: economic and political conflicts kept various bloc possibilities from forming and tore others asunder.

In conceptualizing coalitions or blocs we are faced with a dual task: on the one hand, analysis of class blocs as formed from "the bottom up" and involving group intentions, class situations, tensions, and consciousness at the base; on the other hand, analysis of more tangible power blocs as formed from "the top down" and consisting of organized political activity and interventions, of parties, alliances, policy formation, leadership organizations, and so on. It is primarily in terms of the latter that the coherence and strength of blocs can be evaluated. During the Weimar Republic certain policy issues, decisions, and nondecisions were particularly critical and, as analysis below will demonstrate, blocs formed and dissolved around issues of social policy *(Sozialpolitik)*, trade policy *(Handelspolitik)*, reparations and foreign policy *(Reparationspolitik* broadly conceived), distribution of the national wealth (and burden), democratization (in both the public and private spheres), and the balance between private accumulation and social legitimation. Thus, government coalitions, cooperation and conflict among corporate interest organizations and unions, patterns of social, trade, and fiscal legislation, the policies of state bureaucracies, the public agenda as enunciated by various ideological apparatuses, and the articulation of the tasks at hand by the spokespeople for classes, unions, and parties all help provide the basis for a partially inductive determination of the class coalitions constituting a bloc.

Schematically, for Weimar Germany we can map several blocs composed of rural and urban, dominant and dominated classes. Through these power blocs, the economic sphere, where individuals appear as the carriers of determinate social relations, shaped the political sphere, in which members of all classes appear as equal citizens with equal claims. It was largely through state activity that intrabloc conflicts were mediated and the interests of a bloc as a whole pursued. Although some of the respective blocs here are labeled with dates, these dates only indicate the ascendance, sometimes tacit or de facto, of one or another coalition, not necessarily a formalized shift. The formal goal of the bourgeoisie remained united bourgeois rule, and the form of state might depend on what type of mass base was available for that rule.

In Tables 1–5, we posit five such class blocs. In each schema the hegemonic class or fraction, that is the dominant element within the unity of classes, is represented in capital letters, and ties represented by solid lines are stronger than those represented by dashed lines.

In the bloc formation shown in Table 1, the estate owners and heavy industry together were hegemonic. Their relationship was mediated on the terrain of the state. Export industry, consisting of the more dynamic, new processing industries, was also part of the bloc; it was linked directly to heavy industry. Family peasants too were part of the bloc, although they profited less from their membership. They were linked to the estate owners. Finally, the petty bourgeoisie was an ally of this bloc, profiting as it did from the bloc's social protectionism and antisocialism. Other groups must be considered as having been in opposition.

In the bloc formation shown in Table 2, heavy industry was

Table 1
"Sammlung" Bloc: Pre-1914 Bourgeois Bloc:
The "Historical Ruling Bloc"

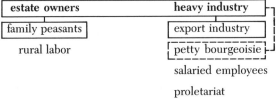

Table 2
Antisocialist Right Bourgeois Bloc: 1922–24:
Rolling Back the Revolution

estate owners	heavy industry
family peasants	export industry
rural labor	petty bourgeoisie
	salaried employees
	proletariat

hegemonic. Export industry was allied to heavy industry in this bloc as well, but it demurred from some of the bloc's economic policies. Again, family peasants were linked via the estate owners. The petty bourgeoisie was lost to the bloc because of the effects of inflation, and other groups were in opposition. This bloc made use of inflation, French occupation of the Ruhr, and aborted communist uprisings to revoke the eight-hour day, lower real wages, and wipe out its debt. By 1924, however, currency stabilization, the massive influx of American capital, and the lifting of trade restrictions led to a realignment.

In the bloc formation shown in Table 3, export industry was hegemonic. Linked to it in the bloc were the organized proletariat (including rural labor) and salaried employees. An expansive economy and liberal social legislation permitted interclass cooperation. Heavy industry, although still within the bloc, had much in the realm of social and economic policy over which to be dissatisfied. Estate owners and family peasants were distinct losers in this arrangement. The petty bourgeoisie became increasingly homeless, as was demonstrated by its accelerating desertion of the primary bourgeois parties. Bloc 3 demonstrated that it was possible for a fraction of the dominant classes to abandon other fractions to a significant extent in favor of a more thoroughgoing collaboration with the organized working class.[47]

Aware of the high costs of the class compromise coalition, prominent figures in export industry and some progressives in heavy industry attempted to form a bloc enjoying mass support but not dependent on the organized working class. Had they succeeded, the bloc would have looked like that shown in Table 4. This bloc formation would have removed the "pernicious" influence of both the "feudal" estate owners and socialist working class. It failed to emerge because the liberal industrialists could not split the peasants from the estate owners and

Table 3
Class Compromise Bloc, 1925–30:
Republican Stability with Democratic Potential

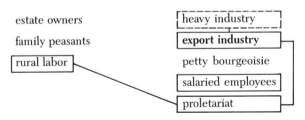

overestimated the republican potential of the petty bourgeoisie. The progressive aspects of the bloc would have linked salaried employees to export industry while the conservative ones would have linked the petty bourgeoisie to heavy industry. [48]

With the end of cooperation with the working class, the failure to build a liberal bourgeois bloc, and the loss of peasant support, the dominant classes by 1932 found themselves in the position of the bloc shown in Table 5. This short-lived bloc formation was like the "Sammlung" bloc except for the important fact that it lacked any base of mass support. After over a decade of republican government it was impossible to stabilize a government that enjoyed no mass support. Further, the agricultural elite was far more dependent on heavy industry that it had been in the prewar bloc.

Tables 6 and 7 introduce the political parties, electoral results, and party coalitions of the Weimar period. Very schematically, we can say that the parties drew their primary electoral support from the following

Table 4
Liberal Bourgeois Bloc (never formed):
The Goal of Liberal Politicians

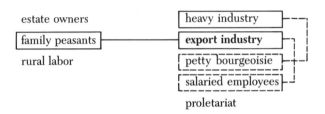

Table 5
Baseless Bloc, 1932: Fascist Potential

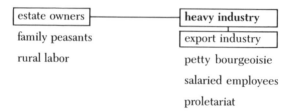

groups: the German Communist party (KPD) from the working class, and the unemployed; the Social Democratic party (SPD) from the working class, urban and rural, and to some extent the middle class; the German Democratic party (DDP) from liberal industry, urban commercial groups, intellectuals, and initially family peasants; the Catholic Center party (Zentrum) from Catholics of all classes, especially workers and peasants; the German People's party (DVP) from urban middle class, "white-collar" groups, mainline industry, and upper bourgeoisie; Economic Party of the Middle Class (Wirtschaftspartei from urban petty bourgeois; the Christian National Peasants and Rural People's party (CNBLP), as its name implies; the German National People's party (DNVP) from various urban middle classes, military and rural elites, and Protestant peasants; the National Socialist German Workers party (NSDAP) from urban and rural Mittelstand, especially Protestant, some from all other groups. The key electoral contribution of the NSDAP consisted of uniting on the basis of an authoritarian populism the various Mittelstand groups (petty bourgeois, peasant, rentier, white collar) who were or had become homeless in the course of economic and political changes and whose economic existence provided no basis for unity.

A note on the Mittelstand and the rapid demise of the DDP: this was the party founded by the most republican industrialists and staffed by liberal intellectuals. Its early electoral strength indicated not so much a left-liberal impulse on the part of its Mittelstand voters as the assumption that the only way to moderate the socialists would be through friendly opposition. In other words, they thought the socialists would be stronger than they actually were. Once the SPD proved irresolute, offensive opposition was the order of the day. By 1924 many of the 1919 DDP (and 1920 DVP) voters voted DNVP. Not at home there either, many voted Wirtschaftspartei in 1928. This was a vote simultaneously against the working class and against big business. On the Zentrum:

the Catholic party was very flexible, partially because of its mixed yet guaranteed constituency. After moving leftward during the war it moved rightward after 1923. From 1918 to 1923 it was allied with the SPD, from 1924 to 1931 with the middle bourgeois parties; by late 1932 it was prepared to form a government with the Nazis alone.

The dotted lines in Table 6 indicate the division of the party arena into left, center, and right—according to the policy behavior of the parties, not necessarily according to the intentions of their electoral supporters. The weakness/disappearance of the center is, of course, the classic story of Weimar Germany. The second classic story is the inability of the left to unite. Consequently, the third classic story is about the instability of cabinets and coalitions. Table 7 examines the vote totals of the three fields and of coalitions other than those actually formed.

Socialist-bourgeois collaboration under socialist leadership was rendered impossible once the Zentrum backed away and moved to the right. Socialist-bourgeois collaboration under bourgeois leadership was rendered impossible by the shrinkage of the DDP and DVP and by the latter's move to the right. Before 1924 and the defeat of the working class, the DVP was not prepared to be part of a "republican bourgeois" arrangement; after 1924 this was the weakest alignment. "Right bourgeois" coalitions were the goal of organized capitalist interests, but the fractiousness of the splinter parties and of the DNVP left them frustrated. Electorally, the most viable possibility remained socialist-bourgeois collaboration under bourgeois leadership; politically the SPD remained willing, but once the economic crisis set in, as it did after 1929, the economic costs it exacted proved intolerable. After 1930 no parliamentary government was possible that excluded both the SPD and the NSDAP. Ultimately, both the SPD and the parliamentary government itself were rejected.

The political interests of classes are generally represented through parties, and it is through the practice of the parties that struggles among the classes may take place. It was characteristic of the last years of the Weimar state that, except for the working class, classes became detached from their parties, which ceased to be viewed as effective representations of class interests. This break in the link between representatives and represented weakened parliament after 1930 and presaged the movement toward what could be called parliamentary idiocy. Concomitant with this was the relative increase in the power of the military, the bureaucracy, and private-interest groups.[49] This shift did not occur entirely against the will of the dominant classes, nor did it indicate a diminution of their power. German industry had, after all, been socially dominant for decades without much of a direct presence

Table 6

Percentage of the Vote Obtained by the Parties and Coalitions Formed

	KPD (USPD)	SPD	DDP	Z (+ BVP)	DVP	Bourgeois splinter parties[a]	DNVP	NSDAP	Not Voting
1919[b]	7.7	37.8	18.6	20.0	4.4	1.6	10.3	—	17.3
1920	20.0	21.7[c]	8.3	18.0	14.0	3.1	14.9	—	21.6
1924 (1)	13.3	20.4	5.8	16.7	9.2	8.2	19.4	6.6	23.7
1924 (2)	9.2	26.0	6.3	17.5	9.9	7.3	20.4[d]	3.0	22.3
1928	10.7	29.8	5.0	15.2	8.6	13.0	14.3	2.6	25.5
1930	13.1	24.6[e]	3.7	14.8	4.6	13.8	7.1	18.3	18.6
1932 (1)	14.3	21.6	1.1	15.7	1.1	3.0	6.0	37.1	16.5
1932 (2)	17.0	20.3	.9	15.1	2.0	3.5	8.5	33.0	20.0
1933	12.2	18.4	.8	14.0	1.0	1.5	7.9	44.2	12.1

Sources: Bernhard Vogel et al., Wahlen in Deutschland (Berlin, New York, 1971), pp. 296, 297; Heinrich Striefler, Deutsche Wahlen in Bilder und Zahlen (Dusseldorf, 1946), pp. 67, 68; Max Schwarz, MdR (Hanover, 1965), pp. 822, 823; S. M. Lipset, Political Man (Garden City, N.Y.: Doubleday Anchor, 1960), pp. 131–51.

Note: Abbreviations from left to right: KPD = German Communist party; USPD = Independent Social Democratic party (with KPD in 1920); SPD = Social Democratic party of Germany; DDP = German Democratic party; Z = Catholic Center party (Zentrum); BVP = Bavarian affiliate of Z; DVP = German People's party; DNVP = German National People's party; NSDAP = National Socialist German Workers party. Cabinet composition did not mirror electoral results directly; frequently there were cabinets of "personalities," for example in 1922–24 and 1930–32. Altogether there were twenty-two governments. The Z was nearly always the fulcrum; after 1924 its right wing tended to dominate. From 1923 to 1930 the DVP enjoyed disproportionate influence. Prosperity and Stresemann's program for reintegrating Germany internationally were essentially responsible for bringing the DVP into the ranks of the "middle parties"; this lasted only as long as they did.

[a] Wirtschafts Partei, Christian National Peasants, and Rural People's party (CNBLP), Volkskonservativen, and regional splinter parties.

[b] The government of revolutionary delegates, declared in November 1918, consisted of 3 SPD and 3 USPD members.

[c] The initial position of the SPD yielded to cabinets strongly influenced by DVP.

[d] DNVP was sometimes in but mostly out of the government.

[e] SPD was not in government, but the government depended on SPD toleration.

Table 7
Vote Totals of Camps and Potential Coalitions

	Left	Center	Right	SOCIALIST[a] bourgeois	Socialist[b] BOURGEOIS	Republican[c] bourgeois	Right[d] bourgeois	Actuale coalition
1919	45.5	38.6	16.3	76.4	80.8	43.0	16.3	76.4
1920	41.7	26.3	32.0	48.0	62.0	40.3	32.0	48/40.3
1924 (1)	33.7	22.5	43.4	42.9	52.1	31.7+	36.8	55.5
1924 (2)	35.2	41.0	23.4	49.8	59.7	33.7+	37.6	41.0
1928	40.7	28.8	29.9	50.0	58.6	28.8+	35.9	58.6
1930	37.7	18.5	43.8	43.1	47.7	23.1+	25.5	36.9
1932 (1)	35.9	16.8	47.2	38.4	39.5	20.9	10.1	—
1932 (2)	37.3	—	—	36.3	38.3	21.5	14.0	41.5

Sources: Vogel et al., *Wahlen in Deutschland*, p. 296, 297; Striefler, *Deutsche Wahlen in Bilder und Zahlen*, pp. 67, 68; Schwarz, *MdR*, pp. 822, 823; Lipset, *Political Man*, pp. 131–51; cf. K. D. Bracher, *Die Auflösung der Weimarer Republik* (Stuttgart, 1955), p. 645. On the parties generally: Sigmund Neumann, *Die Parteien der Weimarer Republik* (Stuttgart, 1965); Bracher, *Die Auflösung der Weimarer Republik* (Bonn, 1965); E. Matthias and R. Morsey, *Das Ende der Parteien, 1933* (Dusseldorf, 1960) pp. 743–94.

[a] SPD + DDP + Z
[b] SPD + DDP + Z + DVP
[c] DDP + Z + DVP
[d] DVP through DNVP
[e] See Table 6

on the political scene or direct management of the state apparatus.[50] The Weimar Constitution had attempted to establish parliamentary government as the locus for resolution of social and interest-group conflicts, but so limited and democratic a system would have left too much to be decided by vote counting. The constitution postulated a kind of super pluralism with equilibrium produced by the continuous collision of conflicting interests, almost all of which would have their inputs.[51]

Additionally, the bourgeois parties from the DDP through the DNVP were singularly incapable of unifying the interests of the dominant classes. Prominent industrialists constantly bemoaned the fragmentation *(Zersplitterung)* and internal conflicts that rendered the bourgeois parties incapable of merging or acting together to dominate the political scene.[52] Of course they were unwilling, once the depression began, to make the kinds of concessions that had enabled Stresemann to act as if such a dominance had been established. The industrialists themselves, however, provided a recalcitrant base for any unified party formation. They rejected political modification of private interests and were "incapable of accepting co-responsibility . . . . for national-political tasks"; they demonstrated irresponsibility and were "incapable of building mass support and providing moral leadership."[53] Back in 1923 industrialists had demonstrated this same selfishness during the Ruhr occupation and inflation. Their selfishness blocked the "national effort" even when the government was headed by a bourgeois-conservative shipping magnate, Cuno. They had favored militant national resistance only to discipline organized labor and then colluded with the French to ameliorate their economic situation.[54]

The contradictory relations among the fractions of the bourgeoisie disabled its own political parties and augmented both the role of the state as the cohesive factor for the bloc of dominant classes and the bourgeoisie's Bonapartist tendencies. Conflicts over political leadership within the industrial bourgeoisie worsened with the start of the agricultural depression in 1928 and became even more acute with the onset of the industrial depression. These conflicts seemed to immobilize not only the parties but also the state itself; state intervention appeared to be—and was—riddled with contradictions.

Nevertheless, as far as the dominant classes were concerned, the state played the role of political organizer of the power bloc. Poulantzas asserts, a bit too glibly, that "the state plays this role because the political parties of the bourgeois fractions are unable to play an autonomous organizational role. [The state's role] emerges as the factor of political unity of the power bloc under the protection of the hegemonic fraction and as organizer of the latter's interests."[55] As the bourgeois parties declined they took on the role of transmission belts, virtually carrying messages from private interest and pressure groups to the state. In turn, the state moved from a parliamentary to a ministerial to a presidential form, each stage being marked by a narrowing of those circles to which the state was responsive. (In 1930 parliament disposed of ninety-eight laws while five were enacted by emergency decree. By 1932, five were enacted by parliament and sixty-six by decree.) The weakening of the bourgeois parties further exposed their essentially class character. Capitalist groups became increasingly concerned with what James O'Connor calls "the private appropriation of state power for particularistic ends."[56] Instead of being populated by citizens, the parties became transparent class representatives. Only the Catholic Zentrum and later the Nazis escaped this fate. The consequence of this demystification was further loss of support, especially from the Mittelstand. Ultimately, however, the Weimar state was unable, in any of its forms, to resolve the contradictions within the bloc of dominant classes. Before it could do so, the victories won by the working class had to be reversed, and the struggle for hegemony within the dominant bloc had to be resolved—both, of course, "in the interests of the nation."

Weimar Stability: Labor-Capital Cooperation

No parliamentary-democratic state system can maintain itself without a mass base. Between 1924 and 1930 the German working class, organized primarily in the SPD, provided a substantial part of this base. The divisions and conflicts within and among the non-working-class strata were such that governing without working-class participation would have been undesirable even had it been possible. Having accepted the rules of the republican game, it was impossible to deny the strength of the working-class party, which shared adherence to those rules. Indeed, the working class's commitment to those rules was greater than that of any other class. It was after 1923, however, that the policy indeterminacy built into those rules became acceptable to the dominant classes. The defeat of the revolutionary working-class impulse had been completed by 1923: local communist uprisings had been suppressed; previous concessions in the realm of wages and hours had been reversed in the context of the Ruhr occupation; the inflation facilitated liquidation of industrial debts; the SPD had rid itself of most of its revolutionaries; *völkisch* radicalism had subsided; radical tax laws were being rewritten, and their author, Matthias Erzberger, had been killed. After 1924, a steady flow of foreign capital facilitated business and industrial expansion.[57] The necessity of governing with labor was recognized by leading industrialists as early as 1924, although initially they meant the Catholic workers organized in the Zentrum. By 1926, a leading industrialist, Paul Silverberg, could tell the annual convention of the League of German Industry (RDI) that government without organized labor (i.e., the SPD) was undesirable, even impossible. In a development that furthered this reorientation, Stresemann had been victorious in 1924 over the rightist, pro-DNVP wing of the DVP.[58] Some steel magnates and other dissidents migrated to the DNVP, while Stresemann found a new source of support in the white-collar employee wing of the party.[59] Stresemann argued that further counter-revolution would strengthen rather than weaken the left and would drive the Catholic Zentrum back in a social-populist direction.

Industrialists and workers each found the other necessary for social stability; their cooperation was mediated, albeit asymmetrically, by the state.[60] Some elements of the dominant bloc objected from the outset, but their opposition was stilled both by apparent economic prosperity and the political stability engendered by cooperation. Some elements of the working class also objected, but even the bulk of the KPD recognized that a period of capitalist stabilization had begun after the thorough defeats of October 1923 and German acceptance of the Dawes Plan in April 1924.[61] Charles Maier employs the somewhat anodyne concept of "corporatist equilibrium" to describe the post-1924 stability. Such a description, however, fails to appreciate the role of the state and its apparatus in organizing the dominant classes. Maier writes:

> What permitted stability after 1924 was a shift in the focal point of decision making. Fragmented parliamentary majorities yielded to ministerial bureaucracies . . . where interest-group representatives could more easily work out social burdens and rewards. This displacement permitted a new compromise: a corporatist equilibrium in which private interests assumed the tasks that parliamentary coalitions found difficult.[62]

As a statement about the consequences of the fragmentation of the bourgeois parties this is correct, although there was nothing new in the German bourgeoisie's reliance on the state organs. As a statement about some kind of neutral or corporate state and a social equilibrium, it is false. There is nothing neutral or classless about organized capitalism.

Although the economic recovery and prosperity of the years 1924–29 were both borrowed and uneven, they were experienced as a real turnaround, despite consistently high unemployment. There were good reasons for this optimistic view. In 1923 German industrial production represented 8 percent of world production compared with a prewar share of 16 percent; the volume of industrial production in 1923 was only 55 percent of the 1913 figure. In addition, Germany had lost 75 percent of its iron ore sources, 31 percent of its blast furnaces, and 23 percent of its other iron and steel facilities in the peace settlement. Yet by 1927 Germany had attained its prewar volume of industrial production; an increase of 3.5 percent in the following year made Germany the world's number-two industrial power. [63] In addition, new investment, rationalization, and concentration enabled German industry to attain a level of productivity formerly unique to the United States.[64] Industrial interests could afford to govern with the working masses and to accede to some of their demands. Between 1925 and 1930 export industry engaged in this kind of Giolittian arrangement in the name of "quality production and expanded trade and consumption."[65] Heavy industry too went along with this, or, more accurately, most of heavy industry went along at best half-heartedly. For organized agriculture, dependent on tariff protection, such an arrangement was intolerable. It had never really recovered and was almost immediately the victim of a price-scissors trend. The agricultural sector became compressed both as consumer and as producer. Production in 1929, for example, was only 74 percent of the 1913 level, and the agricultural, industrial, and total price indices were skewed accordingly (see Table 8).

For the mass of industrial workers and their political (SPD) and economic (ADGB) organs cooperation offered the possibility of both success and stability. In the course of World War I the unions had passed from toleration to recognition, and from 1918 to 1924 unions and entrepreneurs had worked together with partially shared and partially divergent goals in the central joint working groups (*Zentrale Arbeitsgemeinschaften*). Once the revolutionary impulse had been defeated, capital and labor formalized their relations through laws and private agreements. A step-by-step system was devised consisting of collective bargaining, mediation, and compulsory arbitration, which institutionalized a certain amount of economic class conflict while simultaneously softening class conflict in general.[66] The unions themselves came to perceive strikes as a means of last resort to be used only when other means failed to yield a compromise. Only secure unions could indulge themselves in such a routinized policy perspective, one based on three important assumptions: first, that the unions did indeed enjoy full recognition by the state, the industrialists, and the public as a whole; second, that through their assumption of "national" tasks and responsibilities the unions had earned an unassailable, quasi-official or public status; and third, that as institutions they were strong enough to

Table 8
Price Indices 1924–33
(1913 = 100)

	Agricultural prices	Industrial prices	Cost of raw materials	Cost of living	Nominal wages	Real hourly wage rates	Real weekly wage earnings	Level of industrial production
1924	128	137	136	131	91	84	70	77
1925	132	157	133	142	123	100	87	92
1926	132	150	130	142	128	105	90	87
1927	138	148	132	148	145	110	97	110
1928	132	159	134	152	164	117	108	113
1929	126	157	132	154	169	123	110	114
1930	107	154	120	148	155	126	105	99
1931	89	142	108	136	137	127	100	82
1932	77	118	88	121	113	122	94	66
1933	84	111	88	118	115	121	98	74

Source: Gerhard Bry, *Wages in Germany, 1871–1945* (Princeton: Princeton University Press, 1960), pp. 461–67; Deutsches Zentral Archiv, Potsdam (DZA), Büro des Reichspäsidenten/Landwirtschaftsfragen, 332/104; *Statistisches Jahrbuch für das Deutschen Reich, 1926–33,* passim.
Note: Hourly wages tended to be the form of payment for industrial workers, weekly earnings for white collar employees. A reduced work week is also indicated.

weather even severe economic changes.[67] The extent to which such a policy perspective was durable rather than tenuous was a political question; the answer would depend not primarily on industrial or economic class relations but rather on political class relations as evidenced in the parties and in the state. After 1924 the position of the SPD and the working class as underpinnings of the Weimar state appeared to be permanent. Even bourgeois parliamentary governments, such as those that governed from 1924 to 1928, had to respect and make significant concessions to the working class.

An expansive economy, international reconciliation, sweeping social legislation (typified by the unemployment insurance law of 1927 and the acceptance of binding, compulsory arbitration of labor disputes through the Labor Ministry), and vastly increased state welfare expenditures were all part of this collaboration. In a sense, industrialist August Weber was correct when he told fellow members of the RDI that the "whole so-called revolution has become a pure wage movement." Labor abandoned its political struggle while, within limits, its economic struggle was incorporated.[68]

The promises of the Weimar Constitution appeared to be bearing fruit: not only were the unions accorded the right to organize *(Koalitionsfreiheit)*, but the results of collective bargaining were recognized as well. The state was declared committed to *Sozialpolitik*, and according to article 165, capital and labor were to enjoy parity in the determination of economic policy. Despite the obvious and severe setbacks organized labor suffered in the four years following promulgation of the constitution, the ADGB and SPD alike based their efforts on what it, and the democratic republic it signaled, offered. For Rudolf Hilferding, this was the form of state in which the class opposition of workers could be carried furthest without systematic violence; for Hugo Sinzheimer, the privileged position of the unions provided a favorable basis for the further development of society, nation, and state; while for Ernst Fraenkel, the collective rights of labor represented the positive link between the working class and the Republic.

This sense of parity, of labor's co-responsibility for the social, economic, and political common good *(Gemeinwohl)*, came to be conceptualized as "pluralist democracy," according to which the democratization of the state could be followed by a democratization of the economy. Thus, it was in 1928, at the height of Weimar's stability, during the period of cooperation between organized labor and the dynamic-export fraction of industry, that the ADGB put forward its program for *Wirtschaftsdemokratie*, for democratizing the economy. Whether such a program was feasible within a capitalist democracy or would have taken Germany "beyond" capitalism is moot. The advent of economic adversity, a shift in the balance of power within industry, and the beginning of a general capitalist offensive together led not only to the abandonment of any hopes for economic democracy, but also to immobility within both the SPD and ADGB and, ultimately, impotence and despair.

Bourgeois–working-class collaboration during the period of recovery stabilized the dominance of the former by at once rewarding and depoliticizing the latter. Playing by the rules of the game tended to make the SPD a normal, interest-aggregating Volkspartei: Sigmund Neumann has suggested that up to 1930, 25 percent of SPD members and 40 percent of SPD voters were other than working class.[69] Strikes were invariably about wages and other distribution questions; gone were vague political demands and political strikes. Although they retained a more violent tenor and archaic vocabulary, communist-led actions in this period were not much different.[70] The SPD was simply more forthright in representing, together with the unions, the day-to-day interests of the working class in a capitalist society. Thus, the major electoral victory of 1928 was in no way interpreted as a mandate for systemic change. Neither was the repression rather than cooptation of rowdy KPD May Day demonstrations; the SPD would not mobilize forces for change. Finally, in the same line were the toleration of Brüning's nonparliamentary semidictatorship, the support of the reactionary, senile Hindenburg against Hitler for the presidency in 1932, the holding back of the socialist *Reichsbanner* militia, and the politics of the "lesser evil" right up to the final weeks of the Republic.

The bourgeois classes and their political representatives were not unaware of the costs of this collaboration. In a routine and sometimes successful manner, they opposed the "limitless spending" and "stultification of initiative" that were at the heart of SPD programs. What they could not foresee in general was the exact limit of the economy's ability to absorb popular programs. Hence their own credibility was damaged, and much of their opposition appeared sporadic and unprincipled, selfish rather than for the national good. Various conflicts over trade and tariff policy, for example, seemed to underline this selfishness while simultaneously demonstrating how split the dominant classes really were. Important sectors of the Mittelstand came to see themselves as victims of this selfish, weak-kneed policy, and the ranks of the allies and supporters of Germany's social elites were weakened accordingly. The DDP and DVP paid a price in lost support before industry itself concluded that it could no longer afford collaboration.

The major bourgeois electoral victory of 1924 had created the conditions for a popular class state, that is, a state populated by classes rather than equal citizen-atoms, but nevertheless a state where a bourgeois government seemed to be acting in the interests of all citizens and the nation. Sacrifices of various kinds were demanded of all classes for the good of the nation. The cooperation of the bourgeois classes and their various interest groups, however, remained tenuous at best. The interests of the dominant classes were not unified, and the links between representatives and represented remained weak. Although the balance within the bourgeois parties (DDP, DVP, DNVP) shifted to the right, as did the politics of the Catholic Zentrum, they all remained vulnerable to fissures and splits. Despite the absence of the SPD from the government between 1924 and 1928, the internal coherence of the bourgeois parties was not substantially augmented. Thus, the Zentrum was unable to win the support of its Bavarian sister party for the Zentrum's own conservative presidential candidate, Marx, against the northern Protestant Hindenburg in 1925.[71] The DDP's ranks continued to shrink even during the period of stability. Stresemann was constantly under fire from those within the DVP who perceived too many of their individual interests being sacrificed. The DNVP was torn between "abstentionist-rejectionist" and compromise-oriented alternatives as well as between rural and industrial demands. Despite its second-place finish in the 1924 elections, the DNVP participated in the bourgeois government only on two occasions between 1924 and 1928.[72]

Indicative of the bourgeoisie's inability to raise itself from the level of economic-corporate interests to the level of political interests was the continuing growth, even before the depression, of splinter parties, most of which claimed only to represent specific economic groups.[73] The major bourgeois parties never really succeeded in reconciling the various interests of those who comprised their bases. Consequently, the parliamentary and party format for bourgeois–working-class collaboration remained inadequate while it simultaneously aggravated existing cleavages within the bourgeois parties. This was neither the first nor the last occasion when bourgeois political stability was dependent on SPD and union support. The latter, in turn, was conditioned primarily by the bourgeoisie's ability to pay the bill.

The state bureaucracy

The state bureaucracy supplemented parliament and the parties as an arena of class collaboration. Many working-class economic victories, both nationally and in Prussia, were achieved through the agency of the Labor Ministry. Headed most frequently by members of the labor wing of the Zentrum, this ministry tilted toward labor in arbitrating work and contract disputes. Once the depression began it came under constant attack from bourgeois forces. The Labor Ministry was also one of the main sources, along with local government, of the costly social welfare and insurance programs *(Sozialpolitik)*, which assumed tremendous symbolic as well as economic importance.[74] The Economics Ministry served an analogous function in promoting the interests of the industrial classes. It reflected the splits in the industrial camp, however, especially that between export-oriented, small and new industries and domestic-oriented heavy industry.[75] Major industries and cartels supplied the ministry's leadership and staff, much of which moved back and forth between the ministry and the League of German Industry (RDI).[76] A similar situation existed in the Finance Ministry, although there more democratic commercial and banking interests dominated.[77]

In their capacity as ministerial bureaucrats and politicians, these individuals often adopted a certain far-sightedness and autonomy their friends and colleagues back in the interest-group organizations failed to appreciate. Their class origins did not entirely guide their policy formulation.[78] The aristocratic and petty-bourgeois members of the bureaucracy did not behave differently because of their different origins. It is in this sense, too, that the Junkers had functioned as the intellectuals for the dominant industrialists.[79] The relative autonomy enjoyed by the bureaucracy existed as a function of its role within the state. Ostensibly, the bureaucracy represented the needs of the entire nation in a neutral fashion. However, conflicts within the bureaucracy reflected arrangements and conflicts among the dominant class fractions and between them and the working class on the political scene as a whole. The less obvious the dominance of any particular capitalist fraction, the greater the impact of the bureaucracy and of the executive.

The political disorganization of the dominant classes, even during the years of stabilization, rendered the bureaucracy a stronger force in mediating interclass conflicts. Beyond this, Weimar coalition (SPD, DDP, and Zentrum) and socialist governments (as in Prussia) added republican personnel to all the previously antirepublican organs of state and civil society: schools, police, chambers of commerce, judiciary, church.[80] They did not, however, restructure these organs; nor, in the absence of real state power, could they have been expected to do so. Since the working class's political practice did not aim at taking state power, the structures of the capitalist state remained intact, despite the conflicts over leadership within the dominant classes.[81]

Crisis and the End of Stability

The bourgeois governments of 1924–28, under several DVP and Catholic chancellors, were able to compromise and maneuver as much

as they did only at the expense of the parties that constituted the
various coalitions.[82] Cabinets and bureaucracies worked out a host of
compromises, but party life showed signs of becoming moribund as the
transmission of interest-group pressures became an increasingly central activity.[83] Already, formal and real power began to issue from
different sources. Collaboration did not create consensus, and the
centrality of the middle parties masked the decline and splitting of
their constituencies. The political crisis became increasingly acute
after 1928, before the economic crisis had really set in. No member or
fraction of the dominant bloc was capable of imposing its direction on
the other members of the bloc, either through parliament or other
organs of the state. The minimal ideological unity Stresemann was able
to impose dissolved even before his death in October 1929.

The bloc, in brief, could not surmount its own internal contradictions.[84] The political and economic interests of both industry and
agriculture were fragmented along several axes, and despite a plethora
of organizations and pressure groups, no voice was accepted as guiding.
Whereas before 1928 state trade and social and foreign policies had
demonstrated considerable inconsistency and instability, after 1928
incapacitation became more frequent. As the political crisis deepened
and the locus of decision-making narrowed from parliament to cabinet
to presidential circles, the expression of dominant bloc interests actually became more fragmented. Despite the government's increased
emergency powers, it was faced with increased bourgeois disunity.

The SPD electoral victory of 1928 and the Young Plan for reparations
revisions set off the brewing political crisis. Fascism reappeared as a
mass party and as a possible political alternative through which the
interests of the dominant bloc might be represented less directly but
more effectively than they had been. The internal political crisis of the
dominant bloc and its class offensive were intertwined. In some respects the situation after 1928 was like that of 1923 when the conservative shipping magnate, Cuno, had been chancellor: a fragmented
bourgeoisie concerned solely with its particularistic interests prevented the state from formulating a national policy while simultaneously undertaking an offensive against the working class. The SPD
was hardly prepared for such a turn of events: the 1.2-million plus
increase in votes it received in 1928 over 1924 was not a reward for
steadfast opposition to capitalism and bourgeois rule, for such opposition had not been its policy.[85] Despite an initially very strong position
in the cabinet and parliament in 1928, the SPD program consisted only
of the same elements as before: defense of the daily interests of the
organized working class within the capitalist system and continuation of
Stresemann's foreign policy. The SPD was, therefore, inadequately

prepared for the massive lockouts undertaken by employers in Ruhr heavy industry in the fall of 1928. The substantial electoral losses suffered by the bourgeois parties accrued primarily to the benefit of other splinter, rightist, and particularist parties. With prosperity largely mortgaged to American capital through the agency of German finance and industry, the prospects of an SPD government mediating the conflicting needs of the dominant bloc were slim.[86]

The political crisis was fueled by the onset of a fiscal crisis following the collapse of the New York stock market and the subsequent shrinkage of loans. The fiscal crisis served as a pretext for the ouster of Rudolf Hilferding as finance minister and his replacement by the DVP and I. G. Farben representative, Paul Moldenhauer. Reichsbank president Hjalmar Schacht, representing another, still more anti-SPD faction of the dominant bloc, had undermined Hilferding's attempt to restructure government finances in a manner commensurate with the new situation but not entirely at the expense of the working class. Beginning in 1929 unemployment began to rise quickly, and it was over this issue that the Grand Coalition (bloc 3) stretching from the SPD to the DVP collapsed.

With almost 3 million unemployed by March 1930, the DVP refused to agree to an increase in employers' contributions to the unemployment insurance fund, and the coalition collapsed.[87] It was indicative of the SPD's identification with the existing system that it was in no position to ask the working class to accept this setback in the name of a larger struggle. Just prior to his death the previous October, Stresemann had barely convinced his DVP delegation to accept a similar compromise on unemployment benefits and taxation. In the face of substantial opposition to the Young Plan, Stresemann had managed to coerce minimal dominant bloc unity in its favor.[88] With his death, anti-social-collaborationist forces were no longer to be restrained, and the conflicts within the dominant bloc could no longer be held in check.

Industrialists had all along complained of high "political wage rates," but with the onset of the depression the costs of maintaining mass legitimacy through the working class became "excessive." Under the pressure of the heavy-industry fraction, the RDI at its 1929 meetings issued a blistering attack on the policies of the labor-export coalition. Entitled "Recovery or Collapse," it became industry's manifesto for rolling back the gains of organized labor, those obtained both in the workplace and in parliament. Beyond that, however, this and other similar initiatives were part of a campaign by heavy industry (supported by organized agriculture) to remove the dynamic-export fraction from its hegemonic position. These initiatives gained momentum—due both to political developments and to the decline of international trade—and, at the 1931 RDI convention, spokespeople for the dynamic fraction were either ousted from their leadership positions or eased into retirement.

The economic crisis—first in agriculture, then in domestic, and finally in export industry—together with the state's fiscal crisis rendered the costs of social collaboration, reparations fulfillment, and a trade policy based on these two intolerable for the dominant classes. The contradiction between the necessary costs of collaboration and the imperatives of capital accumulation and reproduction could no longer be accepted by a fragmented dominant bloc. Key sectors of capital, including mining, iron and steel, and the whole of agriculture, were in the midst of profitability crises even before the full brunt of the international depression was felt. Partially opposed to these sectors, however, was a prosperous export sector consisting mainly of new industries—ones that had a greater interest in the fulfillment of reparations and a lesser interest in the repression of labor. Some of these industries even subscribed to trade union ideas about the need for increased mass consumption *(Kaufkraft)*. Heavy industry and agriculture were not altogether in agreement either. Whereas industry preferred low food costs and high industrial prices, agriculture preferred just the reverse. Whereas both industrial sectors were operating well below capacity and looked favorably on foreign expansion, pacific or otherwise, agriculture was overproducing and tended toward various autarkic formulas. Once the economic crisis began, it became even more difficult to subsume the diverse economic-corporative interests of the various fractions of the bloc into one political interest. The frequency with which representatives of these fractions found it necessary to remind each other of their common opposition to the organized working class bears witness not only to the depth of hostility toward the SPD and KPD but also to the increased salience and depth of conflicts within the bloc.

Between mid-1930 and the end of 1932 three successive semi- and nonparliamentary governments failed to unify, transcend, or subsume the interests of the dominant fractions while securing for themselves a mass base. Was there no bourgeois political force to organize the political unity of the dominant economic fractions out of the diversity of their economic interests? Was no political unity possible and no mass political support available within the Republic—despite the single-mindedness of elite anti-socialism? Were the maintenance of capitalist economic relations and political democracy so antithetical in this conjuncture that undermining of the Republic was a self-evident necessity for the dominant classes?

Heinrich Brüning, a leader of the Catholic Zentrum party, became chancellor following the collapse of the Grand Coalition in March 1930. He ruled without a parliamentary majority through the semiconstitutional mechanism of presidential decree. The Brüning regime functioned as a surrogate for the bourgeois parties, which had, by this time, lost nearly their entire electoral backing. They had become simple transmission belts for economic interests; under pressure from their industrial backers they had become creatures of "industrial egotism lacking any social concern."[89] A fully inverse relationship had developed between industry's direct influence in a party and that party's electoral viability: the bourgeois parties were now capital's own, and they proved useless. The first year of Brüning's regime was, nevertheless, tolerated by the SPD, which could have toppled him. He attempted to implement a program bridging the differences among the three dominant fractions, and his economic policies were characterized by brutal deflationary budget-balancing and belt-tightening. Brüning's modest efforts to force the estate owners to modernize, give up their huge subventions, or face massive peasant resettlement (land reform) led them to conspire with President Hindenburg's camarilla, and Brüning was abandoned. In fact, however, the heavy-industry fraction had already turned against him because he had not cut himself off entirely from the pressure of organized labor, Catholic and socialist. The dynamic-export fraction of industry, on the other hand, was prepared to continue supporting him, but it was no longer setting the tone or agenda for the dominant classes as a whole. [90]

Brüning was succeeded in May 1932 by a cabinet of barons headed by Franz von Papen. Papen's government was heralded as being fully authoritarian and national, but throughout its six-month tenure it lacked any base of mass support and failed to unify the interests of the dominant fractions. It catered almost exclusively to the protectionist and autarkic strivings of the rural elite and heavy industry while failing to integrate the Nazi party as a junior member of the government. Papen was even less able than Brüning to harmonize the interests of the three dominant fractions, although he was certainly more energetic and effective in his repression of the SPD and unions. Because he incurred the wrath of the dynamic-export fraction and failed to split and enlist part of the Nazi party, Papen was replaced in early December 1932 by General von Schleicher.

Schleicher's failings were a mirror image of his predecessor's: if Papen erred on the side of estate owners, deflation, domestic-oriented heavy industry, autarky, and failure to seek a mass base, then Schleicher and his left-Keynesian minister for "Work Creation" erred grievously on the side of opposition to the rural elite, inflation, the export industries, and too much dickering with the Nazi "left" and the unions. His public-works program was not unlike that proposed by some union spokespeople. Although both fractions of industry were opposed to an inflation, the prospects of a policy shift in favor of the dynamic-export industries came as a rude shock to those in heavy industry and agriculture who had previously brought about a shift in their own favor. Conflicts rather than joint interest had come to the fore among the dominant fractions. Finally, Schleicher's efforts raised the spectre of state socialism and a possible reparliamentarization of political life, even in military dress. The prospect of a *dirigist* social dictatorship supported by Nazi and union anticapitalist masses was too much to bear: the reentry of the unions into the corridors of power threatened what had been the primary political accomplishment of the previous year and a half, namely, their exclusion.

After the failures of the previous two years it was the political fear inspired by Schleicher's program that was central and that led finally to the appointment of Hitler on January 30, 1933. Papen's program, this time with a mass base and a more imperialist tone, appeared to be the least common denominator for the three dominant fractions. The question remaining was how to reconcile the interests of an autarkic rural elite with the interests of the export-oriented dynamic industries. A program for forming cartels in agricultural production and for guaranteeing prices without altering property relations would satisfy the demands of the estate owners. A program of holding down the costs of production while increasing public spending, especially on armaments, would go some way toward satisfying heavy industry. A vigorous program of trade expansion, especially in middle and southeastern Europe—imperialism—could open avenues for export industry without setting it against either the rural elite or heavy industry. Residual notions of laissez-faire entrepreneurship would have to give way to state guidance; ideological homage to the Mittelstand would be honored, after some early confusion, mostly in the breach; and a republic that could only infrequently muster a majority in its favor, but that was nevertheless divisive and costly, would have to be abandoned. Initially, given an improvement in the international economic situation, "only" the peasantry, the working class, and Germany's neighbors would have to pay.

After 1929 Germany witnessed a continuous narrowing of the locus of decision-making and decision-makers. First parliament ceased to participate in making crucial decisions; then the parties themselves became nearly irrelevant, and finally even the cabinet ministers were shut out. Within the corporate-interest organizations such as the RDI, the general-membership assemblies yielded decision-making power to their presidia and then to a few executive leaders. By the end of 1932, crucial decisions were being made by a handful of men in leadership circles, and one can indeed speak of cliques. Although elections occurred with increasing frequency after 1930, their primary effect was to destabilize the situation further. They served also to indicate that a new Mittelstand mass had been aggregated, more on the basis of ideological and political unity than economic. Since 1924, most industrialists and most bourgeois politicians had remained somewhat aloof from *völkisch* (populist radicalism) and had come to look upon it with disdain. After 1930, however, this new popular mass and the Nazi party it supported became objects of their intense interest. Once they established that both the party and its mass were (or could become) supporters of social order, various governmental possibilities involving the Nazis became feasible. In the eyes of those professional politicians and economic leaders for whom the NSDAP was an exogenous force and its supporters potential revolutionaries, the preferred strategy was to split the party and enlist its masses. It was only reluctantly that the leading industrial circles became receptive to the idea that the entire NSDAP had to be called upon to take charge of the state and provide that popular base that had been lacking since 1930.

But what was the NSDAP to be called on to do? To assume state power, to be the class in charge of the state for the maintenance of the economic and political order? Would the Nazis constitute a class, or would they merely act as an agent for the capitalist class or for some capitalists? Or were the Nazis simply the only acceptable common denominator for stabilizing the political system and guaranteeing the social system? The leading representatives of the dominant classes thought the Nazis manageable, despite their demands for total power. Industrialists and agrarians do not seem to have feared that, like the mid-nineteenth-century bourgeoisie described by Marx, they were about to "give up the right to rule for the right to make money." As guarantors of capitalism, as proponents of a strong, imperialist Germany, the Nazis appeared to be the best available possibility.

The manner in which classes had been organized and inserted into the political struggle up to 1930 led first to success in isolating the economic struggles of the dominated classes from their political struggle and then to the defeat of both facets. But the political unity of the dominant classes was not successfully molded out of the diversity and isolation of their economic struggles.[91] Further, the political support previously tendered by the Mittelstand in exchange for nonsocialist stability evaporated. By 1930 virtually all sections of the dominant bloc agreed that postcrisis Germany must be spared the costliness and unreliability of an ineffective, democratic political structure and a profit-devouring social welfare system. Beyond that, however, there was little clarity: a presidential dictatorship, a military dictatorship, a restructured but suffrage-based republic with vague corporatist over-tones, a government with or without a mass base—all were conceivable though each would necessitate a different base of legitimacy and a different internal arrangement of the dominant bloc.[92]

Thus the rollback of working-class gains, a solution to the fractional struggles inside the dominant bloc, and some settlement with the supporting classes outside the center of the capitalist mode of production (peasants, petty bourgeoisie) were all on the agenda.[93] No one of these tasks required a fascist or imperialist solution; perhaps even all three in their ensemble did not. But the concrete conjuncture and manner in which these tasks appeared heightened such a possibility. As we have seen, the dominant bloc eventually "decided" for fascism, although there may have been other ways out of the economic, political, and social crisis that too would not have violated the fundamental interests of its members.[94]

Notes

This essay is an expanded version of an article of the same title published in *Politics & Society* 7, no. 3 (1977):229–66. I wish to thank Butterworth Publishers for its permission to reprint it here. The perspective and positions adopted in this essay have, for the most part, been further substantiated by the rich body of work that has appeared over the past decade. Apart from a number of footnote references and one significant exception, I have not attempted to integrate that literature here. The exception is Knut Borchardt's discussion of economic depression, accumulation problems, and democratic decay, a discussion that has not appeared in English and whose significance for the issues examined here is so great that addressing it has become essential.

For an overview of some of the recent Weimar-Nazi literature—both that which, in the spirit of recent times, is manifestly apologetic as far as economic elites are concerned, as well as more reliable work—see my Introduction to the Second Edition of *The Collapse of the Weimar Republic: Political Economy and Crisis* (New York: Holmes & Meier, 1986), pp. xv–xli as well as other contributions to this volume.

1. Franz Neumann, *Behemoth: The Structure and Practice of National Socialism* (New York: Harper and Row, 1966), pp. 33, 34. A semi-Marxist example of the "final outcome" bias is Barrington Moore, *Social Origins of Dictatorship and Democracy* (Boston: Beacon Press, 1967). The "organized capitalism" and "corporatism" literature is discussed below.

2. Recent debates on "refeudalization" or "repoliticization" concern themselves precisely with the question of whether or how economic relations are again dependent on political ones. Both those supporting the theory of state monopoly capitalism and those opposing it argue that the state has been drawn directly into the process of economic reproduction. See Claus Offe, *Strukturprobleme des kapitalistischen Staates* (Frankfurt: Suhrkamp, 1972), and, on its historical development, H. A. Winkler, ed., *Organisierter Kapitalismus: Vorahsetzungen und Anfänge* (Gottingen: Vandenhoeck & Ruprecht, 1974), esp. the contributions by Winkler, Kocka, and Wehler.

3. On the limits to this autonomy and indeterminacy, see Ralph Miliband, *The State in Capitalist Society* (London: Weidenfeld and Nicholson, 1969), esp. chs. 2, 6.

4. Nicos Poulantzas, *Political Power and Social Classes* (London: NLB, 1973), p. 189. For a different formulation of the same view, see Georg Lukács, *History and Class Consciousness* (London: Merlin Press, 1971), pp. 65ff. Antonio Gramsci, *Prison Notebooks* (New York: International Publishers, 1971), pp. 181, 370, labels the selfish level "economic-corporative" and the organized level "ethical-political." It is only at the latter level that hegemony, active consent, can be established.

5. A position too close to individual capitalists is at minimum considered corruption. Engels' remark that "Bonapartism is the religion of the bourgeoisie" must be understood to encompass almost all forms of the bourgeois state, not just the strictly Bonapartist.

6. On this, see Jürgen Habermas, *Legitimation Crisis* (Boston: Beacon Press, 1975); Offe, *Strukturprobleme des kapitalistischen Staates;* Claus Offe, *Contradictions of the Welfare State* (Cambridge: MIT Press, 1984); and John Goldthorpe, ed., *Order and Conflict in Contemporary Capitalism* (Oxford: Clarendon Press, 1984).

7. A strong argument for the growth of such tendencies is made by Charles Maier, *Recasting Bourgeois Europe* (Princeton: Princeton University Press. 1975), esp. pp. 545ff.

8. There is a vast literature on the role of the Prussian-German state in industrialization; see note 35.

9. Herman Müller was the head of the Grand Coalition and the last SPD chancellor, in office from June 1928 to March 1930. Heinrich Brüning was a leader of the Catholic Zentrum party and chancellor of the first "government by emergency decree" from March 1930 through April 1932; Baron Franz von Papen headed the avowedly authoritarian government of April–November 1932; General Kurt von Schleicher was chancellor in December 1932 and January 1933, immediately before Hitler's appointment. I shall discuss their policies toward the end of this essay.

10. Hans Jürgen Puhle, *Politische Agrarbewegungen in kapitalistischen Industriegesellschaften* (Gottingen: Vandenhoeck & Ruprecht, 1975), p. 29.

11. Nicos Poulantzas, "L'examen marxiste du droit," *Les Temps modernes* 219, 220 (1964); and Otto Kirchbeimer and Franz Neumann, *Social Democracy and the Rule of Law* (London: Allen & Unwin, 1987).

12. James O'Connor, *The Fiscal Crisis of the State* (New York: St. Martin's, 1973), pp. 8, 36. These costs are not just infrastructural but also ongoing and social (social capital and social investments). Ibid., p.6.

13. These points are elaborated upon by Offe, *Strukturprobleme des kapitalistischen Staates,* pp. 21–25.

14. The activities and reports of both the parliamentary Enquête Ausschuss study of the entire economy and the semiacademic Friedrich List Gesellschaft verify rather than contradict this contention.

15. The identity between the economy and the owners of the means of production is even clearer in the German: *die Wirtschaft* means both.

16. Cf. Karl Mannheim, *Ideology and Utopia* (New York: Harcourt, Brace and World, 1936), pp. 203, 146, where this process is described.

17. Eugene Varga made much of this dilemma in analyzing the victory of Italian fascism. His 1927 article appears in Theo Pirker, ed., *Komintern und Faschismus: Dokumente* (Stuttgart: Deutsche Verlags Anstalt, 1966), pp. 131ff.

18. O'Connor *(Fiscal Crisis)* develops this thesis for the fiscal crisis of contemporary America, but in Germany this was only one aspect of the multiple crisis. For Germany, the benefits of imperialism appeared only after 1932.

19. Gathered together in *Wachstum, Krisen, Handlungsspielräume der*

Wirtschaftspolitik (Göttingen: Vandenhoeck & Ruprecht, 1982). The core, and per-haps most provocative parts, of the argument were first presented as addresses and then published as "Zwangslagen und Handlungsspielräme in der grossen Wirtschaftskrise der frühen dreissiger Jahre," in *Jahrbuch der Bayerischen Akademie der Wissenschaften* 1979, pp. 87–132, and "Wirtschaftliche Ursachen des Scheiterns der Weimarer Republik," in K.D. Erdmann and H. Schulze, eds., *Weimar: Selbstpreisgabe einer Demokratie* (Düsseldorf: Droste, 1980), pp. 211–49. They have been restated in "Inflationsgefahren in der Weltwirtschaftskrise?" in W. Engels, A. Gutowski, and H. Wallich, eds., *International Capital Movements, Debt and Monetary System* (Mainz: Hase & Koehler, 1984), pp. 21–42. The argument was briefly summarized on a full page in the *Frankfurter Allgemeine Zeitung*, 29 January 1983, p. 13. See also, "Zum Scheitern eines produktiven Diskurses über das Scheitern der Weimarer Republik," *Geschichte und Gesellschaft* 9 (1983): 124–37. The latter two make frequent favorable reference to my *Collapse of the Weimar Republic*.

20. See his highly complimentary review of *Collapse of the Weimar Republic* and the perspective adopted here in the *Historische Zeitschrift* 236 (1983): 483–86.

21. The Borchardt theses have now witnessed a great deal of debate. See, Claus-Dieter Krohn, "'Ökonomische Zwangslagen' und das Scheitern der Weimarer Republik," *Geschichte und Gesellschaft* 8(1982):415–26, Carl-Ludwig Holtfrerich, "Zu hohe Löhne in der Weimarer Republik?" *Geschichte und Gesellschaft* 10(1984):122–41, Holtfrerich, "Alternativen zu Brünings Wirtschaftspolitik in der Welt-wirtschaftsikrise," *Historische Zeitschrift* 235(1982):605–31. Much of what became Borchardt's argument "for" Brüning was presciently criticized by Gerhard Schulz, "Reparationen und Krisenprobleme nach dem Wahlsieg der NSDAP 1930," *VSWG* 67(1980):200–22. Concretely, Holtferich, argues the following, "Zu hohe Löhne," pp. 137–40: Between 1907 and 1925 the number of salaried employees and officials doubled while the number of wage workers remained constant (from 10.3 to 17.3 percent and 54.9 to 49.2 percent of the labor force, respectively), and this accounted for much of the apparent increase in wages. In other words, increases went to *unproductive* labor. Further, increased shares of the national wealth distributed to labor tended to come not from industry but from agriculture, the petite bourgeoisie, and especially rentiers. This also marked a shift in wealth from *investing* strata to *consuming* strata, thereby disproportionately raising consumption but reducing savings and forcing up interest rates. For Holtfrerich, the proper approach to recovery would have begun by encouraging or inducing investment through mecha-nisms such as employee savings and investment funds. In the end, Holtfrerich's recommendation is remarkably like those being put forward in Sweden during the current crisis and those I have myself adumbrated; see my "Labor's Way: The Successes and Limits of Socialist Politics in Germany," *International Labor and Working Class History* 28 (1985):1–24.

22. See, for example, Eugen Varga's essays collected as *Die Krise des Kapitalismus und ihre politischen Folgen* (Frankfurt: Europäische Verlagsanstalt, 1969), esp. part II. Raford Boddy and James Crotty, "Class Conflict and Macro-Policy: the Political Business Cycle," *Review of Radical Political Economics* 7 (1975): 1–30; Andrew Glyn and Bob Sutcliffe, "The Critical Condition of British Capital," *New Left Review* 66(1971) and *British Capitalism, Workers and the Profit Squeeze* (London: Penguin, 1972).

23. Krohn is particularly adamant on the neo-liberal message of Borchardt's argument—delivered in a context where big businessmen themselves were "authoritarian cap-italists" and real market capitalism no longer existed. For his part, Krohn (pp. 418ff.) stresses overcapacity, the rapidity of capital intensification, and weak demand in the

Weimar economy along with protectionist policies abroad. In addition, he empha-
sizes that a goodly portion of public expenditure subsidized the private sector;
Weimar state activity *countered* the economy's weaknesses rather than *aggravating*
them.

24. The three essential discussions of the logic and predicaments of capitalist democracy
are Adam Przeworksi, *Capitalism and Social Democracy* (New York: Cambridge
University Press, 1985): Offe, *Contradictions of the Welfare State*; and Joshua Cohen
and Joel Rogers, *On Democracy* (New York: Penguin, 1983).

25. Thus Holtfrerich, "Alternativen," p. 627, citing the discussion in chapter 3, section 6
of *Collapse*, writes, "Abraham has clearly demonstrated that industrial opposition,
for example to the work creation measures proposed by the ADGB was directed not
so much at the measures themselves as at the organizations of the 'class enemy' and
at the political system which had secured workers such broad social and political
rights." In "Zu hohe Löhne," p. 141 he makes reference to efforts aimed at "democratization of the economy." For an extension of the discussion of "economic democracy" begun in *Collapse*, see my "Labor's Way," pp. 7–18.

26. Not a very enticing prospect at the time, but it is difficult to imagine anything worse
than the ultimate outcome.

27. This catastrophism was the dominant motif in the Comintern's analysis of Western
Europe, especially after 1928; once the big depression came, the revolution would
surely follow. This view succeeded in pushing other, more penetrating analyses aside
and ultimately produced the fatal logic of "the worse, the better." Cf. Nicos Poulantzas, *Fascisme et dictature* (Paris: Maspero, 1970), pp. 43ff.

28. E.g., Karl Marx, *Capital*, vol. 3 (New York: International Publishers, 1967), p. 791;
idem, *The German Ideology* (New York: International Publishers, 1960), pp. 7–16.

29. This is of course the view derived from the structuralist reading of Marx; cf. Louis
Althusser, and Etienne Balibar, *Reading Capital* (London: NLB, 1970), pp. 225–53;
Louis Althusser, *For Marx* (New York: Random House, 1970), pp. 104–28; and
explicitly, Poulantzas, *Political Power*, pp. 74–76.

30. For a differing view, see Henri Lefebvre, *The Sociology of Marx* (New York: Random
House, 1969), pp. 104–12.

31. This view rejects the "class in itself"/"class for itself" dichotomy. The former simply
does not exist, since without consciousness, without politics, there is no constitution
as a class; there is simply a shared relationship to the means of production.

32. This is perhaps the litmus test for whether a dominant social class is hegemonic,
capable of eliciting spontaneous loyalty. Cf. John Cammett, *Antonio Gramsci and
the Origins of Italian Communism* (Stanford: Stanford University Press, 1967),
p. 204.

33. Or, in different formulation, the uneven development of the different levels of a
social formation leads to the overdetermination of its contradictions and their con-
densation in one of them. Thus, economic contradictions may appear as political
ruptures. Cf. Althusser, *For Marx*, pp. 200–16, 250ff.

34. Preface to the first German edition of Marx, *Capital*, vol. 1 (New York: International
Publishers, 1967), p. 9.

35. There exists a substantial literature on this subject, e.g., Thorstein Veblen, *Imperial
Germany and the Industrial Revolution*, 2nd ed. (New York: Viking Press, 1939);
Hans Ulrich Wehler, *Bismarck und der Imperialismus* (Cologne: Kiepenheuer &
Witsch, 1969), and *Krisenherde des Kaiserreichs* (Gottingen: Vandenhoeck &
Ruprecht, 1970); Helmut Plessner, *Die verspätete Nation* (Stuttgart: W. Kohlham-
mer, 1959); Joseph Clapham, *The Economic Development of France and Germany*
(Cambridge: Cambridge University Press, 1936); W.O. Henderson, *The State and
the Industrial Revolution in Prussia* (Liverpool: Liverpool University Press, 1958).

36. Gramsci, *Prison Notebooks*, p. 19.
37. On the extended cultural dominance of the nobility, see Ernest K. Bramstead, *Aristocracy and Middle Classes in Germany* (Chicago: University of Chicago Press, 1964). On the political "monopoly" see Maxwell Knight, *The German Executive* (Stanford: Stanford University Press, 1952).
38. The origins and political consequences of a certian philistinism are analyzed in Max Weber, "National Character and the Junkers," in *From Max Weber*, ed. Hans Gerth and C. Wright Mills (New York: Oxford University Press, 1958), pp. 386–95.
39. Gustav Stresemann was a spokesman for the dynamic and export branches of industry. After 1923 and until his untimely death in October 1929 he led the chief party of industry, the German People's party (DVP). He "forced" his party and recalcitrant industrialists to unite behind his policy of reintegrating Germany into the international economy and concert and cooperating at home with the SPD. He was foreign minister throughout the period and linked trade and social policy together.
40. Poulantzas, *Political Power*, pp. 239, 283. Conflicts among the dominant fractions and the effects of those conflicts are examined in detail in Abraham, *Collapse of the Weimar Republic*, chaps. 3–6.
41. According to the liberal, DDP-oriented, *Berliner Tageblatt*, 12.12.29.
42. H.A. Winkler, *Mittelstand, Demokratie und Nationalsozialismus* (Cologne: Kiepenheuer & Wirtsch, 1972). Theodor Geiger, *Die Soziale Schichtung des Deutschen Volkes* (Stuttgart: Ferdinand Enke, 1932) pp. 106–8, distinguished among "old, new and proletaroid" Mittelstand, with the first two about 18 percent of the population and the last, overlapping with the other two, about 12 percent. H.A. Winkler, "From Social Protectionism to National Socialism," *Journal of Modern History* 48, no. 1 (March 1976): 1–18 stresses the authoritarianism of much of the Mittelstand and the tenuousness of its link to the bourgeois parties.
43. Correspondence between the central leadership and local and occupational representatives of the DDP, DVP, DNVP, and other bourgeois parties documents this trend.
44. Jürgen Kocka, "Zur Problematik der deutschen Angestellten, 1914–1933," in Hans Mommsen, ed., *Industrielles System und politische Entwicklung in der Weimarer Republik*, (Dusseldorf: Droste Verlag, 1974), pp. 792–811, reaffirms this.
45. Theodor Geiger, "Die Panik im Mittelstand," *Die Arbeit* 7 (1930): 637–54. Numerous voting studies confirmed Geiger's analysis; cf. S.M. Lipset, *Political Man* (Garden City, NY: Doubleday, 1963), pp. 138–52.
46. Rudolf Herberle, *From Democracy to Nazism* (Baton Rouge: Louisiana State University Press, 1945) details the entire process for Schleswig-Holstein. Though peasants were by no means any longer a "sack of potatoes," Marx's characterization remained partially correct: "they are incapable of enforcing their class interest in their own name. . . . Their representative must at the same time appear as their master, as an authority and power that protects them against the other classes and sends them rain and sunshine from above." *The 18th Brumaire* (New York: International Publishers, 1963), p. 124. The announcement metaphor is, of course, also from the same text.
47. During the period of the export-labor coalition, organized labor, through the SPD, was more than a support for the power bloc; as junior ally to the dynamic, export fraction it was in the power bloc. The proletariat derived more from the policies of bloc 3 than did heavy industry, which reluctantly accepted the arrangement because exports were booming and certain agreements had been reached with the export branches allowing heavy industry to share the financial profits. After 1928 heavy industry actively sought to break the labor-export coalition. The usage here of the terms "ally" and "supporter" thus differs somewhat from that of Poulantzas.

48. Representatives of export industry waged an intensive propaganda and organizational campaign between 1928 and 1931 designed to split the peasants from the integration/dependence mechanism that bound them to the estate owners. Ultimately they were unsuccessful because their modernization program could not match the benefits peasants obtained from a strategy of a "united rural sector" led by the estate owners in the name of autarky. See Abraham, *Collapse*, chap. 2.
49. Gramsci, *Prison Notebooks*, p. 210.
50. On something called a German aversion to a conflict-based constitution of liberty, see Ralf Dahrendorf, *Society and Democracy in Germany* (Garden City, NY: Doubleday, 1967), pp. 137–40, 183–90. On absorption by the state of the practical (in our terms economic-corporative) but not political demands of the German bourgeoisie, see Leonard Krieger, *The German Idea of Freedom* (Boston: Beacon Press, 1957), pp. 277, 428, 469ff. Both Krieger and Dahrendorf appreciate the importance of the failure of the German bourgeoisie to bring liberty to Germany. Krieger, however, does not make Dahrendorf's mistake of making the "constitution of liberty" a virtual bourgeois monopoly.
51. Cf. Arthur Rosenburg's comments on the Weimar Constitution, *Geschichte der Weimarer Republik* (Cologne: Pahl-Rugenstein, 1961), p. 61. Proportional representation increased the tendency for parties to represent narrow, fractional interests.
52. Again, the correspondence between various industrialists and the beleaguered chairmen of the bourgeois parties is full of this concern. See note 40.
53. This was Sigmund Neumann's verdict in 1930 already; *Die Parteien der Weimarer Republik* (Stuttgart: W. Kohlhammer, 1965), pp. 24, 54, 96.
54. Rosenberg, *Geschichte der Weimarer Republik*, pp. 178–83; Maier, *Recasting Bourgeois Europe*, pp. 364–73, 402. France occupied the Ruhr when Germany attempted to evade or default on reparations payments. First, German capital successfully whipped up a national fury (which the KPD attempted to outdo!) and used the national crisis to rescind the eight-hour day, lower wages, and accelerate the inflation. Then, after German industry reached private accords with the French, the whole thing was called off. Even bourgeois politicians such as Stresemann and Cuno were surprised by the selfishness of the industrialists.
55. Poulantzas, *Political Power*, p. 299. One may easily quarrel with Poulantzas's contention that the state "plays the role of organizer" of the power bloc, rather than simply providing the terrain. It is by no means self-evident that this was the case in Weimar Germany—either before or during 1932. One can also question his contention that there is no parcelling out of power, that power is always unitary under the hegemonic fraction. This latter argument leads to a hidden form of state monopoly capitalism—a view not borne out by our analysis. See Anson Rabinbach, "Poulantzas and the Problem of Fascism," *New German Critique* 8 (Spring 1976): 157–70. Rabinbach's critique of structuralist Marxism is quite trenchant.
56. O'Connor, *Fiscal Crisis*, p. 9.
57. The flow of foreign capital was immense. By 1930 a total of 27 billion marks had been borrowed. The exact figures differ by source; cf. Charles Bettelheim, *L'Economie allemande sous le nazisme* 1 (Paris: Maspero, 1971): 22–24. On the expansion and overexpansion of the industrial structure and plant, see Robert Brady, *The Rationalization Movement in German Industry* (Berkeley: University of California Press, 1933).
58. Paul Silverberg's remarks to the convention of the League of German Industry (RDI) in Dresden, September 1926. His remarks were not universally accepted; in fact, he came in for considerable criticism, but his line did prevail. Maier, *Recasting Bourgeois Europe*, p. 443, discusses the 1924 defection of Vögler and others from the national-liberal caucus in an attempt to drive the counterrevolution still further.

Adam Stegerwald, head of the Catholic unions and later labor minister (1930–32), greeted Silverberg's remarks by announcing gleefully that "Industry is holding its hand out to Labor." Cited in the Pressarchiv of the Reichslandbund/DZA, series 148, 8:21. Organized agriculture was not pleased with either pronoucement, and agrarian newspapers attacked Silverberg's pronouncement as did the KPD's *Rote Fahne*, 14.9.26, which spoke of a "Silverberg-Severing alliance" (p. 26), that is an alliance between the dynamic fraction of industry and the SPD.

59. Cf., eg., Larry Jones, "The Crisis of White Collar Interest Politics," in Mommsen, ed., *Industrielles System und politische Entwicklung*. pp. 812–16.

60. The middle Weimar years were not the first time that industry and labor had worked together for their mutual benefit. Gerald Feldman describes a joint triumph of heavy industry and labor during the first years of World War I, *Army, Industry and Labor in Germany, 1914–1918* (Princeton: Princeton University Press, 1966), pp. 150–248.

61. See the evaluations and lessons of October by Ruth Rischer for the KPD left and August Thalheimer and H. Brandler for the KPD right, *Die Internationale* 6, Ergänzungsheft no. 1 (January 1924); parts reprinted in Helmut Gruber, ed., *International Communism in the Era of Lenin*, Helmut Gruber (Garden City, NY: Doubleday, 1972), pp. 377–85.

62. Maier, *Recasting Bourgeois Europe*, p. 353. "Organized capitalism" may be a less opaque concept than corporatism.

63. Ralf Beckenbach, *Der Staat im Faschismus* (Westberlin: Verlag für das Studium der Arbeiterbewegung, 1974), p. 39. The expansion of American power is indicated by comparable figures for the United States: America's share of world industrial production rose from 36 to 50 percent, and production in 1923 was 141 percent of the 1913 figure.

64. Brady, *Rationalization Movement*, p. 347. Using 1924 as a base year, productivity by 1929 had reached an index value of 140.

65. That oft-repeated phrase was first used by the chairman of the Reichsleague of Industry, Ludwig Kastl, at its 1927 convention. It was at about this time that the dynamic and export industries captured the leadership of the organization. There was no shortage of hard-line dissidents, especially in heavy industry.

66. The *Gemeinschaften* and the step-by-step approach originated in the agreements reached already in mid-November 1918 between Hugo Stinnes for the industrialists and Carl Legien for the unions (ADGB). Cf. Maier, *Recasting Bourgeois Europe*, p. 59.

67. Walter Müller-Jentsch, "Zum Verhältnis von Staat und Gewerkschaften," in Claudio Pozzoli, ed., *Rahmenbedingungen und Schranken staatlichen Handelns* (Frankfurt: Suhrkamp, 1976), p. 151.

68. Weber's statement parallels the critique of economism voiced in 1927 by Eugen Varga, who maintained that a series of economic gains won by the working class unaccompanied by political, structural victories would prove worse than worthless. Sooner or later much costly gains would elicit sharp repression by the bourgeoisie. *Die Krise des Kapitalismus und ihre politischen Folgen* (Frankfurt: Europäische Verlagsanstalt, 1969), esp. pp. 231–60.

69. Neumann, *Parteien der Weimarer Republik,* p. 33; Hans Neisser, "Sozialistatistische Analyse der Wahlergebnisse," *Die Arbeit* 7 (1930): 658. But, pressure from the KPD caused the SPD to be very militant in its defense of the daily interests of the working class.

70. Cf. Ossip Flechtheim, *Die KPD in der Weimarer Republik* (Frankfurt: Europäische Verlagsanstalt, 1969), p. 244.

71. Georges Castellan, *L'Allemagne de Weimar* (Paris: Presses Universitaire de France, 1969), pp. 91–95.

72. For a summary of these developments, see Larry E. Jones, *The Dying Middle: German Liberalism and the Dissolution of the Weimar System* (Chapel Hill: University of North Carolina Press, 1988).

73. Among others, the Economic Party of the Middle Class (Wirtschaftspartei), which claimed to represent small business and the victims of the inflation, and the Christian National Peasants and Rural People's party (CNBLP), representing southern and central peasants and several others of less importance and devoted to, among other things, upward revaluation. Cf. Neumann, *Behemouth,* pp. 64–67; Martin Schumacher, "Mittelstandsfront und Republik," in *Industrielles System und politische Entwicklung,* ed. Mommsen, pp. 823–35; and Thomas Childers, *The Nazi Voter* (Chapel Hill: University of North Carolina Press, 1983), pp. 119–91.

74. Cf. Ludwig Preller, *Sozialpolitik in der Weimarer Republik* (Stuttgart: Franz Mittelbach Verlag, 1949), pp. 296–387.

75. It is instructive that Stresemann's friend and ally Julius Curtius experienced difficulties heading this ministry that paralleled Stresemann's own problems with fractious industrialists.

76. Lothar Albertin, "Faktoren eines Arrangements zwischen industriellem und politischem System," in *Industrielles System und politische Entwicklung,* ed. Mommsen, pp. 658–75. The argument that the state sector and the monopoly sector grow together (if not fully in tandem), though essentially correct, is less true for Germany than for the USA with its underdeveloped state.

77. See., e.g., Dieter Fricke, ed., *Die bürgerlichen Parteien in Deutschland* (Berlin: Das Europäische Buch, 1968) 1: 317–28.

78. Interesting changes in the composition of the political "agents" or "subelite" from 1880 to 1933 are analyzed by Knight, *German Executive,* esp. pp. vi, 6, 22, 28, 33, and 45.

79. Poulantzas, *Political Power,* pp. 336, 337.

80. One very crucial and unreformed institution that acted as a constraint on the left during the stable years and later collaborated in undermining the republic was the Reichswehr. On the military during the stable years, see F. L. Carsten, *The Reichswehr and Politics, 1918–1933* (London: Oxford University Press, 1966), pp. 163–308. See also Harold Gordon, *The Reichswehr and the German Republic 1919–1926* (Princeton: Princeton University Press, 1957); and Michael Geyer, *Aufrüstung oder Sicherheit* (Dusseldorf, 1981).

81. Without speculating as to precisely what it would have meant for the working class to take state power or the strategies and mechanisms involved in doing so, it is nevertheless clear that the SPD was determined to be not only "the doctor at the sickbed of capitalism" but the savior of the bourgeois parliamentary republic as well. For the SPD, not socialism but organized capitalism and, at most, economic democracy were on the agenda; even nostalgic talk of the soviets *(Räte)* of 1918 was heresy. The SPD might have possessed the capacity to bleed German capitalism dry, but it did not have the capacity to capture its state.

82. Of the five cabinets in office between June 1924 and June 1928, only two received an actual vote of confidence on being presented. Two received a weaker "acceptance vote," and the fifth earned a mere "acknowledgment."

83. Michael Stürmer, *Koalition und Opposition in der Weimarer Republik, 1924–1928,* Beiträge zur Geschichte des Parlamentarismus und der politischen Parteien (Dusseldorf: Droste Verlag, 1967) 36: 280–83 and Abraham *Collapse,* chap. 6.

84. Poulantzas, *Fascisme et Dictature,* p. 72.

85. Rosenberg, *Geschichte der Weimarer Republik,* p. 140.

86. Cf. Werner Link, "Der amerikanische Einfluss auf die Weimarer Republik: Elemente eines penetrierten Systems," in Mommsen, ed., *Industrielles System und politische Entwicklung*, esp. pp. 489–93.

87. Cf. Helga Timm, *Die deutsche Sozialpolitik und der Bruch der Grossen Koalition im März, 1930*, Beiträge zur Geschichte des Parlamentarismus und der politischen Parteien, vol. 1 (Dusseldorf: Droste Verlag, 1952).

88. The Young Plan was drafted by American bankers and government officials to revise the schedule for German reparations payments so as not to force Germany to default. After a grace period, its payments would be lessened but extended till 1987. In June 1929 the RDI decided not to take an official stand on the Young Plan. Divisions were very sharp although much of the leadership and most of the membership favored acceptance. In July the Rhenish-Westfalian industrialists *(Langnamverein)*, under the influence of Ruhr heavy industry, resolved to oppose the Young Plan, as did the Green Front, the latter purporting to represent all of agriculture.

89. The leaders of the bourgeois parties tried constantly but generally unsuccessfully to balance their concern for the "health of industry and economy" with the "social concern" necessary to win votes. This was clearest in the case of the chief party of industry, the DVP (German People's party)! A thorough analysis has been undertaken by Lothar Döhn, *Politik und Interesse* (Meisenheim/Glan: Verlag Anton Hain, 1970). On this period in general, see K. D. Bracher, *Die Auflösung der Weimarer Republik*, Part III (Stuttgart: Ring Verlag, 1955).

90. On the relationship of industrial organization and camps to the Brüning government and its successors, see Reinhard Neebe, *Grossindustrie und Nationalsozialismus* (Gottingen: Vandenhoeck & Ruprecht, 1981) and Abraham, *Collapse*, chaps. 3, 6.

91. See Poulantzas, *Political Power*, p. 137, for the two functions of the political practice of the dominant classes.

92. Even before the crisis a number of schemes, largely reactionary, for reorganizing the state structure had been entertained by prominent political and economic figures. Almost all intended to alter federal-state relations and the bicameral legislative structure. Among the more prominent was the League for Renewal of the Reich headed by former DVP politician, chancellor, and Reichsbank president Luther. Cf. *Die bürgerlichen Parteien*, ed. Fricke, I: 195–200.

93. Postwar blocs had failed to integrate the Mittelstand (small property owners, shopkeepers, small commodity producers, later joined by peasants and some salaried employees and officials), groups enjoying little *economic* unity but reaggregated and organized *politically*, outside any of the blocs, by the Nazis. The dominant classes had to reach some kind of settlement with these groups. Despite their age, the two best analyses of the relationship between the fascist mass movements and the capitalist offensive remain Otto Bauer, "Der Faschismus," and Arthur Rosenberg, "Der Faschismus als Massenbewegung," in *Faschismus und Kapitalismus*, ed. Wolfgang Abendroth (Frankfurt: Europäische Verlagsanstalt, 1967), pp. 114–67.

94. Cf. Mihaly Vajda, *Fascism As a Mass Movement* (New York: St. Martin's, 1976), esp. pp. 68–90. A very insightful contemporary analysis of the needs of the capitalist class and the various ways in which those might be met was provided by Paul Sering [Richard Löwenthal], "Die Wandlungen des Kapitalismus," originally in *Zeitschrift für Sozialismus* (1935), reprinted with the deceptive title *Faschismus und Monopolkapitalismus* (Berlin, 1967), pp. 1–22, 63–79.

What Produces Fascism: Preindustrial Traditions or a Crisis of the Capitalist State?

Geoff Eley

I

The aim of this essay is to explore some of the emerging emphases in current discussions of fascism. In some ways that discussion has entered the doldrums. There was a certain high point in the late 1960s, when the subject was first properly opened up, and when the generalizing ambitions of social scientists and historians briefly converged. Ernst Nolte's *Der Faschismus in seiner Epoche*, translated with exceptional speed as *Three Faces of Fascism: Action Française, Italian Fascism, National Socialism*; general surveys by Eugen Weber, Francis L. Carsten, and John Weiss; an anthology on the European right edited by Eugen Weber and Hans Rogger; the thematic first issue of a new periodical, the *Journal of Contemporary History*; Barrington Moore, Jr.'s vastly influential *Social Origins of Dictatorship and Democracy* (1966); the *Das Argument* discussions of the German new left; and three international conferences in Seattle (1966), Reading, England (1967), and Prague (1969)—all these imparted an excitement and vitality to work on the subject.[1] In retrospect there is an air of innocence to this activity, and its intense preoccupation with comparison, generalization, and theory has tended not to survive the subsequent growth of empirical research. These days people are far more cautious, because the accumulated weight of historical scholarship has seemed to compromise the explanatory potential of the old theorizations.

So what is left, once certain old certainties (like totalitarianism or the orthodox Marxist approaches) have been abandoned? The answer, if we consult the most recent publications, is not very much. We know far better which theories do not work (totalitarianism, the 1935 Dimitrov formula, the authoritarian personality, the mass-society thesis, monopoly-group theory, and so on) than those that do.[2] There have been certain major interventions—the work of Nicos Poulantzas and the controversy surrounding Renzo De Felice are two that come to mind—but on the whole they have not sparked much widespread debate.[3] Most writers have tended to settle for a typological approach to the definition of fascism, by using certain essentially descriptive criteria (ideological ones have tended to be the most common) as a practical means of identifying which movements are "fascist" and which are not. Yet this begs the more difficult conceptual issues and leaves the stronger aspects of definition (such as the dynamics of fascism's emergence, and its relation to class, economics, and political development) to the concrete analysis of particular societies.[4]

Understandably, this is an outcome with which historians can live. In fact, the enormous proliferation of empirical work over the past ten to fifteen years has concentrated overwhelmingly on more immediate problematics, normally with a national-historical definition (for example, of Nazism or Italian fascism rather than fascism in general). We "know" far more than ever before, but this remains the knowledge of highly particularized investigations. Not surprisingly, a common response has been the philistine cry of despair (or perhaps of triumph): "reality" is simply too "complex." Radical nominalism easily follows, and there is precious little agreement as to whether fascism even exists as a general phenomenon.[5]

At the same time, there is now a large body of excellent work that lends itself to theoretical appropriation. Some of this is on the less significant fascisms of the north and west of the European continent or on the larger but ambiguous "native fascisms" of the East, and facilitates a stronger comparative dimension to the discussion. Other contributions are on specific aspects of German and Italian history, including the structure of interest representation, the sociology of the Nazi movement and the nature of the Nazi electorate in Germany, or the precise dynamics of the post-World War I crisis in Italy. In the longer term this intensive reworking of the empirical circumstances of the fascist victories, on the basis of exceptionally elaborate primary research, often sophisticated methodologies, and "middle-level generalizations," promises to reconstruct our theoretical understanding of fascism. My own object is more modest. It is clear that the coherence of current research relies on a number of organizing perspectives that derive from the older theoretical literature. These run through the analytical structures of particular works with varying degrees of explicitness and self-conscious utilization. The aim of this essay is to identify some of the perspectives, to explore their strengths and weaknesses, and by drawing on the more recent theoretical discussions, perhaps to suggest where future interest might fruitfully be directed.[6]

II

One of the commonest emphases in the literature is a kind of deep historical perspective, which proceeds from the idea of German, and to a lesser extent Italian, peculiarity when compared with the "West." In this case the possibility of fascism is linked to specific structures of political backwardness. These are themselves identified with a distinctive version of the developmental process, and are thought to be powerful impediments to a society's ultimate "modernization."

This "backwardness syndrome" is defined within a global conceptual framework of the most general societal comparison. It stresses "lateness" of industrialization and national unification and their complex interaction, predisposing toward both a particular kind of economic structure and a far more interventionist state. The divergence from Western political development is usually expressed in terms of the absence of a successful "bourgeois revolution" on the assumed Anglo-French model, an absence that facilitates the dominance after national unification of an agrarian-industrial political bloc with strong authoritarian and antidemocratic traditions. The failure to uproot such preindustrial traditions is thought to have obstructed the formation of a liberal-democratic polity, and in general this is taken to explain the frailty of the national liberal traditions, and their inability to withstand the strains of a serious crisis. In recent social science this perspective stems from (among others) Barrington Moore, Alexander Gerschenkron, and the discussions sponsored by the Social Science Research Council's Committee on Comparative Politics. In contemporary Marxism it has drawn new impetus from discussion of the ideas of Antonio Gramsci. In both cases the analysis may be traced back to the end of the last century.[7] It exercises a profound influence on how most historians tend to see the problem of fascism, though frequently at a distance, structuring the argument's underlying assumptions rather than being itself an object of discussion.

The argument was put in an extreme, discursive form by Ralf Dahrendorf in *Society and Democracy in Germany*, which deeply influenced a generation of English-speaking students of German history. It has also functioned strategically in a large body of work dealing with the imperial period of German history (1871–1918), whose authors write very much with 1933 in mind. One of the latter, Jürgen Kocka, has recently reaffirmed Dahrendorf's argument in a particularly explicit way, which highlights the specific backwardness of German political culture. Thus in Kocka's view "German society was never truly a bourgeois society," because the "bourgeois virtues like individual responsibility, risk-taking, the rational settlement of differences, tolerance, and the pursuit of individual and collective freedoms" were much "less developed than in Western Europe and the USA." Indeed, the chances of a "liberal-democratic constitutional development" were blocked by a series of authoritarian obstacles. Kocka lists

the great power of the Junkers in industrial Germany and the feudalizing tendencies in the big bourgeoisie; the extraordinary power of the bureaucracy and the army in a state that had never experienced a successful bourgeois revolution and which was unified from above; the social and political alliance of the rising bourgeoisie and the ever-resilient agrarian nobility against the sharply demarcated proletariat; the closely related anti-parliamentarian, anti-democratic, and anti-liberal alignment of large parts of the German ruling strata.[8]

In fact, the "powerful persistence of pre-industrial, pre-capitalist traditions" preempted the legitimacy of the Weimar Republic and favored the rise of right-wing extremism.

These arguments, which are conveniently summarized in Kocka's essay, are representative of the generation of German historians who entered intellectual maturity during the 1960s, in a fertile and (for the time) liberating intellectual encounter with the liberal social and political science then in its North American heyday. This is particularly true of those historians who have explicitly addressed the question of Nazism's longer-term origins, for whom such figures as Karl Dietrich Bracher, Wolfgang Sauer, Ernst Fraenkel, Martin Broszat, M. Rainer Lepsius, and Dahrendorf provided early intellectual examples.[9] Here, for instance, is Hans-Jürgen Puhle summarizing the argument in terms that correspond precisely to the ones used by Kocka. Fascism is to be explained by the specific characteristics of a society "in which the consequences of delayed state-formation and delayed industrialization combined closely together with the effects of the absence of bourgeois revolution and the absence of parliamentarization to form the decisive brakes on political democratization and social emancipation."[10]

It should be noted that this approach to the analysis of fascism is advanced as an explicit alternative to Marxist approaches, which for this purpose are reduced by these authors polemically and rather simplistically to a set of orthodox variations on themes bequeathed by the Comintern, in a way that ignores the contributions of (among others) Poulantzas, the Gramsci reception, and Tim Mason.[11] Thus in a labored polemic against the German new left Heinrich August Winkler gives primary place in his own explanation of Nazism to preindustrial survivals, which in other (healthier) societies had been swept away. This was the factor that explained "why certain capitalist societies became fascist and others not."[12] Or, as Kocka puts it, adapting Max Horkheimer's famous saying: "Whoever does not want to talk about pre-industrial, pre-capitalist and pre-bourgeois traditions should keep quiet about fascism."[13]

Kocka specifies this argument in a detailed study of American white-collar workers between 1890 and 1940, which is motivated by an explicit comparison with Germany.[14] He begins with a well-known feature of Nazism, namely, its disproportionate success among the lower middle class or petty bourgeoisie, and among white-collar workers in particular. He then abstracts a "general social-historical hypothesis" from this—namely, that the lower middle classes develop a "potential susceptibility to right-wing radicalization as a consequence of transformation processes which typically appear at advanced stages of capitalist industrialization"—and proceeds to test it against the experience of American employees in retailing and industry between the end of the nineteenth century and World War II.[15] After careful discussions of social origin, educational background, income differentials, organizational experience, and status consciousness, he concludes that American white-collar workers showed a much lower propensity to see themselves as a distinct class or status group superior and hostile to the working class. This "blurring of the collar line" helps explain the absence of "class-specific" political tendencies comparable to those of German employees, because while the latter turned to the Nazis in large numbers, their American counterparts joined with manual workers in support of the New Deal. Thus the comparable socioeconomic situations of white-collar workers in the two countries failed to produce identical ideological or political orientations. If this is so, Kocka argues, perhaps the general hypothesis, which seeks to explain the rise of fascism by the "changes, tensions, and contradictions inherent in advanced capitalist societies," needs to be qualified.[16]

Kocka considers a number of explanations for the divergence, juxtaposing German and American particularities in each case. Thus the socialist consciousness and greater independence of the German labor movement, which led to its deliberate isolation in the political system, was not replicated in the United States and American white-collar workers had far less reason to construct ideological defenses against the left. Second, ethnicity fragmented the potential unity of both workers and petty bourgeoisie in the United States far more than religious or ethnic differences did in Germany. Third, the swifter emergence of the interventionist state in Germany tended to emphasize the importance of the collar line and legally cemented the lines of differentiation (for example, through the separate insurance legislation for white-collar employees), while, fourth, the existence of "a stratified educational system" tended to strengthen the barriers between occupations by lowering the mobility between manual and nonmanual jobs. Each of these points is well taken, though the enormous expansion of tertiary employment in Germany after the turn of the century (and hence the broadly based recruitment of the white-collar labor force), is probably understated, as are the conceptual difficulties in mobility studies, which Kocka takes rather uncritically on board.[17]

Kocka reserves his major explanation for a fifth factor, namely, "the continuing presence or absence of pre-industrial corporatist/ bureaucratic traditions at advanced stages of industrialization."[18] In the United States the absence of feudal traditions has long been seen as a crucial determinant of the country's political culture, permitting the hegemony of democratic citizenship ideals and the containment of class animosity.[19] In Germany, by contrast, the political culture suggests a "deficit in some essential ingredients of a modern bourgeois or civil society that was closely but inversely related to the strength of Germany's pre-industrial, pre-capitalist, and pre-bourgeois traditions." In the case of white-collar workers this created much ready support for the fascists.[20]

There is much to agree with in Kocka's account, which is exactly the kind of controlled comparison the field so badly needs. By taking the idea of preindustrial continuities and arguing it through in a very specific context he enables us to see more clearly its attractions and disadvantages. The very concreteness of the analysis allows the case for the German *Sonderweg*—for German exceptionalism—to be made more convincingly probably than ever before. At a general level his conclusions seem unimpeachable. This applies most certainly to his stress on "the relative autonomy of social-structural and socio-cultural developments" within the larger process of capitalist industrialization. As the American material shows, there is nothing in the logic of the latter per se to send industrial workers automatically to the left and nonmanual ones automatically to the right of the political spectrum (or, one might add, to associate specific ideologies or political attitudes necessarily with any particular social group).

At the same general level, it is hard to quarrel with Kocka's formulation of the pre-industrial argument:

The uneasy coexistence of social structures that originated in different eras, the tense overlayering of industrial capitalist social conflicts with pre-industrial, pre-capitalist social constellations—the "contemporaneity of the uncontemporary"—defined Germany's path to an industrial society, but not America's.[21]

His practical elaboration of this point, however, is not wholly convincing. To single out the primacy of preindustrial traditions from the larger explanatory repertoire seems arbitrary, not least because some of the major German particularities in Kocka's list—for example, the rise of the Social Democratic party (SPD), or the constitution of *Angestellten* (employees in the private sector and low-status public employees) as a separate social category by the interventionist state—are formed during industrialization rather than before it.[22] Moreover, though Kocka seeks to establish German peculiarity compared with the "West", what he actually shows with most of his argument is American peculiarity with Europe, certainly with the European continent and in many ways with Britain too.

Ultimately Kocka's view of fascism is confusing. On the one hand, he upholds the relationship between capitalism and fascism ("the susceptibility of the new middle class to right-wing extremism . . . would not have existed without the changes, tensions, and crises that accompanied the creation of an industrial capitalist society"), pointing only to its interaction with older preindustrial traditions in a complex causal dialectic ("the tension and crises inherent in industrial capitalist systems on one side, and the repercussions of the collision of older traditions with industrialization and modernization, on the other").[23] On the other hand, the main logic of his argument definitely gives analytical priority to the preindustrial part of the equation, making it the real difference between Germany (which went fascist) and other countries (which did not).[24] However, all capitalist societies are forged from precapitalist materials, and this is as true of the United States (with its nonfeudal configuration of property-owning white democracy) as it is of Germany (with, if we follow Kocka for the sake of argument, its feudal legacy of military and bureaucratic traditions) and elsewhere. In the period of industrialization itself the implied ideal of a "pure" capitalism without precapitalist admixtures (the "modern bourgeois or civil society" that Germany is supposed not to have been and against which German history is measured) never existed. That being the case the crucial problem becomes that of establishing how certain "traditions" became selected for survival rather than others—how certain beliefs and practices came to reproduce themselves under radically changed circumstances, and how they became subtly transformed in the very process of renewal. Preindustrial values had to be rearticulated in the new conditions of an industrial-capitalist economy. It is this process of active reproduction through a succession of new conjunctures between the 1870s and 1930s, surely, that has first claim on our attention.

In other words, Kocka's argument can be tested only on the terrain he deliberately abandons, namely the immediate context of the Weimar Republic. It is here that white-collar attitudes acquired their specific content and political effectiveness, in the vicissitudes of the capitalist economy and the permanent political uncertainty after 1918, for to ensure their disproportionate right-wing orientation (and eventually to harness a fascist potential) required a positive ideological labor, on the part of employers, the state, and the right-wing parties.

One of the least satisfactory aspects of the preindustrial argument is a kind of inevitabilism—a long-range sociocultural determinism of preindustrial traditions—that implies that German white-collar allegiances were just never available for left-wing politics until after 1945. This is partly belied by the manifest dividedness of white-collar allegiances until the late 1920s, and once we concede the existence of significant exceptions, as in any historical argument indeed we must (for example, why did the causal chain of preindustrial status mentalities and right-wing proclivities work for some white-collar groups at different times but not for others?), the preindustrial argument looks far less compelling. In fact, there is much evidence that in the earlier circumstances of the German Revolution many white-collar workers moved significantly to the reformist left. That the left-wing parties (especially the SPD) failed to respond creatively to these possibilities was less the result of German white-collar workers' ineluctable conservatism (bequeathed by the absence of bourgeois revolution, and so on), than of specific political processes and their outcomes, which were themselves naturally subject to the disposing and constraining influence of social and economic determinations.

Similarly, we can scarcely understand the nature of the collar line unless we also examine the technical division of labor, the social context of the workplace, and the position of white-collar workers in the labor process—all of which were experiencing some basic changes in the early twentieth century, in Germany no less than in the United States, but which are strangely absent from Kocka's final account. In the end the invocation of preindustrial ideological continuities confuses these issues, though the argument is handled more constructively in Jürgen Kocka's text than in most others.

III

One point emerges clearly enough from Kocka's account, and that is the limited explanatory potential of a sociological approach to fascism. This should not be misunderstood: I am not voicing hostility to sociology per se, either to the use of different kinds of social theory or to the adoption of social-scientific methodology, quantitative or otherwise. Nor am I suggesting that sociological approaches to fascism in particular are completely lacking in value. Quite the contrary, in fact. The careful dissection of the fascist movement's social composition through analysis of the leadership, activists, and ordinary membership, and through a long tradition of sophisticated electoral analysis, has been an essential feature of recent research. It has generated an enormous amount of information and many new questions, providing the indispensable foundation for any intelligent reflection.[25]

The problems arise with the larger conclusions. Writers move too easily from an empirical sociology of the fascist movement and its electorate to a general thesis concerning its origins and conditions of success, which is usually linked to conceptions of modernization, social change, and the impact of economic crisis. Such conceptions combine with the deep historical perspective identified above to suggest that fascism is structurally determined by a particular developmental experience. This is powerfully represented, for instance, in Barrington Moore's celebrated arguments about the relationship of different developmental trajectories ("dictatorship" and "democracy") to the societal dominance of different types of modernizing coalitions (based on specific configurations of land-owning and urban-bourgeois elements and their links to popular forces). In German historiography especially, it is strongly implied that fascism follows logically from patterns of partial or uneven modernization, which throw unreformed political institutions and "traditional" social structures into contradiction with the "modern" economy. In some versions this effectively redefines fascism as a more general problem of political backwardness.

In this sort of thinking the notion of traditional strata, which are unable to adjust to modernization for a mixture of material and psychological reasons, has tended to play a key part. Since the 1920s, for instance, there has been general agreement that fascism originates socially in the grievances of the petty bourgeoisie or lower middle class. In the words of Luigi Salvatorelli in 1923, fascism "represents the class struggle of the petty bourgeoisie, squeezed between capitalism and the proletariat, as the third party between the two conflicting sides."[26] This was the commonest contemporary judgment and has been pursued repeatedly by both historians and sociologists, Marxist and non-Marxist alike. Most of the accumulated evidence (and a mountain of continuing research) is assembled in an enormous collection of essays recently edited by Stein Ugelvik Larsen, Bernt Hagtvet, and Jan Petter Myklebust, *Who Were the Fascists: Social Roots of European Fascism* (1980), and while the aggregate effect of around 800 pages is hard to assess, it seems to confirm the received assumptions. There have been attempts to suggest that other social groups were ultimately more important in the fascists' makeup, or that class was less important than "generational revolt."[27] On the evidence of *Who Were the Fascists,* however, the fascist movement's social composition seems to have been disproportionately weighted toward the petty bourgeoisie (that is, small-scale owners and producers, together with the new strata of salaried employees, including lower grade civil servants, junior managerial and technical personnel, teachers, clerical workers, and parts of the professions).[28]

At the same time, to call fascism flatly a protest movement of the petty bourgeoisie is clearly an oversimplification. As David Roberts observes in an excellent discussion of petty bourgeois fascism in Italy, the tendency is to "assume that if we can find social categories enabling us to distinguish fascists from non-fascists, we have the key to explaining the phenomenon," with consequences that are potentially extremely reductionist.[29] As Roberts continues, historians of Italian fascism habitually analyze it "in terms of socio-economic crisis and the traumas and frustrations which industrial modernization causes the lower middle class," and the same is equally true of writers on Nazism.[30] As suggested above, this argument conjoins with another popular thesis concerning the relationship of fascism to modernization, where the movement's specificity derives from "its appeal to certain kinds of people who see themselves as losers in modern technological civilization," who rejected "the modern industrial world" and took refuge in an ideology of "utopian anti-modernism."[31] The problem here is that the correlations between fascist ideology, the support of the petty bourgeoisie, and general economic trends are drawn in a way that is too general and mechanical. Though the casualties of capitalist industrialization were certainly prominent among the radical right's supporters, this was by no means the whole story.

As David Roberts reminds us, the deficiencies in this standard view "stem not from the insistence on the petty bourgeois role in fascism, but from the inferences about motiviation that are made from this fact of social composition."[32] Summarizing his own argument in *The Syndicalist Tradition and Italian Fascism* he highlights a quite different ideological tendency in the petty bourgeoisie: so far from "trying to preserve traditional values and repudiate the modern industrial world," its exponents were firmly committed to a heavily productivist vision of industrial progress, and harboured few "backward-looking" anxieties about the modern world in the way normally attributed. In fact, they were preoccupied less with the socioeconomic problems of declining preindustrial strata than with the long-term political questions of Italy's national integration and cultural self-confidence. Their resentments were aimed less at the bearers of capitalist industrialization than at the representatives of a narrowly based parliamentary liberalism (not forgetting, of course, the socialist left, whose growth the latter seemed irresponsibly to permit). In Roberts' view, petty-bourgeois fascism emerged as a critique of "Italy's restrictive transformist political system" under the radicalizing circumstances of World War I. As "political outsiders," its spokespersons presented themselves as a new populist "vanguard" capable of providing the ideological leadership effectively abdicated (as they saw it) by the old Giolittian establishment. Moreover, their urgency stemmed not just from the shattering experience of the war, but from the ensuing crisis of the *biennio rosso,* with its alarming evidence of Socialist electoral gains, working-class insurgency, and ambiguous Popolare radicalism.[33] Under these circumstances radical nationalism was an intelligible response to the social dynamics of national disintegration. Affirming the virtues of industrial power, productivism, and class collaboration, its architects offered a program of national syndicalism, which "could mobilize and politicize the masses more effectively and thereby create a more legitimate and popular state."[34]

In other words, it is worth considering the possibility that fascism was linked as much to the "rising" as to the "declining" petty bourgeoisie. Now, on past experience (the celebrated "gentry controversy" in Tudor-Stuart historiography is a good example), this kind of terminology may create more trouble than it is worth,[35] so let me explain carefully what I mean. Both Germany and Italy were societies experiencing accelerated capitalist tranformation, through which entire regions were being visibly converted from predominantly rural into predominantly urban-industrial environments. In both cases the process was extremely uneven (in vital ways functionally so), with equally large regions trapped into social and economic backwardness (the south in Italy, or the East Elbian parts of Prussia and the Catholic periphery of the south, south-west, and extreme west of Germany). In Italy the process was the more concentrated and dramatic, producing interesting similarities with Tsarist Russia: for example, the massive spurt of growth from the 1890s to World War I; the very high levels of geographical, structural, and physical concentration of industry, which brought masses of workers together in a small number of centers and created new conurbations with politically volatile populations; the interventionist role of the state, linked to a powerful complex of railway, heavy-industrial, shipbuilding, engineering, and hydro-electrical interests, the selective involvement of foreign capital, and a well-knit oligopoly of government, industry, and banks; an exclusivist and oligarchic political system; and a dramatic discrepancy between north and south, between a dynamic industrial sector that in all respects was highly advanced and an agricultural one that was equally and terribly backward.

This situation produced complex political effects. Simplifying wildly, we might say that the pace of social change outstripped the adaptive capabilities of the existing political institutions, particularly when the latter were called on to be responsible to new social forces—agricultural populations concerned for their future in an economy increasingly structured by industrial priorities, urban populations demanding a more rational ordering of their hastily improvised city environment, a potential chaos of private economic interests, the mass organizations of the industrial working class, and the more diffuse aspirations of the new professional, administrative, and managerial strata of the bourgeoisie and petty bourgeoisie. It is the last of these groups that interests me here.

For in a situation of widespread political uncertainty—in both Germany and Italy (and, we might add, Austria, Hungary, and Spain) an existing political bloc of industrial, agrarian, and military-bureaucratic interests entered a protracted period of instability and incipient dissolution in the 1890s from which it never really recovered—large numbers of the educated citizenry experienced a radical skepticism in the appropriateness of the existing political forms, which were largely liberal and parliamentary in type. Acutely conscious of the sociocultural fissures in their newly unified nations, such people took recourse to a new kind of radical nationalism, which stressed the primacy of national allegiances and priorities (normally with a heavily imperialist or social-imperialist inflexion) over everything else. Under circumstances of unprecedented popular mobilization, in which socialists and other "antinational" elements achieved an increasingly commanding position for themselves, this lack of confidence in the unifying imagination of the liberal and conservative political establishment acquired an extra political edge. From the turn of the century radical-nationalist voices called for a new drive for national unity, at first as a kind of dissenting patriotic intelligentsia, but more and more from an independent political base, with its own organized expressions and wider social resonance.

In my own work on Germany I have tried to characterize this dissenting radical-nationalist politics as a new kind of right-wing populism.[36] It was to be found above all in the ideology and mass agitational practice of the nationalist pressure groups, for whom the Pan-German League may be considered a vanguard, but which included the Navy League, the Defence League, the anti-Polish movement, and a variety of other organizations. Originating in the regional and local dissolution of the old Bismarckian power bloc (essentially an industrial-agrarian coalition, hegemonically ordered by a right-wing liberal politics), it created a new space for disinterested patriotic activism. Though aimed at the directly "unpatriotic" activities of the socialists, ultramontanes, and national minorities (especially the Poles), this was also motivated by a growing anger at the alleged faintheartedness of the constitutional government, the old-style conservatives, and above all the liberal parties from whom many of the radical-nationalist activists came by personal background, family, or general milieu.

In other words, radical-nationalists raised a radical right-wing challenge, at first obliquely and then openly, to the established political practices of the dominant classes. If Germany was to enter into its imperialist heritage, they argued, if patriotic unity was ever to be achieved and domestic squabbling overcome, if the work of national unification was to be completed and the nation's internal divisions healed, above all if the challenge of the left was to be met, then a new political offensive to regain the confidence of the people was required. This demand—for a radical propagandist effort to win the right to speak for the "people in general"—I have called "populist."[37] At its height this radical-nationalist agitation produced a generalized crisis of confidence in the existing political system, which undermined the latter's hegemonic capability—the ability, that is, to organize a sufficient basis of unity among the subordinate classes to permit stable government to continue. In Germany this point was reached around 1908–09, and arguably opened the way for a far-reaching reconstitution of the party-political right over the next decade. In Italy the process was more strung out, extending from the intellectual nationalist ferment of the early 1900s to the interventionist drive of 1914–15. Arguably a similar process was unleashed by Spanish Regenerationism after the Spanish-American War.[38]

My suggestion is that we can explain the attractions of radical nationalism (and by extension those of fascism without recourse to the cultural and economic "despair" of threatened "traditional" strata, to concepts of "anti-modernism," or to the persistence of Kocka's "preindustrial traditions." Those attractions may be grasped partly from the ideology itself, which was self-confident, optimistic, and affirming. It contained an aggressive belief in the authenticity of a German/Italian national mission, in the unifying potential of the nationalist panacea, and in the popular resonance of the national idea for the struggle against the left. Radical nationalism was a vision of the future, not of the past. In this sense it harnessed the cultural aspirations of many who were comfortably placed in the emerging bourgeois society, the successful beneficiaries of the new urban-industrial civilization, whose political sensibilities were offended by the seeming incapacitation of the establishment before the left-wing challenge. While I would concur with Roberts that this outlook possessed a definite appeal to a certain type of patriotic intellectual or activist, it is also likely that in times of relative social and political stability the ideology in itself could achieve only a limited popular appeal. But in times of crisis, which brought the domestic unity, foreign mission, and territorial integrity of the nation all into question, this might easily change. The dramatic conjuncture of war and revolution between 1914 and 1923 produced a crisis of exactly this kind.

Given the operation of certain recognized social determinations (like the status distinctions between white-collar and manual work, or the deliberate fostering of white-collar consciousness by employers and the state), we should concede a certain effectivity to this specifically political factor when trying to explain the radical right-wing preferences of large sections of the new petty bourgeoisie. There is no space to develop this argument more fully here, and in some ways the knowledge to do so is not yet assembled, given the general paucity of research in the area. Though we are well equipped with data concerning the voting patterns in Weimar elections, for instance, or the relative prominence of different occupations among the Nazi party members, we are still very ignorant about the social histories of the particular professions and categories of white-collar employment. What we do know certainly suggests that the avenue of inquiry is worth pursuing. The presence of professionals, managers, and administrators among Nazi activists is now well attested, and the Nazi state provided plenty of scope for the technocratic imagination—in industrial organization, public works, social administration, and the bureaucracy of terror.[39] This sort of evidence moves securely with the direction of the above remarks. At the very least the grievances of the "traditional" petty bourgeoisie coexisted in the fascist movements with other aspirations of a more "forward-looking" and "modernist" kind.

IV

This critique of the "petty-bourgeois thesis" can be further developed. Despite the overrepresentation of the petty bourgeoisie, fascist parties were always more eclectic in their social recruitment than much of the literature might lead us to suppose. Two observations in particular might be made. On the one hand, peasants proved especially important to a fascist party's ultimate prospects, because the transition from ideological sect to mass movement was achieved as much in the countryside as the towns. This was true of both Italy (1920–21) and Germany (1928–32). Conversely, some of the smaller fascist movements owed their weakness to the country population's relative immunity to their appeals. This applied to both Norway and Sweden, where farmers kept to the established framework of agrarian-labor cooperation, and to Finland, where neither the Lapua movement (1929–32) nor its successor, the Patriotic National Movement (Isänmaallinen Kansanliike—1KL; 1932–44), could break the hold of the Agrarian Union and Coalition Party on the smaller farmers.[40]

On the other hand, it is also clear that many fascist parties acquired significant working-class support. The best example is the Nazi party itself, with its 26.3 percent workers in 1930 and 32.5 percent in 1933. But though higher than the working-class membership of the Italian Fascist party (15.4 percent in 1921), this was by no means exceptional. Both Miklós Lackó and György Ránki show that the Hungarian Arrow Cross won much support from workers, in both the more proletarian districts of Budapest and the industrial areas of Nógrád, Veszprém, and Komárom-Esztergom.[41]

There is a tendency in the literature to play down the importance of this working-class support in the interests of the petty-bourgeois thesis, especially in the German case, where the research is extensive. Certainly, we can admit that the Nazis made most progress among specific types of workers. Tim Mason lists "the volatile youthful proletariat" in the big cities, who went straight from school to the dole, who lacked the socializing education of a trade-union membership, and who provided much of the Sturmabteilung (SA) rank-and-file support; the "uniformed working class" in public employment, especially in the railways, post office, and city services; and those in the small-business sector of provincial Germany, "where the working-class movement had not been able to establish a stable and continuing presence."[42] It seems clear that the Nazis failed to breach the historic strongholds of the labor movement—the urban industrial settings that contained the 8 million or so wage earners who voted habitually for the SPD and the German Communist party (KPD)—and had to be content with those categories of workers the left had failed (or neglected) to organize.

Yet this was surely significant enough. Though not a sufficient basis for contesting the left's core support, it deprived the latter of a necessary larger constituency. As Mason points out, between 1928 and July

1932 the combined popular vote of the SPD and KPD fell from 40.4 percent to 35.9 percent, and it was progressively unclear how they were to break through the "sociological, ideological, religious and, not least sex barriers" that defined the "historic" working class in Germany. Mason suggests, in fact, that under the conditions of economic crisis after 1929 these barriers were virtually impassable. By eliminating the chances for either reformist legislation or effective trade-union economism, the depression "robbed the working-class movement of its anticipatory, future-directed role for the working class in general," and "to the degree that industry and trade shrank, the potential constituency of the workers' parties stagnated." The effect, Mason concludes, was a disastrous "narrowing of the political arena of the working class movement."[43]

This brings us to an interesting problem. In effect, the SPD and KPD were facing under particularly extreme, urgent, and dramatic circumstances the classic dilemma of the European left in the general period after the stabilization of 1923–24: how to win popular support for socialism by electoral means, at a time (contrary to earlier predictions) when the industrial proletariat in the classical sense had little chance of becoming a numerical majority of the voting population, and when a reformist practice had ceased to show tangible returns. In the crisis of Weimar, moreover, the cause of socialism had become inextricably linked to the defense of democratic gains. It became imperative for the left to break out of the class-political ghetto for which its entire previous history had prepared it, by building broader political alliances and appealing not only to workers, but to white-collar employees, small owners, pensioners, professional people, students, and so on. Most of all, it was vital to conceive of other than class collectivities, by rallying the people as consumers, as women, as taxpayers, as citizens, and even as Germans—not as some opportunist and eclectic pluralism of discrete campaigns, but as the coherent basis for the broadest possible democratic unity. Yet it was in this democratic project that the politics of the left proved most lamentably deficient, at least until after 1935, when the Popular Front revealed a new strategic perspective. It was less the left's inability to carry the working class itself (though, as Mason points out, in 1930–32 about half the wage-dependent population voted for other parties) than its abdication from this wider popular democratic mobilization that proved most fatal to the Republic's survival.[44]

Arguably, it was precisely here that fascism showed its superiority. In the end, the most striking thing about the National Socialist German Workers party (NSDAP), for instance, was not its disproportionate dependence on a particular social group (the petty bourgeoisie), but its ability (by contrast with the two working-class parties) to broaden its social base in several different directions. The promiscuous adaptability of Nazi propaganda has often been noted, and it was certainly adept at tapping manifold popular resentments, promising all and nothing in the same breath. This remarkable diversity of social appeal can, however, easily mislead. Though both cynical and opportunist, Nazi eclecticism was also a major constructive achievement. The Nazis rallied a disparate assortment of social and political elements that lacked strong traditions of cooperation or effective solidarity in the political sphere, and often surveyed long histories of hostility and mutual suspicion. From September 1930 to January 1933 the NSDAP was a popular political formation without precedent in the German political system. It not only subsumed the organizational fragmentation of the right. It also united a broadly based coalition of the subordinate classes, centered on the peasantry and petty bourgeoisie but stretching deep into the wage-earning population.

It did so on the terrain of ideology, by unifying an otherwise disjointed ensemble of discontents within a totalizing populist framework—namely, the radicalized ideological community of the German people-race. The resulting combination was extraordinarily potent—activist, communitarian, antiplutocratic, and popular, but at the same time virulently antisocialist, anti-Semitic, intolerant of diversity, and aggressively nationalist. In Germany this right-wing Jacobinism was all the more complex for the absence of a strong existing tradition of popular radical nationalism, though as I have tried to argue above, one had begun to take shape since the start of the century. In Italy, for example, as David Roberts argues, the fascists had access to the suppressed Mazzinian tradition of unfulfilled radical-nationalist expectations, which they could then recover and transform. In Germany, in the absence of something similar, the recourse to new synthetic solutions (anti-Semitism, the race-mission in the East, "national socialism") was correspondingly all the more important. There was perhaps something of the same contrast in the difference, say, between the authoritarianism of a Pilsudski in Poland, which could conjure memories of national democracy for its present purposes, and the more radical innovations of the Arrow Cross and Iron Guard in Hungary and Romania. This goes some way to explaining the greater radicalism of Nazi racialism and the apparent irrationalism of the program's implementation during World War II.

This line of argument reinstates the importance of ideology for our understanding of fascism. In particular, it directs us to the contested terrain of popular-democratic aspirations, where the socialist left proved most deficient, the fascist right most telling in their mode of political intervention. Where the left, in both Italy and Germany, kept aggressively to a class-corporate practice of proletarian independence, the fascists erupted into the arena and appropriated the larger popular potential.[45] Of course, putting it like this presupposes an expanded definition of ideology, where it means something more than what happens inside a few literati's heads and is then committed to paper and published for wider consumption. In other words, I mean something more than the well-tried intellectual history so popular with many Germanists during the 1950s and 1960s—that is, not just ideas and attitudes, but also types of behavior, institutions, and social relations, so that ideology becomes materially embodied as well as just thought about (for example, not only the fascist movement's formal aims, but its style of activism, modes of organization, and forms of public display). On this basis fascism becomes primarily a specific type of politics, involving radical authoritarianism, militarized activism, and the drive for a centralist repressive state, with a radical-nationalist, communalist, and frequently racialist creed, and a violent antipathy for both liberal democracy and socialism. Providing these elements are treated not as some revealed unity, but as a set of potentials whose concrete substance may be unevenly and partially realized in "real" (particular, historical) fascisms, a definition of this kind could be quite serviceable.

V

It is time to draw some of these threads together. My comments have clearly been concerned mainly with the strong German and Italian cases, with occasional reference to fascist movements elsewhere. I have also (mindful of the typology referred to in note 4) confined myself to a particular aspect of the overall problem, namely the "coming to power" of indigenously generated fascist movements, rather than the less compelling examples of the smaller imitative or client movements, or the dynamics of established fascist regimes. In so doing I suggested that the specificity of the fascist movements resided in a particular capacity for broadly based popular mobilization—a distinctive ideology or style of politics, as the preceding paragraph puts it. Fascism is more extreme in every way. It registered a qualitative departure from previous conservative practice, substituting corporatist notions of social place for older hierarchical ones, and ideas of race community for those of clerical aristocratic and bureaucratic authority. These and other aspects of fascist ideology are intimately linked to its broadly based popular appeal. Fascism is an aggressively plebeian movement, espousing a crude and violent egalitarianism. Above all, fascism stands for activism and popular mobilization, embracing everything from paramilitary display, street fighting, and straightforward terror to more conventional forms of political activity, new propagandist forms, and a general invasion of the cultural sphere. It is negatively defined against liberalism, social democracy, and communism, or any creed that seems to elevate difference, division, and conflict over the essential unity of the race-people as the organizing principle of political life.

At the same time, fascism was not a universal phenomenon, and appeared in strength only in a specific range of societies. In explaining this variation there are two main emphases. One is the deep historical perspective discussed in relation to Jürgen Kocka. At some level of explanation the structural factors stressed by the latter are clearly important and might be summarized as follows: (1) accelerated capitalist transformation, in a dual context of simultaneous national state formation and heightened competition in the imperialist world economy; (2) the coexistence in a highly advanced capitalist economy of large 'traditional' sectors, including a small-holding peasantry and an industrial-trading petty bourgeoisie, "deeply marked by the contradictions of capitalist development";[46] and (3) the emergence of a precocious socialist movement publicly committed to a revolutionary program. This complex overdetermination (the "contemporaneity of the uncontemporary," or "uneven and combined development") characterized both German and Italian history before World War I, articulated through the interpenetration of national and social problems. Most of the primary analytical traditions share some version of this framework (for example, the political science literature on state formation and the related theories of developmental crises, the particular works of Gershenkron and Barrington Moore, and most of the analogous literature within Marxism).

However, German historians have given this structural argument an additional formulation, which is far more problematic. Evaluating German development (or "misdevelopment," as they call it) by an external and linear model of "modernization," which postulates an ultimate complementarity between economic growth and political democratization (which in Germany, for peculiar reasons, was obstructed), such historians stress the dominance in German public life of preindustrial ideological traditions. The absence of a liberal political culture is thought to have permitted the survival of traditional authoritarian mentalities that enjoyed strong institutional power bases, and could then be radicalized under the future circumstances of an economic or political crisis. Thus a "reactionary protest potential" is created.[47] Fascism draws its support either directly from traditional social strata, or from newer strata (such as white-collar employees) supposedly beholden to traditional ideals. This essentially is Jürgen Kocka's argument.

Though not incompatible with a modified version of the above, the second approach stresses the immediate circumstances under which the fascists came to power. Here it is necessary to mention the impact of World War I, the nature of the postwar crisis in the European revolutionary conjuncture of 1917–23, the unprecedented gains of the left (both reformist and revolutionary), and the collapse of parliamentary institutions. Together these brought a fundamental crisis in the unity and popular credibility of the dominant classes, which opened the space for radical speculations. Here again, although one was the major defeated party and the other a nominal victor in World War I, the German and Italian experiences were remarkably similar in these respects. In both cases the radical right defined itself against the double experience of thwarted imperialist ambitions and domestic political retreat, each feeding the other. In both cases the postwar situation was dominated by the public accommodation of labor, whose political and trade-union aspirations appeared to be in the ascendant: trade unions acquired a new corporative legitimacy; socialists attained a commanding presence in large areas of local government; the national leaderships of the SPD and Italian Socialist party (PSI) occupied the center of the political stage; and substantial movements to their left (first syndicalist and then communist) added an element of popular insurgency. In both cases, too, liberal or parliamentary methods of political containment were shown to have exhausted their potential, guaranteeing neither the political representation of the dominant classes nor the mobilization of popular consent. In such circumstances fascism successfully presented itself as a radical populist solution.

In other words, fascism prospered under conditions of general political crisis, in societies that were already dynamically capitalist (or at least possessed a dynamic capitalist sector), but where the state proved incapable of dispatching its organizing functions for the maintenance of social cohesion. The political unity of the dominant classes and their major economic fractions could no longer be organized successfully within the existing forms of parliamentary representation and party government. Simultaneously the popular legitimacy of the same institutional framework also went into crisis. This way of formulating the problem—as the intersection of twin crises, a crisis of representation and a crisis of hegemony or popular consent—derives from the work of Nicos Poulantzas and its subsequent reworking through the extensive and continuing reception of Antonio Gramsci's ideas into the English language. It has been formulated with exemplary clarity for the case of Nazism by David Abraham:

Could no bourgeois political force organize the political unity of the dominant economic fractions out of the diversity and factiousness of their economic interests? Was no political unity possible and no mass political support available within the Republic, despite the singlemindedness of the dominant classes' anti-socialism? Were the maintenance of capitalist economic relations and political democracy so antithetical in this conjuncture that abandonment and undermining of the Republic were self-evident necessities for the dominant classes?[48]

In the context of the Weimar crisis, adjustments within the existing institutional arrangements looked increasingly untenable, and more radical solutions beyond the boundaries of the existing political system consequently became more attractive.

The problem of defining fascism is therefore not exhausted by describing its ideology, even in the expanded sense of the latter intimated above. Fascism was not just a particular style of politics, it was also inscribed in a specific combination of political conditions (themselves the structured, mediate effect of complex socioeconomic determinations), namely the kind of dual crisis of the state just referred to. Now, that kind of crisis is normally associated with the Great Depression after 1929, but the postwar crisis of political order between 1917 and 1923 was equally important. The global ideological context of the Bolshevik Revolution and its international political legacy gave enormous impetus to the radicalization of the right, and the more vigorous fascist movements generally arose in societies that experienced serious left-wing insurgencies after 1917–18. As well as Italy and Germany, Hungary, Austria, Finland, and Spain are all good examples. Although the recent tendency has been to accept that "Francoism was never really fascism but rather some variant of limited, semi-pluralist authoritarianism," for instance, Paul Preston has argued convincingly that it *was* (at least between the mid-1930s and mid-1950s), and does so partly on the basis of "the Spanish crisis of 1917–23," which was "analogous to the Italian crisis of 1917–22."[49] Moreover, this approach supplies criteria for assessing the seriousness of other crises elsewhere. Thus the formation and fleeting victory of the Popular Front in 1934–37 threatened to create a comparable situation in France, until the breakup of the left government dissipated the gathering concentration of radical right-wing forces.

The operative circumstances were ones that made it possible for the dominant classes to take extreme or exceptional solutions seriously, though never without well-founded hesitation. One such circumstance was obviously the very emergence of the fascists as a credible mass movement, for without the popular materials an "extra-systemic solution" (in Abraham's phrase) was clearly a nonstarter.[50] But, as a generalization, recourse to the fascist option was politically most likely where the left had achieved significant inroads into the administration of state power and the limitation of private capitalist prerogative, or where combinations of entrenched left-reformism and concurrent revolutionary activity seemed to obstruct the resolution of economic crisis and the restoration of order. For example, the most persuasive reading of the crisis of Weimar stresses the importance of a kind of social-democratic corporatism (embodied in trade-union legislation, a ministry of labor, compulsory arbitration procedures, unemployment insurance, other welfare legislation, and so on), whose defensive strengths could not be dismantled within the existing constitutional framework of parliamentary decision-making. The structural necessity of fascist remedies (given certain inflexible commitments and requirements among the most powerful fractions of the dominant classes) can then be located in the labor movement's ability to defend the institutional advances of the 1918 revolution (or more accurately, of the political settlement of 1918–23).[51] When we add the SPD's strong position in provincial and local government, the impressive militancy of the Reichsbanner militia, and the continued vitality of a strategic Marxist-reformist vision among the party intelligentsia, the appeal of a radical authoritarian solution becomes all the more intelligible.[52]

This idea of a defensive social-democratic corporatism, which within the limits of this essay has to remain theoretically underdeveloped, may well be a fruitful one for the discussion of fascism. It lends a formal unity to the political crisis of Weimar, between the foundering of the Grand Coalition in March 1930 on the issue of insurance legislation, and the precipitation of the von Papen-Hitler maneuver in December 1932–January 1933 by General Kurt von Schleicher's renewed corporatist exploration. *Mutatis mutandis*, the argument also works for the Italian situation in 1918–22, where the presence of a mass socialist party publicly committed to a revolutionary program (however rhetorically) had effectively thrown the state into paralysis. Here the growing popular strength of the left, its aggressive use of the workers' councils in Milan and Turin, its commanding position in northern local government, and its massive concentrations of regional support provoked a massive counterrevolutionary backlash, organized through Mussolini's fascists. In both Germany (1918–33), and Italy (1918–22), and for that matter in Spain (1931–36), we are dealing in effect with limited socialist enclaves (some of them physical, some institutional, some merely attitudinal or ideological) within the existing state, which constituted intolerable obstructions to the kind of stabilization a powerful coalition within the dominant classes was increasingly pursuing. Arguably a comparable situation threatened to arise in the wake of the Popular

Front in France (1934–37), and if the Labour Government had chosen to conduct a stubborn resistance to the demands for conservative stabilization in 1931 instead of capitulating, similar circumstances might have materialized in Britain as well. As Joseph Baglieri says of Italian fascism:

> The movement's functional role against the socialists and the Popolari attracted the sympathies and support of all those interests which felt threatened by the post-war mobilization of the lower classes, the incipient process of economic and political democratization, and the breakdown of traditional authority. In the process of crushing the left, the fascists succeeded in offering these interests an alternative sovereignty which successfully stood in for the crumbling Liberal state.[53]

Fascism may be best understood, therefore, as primarily a counter-revolutionary ideological project, constituting a new kind of popular coalition, in the specific circumstances of an interwar crisis. As such it provided the motivational impetus for specific categories of radicalized political actors in the immediate aftermath of World War I, embittered by national humiliation, enraged by the advance of the left. As working-class insurgency defied the capacities of the existing liberal politics to achieve the necessary stabilization, this radical-nationalist cadre became an important pole of attraction for larger circles of the dominant classes and others who felt threatened by the reigning social turbulence. In Italy, where the socialist movement was generally further to the left than in Germany, and where no equivalent of the SPD functioned as a vital factor of order, this process of right-wing concentration around the redemptive potential of a radical-nationalist anti-socialist terror was far more advanced. But later, in the renewed but differently structured crisis of 1929–34, a recognizable pattern recurred. Elsewhere a similar scenario was scripted, but indifferently played out. Spain and possibly Austria were the closest examples of a similarly enacted fascist solution. Other countries certainly generated their own fascist cadres—in some cases very large (France, Finland, Hungary, Romania), in some quite small (Britain, Scandinavia). The severity of the political crisis, and the resilience of established political forms, determined the broader attractions of the fascist ideology.

In the end both perspectives are necessary—the deep historical or long-term structural one and the stress on the immediate crisis, but we have to be clear about what exactly each may reasonably explain. In particular, the causal primacy of "preindustrial traditions" threatens to become both teleological and heavily determinist, locating the origins of fascism somewhere in the middle third of the nineteenth century, when Germany (and Italy) failed to take the "long hard road to modernity," in Dahrendorf's phrase.

Much of this would be perfectly acceptable and in the most rounded of analyses, should be complementary to the other type of approach rather than antithetical. Yet in the works of Jürgen Kocka and other German historians the explanatory claims are far more aggressive than this. The "preindustrial traditions" are given a privileged place in the causal repertoire in a way that specifically displaces certain other approaches—those beginning with the interior dynamics of the immediate fascism-producing crisis. What is seen to be the driving contradiction of the latter—the antidemocratic mentalities that left various social groups so receptive to the fascist appeal—is displaced from its own contemporary context onto a much deeper argument about the course of German history and its singularity. This is accompanied by a clearly stated polemical purpose: fascism is to be explained not by its capitalist present, but by the baleful influence of the feudal past. Winkler is quite explicit on this score. The antidemocratic outcome to the world economic crisis in Germany, as opposed to "the other developed industrial societies," had "less to do with the course of the crisis itself than with the different pre-industrial histories of these countries. The conditions for the rise of fascism have at least as much to do with feudalism and absolutism as with capitalism."[54]

This is unnecessarily restrictive. Older attempts to take the relationship between fascism and capitalism as the primary causal nexus were indeed inadequate, but that is no excuse for evading the challenge of more recent discussions of fascism or more general theories of the state, forms of domination, and so on. Historical discussions of the relationship between capitalism and fascism are actually proceeding with an unprecedented intensity, as the most cursory glance at current research on the Weimar Republic or the final years of liberal Italy will quickly reveal. But they are doing so in an almost wholly "empirical" or "practical" way, without any guiding reference to the larger theoretical issues discussed in this essay. If we are truly to understand the problem, I would argue, it is here, by theorizing fascism in terms of the crisis that produced it—that we shall have to begin.

Notes

This essay originally appeared in *Politics and Society* 12, no. 1 (1983): 53–82, and subsequently as a chapter in *From Unification to Nazism: Reinterpreting the German Past*, by Geoff Eley, published by George Allen & Unwin in 1986. It is reprinted with permission from George Allen & Unwin.

Whatever coherence and value the text may possess owes a great deal to the thoughts and writings of those who have labored longer and more directly on the subject of fascism than I have myself. My main intellectual debts should be clear from the notes but my thinking has been shaped over a period of time by the work of three friends and colleagues in particular, who may not always recognize their own ideas after I have finished with them, but who deserve to be handsomely thanked: Jane Caplan, Michael Geyer, and Tim Mason.

1. See Ernst Nolte, *Three Faces of Fascism* (London: Weidenfeld and Nicolson, 1965); Eugen Weber, *Varieties of Fascism* (New York: Krieger, 1964); Francis L. Carsten, *The Rise of Fascism* (Oxford: Clarendon Press, 1967); John Weiss, *The Fascist Tradition* (New York: Harper & Row, 1967); Hans Rogger and Eugen Weber, eds., *The European Right* (London: Weidenfeld & Nicolson, 1965); *Journal of Contemporary History* 1 (January 1966), special issue entitled "International Fascism, 1920–45." The *Journal of Contemporary History* published a second special issue ten years later called "Theories of Fascism" 11 (October 1976). Selections from both issues have been published as G. L. Mosse, ed., *International Fascism: New Thoughts and New Approaches* (London: Sage Publications, 1979); Barrington Moore, Jr., *Social Origins of Dictatorship and Democracy* (Boston: Beacon, 1966). The three international conferences produced the following volumes of proceedings: P. F. Sugar, ed., *Native Fascism in the Successor States, 1918–1945* (Santa Barbara: University of California Press, 1971); S. J. Woolf, ed., *European Fascism* and *The Nature of Fascism* (New York: Random House, 1968); Institute of History, Czechoslovak Academy of Sciences, ed., *Fascism and Europe* (Prague, 1970), 2 vols. The first of the two Woolf volumes was recently reissued in a slightly revised form as *Fascism in Europe* (London: Methuen, 1981).

2. By now there are many critiques of these older approaches. Among the best are B. Hagtvet, "The Theory of Mass Society and the Collapse of the Weimar Republic: A Re-examination," in S. U. Larsen, B. Hagtvet and J. P. Myklebust, eds., *Who Were the Fascists: Social Roots of European Fascism* (Bergen: Universitetsfarlaget, 1980), pp. 66–117; and M. Clemenz, *Gesellschaftliche Ursprünge des Faschismus* (Frankfurt: Suhrkamp, 1972), pp. 26–57, 96–126, 235–49. In some ways totalitarianism theory in particular has fallen more to the relentless accumulation of monographic research than to frontal critique. For an introduction to that scholarship see Jane Caplan, "Bureaucracy, Politics and the National Socialist State," in P. Stachura, ed., *The Shaping of the Nazi State* (London: Croom Helm, 1978), pp. 234–56; and H. Mommsen, "National Socialism—Continuity and Change," in W. Laqueur, ed., *Fascism: A Reader's Guide* (London: Wildwood House, 1976), pp. 179–210.

3. Nicos Poulantzas, *Fascism and Dictatorship* (London: NLB, 1974); R. De Felice, *Fascism: An Informal Introduction to Its Theory and Practice* (New Brunswick, NJ: Rutgers University Press, 1976). Poulantzas' book on fascism has excited little formal discussion by comparison with his other writings, with the major exceptions of an excellent short essay by Jane Caplan appearing in this volume, and a more abstract piece by Ernesto Laclau. Likewise, De Felice's work has not had a great deal of impact outside the specifically Italian discussion. See E. Laclau, "Fascism and Ideology," in *Politics and Ideology in Marxist Theory* (London: NLB, 1977), pp. 81–142; and M. Ledeen, "Renzo De Felice and the Controversy over Italian Fascism," *Journal of Contemporary History* 11 (October 1976): 269–82.

4. For example, see S. Payne's useful general text, *Fascism: Comparison and Definition* (Madison: University of Wisconsin Press, 1980), pp. 195ff., 6ff., where he proposes a "descriptive typology" based on "(a) the fascist negations, (b) common points of ideology and goals, and (c) special common features of style and organization." The negations involve antiliberalism, anticommunism and qualified anticonservatism. The common goals include a new kind of "national authoritarian state," a "new kind of regulated, multi-class, integrated national-economic structure," a radical foreign policy, and "an idealist, voluntarist creed." The stylistic and organizational features

are "an aesthetic structure of meetings, symbols and political choreography"; militarized forms of mass mobilization; a stress on violence, masculinity, and youth; and a "tendency towards an authoritarian, charismatic, personal style of command."

This is very similar to the approach of Juan Linz, who has published a number of widely cited and influential essays proposing "a multi-dimensional typological definition" of fascism. (see his "Some Notes toward a Comparative Study of Fascism in Sociological Historical Perspective," in Laqueur, ed., *Fascism*, pp. 3–121). Personally, though there are many valuable insights to be culled discretely from his work, I find Linz's general argument obscure, inconclusive, and confusing in the density of its cultivated empirical complexity. Moreover, the typology described above needs to be extended by a further set of distinctions between the different kinds of fascist movements. One possibility would be the following: (1) indigenously generated movements that successfully came to power (Italian Fascism, Nazism, Francoism); (2) small imitative movements that achieved no particular popularity in their home societies (e.g., the British Union of Fascists, or the various Scandinavian Nazi groups); (3) larger indigenous movements with strong similarities of ideology, sociology, and style, but that originated independently of Italian or German sponsorship in a different configuration of social forces, and never took power under peacetime conditions (e.g., Arrow Cross in Hungary, or Iron Guard in Romania); (4) finally, the so-called Quisling regimes installed by the Germans during the war.

5. For a particularly pointless such discussion, see G. Allardyce, "What Fascism Is Not: Thoughts on the Deflation of a Concept," *American Historical Review* 84 (April 1979): 367–88.

6. A familiar but nonetheless important disclaimer should be entered here: by making certain criticisms of existing works, I am *not* trying to discount their value or consign them to the scrap-heap. The point is to open up discussion, nothing more. In certain ways this essay connects with a larger intellectual project, concerned with redrawing the agenda of German historical discussion for the late nineteenth and early twentieth centuries. See D. Blackbourn and G. Eley, *Mythen deutscher Geschichtsschreibung: Die gescheiterte bürgerliche Revolution von 1848* (Frankfurt: Ullstein, 1980), and the controversy it has aroused. This book has now appeared in an expanded and revised English edition as *The Peculiarities of German History: Bourgeois Society and Politics in Nineteenth-Century Germany* (Oxford: Oxford University Press, 1984). This essay originated in a review essay for another journal, and it is only fair to mention the texts that originally provoked it, as they clearly helped formulate the judgments on which the following exposition rests. They include: Laqueur, ed., *Fascism;* Mosse, ed., *International Fascism;* Payne, *Fascism;* Larsen, Hagtvet, and Mylkebust, eds, *Who Were the Fascists;* H. A. Winkler, *Revolution, Staat, Faschismus: Zur Revision des Historichen Materialismus* (Gottingen, 1978); and J. Kocka, *White Collar Workers in America 1890–1940: A Social-Political History in International Perspective* (London, 1980).

7. For discussions of these analytical traditions, see Blackbourn and Eley, *Mythen deutscher Geschichtsschreibung*, and J. A. Davis, ed., *Gramsci and Italy's Passive Revolution* (London: Croom Helm, 1979). For valuable examples see A. Gerschenkron, *Economic Backwardness in Historical Perspective* (Cambridge: Harvard University Press, 1962); Barrington Moore, *Social Origins of Dictatorship and Democracy* (Boston: Beacon, 1966); Charles Tilly, ed., *The Formation of National States in Western Europe* (Princeton: Princeton University Press, 1975); R. Grew, ed., *Crises of Political Development in Europe and the United States* (Princeton: Princeton University Press, 1978); and B. Hagtvet and S. Rokkan, "The Conditions of Fascist Victory," in Larsen, Hagtvet, and Myklebust, eds., *Who Were the Fascists*, pp. 131–52, which links the "violent breakdown of competitive mass politics" to a

complex "geoeconomic-geopolitical model," in which a country's early "geopolitical position," its "semi-peripheralization" in the world economy, and its manner of unification supply the vital preconditions for the emergence of fascism.

8. See Ralf Dahrendorf, *Society and Democracy in Germany* (Garden City: Doubleday, 1967). J. Kocka, "Ursachen des Nationalsozialismus," *Aus Politik und Zeitgeschichte*, June 21, 1980, pp. 9–13, reaffirmed Dahrendorf's argument.

9. K. D. Bracher, *The German Dictatorship: Origins, Structure and Consequences of National Socialism* (Harmondsworth, Middlesex: Penguin, 1973; original German edition 1969); W. Sauer, "National Socialism: Totalitarianism or Fascism?" *American Historical Review* 73 (1967): 404–24, and "Das Problem des Deutschen Nationalstaats," in H.-U. Wehler, ed., *Moderne deutsche Sozialgeschichte* (Cologne: Kiepenheuer & Witsch, 1966), pp. 407–36; E. Fraenkel, *The Dual State* (New York: Oxford University Press, 1941); M. Broszat, *Der Nationalsozialismus: Weltanschauung, Programm und Wirklichkeit* (Stuttgart: Deutsche Verlags-Anstalt, 1960); M. R. Lepsius, "Parteiensystem und Sozialstruktur: Zum Problem der Demokratisierung der deutschen Gesellschaft," in G. A. Ritter, ed., *Deutsche Parteien vor 1918* (Cologne: Kiepenheuer & Witsch, 1973), pp. 56–80; Ralf Dahrendorf, *Society and Democracy in Germany* (Garden City: Doubleday, 1967). By "German historians" in this context I mean historians in West Germany. It is hard to say exactly how broad this generational experience was, partly because the ideological fronts have changed again since the early 1970s, leaving the most self-conscious exponents of avowedly "social-scientific" history (e.g., as represented in the controlling group of the journal *Geschichte und Gesellschaft*) feeling relatively isolated within the West German historical profession as a whole. But for a fairly representative example of literature and authors at the height of the earlier liberalizing trend (several of the contributors have since moved quite markedly to the right), see M. Stürmer, ed., *Das kaiserliche Deutschland: Politik und Gesellschaft 1870–1918* (Dusseldorf: Droste Verlag, 1970).

10. H.-J. Puhle, *Von der Agrarkrise zum Präfaschismus* (Wiesbaden: F. Steiner, 1972), p. 53. The constipated nature of this sentence is an accurate (even benevolent) reflection of the original German.

11. The literature on Gramsci is now enormous. Among the most useful discussions of what he had to say about fascism in particular are the following: A. Davidson, *Antonio Gramsci: Towards an Intellectual Biography* (London: Merlin Press, 1977), pp. 185–201; W. L. Adamson, *Hegemony and Revolution: Antonio Gramsci's Political and Cultural Theory* (Berkeley: University of California Press, 1980), pp. 71–101; C. Buci-Glucksmann, *Gramsci and the State* (London: Lawrence and Wishart, 1980), pp. 295–324; P. Spriano, *Antonio Gramsci and the Party: The Prison Years* (London: NLB, 1979): and Davis, ed., *Gramsci and Italy's Passive Revolution*. For the work of Tim Mason the following are most important: "The Primacy of Politics—Politics and Economics in National Socialist Germany," in Woolf, ed., *Nature of Fascism*, pp. 165–95; *Sozialpolitik im Dritten Reich* (Cologne: Westdeutscher Verlag, 1977); "Zur Entstehung des Gesetzes zur Ordnung der nationalen Arbeit vom 20. January 1934: Ein Versuch über das Verhältnis 'archäischer' und 'moderner' Momente in der neuesten deutschen Geschichte," in H. Mommsen, D. Petzina, and B. Weisbrod, eds., *Industrielles System und politische Entwicklung in der Weimarer Republik* (Dusseldorf: Droste, 1974), pp. 322–51; "Intention and Explanation: A Current Controversy about the Interpretation of National Socialism," in G. Hirschfeld and L. Kettenacker, eds., *Der "Führerstaat": Mythos und Realität* (Stuttgart, 1981), pp. 21–42; "Open Questions on Nazism," in R. Samuel, ed., *People's History and Socialist Theory* (London: Routledge and Kegan Paul, 1981), pp. 205–10.

12. H. A. Winkler, "Die 'neue Linke' und der Faschismus: Zur Kritik neomarxistischer Theorien über den Nationalsozialismus," in *Revolution, Staat, Faschismus*, p. 116, and esp. pp. 74–83. Winkler's essay "German Society, Hitler and the Illusion of Restoration, 1930–33," in Mosse, ed., *International Fascism*, pp. 143–60, puts a similar point of view.

13. Kocka, "Ursachen des Nationalsozialismus," p. 11. For exactly similar arguments, see Puhle, *Von der Agrarkrise*, p. 53, and H.-U. Wehler, *Das deutsche Kaiserreich 1871–1918* (Gottingen: Vandenhoeck & Ruprecht, 1973), pp. 238ff., 226.

14. Kocka, *White Collar Workers*. The original German edition appeared as *Angestellte zwischen Faschismus und Demokratie. Zur politischen Sozialgeschichte der Angestellten: USA 1890–1940 im internationalen Vergleich* (Gottingen: Vandenhoeck & Ruprecht, 1977). Kocka has by this time accumulated a small mountain of publications on the subject of white-collar workers in one way or another. Among the most important are *Unternehmungsverwaltung und Angestelltenschaft am Beispiel Siemens 1847–1914: Zum Verhältnis von Kapitalismus und Bürokratie in der deutschen Industrialisierung* (Stuttgart: Klett, 1969); "Vorindustrielle Faktoren in der deutschen Industrialisierung. Industriebürokratie und 'neuer Mittelstand'" in Stürmer, ed., *Das kaiserliche Deutschland*, pp. 265–86; and *Klassengesellschaft im Krieg: Deutsche Sozialgeschichte 1914–1918* (Gottingen: Vandenhoeck und Ruprecht, 1973), esp. pp. 65–95.

15. Kocka, *White Collar Workers*, p. 5.

16. Ibid.

17. Kocka concedes that the inadequacy of the evidence may ultimately vitiate the comparison in this respect. Moreover, until Hartmut Kaelble's work the more recent research was mainly on the American side. See Kaelble, "Sozialer Aufstieg in den USA und Deutschland, 1900–1960: Ein vergleichendes Forschungsbericht," in H.-U. Wehler, ed., *Sozialgeschichte Heute. Festschrift für Hans Rosenberg zum 70. Geburtstag* (Gottingen: Vandenhoeck und Ruprecht, 1974), pp. 525–42, and Hartmut Kaelble, *Historical Research on Social Mobility* (New York: Columbia University Press, 1981).

18. Kocka, *White Collar Workers*, p. 265.

19. For a recapitulation of these debates, see J. Karabel, "The Failure of American Socialism Reconsidered," *Socialist Register 1979* (London: Merlin Press, 1979), pp. 204–27.

20. Kocka, *White Collar Workers*, p. 266.

21. Ibid., pp. 281f. The phrase "contemporaneity of the uncontemporary" originates with Ernst Bloch. In some ways it corresponds to Trotsky's "uneven and combined development" and the Althusserian "overdetermination."

22. In other ways the argument seems strained. Thus the suggestion that "corporatist remnants in German society help explain why working-class status in itself was more important than differences between crafts and occupations" seems both eccentric and obscure, as does the reference to "the relative insignificance of the line between skilled and unskilled workers in German trade unions and social structure" (ibid., p. 265).

23. Ibid., pp. 282ff.

24. This is also true of Winkler, "Die 'neue Linke' und der Faschismus," p. 83.

25. Aside from the voluminous contents of Larsen, Hagtvet, and Myklebust, eds., *Who Were the Fascists*, there is a useful introduction to such research in R. Mann, ed., *Die Nationalsozialisten: Analysen faschistischer Bewegungen* (Stuttgart, 1980).

26. Quoted by D. D. Roberts, "Petty-bourgeois Fascism in Italy: Form and Content," in Larsen, Hagtvet, and Myklebust, eds., *Who Were the Fascists*, p. 337.

27. Several authors have suggested that the working class was more important to the

social base of the Nazis. See M. Kele, *Nazis and Workers, 1919–1933* (Chapel Hill: University of North Carolina Press, 1972); and C. J. Fischer, "The Occupational Background of the SA's Rank and File Membership during the Depression Years, 1929 to Mid-1934," in Stachura, ed., *Shaping of the Nazi State*, pp. 131–59. More recently R. F. Hamilton, *Who Voted for Hitler?* (Princeton, NJ: Princeton University Press, 1982), has shifted the focus to the "upper classes" as the decisive factor. The "generational-revolt" argument has been advanced very unconvincingly by P. Merkl, "Comparing Fascist Movements," in Larsen, Hagtvet, and Myklebust, eds., *Who Were the Fascists*, pp. 753–83.

28. The volume is extraordinarily useful from this point of view, not least because of its genuinely comprehensive coverage of the European continent. P. Schmitter on Portugal, D. Wallef on *Christus Rex* in Belgium , and H. van der Wusten and R. E. Smit on Holland are particularly useful, as are the ten sophisticated essays on Scandinavia.

29. Roberts, "Petty-bourgeois Fascism in Italy," p. 337.

30. Ibid., p. 338.

31. E. Tannenbaum, *The Fascist Experience: Italian Society and Culture 1922–1945* (New York: Basic Books, 1972), p. 4; Henry A. Turner, Jr., "Fascism and Modernization," in Turner, ed., *Reappraisals of Fascism* (New York: Watts, 1975), pp. 133ff. The view was put in Wolfgang Sauer's seminal article of 1967 and in several of the discussions at the 1967 Reading Conference. See Sauer, "National Socialism"; A. F. K. Organski, "Fascism and Modernization"; and G. Germani, "Fascism and Class," in Woolf, ed., *Nature of Fascism*, pp. 19–41, 65–96.

32. Roberts, "Petty-bourgeois Fascism in Italy," p. 337. The following quotations come from the same essay. See also David Roberts, *The Syndicalist Tradition and Italian Fascism* (Chapel Hill: University of North Carolina Press, 1979).

33. The Partito Popolare Italiano (Popular Party), formed in 1918–19, was Italy's first Catholic party and the political ancestor of Christian Democracy. In the years 1919–22 it became the vehicle for a variegated movement of agrarian radicalism, although the various forces acting to control the latter always ensured that it could never become a peasants' party as such.

34. Roberts, "Petty-bourgeois Fascism in Italy," p. 345. This recourse to Mazzini was anything but traditional or "backward-looking" in the sense normally intended by such descriptions. As Roberts says: "In Italy, after all, nationalism was hardly traditional for the society as a whole, and it could still have progressive consequences in such a context. Since these fascists were seeking alternatives to the political patterns that had developed because of the way Italy was unified, it was plausible for them to turn to Mazzini, who represented all the unfulfilled promise of the Risorgimento; his vision of a more popular kind of Italian unity had not been achieved, so it was not merely reactionary nostalgia that led fascists to look to him for ideas and inspiration as they sought solutions to contemporary problems." For a similar argument in the context of German radical nationalism, see G. Eley, *Reshaping the German Right: Radical Nationalism and Political Change after Bismarck* (New Haven: Yale University Press, 1980), esp. ch. 5, pp. 160–205.

35. There is a useful introduction to the gentry controversy and its historiographical context in R. C. Richardson, *The Debate on the English Revolution* (London: Methuen, 1977), pp. 90ff. The problematic nature of trying to establish precise causal correlations between "rising" or "declining" social forces and specific ideologies or political movements should be plain. My aim is not to exchange the "threatened traditional strata" type of explanation for fascism for an equivalent reductionism based on the idea of "rising new strata" of the white-collar petty bourgeoisie. The point is to think carefully about why exactly radical nationalism

(and other aspects of the fascist ideological project) proved so appealing to *different* categories of people. The interesting thing about radical nationalism in Germany was its ability, in a complicated process covering the first two decades of the century, to harness the aspirations of both the old petty bourgeoisie and the new—both the small producers, traders, and businessmen in town and country, and the new technocracy of the professional and managerial intelligentsia. If I understand Roberts correctly, his work lends itself to a similar sort of argument in Italy. The problem of fascism then becomes in part the process of unifying, or at least combining on a stable basis, the disparate aspirations of a variegated social base.

36. Eley, *Reshaping the German Right.* The argument is also summarized in Eley, "Some Thoughts on the Nationalist Pressure Groups in Imperial Germany," in P. Kennedy and A. J. Nicholls, eds., *Nationalist and Racialist Movements in Britain and Germany before 1914* (London: Macmillan, 1981), pp. 40–67.

37. My use of the term is not intended to invoke a specific historical experience, like that of Russian or North American Populism in the later nineteenth century. It refers to a broadly based appeal to "the-people-in-general" against unrepresentative, ineffectual, and morally flawed dominant interests. As such, it could become articulated into both a politics of the right and a politics of the left. For the key text in stimulating this specific theoretical usage, see E. Laclau, "Towards a Theory of Populism," in *Politics and Ideology in Marxist Theory*, pp. 143–99. See also S. Hall, "Notes on Deconstructing 'the Popular,'" in Samuel, ed., *People's History and Socialist Theory*, pp. 227–40.

38. For Italy see A. DeGrand, *The Italian Nationalist Association and the Rise of Fascism in Italy* (Lincoln: University of Nebraska Press, 1978); W. Alff, "Der Begriff Faschismus" and "Die Associazione Nazionalista Italiana von 1910," in *Der Begriff Faschismus und andere Aufsätze zur Zeitgeschichte* (Frankfurt: Suhrkamp, 1971), pp. 14–95. For Spain: J. C. Ullmann, *The Tragic Week: Anticlericalism in Spain, 1876–1912* (Cambridge: Harvard University Press, 1968).

39. See the following: F. Zipfel, "Gestapo and the SD: A Sociographic Profile of the Organizers of Terror," in Larsen, Hagtvet, and Myklebust, eds., *Who Were the Fascists*, pp. 301–11; G. C. Boehnert, "The Jurists in the SS-Führerkorps, 1925–1939," in Hirschfeld and Kettenacker, eds., *Der 'Führerstaat'*, pp. 361–74; Mason, "Zur Entstehung des Gesetzes zur Ordnung der nationalen Arbeit"; K.-H. Ludwig, *Technik und Ingenieure im Dritten Reich* (Dusseldorf: Droste, 1976); and A. D. Beyerchen, *Scientists under Hitler: Politics and the Physics Community in the Third Reich* (New Haven: Yale University Press, 1978). See also K.-J. Muller, "French Fascism and Modernization," *Journal of Contemporary History* 11 (October 1976): 75–108.

40. For discussions of agrarian fascism in Italy and Germany, see J. Baglieri, "Italian Fascism and the Crisis of Liberal Hegemony, 1901–1922," and N. Passchier, "The Electoral Geography of the Nazi Landslide," in Larsen, Hagtvet, and Myklebust, eds., *Who Were the Fascists*, pp. 327ff., 283ff. The Scandinavian essays in the same volume are especially useful and show how illuminating the comparison with smaller and more marginal fascisms can be. For Norway: J. P. Myklebust and B. Hagtvet, "Regional Contrasts in the Membership Base of the *Nasjonal Samling*"; H. Hendriksen, "Agrarian Fascism in Eastern and Western Norway: A Comparison"; and S. S. Nilson, "Who Voted for Quisling?" For Sweden: B. Hagtvet, "On the Fringe: Swedish Fascism 1920–45." For Finland: R. Alapuro, "Mass Support for Fascism in Finland"; R. E. Heinonen, "From People's Movement to Minor Party: The People's Patriotic Movement (IKL) in Finland 1932–1944." See Larsen, Hagtvet, and Myklebust, eds., *Who Were the Fascists*, pp. 621–50, 651–56, 657–66, 735–38, 678–84, 689ff.

41. Figures for Germany and Italy are taken from Payne, *Fascism*, pp. 60ff. An additional 23.4 percent could be considered in the Italian case, accounting for agricultural laborers. For Hungary, see M. Lacko, "The Social Roots of Hungarian Fascism: The Arrow Cross," and G. Ranki, "The Fascist Vote in Budapest in 1939," in Larsen, Hagtvet, and Myklebust, eds., *Who Were the Fascists*, pp. 395–400, 401–16.
42. T. Mason, "National Socialism and the Working Class, 1925–May 1933," *New German Critique* 11 (Spring 1977): 60–9.
43. Ibid., pp. 59, 65.
44. Ibid., p. 60.
45. The argument in this and the previous two paragraphs owes much to Laclau, "Fascism and Ideology."
46. R. Fraser, "The Spanish Civil War," in Samuel, ed., *People's History and Socialist Theory*, p. 197.
47. Kocka, *White Collar Workers*, p. 252.
48. D. Abraham, *The Collapse of the Weimar Republic: Political Economy and Crisis* (Princeton: Princeton University Press, 1981), p. 287.
49. P. Preston, "Spain," in Woolf, ed., *Fascism in Europe*, p. 332. See also Preston's *The Coming of the Spanish Civil War* (London: Macmillan 1978); R. Carr, *Modern Spain 1875–1980* (Oxford: Oxford University Press, 1980), pp. 81–97; and G. H. Meaker, *The Revolutionary Left in Spain 1914–1923* (Stanford: Stanford University Press, 1974).
50. The phrase comes from the title of the penultimate section of Abraham's final chapter, "Towards the Extra-systemic Solution," in *Collapse of the Weimar Republic*, pp. 313–18.
51. Here I am abstracting from a number of recent works, which are separated by numerous specific differences and whose authors may not share the particular formulations I have chosen. See, in particular, B. Weisbrod, *Schwerindustrie in der Weimarer Republik: Industrielle Interessenpolitik zwischen Stabilisierung und Krise* (Wuppertal: P. Hammer, 1978); and "Economic Power and Political Stability Reconsidered: Heavy Industry in Weimar Germany," *Social History* 4 (May 1979): 241–63; Abraham, *Collapse of the Weimar Republic*; D. Stegmann, "Kapitalismus und Faschismus 1929–34; Thesen und Materialien," in H. G. Backhaus ed., *Gesellschaft: Beiträge zur Marxschen Theorie* (Frankfurt, 1976), vol. 6, pp. 14–75; C. D. Crohn, "Autoritärer Kapitalismus: Wirtschaftskonzeptionen im Übergang von der Weimarer Republik zum Nationalsozialismus," in D. Stegmann, B.-J. Wendt and P.-C. Witt, eds., *Industrielle Gesellschaft und politisches System* (Bonn and Bad Godesberg: Verlag Neue Gesellschaft, 1978), pp. 113–29; and Charles S. Maier's summing up at the 1974 Bochum conference on the Weimar Republic, in Mommsen, Petzina and Weisbrod, eds., *Industrielles System und politische Entwicklung*, pp. 950ff.
52. See W. Luthardt, ed., *Sozialdemokratische Arbeiterbewegung und Weimarer Republik: Materialien zur gesellschaftlichen Entwicklung 1927–1933* (Frankfurt: Suhrkamp, 1978), 2 vols.
53. Baglieri, "Italian Fascism and the Crisis of Liberal Hegemony," p. 333.
54. Winkler, "Die 'neue Linke' und der Faschismus," p. 83.

Bonapartism, Fascism, and the Collapse of the Weimar Republic

Derek S. Linton

In a survey of theories of fascism, the historian Martin Kitchen divided them into three types: "heteronomic," "autonomic," and "syncretic." Included in the first type were those theories "which assert that fascism is determined and produced by capitalism (or to use the somewhat euphemistic terms, 'industrial society', 'modern society', 'the age of the masses' or 'modernisation') . . . whereas those in the second hold that fascism was an independent force which was able to determine the course of capitalist development."[1] Syncretic theories combine aspects of the first two. Although these distinctions have seldom been absolute, they do indicate general tendencies found in the literature on fascism, whether Marxist or non-Marxist. This essay will explore one set of basically syncretic theories within the Marxist tradition, the set of analyses of National Socialism that derived from Marx's and Engels' accounts of Bonapartism in nineteenth-century France.[2]

The exploration will proceed in three parts. First, I will outline the conditions of emergence of the Bonapartist perspective on fascism from the debates within the Communist International during the 1920s. Second, I will examine some of the elements of Marx's and Engels, concept of Bonapartism that proved especially stimulating and fruitful in framing a Marxist explanation of National Socialism. Finally, I will exposit, compare, and contrast the leading Bonapartist perspectives of the 1930s, those of August Thalheimer, Leon Trotsky, and Otto Bauer. Throughout, I will be largely, although not exclusively, concerned with the explanatory framework of the theories rather than their political functions or strategic implications.

The Bonapartist Perspective on Fascism

The triumph of Mussolini's Fascist movement in Italy in 1922 and the stunning defeat and brutal suppression of Italy's militant and powerful labor movement were experienced by European Marxists as cataclysmic shocks.[3] These serious reversals as well as the unexpected strength of counterrevolutionary movements in postwar central Europe shattered apocalyptic hopes among members of the Comintern for rapid proletarian victories modeled on the Bolshevik example and prodded some thoughtful social democrats to reconsider their strategies for a purely peaceful parliamentary road to socialism. These shock experiences also sparked considerable debate and theoretical controversy about fascism and counterrevolution within the European left, which established the parameters for subsequent Marxist interpretations of German National Socialism.

Already in the mid-1920s, the complex of problems and questions arose that would be central to Marxist theorizing on what constituted fascism. First, in what temporal trajectory of capitalist development should the fascist phenomenon be placed? Was it the product of the epoch of imperialism and capitalist decay, an aberration of belated and incomplete capitalist development, the offspring of postwar social displacement, disorientation, and economic crisis, or a complex hybrid of these possibilities? Second, what accounted for the political geography of fascism? Why had it taken root in Italy rather than elsewhere? Was fascism merely a local phenomenon, the outcome of a specific configuration of class forces and political crisis confined to Italy? Or was fascism likely to spring up in other countries with relatively weak industrial development and large transitional classes (landowners, peasants, artisans, small shopkeepers)? Could it even be a general form of counterrevolutionary movement common in varying degrees to all capitalist nations? Third, what constellation of class forces made fascism possible? What was the relation of the fascist movement to the large-scale capitalists, the landowners, the old and new lower middle class, the peasantry and labor? How was it related to the postwar labor offensive and the capitalist counterattack? Was it essentially the counterrevolutionary instrument of big capital and the agrarians or was it a semi-autonomous movement of the petty bourgeoisie and declassé elements? Finally, what was the political nature of fascism? What was its relation to the preexisting political system, the parties, and the state? Once in power, was the fascist state a new form of class rule, the direct instrument of monopoly capital, or was it analogous to the Bonapartist regime described by Marx? Divergent answers to these questions generally implied alternative strategies for combating fascism as well.

Although the Fifth Congress of the Communist International in 1924 attempted to settle these issues by resolving that "fascism is the instrument of the big bourgeoisie for fighting the proletariat, when the legal means available to the state have proved insufficient to subdue them,"[4] even within European Communist parties answers to these questions continued to be quite diverse and leading Communists openly dissented from this resolution. Thus, for example, as late as 1928 the Italian Communist leader Palmiro Togliatti considered fascism a largely Italian phenomenon and warned against diluting the concept by applying it to all forms of reaction.[5] In Italy the intermediate and transitional classes had been especially strong and the specific constellation of class relations was unlikely to occur elsewhere. Moreover, fascism was originally to some degree autonomous from capitalist interests. According to Togliatti, while the attacks of fascist gangs on the organizations of workers and peasants

> worked naturally to the advantage of industrial and financial capital . . . fascism was not simply capitalist reaction. It embraced many other elements at the same time. It comprised a movement of the rural petty bourgeois masses; it was also a political struggle waged by certain representatives of the small and middle bourgeoisie against a section of the traditional ruling class, . . . finally it was a military organization which claimed the ability to take on the regular armed forces of the state with some probability of success.[6]

Once in power, claimed Togliatti, fascism became "a center of political unity for the dominant classes but only after a far-reaching transformation in its structure and social compositions." Fascism also differed from other forms of reaction in its savage suppression of democratic rights and its thoroughgoing extirpation of all autonomous mass organizations including those of the Socialists, which the Comintern resolution had maligned as instruments of capitalist dictatorship and twins of fascism.

After 1928, however, such relatively sophisticated and complex analyses became anathema within the Comintern. As the Soviet leadership under Stalin became increasingly preoccupied with the domestic tasks of "building socialism in one country," it stringently disciplined and purged foreign Communist parties in order to compel them to conform to the shifting policies of the Communist party of the Soviet Union.[7] Henceforth, virtually unquestioning orthodoxy was enforced within the Comintern.

In the case of the Comintern analysis of fascism, orthodoxy meant that the dubious propositions already advanced in the 1924 resolution now congealed into frozen verities. First, fascism was held to be a product of monopoly capitalism in the epoch of decay. "It is based on the concentration and centralization of capital and the associated development of trusts and cartels, and leads to the massive centralization of the whole apparatus of mass oppression—including the political parties, the Social Democratic apparatus, the reformist trade unions, the cooperatives, etc."[8] Second, fascism was declared a general phenomenon common to all capitalist nations: "The totality of modern capitalist states constitutes a varied amalgam of fascist countries (Italy, Poland) and bourgeois democracies containing fascist elements and standing at different stages of the fascisation process." Third, the social base of fascist movements was said to be "the petty bourgeois masses, and the corresponding strata of white collar workers and officials," largely manipulated and deployed by the high bourgeoisie for counterrevolutionary goals.[9] Finally, the Soviet Comintern delegate Dmitril Manuilski avowed,

> Political reaction as a form of government has advanced continuously with the development of imperialism in all capitalist states and has become the counterpart to imperialist aggression. The fascist regime is not just any new type of state; it is one of the forms of bourgeois dictatorship characteristic of the imperialist epoch. Fascism grows organically out of bourgeois democracy. The process whereby bourgeois dictatorship switches to an open form of suppression of the workers thus represents the essence of the fascisation process.[10]

This Comintern version of fascism was, as Kitchen remarks, "the extreme form of the heteronomic theory."[11]

Two further elements of this orthodoxy, which reigned in the Comintern and German Communist party (KPD) from 1928 to 1935 and which contributed indirectly but substantially to Hitler's victory, deserve emphasis.[12] First, any repressive and antilabor regime was labeled "fascist." Hence, the conservative and authoritarian governments of Chancellors Henrich Brüning, Franz von Papen, and General Kurt von Schleicher in Germany between 1930 and 1932 were described as already fascist, thus trivializing the danger of Hitler's accession to power. Second, the Social Democrats were branded a twin of the moderate wing of fascism. Indeed, since Socialists, unlike the Nazis, supposedly successfully deceived the workers, they were desig-

nated the primary enemies of the Communists. Such a position obviously precluded any common action with organized socialists against
the Nazis. Thus in February 1932, less than a year before the Nazi
seizure of power, Ernst Thälmann, the leader of the German Communist party, could still stamp the national Brüning government and the
Social Democratic-dominated government of Otto Braun in Prussia
fascist for such antilabor measures as cutting welfare payments and
curbing strikes.[13] He could complacently denounce what he called the
"opportunistic overestimation of Hitler fascism" and blithely assert that
Social Democracy was the most active element in the fascisation of
Germany and hence the KPD's most dangerous enemy.

Consequently, during the period of the rise of Hitler, Marxist analyses treating the Nazi movement as anything other than the pliable and
bribed instrument of German big business and the Junkers were
formulated outside of and in opposition to the official Comintern position, as were antifascist strategies based on a united front of the
German Social Democratic party (SPD), Communists, and trade
unions. The three key figures who posed comprehensive alternative
analyses and strategies were the German right communist August
Thalheimer, the expelled Soviet left-oppositionist Leon Trotsky, and
Otto Bauer, the foremost theoretician of the Socialist party of Austria.
Despite quite significant differences in their theories of fascism, all
three, for reasons to be explored, took Marx's and Engels' writings on
nineteenth-century Bonapartism as their point of departure. By em-
ploying the concept of Bonapartism, all three developed extensive
interpretations of the collapse of the Weimar Republic and the Nazi
seizure of power that compared favorably both in subtlety and political
acumen with the crude instrumentalism of the Comintern.

Bonapartism in Marx and Engels

The French historian Pierre Ayçoberry, in his historiographical study
The Nazi Question, praises August Thalheimer for brilliantly framing
the question "concerning the relative autonomy of the state vis à vis the
dominant economic class.[14] He concludes, however, by contending
that "at bottom, he did not contribute much more than a return to
Marx, the return to origins, a standard tactic of reformers and heretics.
But he was to have many descendants in this regard: the application of
the notion of Bonapartism to German history and the debate on the
reciprocal relations of the Nazi state and the great monopolies originated with him." Such an assessment begs more questions than it
answers. Leaving aside that Thalheimer concentrated on the conditions

leading to the Nazi seizure of power rather than on the Nazi state, it fails to answer the question of "which Marx" Thalheimer and the other Bonapartist theorists returned to.

Thalheimer, Trotsky, and Bauer were all well aware that the instrumentalist conception of the state and politics favored by the Comintern could muster strong textual support, such as the famous passage in the *Communist Manifesto* where Marx wrote, "The executive of the modern State is but a committee for managing the common affairs of the whole bourgeoisie."[15] Although Marx's writings on Bonapartism and the Commune were certainly his most sustained political writings, the decision to privilege these texts over others suggests that Thalheimer, and to a lesser degree Bauer and Trotsky, found either Marx's mode of analysis, the structural characteristics of the events he analyzed, or both, especially germane for understanding National Socialism. Second, neither Thalheimer nor any of the others simply appropriated and applied Marx's model of Bonapartism. Not surprisingly, given Marxist historicism, all of them used it as a starting point but also recognized and emphasized negative analogies between Bonapartism and fascism that depended on the intervening development of capitalism since the mid-nineteenth century. The question to be asked then is: What aspects of Marx's and Engels' accounts of Bonapartism did they find useful? While the answers would be somewhat different for Thalheimer, Trotsky, and Bauer, some elements were shared among the three.

In many respects the historical situation in which Marx originally grappled with the regime of Louis Napoleon presented obvious parallels with the triumph of fascism in Italy or the rise of Hitler, parallels that few well-versed Marxists could overlook. Despite the defiantly optimistic peroration with its ringing prophecy of the downfall of Louis Napoleon's regime, Marx's *Eighteenth Brumaire* portrays a tragedy of working-class defeat, followed by the attrition of a parliamentary republic, culminating in the seizure of power by an unscrupulous and shadowy political adventurer aided by a secret society and backed by the bayonets of the army. The events that brought Louis Napoleon to power were as much a shock to Marx after the heady optimism of the 1848 revolutions as the triumph of fascism was to Marxists in the 1920s. Marx explained these events by closely examining both the cohesion and the fragmentation of the French bourgeoisie.[16]

According to Marx, the dictatorship of Louis Napoleon was in no respect a direct response to a working-class offensive. Indeed, after the crushing defeat of June 1848, when Parisian workers had revolted in an attempt to retain the right of the unemployed to guaranteed jobs in the national workshops, "the proletariat passes into the *background* of the revolutionary stage," although the June Days would haunt "the subsequent acts of the drama like a ghost."[27] The June Days not only catalyzed cohesion in an otherwise fragmented bourgeoisie, which rallied around the slogans "property, family, religion, order," but also traumatized property holders giving rise to a deep-rooted fear of disorder or any sign of reawakening class conflict. This fear, periodically revived by peasant and labor unrest or petty-bourgeois discontent, would condition the willingness of the bourgeois parliamentary bloc to lean on the executive and the army and to undermine and eliminate democratic rights, including universal manhood suffrage. "It understood that all the so-called bourgeois liberties and organs of progress attacked and menaced its *class rule* at its social foundation and political summit simultaneously, and had therefore become '*socialistic*.'"[18] Unable to represent the majority of the nation, the bourgeois parliamentarians would attempt to stifle the political expression of the majority.

Not only were the bourgeois parliamentarians unable to represent the vast majority of the nation, but riven by irreconcilable internal antagonisms, they were unable even to represent the bourgeoisie. Much of *The Eighteenth Brumaire* is taken up with the parliamentary intrigues and machinations of the various factions of the bourgeois parties, the internal disintegration of the party of Order and the consequent crisis of representation. From the outset, the party of Order was, according to Marx, split into two great rival factions, Orleanists and Bourbons, each backing a rival royal house.[19] As is usual with Marx, he treats these factions not merely as political divisions but rather as expressions of social interests, capital and landed property respectively, reinforced by cultural distinctions. The continual squabbles within the party of Order over constitutional issues and the conflicts of this party with the president, Louis Napoleon, who constantly attempted to enlarge his sphere of authority, soon alienated those whom it purported to represent.

> The parliamentary party was not only dissolved into its two great factions, each of these factions was not only split up within itself but the party of Order in parliament had fallen out with the party of Order *outside* parliament. The spokesmen and scribes of the bourgeoisie, its platform and its press, in short, the ideologists of the bourgeoisie and the bourgeoisie itself, the representatives and the represented, faced one another in estrangement and no longer understood one another.[20]

This estrangement increasingly led to a rejection of parliamentary government by the extraparliamentary bourgeoisie and to its support for an authoritative executive in the person of the president, Louis Napoleon. The aristocracy of finance, its business tied up with public credit, "condemned the parliamentary struggle of the party of Order as a *disturbance of order*."[21] The commercial bourgeoisie soon followed suit. In short, the parliamentary party of Order failed to aggregate the heterogenous interests of the bourgeoisie or create the conditions of order and stability that were regarded as necessary for the pursuit of private business affairs.

This crisis of representation and the longing for stability, order, and economic security meant that the bourgeoisie was willing to countenance Louis Napoleon's coup d'état in December 1851. In so doing

> the bourgeoisie confesses that its own interests dictate that it should be delivered from the danger of its *own rule;* that in order to restore tranquility in the country, the bourgeois parliament must first of all be given its quietus; that in order to preserve its social power intact, its political power must be broken: that the individual bourgeois can continue to exploit the other classes and to enjoy undisturbed property, family, religion and order only on condition that their class is condemned along with the other classes to like political nullity.[22]

If the fragmentation of bourgeois interests and the generalized crisis of representation eroded the parliamentary republic and thus made Napoleon's coup possible, there remained the question of how and with what bases of support the adventurer Louis Napoleon was able to seize and retain power. Marx's account of the sources of support for Louis Bonaparte and the social interests that his regime served is extremely complex.[23] According to Marx, the mass base of Louis Napoleon's presidency and coup d'état had been the conservative peasantry, which, inspired by the Napoleonic legend, had elected Bonaparte to the presidency in December 1848. Louis Napoleon's major organizational base of support, however, was the Society of December 10th, a secret society gathered from the declassé flotsam of all social classes, which functioned both as an approving claque simulating public enthusiasm and as a terrorist gang intimidiating political opponents. The second organizational source of support was the army recruited from the peasantry. From 1848 Louis gradually brought the army under his control, replacing parliamentary generals, wining and dining the officer corps, promising future glory.

Marx also detailed the political means employed by Louis Napoleon to strengthen the executive power against the parliament after his election to the presidency in December 1848.[24] Part of his success was attributable to the deficiencies of the Constitution of 1848, which made the president the only official elected directly by the entire nation and invested him with quasi-royal powers. Louis Napoleon's adroit use of these prerogatives combined with the factional disarray of the National

Assembly resulted in a steady increase in the autonomy of executive authority. By the time the parliamentarians decided to oppose his designs for an unconstitutional second presidential term, his tight grip on the levers of power, the army and the bureaucracy, enabled him to carry out a successful coup.

Under Louis Napoleon, the executive power with its army and vast body of officials appeared to have acquired complete autonomy vis-à-vis civil society.[25] Marx considered the appearance of complete autonomy illusory claiming instead that the executive rested on the passive base of the masses of small isolated peasant proprietors. This vast dictatorial power seems to have served no well-defined class interests or indeed any interests apart from those of Louis Napoleon and his immediate entourage. Louis Napoleon pursued contradictory policies and attempted to play off all classes against one another, to conjure and steal "the whole of France in order to make a present of her to France."[26] However, while breaking the political power of the bourgeoisie, "by protecting its material power, he generates its political power anew." This seems, however, to be an inescapable consequence of maintaining bourgeois property relations rather than the willed or forseeable result of conscious policy.

The other *locus classicus* for Bonapartist analyses of fascism was Engels' attempt in the *Origin of the Family, State and Private Property* to generalize the phenomenon of Bonapartism by classifying it as an exceptional form of state in conditions of class balance. According to Engels,

> By way of exception, however, periods occur in which the warring classes balance each other so nearly that the state power, as ostensible mediator, acquires, for the moment, a certain degree of independence of both. Such was the absolute monarchy of the seventeenth and eighteenth century, which held the balance between the nobility and the class of burghers; such was the Bonapartism of the First and still more the Second French Empire, which played off the proletariat against the bourgeoisie and the bourgeoisie against the proletariat. The latest performance of this kind in which ruler and ruled appear equally ridiculous, is the new German Empire of the Bismarck nation; here capitalists and workers are balanced against each other and equally cheated for the benefit of the impoverished cabbage junkers.[27]

While this rather elliptical historical formula sacrificed any sense of the complex internal fragmentation of classes, the importance of transitional classes, or a crisis of representation for the triumph of Bonapartism nonetheless both Otto Bauer and Trotsky would make use of the notion of "class balance."

Thus in summary, the Bonapartist theorists of the 1920s and 1930s could in varying degree draw on some elements of Marx's dissection of Bonapartism: the depiction of Bonapartism as in part a response to working-class defeat accompanied by bourgeois fear and fragmentation; the account of the corresponding crisis of representation, attrition of parliamentary rule, split between public power and private social interest, and autonomization of the executive as the bourgeoisie recognized that its political power was incompatible with preserving social dominance; the portrayal of the opportunities this provided for a declassé adventurer and his followers to seize power. It should be noted, however, that Marx's analysis could be more readily made to yield answers to questions about the social character of fascism and its relation to the political system than about its relation to the historical development of capitalism or fascism's political geography.

Bonapartist Perspectives of the 1930s

The analysis of the attrition of Weimar democracy and the rise of Hitler based most closely on Marx's Bonapartist model was undertaken by August Thalheimer and other contributors to *Gegen den Strom* (Against the Current), the journal of the German Communist party—Opposition (KPD[O]) between 1930 and 1933.[28] Thalheimer, who had been a key theoretician of the German Communist party until his expulsion for outspoken opposition to the Comintern resolution of 1928, warned with prophetic lucidity against the tendency on the part of both Communists and Social Democrats to underestimate the fascist danger. Given the organizational weakness of the KPD(O), however, his clearsighted warnings during the early 1930s would remain Cassandra-like. Although his articles were discovered by the German new left in the 1960s, recent Marxist critics have faulted him for ostensibly failing to relate the orientations and attitudes of classes in Germany to the economic conjunctures of the 1930s and the categories of political economy.[29] This criticism is only partially justified, since it tends to focus myopically on his best-known article, "Uber den Faschismus" (On Fascism), rather than his writings on the political situation in Germany.

It was in "Uber den Faschismus," written in 1928 and published in 1930, that Thalheimer depended most heavily on *The Eighteenth Brumaire*, which he quoted extensively. Nonetheless, he did not equate Bonapartism and fascism, stating instead that "they are related phenomena with common as well as divergent characteristics both of which have to be worked out."[30] Indeed, he proceeded analogically, establishing a series of correspondences and contrasts between these two forms of rule. Among the features they shared, he numbered the autonomy of executive power, "the political subordination of all masses, including the bourgeoisie itself, under the fascist state power but with the social dominance of the large bourgeoisie and large landowners," and the attempt to appear as the benefactor of all classes.[31] Even the dynamics of class struggle that brought both regimes to power were similar, a defeat of a working-class offensive and the exhaustion of the bourgeoisie, which searched for a savior to preserve its social power. The nationalism and imperialist aspirations of both regimes as well as their internal contradictions propelled both to war.

However, a number of features distinguished the two regimes as well.[32] Some of these stemmed from the different national histories of France and Italy, as for example Louis Napoleon's use of the Napoleonic legend as opposed to Mussolini's more artificial attempt to recall the glory of ancient Rome. "More important, however, are the distinctions which stem from changes in the general character of capitalism." Louis Napoleon belonged to the age of competitive capitalism and could sometimes advance national liberation, for instance in his aid to Italian independence, whereas Mussolini's foreign policy bore the marks of modern imperialism and was reactionary from the outset. Moreover, the organizational bases of the two regimes diverged in certain respects. Whereas the Society of December 10th was the counterpart of the secret societies of the early French labor movement, the fascist party was the counterrevolutionary counterpart of the Bolsheviks. The mass character of the fascist party "makes it in certain respects stronger, but also increases its internal contradictions, the contradiction between the social interests of these masses and the interests of the dominant class which it serves."[33]

Although Thalheimer did not explicitly emphasize his differences from the Comintern position in this article, they were nonetheless pronounced. While he too related the triumph of fascism to the era of imperialism and monopoly capitalism, albeit somewhat perfunctorily, he pointed out that the nations where fascism had come to power— among which he counted Italy, Poland, and Bulgaria—were not exactly major capitalist societies.[34] While the attempt to dismantle the parliamentary system and create "stronger political guarantees for bourgeois domination" was evident in "such highly developed capitalist lands as England, Germany and France which were more or less socially and economically shaken by the results of the war, that points in the *direction of fascism, it can* lead to forms of open dictatorship of capital in certain critical situations. But these will not *necessarily* be identical with fascism."[35]

Thus while there was a general tendency toward the decline of parliamentary regimes, the subsequent forms of rule were contingent. One explanation for this was that although the bourgeoisie played a central role in the demise of parliament, preparing the conditions for its own political dispossession, it was relatively passive in the actual coups that brought dictatorships to power. Nor could fascism be regarded as the final form of capitalist rule, a position common in the Comintern, with its obvious corollary that after fascism the working class would triumph. Thalheimer reminded his readers that despite Marx's characterization of the Second Empire as the last and rottenest form of state power, it had been followed by a stable parliamentary democracy.[36]

Thalheimer sometimes sounded like an instrumentalist, claiming that fascism was an open dictatorship of capital, but this could presumably be reconciled with his account of political expropriation since the social power of the bourgeoisie not only remained intact but was enhanced by the destruction of all working-class and mass organizations.[37] Thus his account of the social characteristics and political nature of fascism paralleled Marx's account in *The Eighteenth Brumaire* and was considerably more nuanced than the instrumentalist position adopted by the Comintern in 1928. Moreover, in contrast to the dogmatism of the Comintern, Thalheimer left his analysis open-ended by calling for further investigation of the forms of capitalist dictatorship and questioning the possibility of reducing different national experiences and class configurations to a schematic theoretical formula.

Although "Uber den Faschismus" largely discussed Italian fascism, by the time it was published Thalheimer had already written about the crisis of German parliamentary democracy in the spring of 1929 in an article entitled "Die Krise des Parlamentarismus—das Vorspiel zur Krise der bürgerlichen Herrschaft" (The Crisis of Parliamentarianism—a Prelude to the Crisis of Bourgeois Domination).[38] In this article Thalheimer cited numerous attacks by leading journalists and politicians including Chancellor Gustav Stresemann against the dependence of the government on parliamentary parties. Most of these speeches and articles advocated strengthening executive authority and ending "partyism," which pandered to special interests. Thalheimer compared this opposition on the part of the bourgeois spokespersons to their own parties and representatives and the appeal for a more autonomous executive to the preparatory period that had led to Bonapartism in France in the early 1850s or to fascism in Italy in the early 1920s. At the root of the crisis of parliament he detected an offensive on the part of the German trusts, which, faced with worsening international competitiveness, could no longer tolerate the costly and uncontrollable outcomes of the parliamentary process:

The pressure of the trust capital on the masses of people in Germany grows visibly. The "industrial middle class" is ground down, monopoly capital has already created higher profit rates for itself, at the same time putting pressure on wages and social costs. The consequence, a slow but steadily growing counter pressure from under, radicalization of the petty bourgeois and the working class.[39]

This radicalization was already apparent during the elections in May 1928 when both far left and right had gained at the expense of the centrist parties. The bourgeois parties by attacking parliamentarianism were ideologically preparing their own demise. "*The social dominance of the bourgeoisie has fallen into contradiction with its political rule.* It prepares its own political resignation in order to preserve and fortify its class dominance."[40] Thus by selectively deploying elements of Marx's Bonapartism model, Thalheimer described a gathering crisis of parliamentary democracy and bourgeois hegemony well before the onset of the Great Depression and Hitler's electoral breakthrough. Because of the international situation of German capital, large industry was no longer willing to maintain the costly series of political and social compromises such as high welfare payments that had stabilized Germany since 1924.[41] It should be noted, however, that until 1932 Thalheimer, in contrast to Marx in *The Eighteenth Brumaire*, tended to depict capital as a unified political agent arrayed behind the leadership of the major trusts. Moreover, he was vague on the way the needs of German trusts translated into demands by leading politicians for a stronger executive.

Thalheimer's understanding of the crisis of representation enabled him to see through the pseudo-parliamentary trappings of the presidential government Thalheimer regarded as a prelude to fascist dictatorship. Already in spring 1930, Thalheimer affirmed that although Brüning could rely on a majority in parliament he could not rely on a parliamentary majority—since his majority included the Nationalists, who took their lead from the president.[42] In addition, neither the composition nor the policies of the government were controlled by the Reichstag. President Hindenburg had determined the composition of the Brüning government, had mandated agricultural tariffs and the program of aid to the Junkers, and could prorogue parliament at any time using the emergency powers granted in Article 48 of the Constitution. Moreover, the mass of the bourgeoisie had turned increasingly antiparliamentary.

Thalheimer strongly believed that the objective preconditions for a fascist dictatorship were already present in Germany.[43] While the elimination of concessions to labor made during the postwar labor offensive of 1918–20 had in the past been possible under parliamentary democracy, now the broad and systematic attack on German labor, the attack on wages and welfare, was becoming so intense as to be incompatible with the maintenance of democratic rights, especially the right of organization and the right to strike. Second, he argued that while the agency costs of the state might well be higher under a fascist dictatorship, these costs would be more than offset by cuts in social expenditure. Third, he contended that it was not a question of the bourgeoisie voluntarily handing over power to the fascists but rather the unavoidable logic of its position. In Italy the bourgeoisie had only wanted to intimidate labor, to eliminate its organizations, "not the rule of fascism. But to break the organization of labor by systematic terror, it had to accept in the bargain the building, arming, military training of fascist organizations and the tolerance and support for their actions by civil and military authorities." While a sector of the bourgeoisie already openly backed fascism, another sector continued to oppose it, but "against their will they play into the hands of the fascists."[44] Even the Democrats and more liberal members of the Peoples' party were clamoring for a stronger executive authority, while the agrarian wings of the Nationalists, Popular Conservatives, and Center vociferously supported a dictatorship by President Hindenburg.[45]

Again before the Nazi electoral breakthrough, Thalheimer perceived the impending danger. The National Socialists were the most active wing in this weakening of parliamentary rule, cooperating with but simultaneously distancing themselves from the conservative grouping around Hindenburg.[46] Above all, they were using the situation advantageously to build up their party organization in the workplace and governmental apparatus. They were both participating in parliamentary institutions to destroy them and at the same time increasing their extraparliamentary terror against labor. Recognizing that fascism, like Bonapartism, was in part a consequence not of the strength of labor but rather its weakness, internal division, and exhaustion, Thalheimer cautioned against an abstentionist or passive policy on the part of labor, although given the policies of the Communists and Socialists, he appears to have doubted the likelihood of energetic or concerted action.[47] The form of bourgeois rule was not a mere juridical question but one of the balance of class power. Parliamentary democracy was worth defending against fascism, he avowed, but it could be defended only by extraparliamentary means.

While these early articles by Thalheimer stressed the incompatibility of continued parliamentary government and democracy with the onslaught against labor orchestrated by German trusts, during the chancellorships of von Papen and General Schleicher, the final act of the Weimar Republic, Thalheimer and other contributors to *Gegen den*

Strom emphasized the failure of the presidential dictatorship to overcome the economic crisis of capitalism, stabilize the political situation,
attract a mass base, or aggregate the interests of the various fractions of
the high bourgeoisie. In his analysis of the November 1932 elections,
Thalheimer made clear that the authoritarian von Papen-Schleicher
government rested on no base of support either within or outside of
parliament. If it tried to demonstrate that the new Reichstag was
incapable of functioning nothing was gained.

> Capital expects the dictatorial government to create "order." This govern-
> ment, however, is parliamentary scandals, new elections or actions of the
> sort of July 20th or September 12. A dictatorial govenment that is even
> more insecure and weaker than a parliamentary one, which has to stage a
> coup de main every few weeks, is not what the grande bourgeoisie
> expects from a reactionary dictatorship.[48]

While the Nazis had suffered their first major defeat in this election, a
loss of some 2 million votes, Thalheimer attributed this loss to purely
temporary factors.[49] These factors included hopes reposited by the
large and petty bourgeoisie in von Papen's program for economic
revival, the pressure of large landowners in favor of von Papen, the
disappointment of many Nazi followers with the lack of immediate
success by the party, and the extraparliamentary activity of labor. Von
Papen's economic program was failing since he was "paralyzed by his
incapacity to bridge the divisions between industrial and agrarian
capital in the interest of capital as a whole." Moreover, government
instability created an unfavorable business climate. Even the Junkers
whom von Papen favored were increasingly falling away from the
government because of his incapacity to meet their maximum demands. As the von Papen government failed, Nazi voters who were
disappointed by the lack of success in taking power in August would
stream back.

This mode of analysis was continued in December 1932 in the
anonymous article "Von Brüning bis Schleicher" (From Brüning to
Schleicher), which declared that von Papen had brought on the instability by his plans for revising the Constitution and by incurring the
opposition of industrial and commercial capital to the costs of his
agrarian program.[50] While von Papen's downfall once again opened the
prospect for Nazi participation in the government, those at the pinnacle of the state apparatus, especially the generals, were still not prepared to subordinate themselves to the fascists. If anything, despite
initial appearances, General Schleicher's government was even weaker
than his predecessor's. He retreated from von Papen's plans to alter the
Constitution and his program for creating employment and stimulating

the economy was failing even more rapidly than von Papen's. Schleicher tried to play the benefactor of all classes, eliminating the import quotas that damaged industrial interests, promising the agrarians a mandatory mixture of butter and margarine, ending von Papen's wage controls, and promising no further lowering of living standards to labor. His social rhetoric was beginning to be perceived by the bourgeoisie, however, as a disturbing sign of weakness vis-à-vis labor. Nor was Schleicher in a position "to force the various fractions of the bourgeoisie to reduce their particular interests to a common denominator."[51]

The meetings between Hitler and von Papen could be seen as threats to replace Schleicher in the unified interests of large capital. This judgment was reiterated and elaborated in the issue of *Gegen den Strom* that appeared a few days after the formation of the Hitler-von Papen government, a government it described as Nazi-dominated despite the presence of the conservative Nationalist coalition partners. "Von Papen and Schleicher fell because of the antagonisms within the camp of the bourgeoisie . . . because those strata of the bourgeoisie which felt disadvantaged by their policies could play the fascist party off against them. Today, however, the bourgeoisie has handed over power to the fascists and resigned in their favor." The consequence of this would be the complete elimination of the rights of laborers and an unrestrained attack by capital. While the Nazis could not resolve the international capitalist crisis, they could "reduce the living standard of labor to a level of unimaginable misery" while providing subventions to industry and the Junkers.[52] The industrialists had abandoned political power but their control over the workplace would be even more stringent.

There were certainly numerous deficiencies in the analysis of Thalheimer and the KPD(O). The relation between cohesion and fragmentation, particular and common interests within the bourgeoisie, was never clearly spelled out. Sometimes the bourgeoisie appeared as a unified agent subordinate to the interests of the trusts, at other times as a more heterogenous social group, antagonistic to labor and sharing a common interest in order, but otherwise unable to coordinate its manifold economic and political interests. Although there were indications in several articles that the Nazi party garnered cross-class support, there was little concrete investigation of its composition. The strength and lasting contribution of Thalheimer's analysis, however, lay in his often penetrating treatment of the political process and social implications of the steady erosion of parliamentary democracy and the establishment of presidential dictatorship, a treatment derived from the leading motif of *The Eighteenth Brumaire* and rooted in an examination of the ways in which a defense of social and economic interests of the German bourgeoisie had become structurally incompatible with the preservation of democratic rights and norms.

The second major Marxist figure of the 1930s who analyzed the phase of presidential dictatorship in Germany from 1930–33 in terms of Bonapartism was Leon Trotsky. Like Thalheimer and in opposition to the German Communist party (KPD), Trotsky sharply distinguished between the period of presidential dictatorship and fascism and pressed for a united front of labor organizations to halt the Nazis. Trotsky's use of the Bonapartism concept, however, contrasted markedly with that of Thalheimer in several respects. Whereas for Thalheimer fascism was the modern analog of Bonapartism—Bonapartism in the era of mass politics and monopoly capitalism—Trotsky viewed Bonapartism as either a preparatory phase for fascist dictatorship ("preventive Bonapartism") or a degenerate form of fascist rule ("Bonapartism of fascist origin").[53] While Bonapartism could assume many forms depending on concrete historical conditions, the essence of Bonapartism for Trotsky consisted of being a dictatorship resting on the military, police, and bureaucracy:

> a government of the saber as judge arbiter of the nation—that's just what *Bonapartism* is. The saber by itself has no independent program. It is the instrument of "order." It is summoned to safeguard what exists. Raising itself *politically* above all classes, Bonapartism . . . represents *in the social sense*, always and in all epochs the government of the strongest and firmest part of the exploiters; consequently, present day Bonapartism can be nothing else than the government of finance capital which directs, inspires, and corrupts the summits of the bureaucracy, the police, the officers' caste and the press."[54]

Thus for Trotsky, Bonapartism lacked mass support or indeed any firm support outside the state apparatus. A Bonapartist dictatorship was preventive when civil war was threatened, when the working class and fascists were balanced but an open confrontation had not occurred. "As soon as the struggle of two social strata, the haves and have nots, the exploiters and exploited—reaches its highest tension, the conditions are established for the domination of bureaucracy, police, soldiery. The government becomes 'independent' of society."[55] This would be a short-lived and highly unstable form of government. More stable was "Bonapartism of fascist origin," which arose when after seizing power, a fascist party gradually lost its petty-bourgeois mass base as some of its followers were absorbed into the state apparatus and others were disillusioned by the regime's inability to fulfill its social promises. At that point, "fascism is regenerated into Bonapartism."[56] Hence Trotsky placed Bonapartism and fascism in a temporal trajectory of "preventive Bonapartism"—fascist dictatorship—"Bonapartism of fascist origin," all of which socially served finance capital but rested on different social bases and had different relations to the petty bourgeoisie and labor.

This notion of Bonapartism as a short-lived phase of class equilibrium prior to civil war emerged in Trotsky's characterization of the Brüning chancellorship in early 1932.

> The Brüning regime is the regime of bureaucratic dictatorship or, more definitely, the dictatorship of the bourgeoisie enforced by means of the army and police. The fascist petty bourgeoisie and the proletarian organizations seem to counterbalance one another . . . Brüning's dictatorship is a caricature of Bonapartism. His dictatorship is unstable, unreliable, shortlived. Supported directly only by a small minority of Democrats against the will of the workers, threatened by fascism. . . . The dictatorship of bureaucratic impotence fills the lull before the battle, before the forces are openly matched.[57]

If the Brüning government was a caricature of Bonapartism, the governments of von Papen and General Schleicher in late 1932 were the real thing, specifically German forms of Bonapartism. Hindenburg's reelection to the presidency in spring 1932 with the support of the Socialists and Catholic Centrists had the character of a plebiscite against civil war. "But precisely this is the most important function of Bonapartism: raising itself above the two struggling camps in order to preserve property and order. It suppresses civil war, or precedes it or does not allow it to rekindle."[58] Hindenburg permitted the government to appear to have mass support, although Hindenburg himself had broken with the democratic parties and openly served the landowners, industrialists and bankers, while the upper levels of the propertied class were Papen's only base of support. Hence, despite such apparent successes as the coup against the Socialist government in Prussia in July, von Papen's grip on power was precarious. Behind Hindenburg and von Papen stood the state apparatus, the strongest sector of which was the army, embodied by General Schleicher, whom Trotsky viewed as the "core of the Bonapartist combination."[59] While Trotsky regarded the von Papen-Schleicher governments as highly unstable, he expected finance capital to opt for an open fascist dictatorship only if the class struggle intensified.[60]

This proved to be false but was noted by Trotsky without theoretical reevaluation after the Nazi seizure of power. In his own account of the coming to power of the Hitler-Hugenburg government, it was not intensified struggle by the revolutionary working class but rather the fragmentation of the possessing classes that issued in the handing over of power to the Nazis. General Schleicher, in whom Bonapartism assumed its purest form, fell because the passivity of the proletariat "weakened the hoop of fear that binds together the possessing classes, bringing into the open the antagonisms that tear them apart."[61] The economic base for Bismarck's coalition of iron and rye, of heavy industry and large-scale agriculture, no longer existed. Because of its narrow social base, the industrial bourgeoisie needed Junkers and rich farmers, but economically the preservation of agriculture had become a millstone. When Schleicher deserted the agrarians, they engineered his downfall and replaced him with Alfred Hugenburg, who was the embodiment of the Junkers and landed property. Hitler had been added to "decorate the camarilla of property owners with the leaders of a 'national movement,' and secondly, to place the fighting forces of fascism at the direct disposal of the proprietors." Trotsky considered this operation highly risky for the propertied clique around Hugenburg, which he believed held the real posts of power "while the plebians are assigned the decorative or secondary posts." The government was a brittle, contradictory, and internally divided amalgam of representatives of agriculture, industry, and the reactionary petty bourgeoisie. Although Trotsky did not rule out that the clique of property holders would eliminate the Nazis and a return to a Bonapartist regime, he thought more likely a situation of semi-civil war that would make the Nazis indispensable and in which they would displace their "much too corpulent mentors," expropriating them politically.[62]

Although occasionally rising to the rhetorical power of Marx in *The Eighteenth Brumaire*, especially in "What Is National Socialism?" of June 1933, in which he discussed the symbolic manipulation by the Nazi regime, Trotsky was clearly less indebted to Marx's concept of Bonapartism and more dependent on Engels' various formulations for his analysis of fascism than was Thalheimer.[63] Were their differences ultimately more than terminological? Did they have any consequences apart from the fact Trotsky labeled Schleicher a Bonapartist, while Thalheimer regarded the period of presidential dictatorship as a prelude to fascism, the modern variant of Bonapartism? In fact, the terminological differences were closely tied to substantive differences. Thalheimer's account of the increasing autonomy of the executive was much more processual; autonomization was a dynamic response to both a crisis of representation within the bourgeoisie and the incompatability of the maintenance of parliamentary system with the industrialists' offensive, an offensive that reflected both the international position of German capital and the relative weakness of German labor. As a result he paid much more attention to the specific policies of both the bourgeois parties and government and recognized that the steady movement toward fascism was accompanied by a corresponding erosion of labor's power in the face of the capitalist offensive. By contrast, Trotsky's more mechanistic account treated the early 1930s as a period of labor offensive, albeit one thwarted by labor's misleaders and the unstable equilibrium between labor and fascism approaching civil war, a perspective on the nature of the period not far removed from the Comintern's. Nonetheless, both Trotsky and Thalheimer stood far from the Comintern in their recognition that the presidential dictatorship between 1930 and January 1933 was not fascist and that all available means for united labor action had to be utilized to prevent the Nazis from seizing power.

The third major Marxist figure who adopted a Bonapartist perspective was Otto Bauer, the leading theoretician of the Austrian Socialist party.[64] While both Trotsky and Thalheimer treated Bonapartism and fascism as related phenomena, they asserted that key differences depended on contrasts between the phase of competitive capitalism in which Louis Napoleon had operated and monopoly capitalism, but both left the precise nature of this dependence unspecified. In contrast, Bauer attempted to link his Bonapartist analysis of fascism with a closer examination of the structural transformation of the interwar economy, a linkage often obscured by excerpting his chapter on fascism from *Zwischen zwei Weltkriegen?* (Between Two World Wars?) of 1936.[65] Moreover, he strove to place fascism within the framework of a generalized European economic, political, and cultural crisis of the postwar era, a crisis of capitalist civilization, and in doing so developed a far more comprehensive syncretic theory of fascism than did the other two.

Bauer took World War I as the starting point of the crisis of capitalist civilization. The war had disrupted the delicate balance of the international economy, which was never restored in the postwar world. Much of *Zwischen zwei Weltkriegen?* consists of a detailed analysis of the world economy in the 1920s, of international credit and currency problems, the expansion of agricultural output and changes in industrial production processes such as the rationalization movement in Germany.[66] As a consequence of the enormous expansion of production brought on by industrial rationalization coupled with a lagging mass-purchasing power that put downward pressures on prices and profits even during the prosperous late 1920s, the economic crisis of the 1930s was quantitatively more severe than earlier ones. The inability of the leading capitalist powers to reestablish stability in the postwar world, a failure associated with reparations and international credit, also meant that the depression of the 1930s was qualitatively different from earlier cyclical downturns. In the face of falling prices, agriculture and industry had demanded strong measures to protect the domestic market and substantial export premiums.[67] Central banks had adopted monetary regulation to stave off the collapse of their currencies. Everywhere open competition and free trade had been replaced by bureaucratically administered economies that began by regulating currency and foreign trade but soon extended their controls to agricultural production, wages, the labor market, and consumption, ushering in a new neomercantilist phase of capitalism, of which fascist Germany was the most extreme variant.

Fascism too, according to Bauer, was very much a product of closely interconnected social processs caused by the disruptions of the war years and the economic crisis of the postwar period. [68] Both Italian fascism and German National Socialism had recruited their initial followers from among declassé veterans who knew no other existence than war. The ideology and organizational forms of fascist movements were above all military. The war and the postwar economic crisis had also impoverished and embittered many small farmers and petty bourgeois, who then rejected democracy and the middle-class parties they had previously supported and turned instead to fascism. Moreover, the capitalist class had seen its profit rates fall in the postwar crises, and it therefore desired to break the resistance of labor, a desire probably irreconcilable with the continuance of democracy. Fascist movements had been especially strong in Italy and Germany, both of which had weak and belated traditions of parliamentary democracy, had been shaken by their war experiences (domestic opposition to entering the war in Italy, the unexpected military defeat in Germany), and suffered severe economic dislocation in the immediate postwar period.

Although capitalists had not originally encouraged the formation of fascist movements, they quickly discovered that these movements were useful for intimidating labor and driving it on the defensive.[69] In Germany, however, after 1923, when the Ruhr had reverted to national control and the currency and economic recovery had been underwritten by foreign loans, German capital stopped its funding of the paramilitary right and instead bankrolled the bourgeois parties. Even the monarchist Nationalists gradually accepted democratic rules. Only with the onset of the depression in 1929 had German heavy industry and the Junkers rediscovered the usefulness of a fascist movement. "The bourgeois fractions which supported Brüning used the anxiety of the Social Democracy and trade unions at the prospect of a fascist dictatorship in order to extract from them toleration for Brüning's capitalist dictatorship, which with the deflationary policy of its emergency decrees rapidly lowered the living standard of the popular masses."[70] The fact that the Nazis attacked such labor defense organizations as the Reichsbanner and Rotfront ensured favorable handling by the state authorities.

This did not mean, however, that the industrialists or Junkers had become fascists. Indeed, they were largely contemptuous of the plebians who composed the fascist movement.

> But as in Italy the moment came in which the capitalists and Junkers had only the choice of suppressing the fascists, and with that instantly changing the balance of forces in favor of labor, or handing over state power to the fascists. In this situation Hindenburg's Junker cronies decided on the transfer of state power to Hitler. As in Italy representatives of the historic bourgeois parties entered the first fascist government believing that they could subordinate and assimilate the fascists. But more rapidly than in Italy, German fascism used this conquered state power to throw the bourgeois parties out of the government, to dissolve the parties and organizations of the bourgeoisie and to establish its *totalitarian* dictatorship. Here too the class struggle seemed to end when the fascist storm troops set up their domination over all classes.[71]

Although the fascists justified themselves to the bourgeoisie on the grounds of having saved it from Bolshevism, the proletariat had long been on the defensive. The capitalist class and large landowners transfered power not because of a threatened proletarian revolution but rather "to destroy the achievements of reformist socialism."[72] (This emphasis on social-democratic achievements was not surprisingly far more pronounced in Bauer's work than in Trotsky's and Thalheimer's.)

The fascist dictatorship was the outcome of a peculiar balance of class forces that, using Engels, Bauer compared to the balance between the nobility and bourgeoisie that had sustained absolutism or the balance between the bourgeoisie and labor that had resulted in Bonapartism. The capitalists had been too weak to carry through their deflationary and antilabor policies by ideological or legal means, but "strong enough to pay, arm and unleash on the proletariat a lawless, anti-legal private army."[73] Labor, led by the reformist socialists and trade unions, had been strong enough to hinder the deflationary policy but not strong enough to defend itself against force. Since the socialists had supported the democratic republic, peasants, petty bourgeois, and many workers viewed them as an integral part and beneficiary of the hated system that failed to protect these strata from impoverishment during the economic crisis. Therefore these strata flocked to the fascists. "The result of this balance of forces or much more the weakness of both classes is the victory of fascism."[74] Thus while Bauer, like Trotsky, made use of the balance-of-classes notion from Engels, the accounts of the players and relative weights in that balance were quite different.

While the bourgeoisie had been politically dispossessed, its organizations, press, and traditions destroyed, the leading sector of the bourgeoisie rapidly found that the new system of domination would serve its own interests.[75] The fascist dictatorship smashed the unions and other mass organizations that previously inhibited capitalist dominance and by eliminating all democratic rights silenced any possible opposition. It retained a capitalist economy and therefore had to be solicitous about the profitability of industry. Being dependent on the banks and credit system for government financing, the dictatorship had to represent the interests of high finance as congruent with national interest. Moreover, in power the fascist parties suppressed the radical anticapitalist tendencies in their own ranks, Hitler's murder of Sturmabteilung (SA) leaders in June 1934 being a prime example, thus removing the last impediment to bourgeois social dominance.

However, while Bauer, in contrast to Thalheimer and Trotsky, did not ascribe any importance to divisions within the capitalist class for the victory of fascism, once fascism was in power he thought that the development of the administered economy was likely to injure the interests of particular fractions of capital and thereby heighten intracapitalist tensions.[76] Fascist totalitarianism ran counter to the traditions and ideology of many strata of the bourgeoisie. Autarky and preparation for war hurt the export-oriented finished goods industry. Rentiers feared a devaluation of their financial instruments in the event of war. Increasingly the armaments industry and large landowners who were closely related to the officer corps obtained the upper hand. Thus in the final analysis, the fascist dictatorship rested on and served only one fraction of the bourgeoisie, the war-oriented sector. This position approached the definition of fascism announced a year earlier at the Seventh Comintern Congress, where as part of the shift to a strategy of forming Popular Fronts with socialists and liberal parties, the official spokesman Georgi Dmitrov had proclaimed that fascism was "the open terroristic dictatorship of the most reactionary, chauvinist, most imperialist elements of finance capital."[77]

However, in it comprehensiveness, empirical weight, and subtle analysis of the relation between the ruling caste and dominant class under fascism, Bauer's fascism theory was distant from that of the Comintern. Rather than being satisfied with generalities about monopoly capitalism, Bauer undertook a concrete analysis of the strains of the postwar economy. While he believed that there were strong tendencies in all modern capitalist economies toward a bureaucratically administered economic system, these tendencies emerged fully only where fascism was victorious, as in Italy and Germany. To explain why fascism had come to power in these nations, Bauer provided a multicausal interpretation that connected the weakness of parliamentary democratic traditions, the effects of the war, and the specific character of the postwar economic crisis in both countries. Bauer's account of the preconditions, social composition, and appeal of the fascist movements was considerably more intricate than either the position of the Comintern or those of Thalheimer and Trotsky. In accordance wtih earlier Italian analyses like Togliatti's, he acknowledged the relative autonomy of the fascist movement. However, despite his use of a Bonapartist model, Bauer's analysis of the political crisis and presidential dictatorship in Germany was far sketchier than Thalheimer's or Trotsky's and bourgeois fragmentation played no role whatsoever in his chronicle of the triumph of fascism. Nonetheless, Bauer's combined analysis of developmental tendencies in the postwar economy and the internal conditions in Italy and Germany that created a favorable climate for the victory of fascism permitted him to confront the Comintern theory of 1928 on its own terrain and offer a comprehensive alternative to this heteronomic model.

Despite the significant contributions of Thalheimer, Trotsky, and Bauer to a Marxist theory of fascism, in the postwar world, the Bonapartist alternative was largely relegated to oblivion as the historiography of Nazism fell victim to the cold war. Across the military and political barriers of divided Europe, a theory of totalitarianism that equated Nazism and Communism on the basis of purely formal similarities faced an unrevised and mirror-image communist theory that equated fascism with monopoly capitalism in the era of imperialism.[78] Only with the growth of the new left in the 1960s would these Bonapartist analyses be disinterred, reprinted, reexamined, and eventually further elaborated and modified.[79] The appropriation of the Bonapartist theories of the 1930s enabled adherents of the new left to establish contact with a critical Marxist tradition while avoiding the staggering simplifications of the instrumentalist intepretation with its lack of complex mediations between social classes, economics, and political representation still dominant in the East bloc. Presently the impetus for reexamining seems exhausted, but over a fifteen-year period beginning in the mid-1960s historians and political scientists associated with the new left produced a substantial body of work on National Socialism deriving either directly or indirectly from some variant of the Bonapartist perspective. Although much of this work transcended some of the manifest weaknesses of the literature of the 1930s, for example, the relative inattention to Nazi ideology, the thinness of empirical evidence for the divisions between fractions of capital, nonetheless this recent literature testifies to the vitality and rich legacy of this alternative tradition.

Notes

I wish to thank Steven Lee and Craig Rimmerman for having read and commented on earlier drafts of this essay.

1. Martin Kitchen, *Fascism* (London: Macmillan, 1976), p. x.
2. For a brief survey of both Marxists and non-Marxists who made use of the Bonapartist analogy to analyze National Socialism, see Jost Dülffer, "Bonapartism, Fascism and National Socialism," *Journal of Contemporary History* 11 (1976): 109–28, although he omits Otto Bauer.
3. See David Beetham, *Marxists in the Face of Fascism* (Totawa, NJ: Barnes & Noble, 1984), pp. 5–17, 82–148. The socialist parties in both Germany and Austria adopted policies of active defense of democratic institutions in the mid-1920s both as a response to domestic reaction and foreign examples like Italy. For the Austrian case see Charles A. Gulick, *From Habsburg to Hitler*, Vol. I (Berkeley: University of California, 1948), pp. 124–31.
4. "Resolution on Fascism, Fifth Comintern Congress," in Beetham, *Marxists*, pp. 152–53. See also the articles by Gramsci, Togliatti, et al. in Beetham, *Marxists*, pp. 113–48.
5. Palmiro Togliatti, "On the Question of Fascism," in Beetham, *Marxists*, pp. 136–48.
6. Togliatti, "On the Question of Fascism," pp. 138–39.
7. Franz Borkenau, *World Communism: A History of the Communist International* (New York: Norton, 1939), pp. 332–56, and Stephen F. Cohen, *Bukharin and the Bolshevik Revolution* (New York: Alfred A. Knopf, 1973), pp. 329–30.
8. See Dmitril Manuilski's report to the executive committee of the Comintern plenum in April 1931 in Beetham, *Marxists*, pp. 157–58.
9. Ernst Thälmann, "The Revolutionary Way Out and the KPD," in Beetham, *Marxists*, p. 163.
10. Manuilski, "On Fascism," p. 157.
11. Kitchen, *Fascism*, p. x.
12. See Beetham, *Marxists*, pp. 17–25. For a more extensive analysis and documentation see Theo Pirker, *Komintern und Faschismus* (Stuttgart: Deutsche Verlags-Anstalt, 1965), pp. 57–70, 141–85.
13. Thälmann, "The Revolutionary Way Out," pp. 162–67.
14. Pierre Ayçoberry, *The Nazi Question* (New York: Random House, 1981), pp. 62–63.
15. Karl Marx and Frederick Engels, *"Manifesto of the Communist Party"* in *Selected Works* (New York: International Publishers, 1968), p. 37.
16. For the development of Marx's theory of Bonapartism see Maximilien Rubel, *Karl Marx devant le bonapartisme* (Paris: Mouton, 1960). For Marx's shock at Louis Napoleon's coup and the resulting shift in his analysis of recent French history, see Jerrold Seigel, *Marx's Fate* (Princeton: Princeton University Press, 1978) pp. 206–16.
17. Karl Marx, "The Eighteenth Brumaire of Louis Bonaparte," in *Selected Works* (New York: International Publishers, 1968), pp. 103, 168.
18. Ibid; p. 131.
19. Ibid., p. 118–19.
20. Ibid., p. 157.
21. Ibid., pp. 158–59.
22. Ibid., p. 132.
23. Ibid., pp. 138, 171–76.
24. Ibid., pp. 108–09, 136–52.
25. Ibid., p. 171.
26. Ibid., pp. 177–79.
27. Engels, *"Origin of the Family, State and Private Property,"* in *Selected Works*, p. 588.

28. For the KPD(O) see Karl H. Tjaden, *Struktur und Funktion der KPD-Opposition* (Erlangen: Verlag Politladen, 1970).
29. See R. Griepenburg, and K. H. Tjaden, "Faschismus und Bonapartismus," *Das Argument* 41, no. 8 Jg. Dez. (1966): 471–72; and Martin Kitchen, "August Thalheimer's Theory of Fascism," *Journal of the History of Ideas* 34, no. 1 (1974): 77–78. For a critique from an opposite tack, namely being overly "economistic," see Frank Adler, "Thalheimer, Bonapartism and Fascism," *Telos* 40 (1979): 107. "Uber den Faschismus" became readily available when it was anthologized in Wolfgang Abendroth, ed., *Faschismus und Kapitalismus* (Frankfurt: Europäische Verlag, 1967), pp. 19–38. See also the discussion in Beetham, *Marxists*, pp. 25–29.
30. August Thalheimer, "Uber den Faschismus," in Gruppe Arbeiterpolitik, *Der Faschismus in Deutschland* (Frankfurt: Europäische Verlag, 1973), p. 28.
31. Ibid., pp. 39–40.
32. Ibid., pp. 41–42.
33. Ibid., pp. 42–43.
34. Ibid., pp. 35–36. In response to German leftists who comforted themselves with the observation that Germany was not Italy and hence was immune to a fascist victory, Thalheimer and other members of the KPD(O) subsequently modified this position. See, for example, the anonymous article "Deutschland und Italien" of 1933 reprinted from *Gegen den Strom* no. 4 in *Der Faschismus in Deutschland*, pp. 212–18.
35. Thalheimer, "Uber den Faschismus," p. 45.
36. Ibid., pp. 35–39. His attempt to prove that Marx did not really mean that Bonapartism was the final form of bourgeois rule in the *Civil War in France* is highly contrived to say the least. Marx, as Engels later noted, was simply wrong.
37. Thalheimer, "Uber den Faschismus," pp. 43–47. Adler, in "Thalheimer, Bonapartism and Fascism" (p. 107), accuses Thalheimer of lapsing into instrumentalism. There is certainly some slippage as there was in most Bonapartist theories of fascism, but there is no problem with saying that the social power of the bourgeoisie is increased, and its control over the workplace enhanced, even though it has lost its political power.
38. July 20 was the date of von Papen's illegal coup against the socialist-led government of Prussia; September 12 was the date of a vote of no-confidence in von Papen staged by the Nazis in revenge for his refusal to bring Hitler into the government on Hitler's terms. Thalheimer, "Die Krise des Parlamentarismus—das Vorspiel zur Krise der bürgerlichen Herrschaft," in *Der Faschismus in Deutschland*, pp. 49–51.
39. Ibid., p. 52.
40. Ibid.
41. More recent Marxist and non-Marxist histories of the Weimar Republic have tended to confirm that the employers' offensive began in 1927/1928 as they were faced with a profit squeeze, rather than after the onset of the Great Depression. See, for example, David Abraham, *The Collapse of the Weimar Republic* (Princeton: Princeton University Press, 1981), pp. 229–38.
42. Thalheimer, "Grundlagen und Wege der faschistischen Entwicklung in Deutschland," in *Der Faschismus in Deutschland*, pp. 78–79.
43. Ibid., pp. 82–84.
44. Ibid., pp. 87–88.
45. Ibid., p. 86.
46. Ibid., p. 87
47. Ibid., pp. 88–91. Needless to say, for Thalheimer as for Trotsky, the defense of parliamentary democracy was simply a way station on the road to proletarian dictatorship. The example of the Bolsheviks' support of Kerensky against Kornilov was invariably cited.
48. Thalheimer, "Nach den Wahlen des 6. November," in *Der Faschismus in Deu-*

tschland, pp. 186–87. July 20, 1932, was the date of von Papen's illegal coup against the Socialist-led government of Prussia; September 12 of a vote of no confidence in von Papen in the Reichstag staged by the Nazis in revenge for his refusal to bring Hitler into the government on his own terms.

49. Ibid., pp. 188–90.
50. "Von Brüning bis Schleicher," in *Der Faschismus in Deutschland*, pp. 194–95.
51. Ibid., p. 196.
52. "Faschisticsche Diktatur über Deutschland," in *Der Faschismus in Deutschland*, pp. 198–200.
53. Leon Trotsky, "Bonapartism and Fascism," in *The Struggle against Fascism in Germany* (New York: Pathfinder Press, 1971), pp. 441–42. See also Robert S. Wistrich, "Leon Trotsky's Theory of Fascism," *Journal of Contemporary History* 11 (1976): 169–73.
54. Trotsky, "Bonapartism and Fascism," p. 439.
55. Leon Trotsky, "The Only Road," in *The Struggle Against Fascism*, p. 276.
56. Trotsky, "Bonapartism and Fascism," p. 441.
57. Leon Trotsky, "What Next?" in *The Struggle Against Fascism*, pp. 160–61.
58. Leon Trotsky, "German Bonapartism," in *The Struggle Against Fascism*, p. 331.
59. Leon Trotsky, "The German Puzzle," in *The Struggle Against Fascism*, pp. 269–70.
60. Trotsky, "German Bonapartism," pp. 333–34.
61. Leon Trotsky, "Before the Decision," in *The Struggle Against Fascism*, pp. 338–39.
62. Ibid., pp. 340–341.
63. Leon Trotsky, "What Is National Socialism?" in *The Struggle Against Fascism*, pp. 399–407, is one of the few works in which Nazi ideology is treated at length. Trotsky's often insightful observations, however, were not incorporated in any theoretical perspective. This work also often takes on an instrumentalist cast, since Trotsky claims that monopoly capital assigns Hitler his tasks.
64. For the development of Otto Bauer's theory of fascism, see Gerhard Botz, "Genesis und Inhalt. der Faschismustheorien Otto Bauers," *International Review of Social History* 19 (1974): I: 28–53. Botz seems to me to overstate the differences between Bauer's fascism theory in *Zwishcen zwei Weltkriegen?* and his uncompleted final article of 1938 (*Der Faschismus*, p. 41). See also his "Austro-Marxist Interpretation of Fascism," *Journal of Contemporary History* 11 (1976): 129–56.
65. Otto Bauer, *Zwischen zwei Weltkriegen?* in *Werksausgabe* Bd. IV (Vienna: Europa Verlag, 1976), pp. 49–331.
66. Ibid., pp. 55–99, esp. p. 99 for a summary diagnosis of the crisis.
67. Ibid., pp. 99–109.
68. Ibid., pp. 137–39.
69. Ibid., pp. 143–46.
70. Ibid., p. 145.
71. Ibid., p.146.
72. Ibid., p.147.
73. Ibid., p.148.
74. Ibid., p.149.
75. Ibid., pp. 149–53.
76. Ibid., pp. 154–55.
77. Botz, "Otto Bauer's Faschismustheorien," p. 52.
78. Ayçoberry, *The Nazi Question*, pp. xii, 125–37.
79. A first step toward republication of some of the heterodox Marxist theorists of the 1930s was Abendroth's *Faschismus und Kapitalismus*. Trotsky's works on National Socialism were republished in the Federal Republic of Germany in the late 1960s and in English in the early 1970s. During the 1970s the Arbeitsgemeinschaft für die

Geschichte der österreichischen Arbeiterbewegung reprinted the collected works of Otto Bauer. For some of the reception of the Bonapartism literature in the German new left see *Das Argument* 41 (December 1966).

Some recent discussion, uses, or confirmations of the Bonapartist theorists of the 1930s include Kitchen, *Fascism,* pp. 71–82; Reinhard Kühnl, *Formen bürgerlicher Herrschaft* (Reinbek: Rowohlt, 1971), pp. 140–42; Mihaly Vadja, *Fascism as a Mass Movement* (New York; St. Martin's, 1976), pp. 93–104; and much more critically, Nicos Poulantzas, *Fascism and Dictatorship* (London: NLB, 1979), pp. 59–62. Poulantzas seems only to have read Thalheimer's "Uber den Faschismus" and to have misinterpreted that. David Abraham, in *The Collapse of the Weimar Republic,* gives considerable empirical evidence for the divisons between various fractions of capital, divisions that played a key role in Thalheimer's analysis of the relations among the state, large capital, and the Nazi party in 1932–33. Kühnl has devoted considerable attention to Nazi ideology, which was treated peripherally by the theorists of the 1930s.

Theories of Fascism:
Nicos Poulantzas As Historian

Jane Caplan

Within a year of each other, in 1968–69, two political scientists, Nicos Poulantzas and Ralph Miliband, published deeply contrasting studies of the state under capitalism,[1] and thereby embarked on a project of mutual criticism that has had a wide airing among Marxists.[2] This interest was hardly surprising. For one thing, the coincidence of the books' publication broke a relative silence on the theory of the state in Marxism, and a debate of some kind was long overdue. Secondly, the debate they provoked went straight to the heart of an already familiar conflict of political cultures, as a resumé will show.

Poulantzas and Miliband started from theoretical positions that could hardly be more dissimilar, and they became progressively more critical of each other. Miliband's *The State in Capitalist Society* is a work of dissenting radicalism, forceful, incisive, and politically uncompromising. Yet, as a detailed exposure of the composition, mechanics, and style of Western political systems, it stands firmly within the empirical tradition exemplified by the political sociologist to whom it is dedicated, C. Wright Mills. In this sense, its structure, if not its political judgment, conforms to a version of orthodox political theory rooted in Western bourgeois thought. Poulantzas' *Political Power and Social Classes,* on the other hand, is the heir, through critical modification, of the newer and rather less accessible methodological school associated with the name of Louis Althusser. Its entire problematic and vocabulary were far less familiar when it was first published, and correspond to a theoretical rigor quite absent from Miliband's work. The establishment of a strict Marxist theoretical framework was an integral part of Poulantzas' project, and was pursued by him with a special regard for conceptual precision and subtle differentiations.

The two authors themselves were a good deal less dispassionate than this in describing one another's method. In Miliband's eyes, Poulantzas suffered from "an exaggerated fear of empiricist contamination," and was guilty of a "structuralist abstractionism" so abstruse that "it cuts him off from any possibility of achieving what he describes as 'the political analysis of a concrete conjuncture.'"[3] Conversely, Poulantzas accused his critic of capitulating to "the illusions of the evident," and of a neopositivist empiricism that (returning Miliband's own charge of "super-determinism") led to the establishment of "immutable dogmas." In addition, some of Miliband's criticisms struck him as so "utterly absurd" that he declined to respond.[4] It is hardly surprising, then, to find that the two writers have been characterized as working within utterly different systems of knowledge.[5]

I have started my assessment of Poulantzas' work by posing the substance of his argument with Miliband not because I wish to take sides in it, but because I find myself awkwardly poised between the two protagonists—a position of epistemological impurity that would, I fear, commend my remarks to neither. My interest in Poulantzas arises, in fact, precisely from this midway position. In a subsequent defense of his work against Miliband's charge of crippling abstractionism, Poulantzas referred explicitly to his second book, *Fascism and Dictatorship,* which, he claimed, far from eschewing contamination by facts, constituted "a detailed historical analysis of German and Italian fascism."[6] It is this book, and the author's claim, that I want to discuss here; and the major issue is not the absence of "facts," but their very concrete and provocative presence.

My reactions on reading *Fascism and Dictatorship* were mixed. On the one hand, its basic problematic was immediately absorbing: it offered an analysis of fascism set strictly within the terms of the class struggle, but which insisted on the specificity of the political domain, and correspondingly rejected a crudely economistic correlation of class and state. On the other hand, I was surprised, given the ostensible rigor of this methodology, by the carelessness with which Poulantzas treats historical data, and by the extent to which subsequent empirical research has tended to weaken the general analysis of fascism that he proposed. I have since been told that it was naive of me to suppose that a political theorist would have much sensitivity to "real" history; but this dismissal of a genuine problem—the correlation of theory and concrete analysis—hardly seems adequate. Rather, it seems important to explore the paradox that, in Poulantzas, extreme theoretical precision is combined with crude empirical inaccuracy. Without such an attempt, the book might as well be ignored; but with it, there is at least a chance of illuminating the problem.

I will therefore consider *Fascism and Dictatorship* from the standpoint of a historian whose field is the structure of the National Socialist regime in Germany, but *not* in the guise of the outraged specialist rescuing "history" as such from the crude embrace of the political theorist. Thus, although my argument will not primarily be concerned with problems of epistemology, it is bound to bear strongly on them. In this sense, an examination—however preliminary and partial—of some of the historical limitations and errors of Poulantzas' study will, I hope, help to expand the discussion of method among historians, and assist the further articulation of Marxist political history.

My starting point is Poulantzas' own statement of his intentions and method in the Introduction to *Fascism and Dictatorship*. The correct method for analyzing fascism as a political phenomenon, he observes, is "to concentrate on a thorough investigation of where fascism took root, and to analyse concrete situations."[7] He then points out that his book

> is not a historiographical study of German and Italian fascism, but a study in political theory—which of course cannot be carried out without thorough historical research. But the treatment of the material, and in particular the order of exposition, are bound to be different in each case. This study concentrates on elucidating the essential features of fascism as a specific political phenomenon. Historical "events" and concrete details are used here only to the extent that they are relevant illustrations of the subject under discussion [i.e., the essential features of fascism].[8]

As a description of a conventional line of demarcation between history and political theory, this is perfectly clear and unexceptionable (indeed, the traditional invocation of history as the provider of events for pictorial purposes is perhaps somewhat surprising to find in this context, suggesting as it does a discrete object of knowledge defined by chronology). At any rate, although Poulantzas has elsewhere argued that concrete facts "can only be rigorously—that is, demonstrably—comprehended if they are explicitly analysed with the aid of a theoretical apparatus constantly employed through the length of the text," the previous quotation shows his clear acknowledgment that the need for theory does not in itself cancel out the need for soundly derived historical detail.[9] In other words, Poulantzas' discourse explicitly combines the theoretical and the empirical in an alliance in which the former takes primacy.[10]

The order of exposition in *Fascism and Dictatorship* reflects the terms of this alliance. In a series of chapters that analyze in turn the relationship of fascism with each of the classes and conclude with a general treatment of the fascist state, Poulantzas first states his theoretical propositions, and then illustrates them by reference to the Italian and German cases. However, it is not easy to do justice in a short summary to the various themes he develops in this way. His method leads to careful conceptual differentiation, and his propositions are generally stated with powerful clarity; but their exposition is characterized by subtle and exhaustive argumentation that does not lend itself readily to précis. I shall therefore offer only a highly compressed resumé of the main features of Poulantzas' theory of fascism, with a view to making my particular criticisms intelligible.[11]

The central theme of Poulantzas' study is the specificity of fascism as one form of "exceptional capitalist state," namely, of the regimes corresponding to various types or articulations of political crisis under capitalism; other examples would be military dictatorship and Bonapartism.[12] The framework in which its specificity can be established consists, according to him, of (1) the changes in the relations of production, and (2) the developments in the class struggle and their relation to the political crisis. Both these questions are subjected to concentrated theoretical and empirical examination. Only by this means, Poulantzas argues, can the *essential* elements of fascism be identified and distinguished from its secondary, contingent features, and a rigorous specification of the fascist state be accomplished. Thus Poulantzas begins by arguing that fascism cannot be dissociated from the imperialist stage of capitalism; more specifically, the period that saw its first rise was one of transition, in imperialist countries, toward the dominance of monopoly capital. This point alone, however, cannot explain the emergence of fascism, nor finally define its uniqueness in contrast to other types of exceptional state. These matters can only be elucidated by also examining the particular conjuncture of the class struggle, that is, the specific sets of relations of class forces at the given time. Thus an analysis of the class struggle will expose the crisis of the political representation of monopoly capital, and its possible resolution; it will also make the crucial distinction (for working-class strategy) between a political crisis of this kind and a true revolutionary situation.

Poulantzas is particularly concerned to refute a number of contemporary interpretations of fascism adopted on the left: fascism as the direct agent of monopoly capital (the economist line of the Third International); fascism as a system of class equilibrium (a theory elaborated principally by the German right communist August Thalheimer and echoed by many Marxists in one form or another); and fascism as the dictatorship of the petty bourgeoisie (described by Poulantzas as a social democratic interpretation). These three rejected theories are not arbitrarily introduced by Poulantzas, for they correspond to crucial elements in fascism, torn out of context: the role of monopoly capital, the extreme degree of autonomy of the state, and the ties between the fascist party and the petty bourgeoisie. Each of these important facets of the problem of fascism is vulnerable to misconception, especially in the sense that each may be mistaken for the whole, although they are all in fact only parts. Poulantzas' ambition is to correct the errors of emphasis and to reconstruct a relationship between these parts. He theorizes fascism as follows:

> Throughout the rise of fascism and after the conquest of power, fascism (the fascist party and the fascist State) *characteristically* has a relative autonomy from both the power bloc [i.e., the politically dominant classes and/or class fractions, conceived of as an unstable alliance—J.C.] and the fraction of big monopoly capital, whose hegemony [i.e., relative dominance within the alliance] it has established. This relative autonomy stems from two sets of factors:
>   (a) from the internal contradictions among the classes in the power alliance, i.e. from its internal political crisis: the relative autonomy necessary to reorganize this bloc and establish within it the hegemony of the fraction of big monopoly capital;
>   (b) from the contradictions between the dominant classes and fractions and the dominated classes, i.e. from the political crisis of the ensemble of the social formation, and from the complex relation between fascism and the dominated classes. This relation is precisely what makes fascism indispensable to mediate a re-establishment of political domination and hegemony.[13]

"Relative autonomy" is a key concept here. For Poulantzas, the political—state power—is always relatively autonomous from capital itself; in fascism, this autonomy exists in an extreme or an exceptional degree. Thus his formulation avoids both a simplistic association of fascism with a single class, and also the rather more subtle but still inappropriate proposition of class equilibrium. The concept of "hegemony" adds extra definition to his picture of the political: by emphasizing that the power bloc consists of more than one class or class fraction, related in an often problematic and contradictory alliance, Poulantzas disposes of the simplistic notion that capital is an indivisible entity and that "the ruling class" exists as the coherent agent of this entity. Thus, if I may insert the determinant emphases into Poulantzas' own words, the historic achievement of fascism is "to *mediate* a re-establishment of political domination *and* hegemony." In essence, fascism acts as the instrument for the resolution of both of the political crises identified in the whole quotation. It is specified by the identification of those characteristics that fit it for this task.

This preliminary theoretical statement by Poulantzas is typical of the qualities of precision and clarity that make a decisive contribution to the book's value as a whole. Poulantzas' careful distinctions are extremely useful for analyzing the political character of a phenomenon as complex and as misunderstood as fascism, for they break up this congealed notion into conceptually functional pieces. But the full character of such a set of propositions lies, as it were, in their historical intersections. It is precisely the analysis of a concrete historical conjuncture that authorizes its appropriation to theory, for otherwise the theory remains locked within its own potential, its explanatory power unused.

It is in the analysis of the concrete historical conjuncture that Poulantzas' book reveals its weaknesses, however. In other words, the "thorough historical research" deemed an indispensable part of the project turns out in the end to be seriously inadequate: partly in the sense that it is carelessly done, and partly in the sense that it has since proved to be so easily contradicted. To illustrate this, I propose to examine three related aspects of the evidence tendered by Poulantzas in illustration of his theory of fascism, taken from the German case. The area of possible choice for such a critique is wide, for almost no part of Poulantzas' empirical material is free from suspicion. I have therefore made my selection with a view to attempting a progressive critique of some central elements of his theory as it relates to the structure of the fascist state. These are:

1. His periodization and characterization of the relations between the Nazi party and the state.
2. His handling of the term *petty bourgeois* in connection with the personnel of the state apparatus.
3. His ascription to the Nazi regime of a unity of structure and motivation.

Poulantzas' periodization of party-state relations after 1933 suffers from the general incapacity of his theory to accommodate the actual course of events. There are also numerous inaccuracies, which, though often minor in themselves, cumulatively weaken his analysis.

In general terms, Poulantzas' object is to explain the process by which German fascism after 1933 became the means by which big capital established its hegemony within the power bloc and achieved the status of "ruling class" (the class whose political representatives occupy the dominant place on the political scene), while at the same time locating and explaining the relative autonomy of the Nazi state. To do this, he postulates a particular relationship between party and state as well as a particular metamorphosis of the class relations of the party. Poulantzas divides the period of Nazi rule after 1933 into two episodes, an initial and a stabilized stage. He argues that in the first stage the petty bourgeoisie was established as the ruling class, in that the Nazi party was acting as the effective representative of the petty bourgeoisie on the political scene. The political representatives of the (politically incapacitated) fractions of capital were evicted from the political scene: the bourgeois parties were abolished, and their politicians were expelled from power. At the same time, the upper ranks of the state apparatus were, he says, "massively filled" with petty-bourgeois members of the National Socialist German Workers Party (NSDAP).[14] In this sense, the petty bourgeoisie was also established as the "class in charge of the state"—the class from which the personnel of the state is recruited and which subordinates the state apparatus to its own characteristic class ideology.[15]

At a later date, so Poulantzas argues, the first of these two forms of domination by the petty bourgeoisie was dissolved: it ceased to be the "ruling class." In other words, the Nazi party and state leaderships ceased to function as the political representatives of the petty bourgeoisie; what Poulantzas calls "the representational tie" was broken. However, the petty bourgeoisie still continued to act as the class in charge of the state, in the sense that it still provided the personnel for the state apparatus. Concomitantly, the NSDAP itself was reduced to a diversionary or integrationist vehicle for the petty bourgeoisie, and was politically subordinated to the state. Together, these changes in the relationship between party and state, and in the class relations of the party, marked the reestablishment of the dominant roles of big capital. Thus Nazism and monopoly capital had grown closer, but the relationship of the party with the petty bourgeoisie continued to ensure the relative autonomy of the state from big capital. This, then, was the so-called stabilized stage of fascism.[16]

If the summary I have attempted of Poulantzas' analysis appears confusing, this is only partly due to the tendency of any process of compression to produce this effect. In some measure, that is to say, the confusion is inherent in the incorrectness of the analysis. Thus, for example, there is no exploration of the alleged rupture of the representational tie between party/state leaderships and the petty bourgeoisie as a class. The rupture is postulated as an unsubstantiated fact, even though the cause and consequence of this rupture—the reestablishment of the domination of big capital—is one of the crucial elements in Poulantzas' general theory and thus demands explanation. Equally, his

account of the transition and difference between the initial and stabilized stages is almost impossible to follow in detail, owing to his
failure to explain what he means by the terms "party" and "state," and
to define their relationship with "fascism" as he uses this term.

It is not surprising, then, that the evidence offered in illustration of
this highly demanding and to some extent misleading analysis is inadequate to represent it.

To start with, the postulation of a two-stage periodization of fascism
in power is clearly crucial to Poulantzas' analysis, because it defines
fascism's mediating role, and locates its relative autonomy. Yet his
account contains elementary errors of dating that are bound to call his
whole treatment into question. He writes that in 1933–34 "the last of
the bourgeois politicians (von Papen, Hugenberg, von Neurath) were
expelled from the government," his way of presenting an important
illustration of the initial stage of fascism in power, namely, the political
eviction of the bourgeoisie. But the fact is that one of this trio, Konstan-
tin von Neurath (foreign minister), did not leave his ministry until
1938. Moreover, a significant group of other unmistakably bourgeois
politicians survived up to this date, and even beyond it: Lutz Schwerin
von Krosigk, Franz Gürtner, Paul von Eltz-Rübenach, Werner von
Blomberg, and Hjalmar Schacht, who held, respectively, the ministries
of finance, justice, transportation, armed forces, and economics/
Reichsbank presidency—hardly a negligible list of political offices. It is
as if Poulantzas defined his bourgeois politicians solely by reference to
their party membership, and then assumed that they ceased to be
bourgeois politicians after 1934 because their parties had by then been
abolished. This is an evident absurdity, yet it is the only way to make
logical sense of his argument, unless (as is more probably the case) he
was simply ignorant of the survival of a significant bourgeois element in
the Nazi regime until the year 1938.

This initial error, though it might appear trivial, has far-reaching
consequences. Not only does it obviously subvert the particular
periodization proposed, but it also threatens part of the general interpretation advanced by Poulantzas. For this reason, the issue is more
than just a pedantic quibble about dates. In the first place, Poulantzas'
supposition that 1934 marks the date of the defeat of the bourgeois
power bloc hides from him the actual significance of one of the crucial
political events of that year—the purge of the Nazi party's mass base,
the Sturmabteilung (SA), which had been intensifying its clamor for a
second, populist revolution. The liquidation at Hitler's orders of the SA
leadership (by the Schutzstaffel, or SS, with army connivance), and the
elimination of the SA as an effective political force, must be seen
primarily as a consequence of Hitler's early weakness vis-à-vis the old

bourgeois power bloc (especially the army). The purge of the SA represented the terms of this initial compromise into which Hitler was forced, though the relationship was, to be sure, a complex one: a coup by Hitler against the fascist movement as such, in order to forestall a possible conservative-military coup against the new regime. In other words, Hitler was obliged initially to move his regime not against but *toward* the old power bloc, establishing an uneasy tactical compromise from which he did not fully emancipate the regime until 1938. Although Poulantzas evidently understood the populist character of the SA, he mistook the full context of the 1934 purge: the result is a tangle in which 1934 is postulated as the date of defeat both of the radical petty bourgeoisie (the SA purge) and of the old bourgeois bloc (the alleged expulsion of bourgeois politicians).

If, however, we grasp the true significance of the SA purge, and also correct Poulantzas' dating errors, then we can appreciate an important fact that remained hidden from him: the considerable continuity of bourgeois representation on the political scene, throughout almost the whole decade of the 1930s. By missing this, Poulantzas reduces to invisibility a political tendency in the regime that ran to some extent counter to fascism, in that it maintained (if indirectly) a certain link with pre-1933 attempts to resolve the crisis without recourse to fascism. This bourgeois-conservative tendency progressively lost ground as the regime developed, through an extremely diffuse and undirected process of political subversion, its full "fascist" character: extreme political autonomy. In 1938 this process culminated in a visible change in the status of the bourgeois-conservative politicians in the regime. Either they were ousted from ministerial power or, if they remained (as did ministers Krosigk and Gürtner, for instance), they were driven unmistakably onto the defensive in government and administration, forfeiting political initiative and clout. A more far-reaching example of this same process was Hitler's purge of the military leadership early in 1938, and his assumption of direct personal command of the armed forces: here was the decisive break with the old-guard generals, leading ultimately to a war conceived and conducted in unprecedented defiance of conventional military strategy. Thus all the evidence points to the period around 1938 as a major watershed in the political constitution of the Nazi regime—though not the last one, as what follows will suggest.

Poulantzas' proposition that the stabilized stage of fascism was marked by "the subordination of the NSDAP to the Nazi state apparatus in the strict sense of the term" (i.e., to the state bureaucracy) is also open to serious challenge.[17] The main objection to this formulation is that it rests on a highly dubious characterization of the Third Reich as "a monocratic administrative state." Poulantzas quotes this phrase from Karl Dietrich Bracher, who has carried out pioneering research into the Nazi regime, but this judgment is not one of his more successful achievements.[18] Subsequent research into the workings of Nazi government strongly suggests that it was characterized by an extreme diffusion and dislocation of authority, and a highly disordered proliferation of agencies and hierarchies. In this context, it becomes extremely difficult to speak with any confidence of "the subordination of the party to the state," for such a description must rely on a secure definition of its two terms that is not empirically available. A concrete example will suggest the nature of the problem.

According to Poulantzas, "the party's general secretary, Rudolf Hess, was allowed into the government for purely decorative purposes," all important political decisions being actually taken by the state apparatus. This misses an important point. It is true that Hess himself was not personally an outstandingly effective political figure. The office he headed as Führer's deputy and minister without portfolio (not "general secretary") had powers, however, which it *did* use, to vet all government enactments in draft, to propose legislation itself, and also to vet senior civil service appointments. After his flight to England in May 1941, Hess was replaced by his erstwhile deputy Martin Bormann, a far more determined figure who worked (with some success) to concentrate greater political authority in his hands, and who based this evolving system of power on what could be seen, for the first time, as a genuinely organized party structure. To describe Hess as "decorative," and to leave out subsequent developments entirely, is therefore misleading—the analysis is broken off at an arbitrarily defined terminal point. Moreover, the structure and personnel of the Hess/Bormann office itself reflected the complex and shifting structural relationships and identity of the regime. It was in his capacity as minister without portfolio that Hess built up his office, though it was called the Staff of the Führer's Deputy. After Bormann took over in 1941, it was renamed the Party Chancellery, and in 1943 Bormann acquired the title of secretary of the Führer—a sequence of names that demands to be pondered. Moreover, the staffing of the office was far from simple: finance seems to have come from unidentified NSDAP sources, while almost all the officials were trained civil servants as well as NSDAP stalwarts.

This dense web of connections represents only a partial reconstitution of a single aspect of the regime's political structure, yet it already suggests that Poulantzas' static analysis of this structure is suspect. He cannot, of course, be held responsible for those deficiencies of his approach that have been brought to light by later research; and indeed the main historical monographs supporting the alternative characterization of the regime I have proposed were not published when Poulantzas was writing *Fascism and Dictatorship*.[19] It is, nevertheless, striking that a central part of his analysis should so completely fail a later empirical test. Information of the kind needed to back a general analysis is, of course, assembled piecemeal, and its implications can be recovered only with some difficulty—a condition of historical research that Poulantzas, to his own cost, ignores.

The role of the petty bourgeoisie in the fascist regime is a crucial one in Poulantzas' scheme, as is evident from the brief summary above. The petty bourgeoisie is, in a sense, the condition of mediation for fascism and big capital; it is also explicitly the condition of the fascist state's relative autonomy from big capital. At the same time, it is clearly the most difficult class to analyze and to place in a historical conjuncture, owing to its ambiguous position in the capitalist mode of production. Poulantzas insists that, in Marxist theory, economic relations alone are inadequate for a definition of the petty bourgeoisie, and that ideological and political relations are indispensable in arriving at a definition.[20] Inescapable though this fact may be, it is also bound to be the source of much debate, since it so enlarges the scope for investigative interpretation. In particular, it must raise the question of the relationship between the theoretical and the empirical, for an understanding of the nature and status of the petty bourgeoisie is likely to depend on a set of conceptual distinctions that will have to be carefully recombined in any concrete analysis.

In the present case, the issue is the relationship between a number of concepts elaborated by Poulantzas and their status with regard to empirical detail. First, Poulantzas makes the distinction, mentioned already, between the ruling class and the class in charge of the state— that is, between (1) the class whose representatives occupy the dominant place on the political scene, and (2) the class that provides the personnel of the state apparatus. Second, Poulantzas operates with a distinction between a class and a social category. Class is defined primarily (though not exclusively) by reference to position in the mode of production. A social category, on the other hand, is a group defined primarily by politics and ideology. The components of a social category do not, of course, escape class status, but they are corporately recognizable as a particular group in the sense that they possess a degree of internal unity and autonomy and express this to visible social or political effect.[21]

These two sets of definitions come into combination when the relationship of the petty bourgeoisie and the state is under discussion.

Poulantzas defines the petty bourgeoisie as a class composed of two groups: (1) the traditional petty bourgeoisie of small-scale producers and owners, not exploiting wage labor, and (2) the "new" petty bourgeoisie of nonproductive salaried employees. This definition is familiar, and in general useful. Within group (2), as Poulantzas points out, are numbered the personnel of the state, or civil servants; these are "nonproductive employees whose function is to ensure, through the role of the State, the *reproduction* of the conditions of production of surplus value."[22] At the same time, however, the civil service also stands as a classic example of the social category (a fact Poulantzas adduces as the source of the misconception that proposes the civil service itself as a "new class"). In concrete terms, the common ideology of the civil service as a social category will include a degree of "statolatry" (idolization of the state), and more specifically a tendency to see the state as the necessarily powerful, but still neutral, executant of "the common good." Civil servants may also appear (to themselves and to others) as a group uniquely poised "above" conflicts of class or interest, and they may well be amenable to political invocations of this virtuous role. Beyond this, they may also see themselves as constituting a pseudo-class, possessing a distinct set of corporate interests.

The civil service is also subject to a third definitional system, in addition to its status within the petty bourgeoisie and its homogeneity as a social category. Poulantzas, following Marx, agrees that a civil service can also be viewed in terms of the class *origin* of its members.[23] Thus Marx offered the example of a civil service whose upper ranks are recruited from the landed nobility and the bourgeoisie, with the middle and lower ranks petty bourgeois in origin.

How do these concepts, separately defined, operate together in practice to illuminate the relationship between the petty bourgeoisie and the personnel of the state? In the course of his discourse on the theory of state power in *Political Power and Social Classes*, Poulantzas used them effectively to invalidate any theory seeking to locate a *source* of power in the civil service itself. Yet the sensitivity he showed when handling this initial case is not, unfortunately, reproduced in the historical passages of *Fascism and Dictatorship*. Here, where discussion ought to rest on a careful specification of the terminology in use and the concepts to which it refers, Poulantzas actually shifts his discourse through all four modes. In other words, there is no clarification of the actual relationships or overlaps on the civil service field between the concepts of (1) class in charge of the state, (2) petty bourgeoisie as class, (3) civil service as social category, and (4) class origins of civil servants.

For example, the actual significance of the petty bourgeoisie's alleged invasion of the "upper ranks" of the German state apparatus after 1933 cannot be assessed without a prior knowledge of the class origin of those evicted.[24] The practical relationship between class status and class origins must also be established for this purpose, as also the actual context in which the inherently subjective concept of the "social category" is operative—and all this through rigorous reference to the concrete conjuncture under scrutiny. Yet Poulantzas, far from acknowledging the specificity of each of his concepts, tends to employ them as if they are interchangeable. Thus the initial acquisition of ruling-class status by the petty bourgeoisie, and its subsequent demotion to acting as the class in charge of the state, are voided of meaning if the state personnel is, in another definitional system, regarded as part of the petty bourgeoisie in any case.[25] Furthermore, the persistence within the state apparatus of what Poulantzas describes as "contradictions of the 'corporative' type, between social categories" becomes inexplicable.[26] It is assigned, without discussion, to the level of a secondary and nondetermining feature of the fascist regime. Thus the discourse threatens to remain a competition of categories, whose contradictions in historical combination are not forced into yielding up their political significance.

Here is a case where empirical research (however prosaic) is indispensable in order to anchor the discussion. When Poulantzas speaks of a "massive" filling of the "top ranks" of the state apparatus by petty-bourgeois members of the NSDAP, we need to know what "massive" connotes, what the "top ranks" are, and whether the class origin of the party members is fully established. Of course, if Poulantzas were relying on a widely known corpus of firm evidence, these matters would be less important. In fact, however, his assertions are highly controversial: they are not supported by evidence, and to the best of my knowledge would be hard to prove in any case. The necessary recovery of appropriate information on the class origin, party affiliation, and administrative rank of public service recruits as a whole from 1933 has not yet been carried out, not least owing to the difficulty of access to the relevant documentation. In the meantime, it seems to be the case that the "top ranks" of the civil service (i.e., *Regierungsrat* upward) were in general relatively successful in resisting the alleged invasion of the petty bourgeoisie—but at a fatal price of being progressively outflanked, as an external redisposition of political forces took place in the kaleidoscopic shifting of institutional structures and relationships.

I do not mean here to deny the force of Poulantzas' statement that "institutions do not determine social antagonisms: it is the class struggle which governs the modifications in the State apparatuses."[27] The primacy thus established is correct and important. My point is that Poulantzas' specific understanding of the class struggle is, in this context, incorrect, as adequate research might have demonstrated. In general terms, the class struggle in the Nazi state revealed itself in the relations within and between state institutions in the plural, as well as in a state system conceived of as a whole. Thus, for example, a sector of the bourgeoisie (that which had traditionally provided personnel for the upper civil service) continued in certain institutions to "function as a social force" in the sense suggested by Poulantzas;[28] his exclusive consignment of the state apparatus to the petty bourgeoisie in its various manifestations is too crude.

As a final point, there is in any case an unexamined tension in Poulantzas' general presentation of the petty bourgeoisie, namely, his failure to consider the contradictory tendencies in petty-bourgeois ideology toward both statolatry *and* violent individualism. This is important in the context of the civil service, for these tendencies find one of their most characteristic expressions in the tortured mental postures of petty state officials—the ideological tension between the service they offer and the status they claim.

Generally, then, Poulantzas' attempt to construct the role of the petty bourgeoisie in the Nazi state is broadly unsuccessful and suggests an oversimplification of political and ideological categories. This is largely due to the absence of an empirical location for his typology—a location that would extract and expose the actual contradictions in this class's situation, rather than those visited on it in the name of method.

My final criticism is that Poulantzas treats the Nazi regime implicitly as a unity, with its own firm line of determinate policy. In other words, he appears to endow the regime with an unquestioned capacity for intention and execution. I use the words "appears to" deliberately, for I think that his treatment follows logically from a methodological position, and is not a conclusion he draws from a process of research. I will return to this problem below, but first I want to present a preliminary case against what is, in effect, Poulantzas' central thesis: that fascism's historic function is the performance of a service of mediation to monopoly capital, which it achieves partly by means of preserving its relative autonomy from capital. Manifestly, this endows fascism with an objective role in the resolution of the dual political crisis of the dominant class, a crisis whose initial establishment by Poulantzas is one of the most successful achievements of the book. However, it also appears that his version of the resolution of the crisis is at least partly based on an assumption about the Nazi regime's integrity that cannot be proven historically.

The substance of my doubts about the correctness of Poulantzas' interpretation is this: the degree of political dislocation in the structure of the state after 1933 was such that, if it did not amount to a "primacy of politics," it at least constituted an extension of political autonomy to a degree that calls into question the alleged historic service of fascism to capital.[29] In other words, the political developments after 1933 strongly suggest that the fascist period in Germany was a part rather than a resolution of the political crisis of representation of the early 1930s. It is Poulantzas, postulation of a *successful* mediation by fascism that, in this sense, lies at the root of the distortions, contradictions, and confusions of his study.

In fact, the correct conclusion seems at times to be forcing its way into Poulantzas' discussion—hence, for instance, his unexplored and unexplained treatment of the fascist party and fascist state in Germany as, variously, correlates, synonyms, and opposites.[30] Take also his pair of propositions that (1) "big capital used the fascist party, the fascist State and fascist ideology to impose a general policy which unified the power bloc," and (2) "the continuous contradictions between big capital and the Nazi party-state [were] part of the 'game' which national socialism was playing, juggling big capital with the other classes and fractions of the power bloc, and the power bloc with the masses."[31] These two propositions contain a clear contradiction, which can hardly be disguised by describing National Socialist policy as a "game." Contradictions of this kind cannot be denied, and it is quite correct that they should make their existence felt in such passages. However, the only way they can be "made sense of" is by acknowledging that the political tensions that Poulantzas continuously judges as "secondary" after 1933 were, in fact, of primary and fundamental significance for assessing the nature of the fascist regime in Germany.

It seems in any case that any examination of exceptional states must always bear in mind the possibility that it is dealing with a stage of crisis in conjunctural terms, and not an end to it. This possibility is surely inherent in the concept of the exceptional state as such. An adequate examination of the "concrete facts" of the fascist period in Germany would suggest the aptness of this conclusion in this case, but Poulantzas is not concerned to examine the full career of fascism in either Germany or Italy. In the German case, his research and exposition cease, broadly speaking, at the mid-1930s, because he is interested only in establishing fascism up to its so-called stabilized stage, that is, up to about 1934 in Germany. Stabilization is thus enthroned as a historical and analytic end-point beyond which nothing more need be said about the phenomenon of fascism. True, he occasionally lifts a corner of the veil that shrouds the later 1930s and the war years, with, for example, an observation on the displacement of the class struggle, or on the nature of the contradictions found in the Nazi state.[32] But these hints are never followed up. Instead, their significance remains a shadow, and we are left with a stronger memory of much blander assertions, such as that "the characteristic features of [petty-bourgeois] ideology correspond completely to the interests of big capital."[33]

Clearly, one objection to such a half-finished exposition of fascism is that it rules out any explanation of its collapse, and is therefore inadequate. This objection cannot be dismissed as stemming from teleology: it is not a bid to read the outcome back into the origin, and compress these as stages in a single process. Rather, the objection is founded on the more secure procedure of deriving fascism's collapse from fascism's contradictions, and not the contradictions from the collapse. This theoretical approach suggests that one must grasp fascism in its process as well as its structure, and thus examine its full trajectory. In historical terms, the fascist *regime* must be independently specified, and not simply allowed to follow from an analysis—however acute—of fascism before it comes into political power. Though Poulantzas is partly aware of the significance of the transition, his basically structural approach prevents him from subjecting fascism-in-power to the same detailed examination he makes of fascism before it constitutes its regime. Consequently, his characterization of fascism is incomplete. In addition, it would be enormously difficult to derive from his analysis an explanation of the collapse of fascism that did not contradict his account at crucial moments. On the contrary, an entirely new system of explanation would have to be developed from scratch.

An interpretation of fascism developed from this method would, I think, run along the following lines. The starting point could be Poulantzas' acute diagnosis of the crisis of representation of the power bloc, but fascism, as I have indicated, would have to be seen as a further stage in this crisis, not its resolution. Fascism is the most extreme form yet observed of the exceptional capitalist state, and the essential contradiction of exceptional states is that they represent a type of coercive structure in which the control of the extraction of surplus value is displaced from the labor process to the political process, in a vast enhancement of the state's role. The fascist regime is the extreme form of the autonomization of politics under capitalism. It is the product of an immense dislocation of the capitalist mode of production, and although it may appear to the economically and politically distressed power bloc as the only short-term solution, this fascist resolution is unlikely to persist in the long term, for it manifestly bristles with contradictions. As a system, it cannot be other than permanently fraught with its own downfall, for politically it has forfeited (by exceeding) the state's brief under capitalism: to act as the guarantor of the conditions for the reproduction of the conditions of production of surplus value—the rest being up to capital.

This delicately distanced relationship of the political and the economic is explosively compressed under fascism, and the political is enthroned in a threatening autonomy. (The only rational version of such an autonomy in the capitalist stage of production is, of course, the *deliberate* political subversion of capitalism—revolution.) This is not to deny, however, that there will be steps in the fascist process that will be beneficial to capital, but these will measure only a temporary masking of the fundamental contradiction, and not (as in a model of "normal" capitalism) a strategic adaptation to the contradictions of the mode of production. The self-destruction of fascism is therefore inherent in its political status, and to the extent that it embodies the purely political, so it will bring down the social formation with it.

This interpretation follows logically from an understanding of the significance of the labor process under capitalism, as the characteristic locus of capital's domination over labor. It underlines the need to concentrate more research specifically in this area, and to take this premise generally as an appropriate explanatory starting point for the political history of capitalism. In the case of fascism, the characterization I have outlined in these terms could be followed through historically in a number of ways, of which only a few can be suggested here. Under National Socialism, for example, one term of the fundamental contradiction in the role of the state is expressed in the tendency toward the ultimate autonomization of the political police, with its disruptive implications for the process of production. Of course, we can also locate in National Socialism the alternative tendency toward disciplining the labor force through the labor process too, visible for example in the compulsory membership of workers in the Labor Front, the various forms of corporative organization, the much-publicized attention to working conditions, and so on. These tendencies are often seen as the "rational" or "modern" side of fascist regimes, whereas in fact they are developmental tendencies of *capitalism* at a certain stage of the class struggle. Their appearance is thus not generic to fascism, though under fascism they take a particular form (e.g., corporate rather than independent labor unions). This so-called rational aspect of fascism must be compared with similar developments in other capitalist countries, and when this is done, the preponderance in fascist states of the machinery of *political* control will emerge as the determining characteristic, and the pace at which this machinery operates will be seen to accelerate as the contradictions established in fascism become more acute. It is for this reason that the executions mount, the con-

centration camps fill, the police system takes off into total independence, and, at the most extreme and comprehensive level, war engulfs
society, as the Nazi regime "matures" into the full expression of its
contradictions.

Other historical moments through which the characteristic political
nature of fascism might be investigated and specified include, for
example, in the German case the successive and fumbling attempts by
capital to avoid recourse to the political after 1930 (the administrative
autocracy of the Brüning and Papen governments); the actual process
by which the NSDAP established itself as a political alternative; the
enthronement of ideology after 1933; and, connected with this, the
"archaisms" of Nazism, such as its invocations of feudal and even
Germanic-tribal community models (tendencies often dismissed as
simply absurd, but that might perhaps be logically related to the
genuinely anachronistic political status claimed by a fascist regime in
capitalism). The complicated and ambiguous subformations of the system need rigorous identification, as, for example, the role of the SS in
the system of production. The "post-history" of fascism is another
indispensable field of study: for example, the connection between the
developments of the Nazi era and the extraordinary degree to which
class struggle in West German capitalism since the later 1940s has been
de-politicized. The Italian case could also be studied in similar detail,
as an apparently "weaker" instance of the model I have outlined.
Finally, the value of such studies ought not be vitiated by failing to
specify fascism in comparison with developments in those capitalist
societies that have not undergone a fascist period, or have experienced
exceptional regimes of a nonfascist type.

The above forms an incomplete and partly speculative list of points
thrown up by what I believe to be a fruitful approach to the analysis of
fascism: both the list and my general propositions would have to be
refined and modified by reference to the concrete. Only in this way,
however, can we arrive at a genuine distinction between the essential
and the secondary elements of fascism, and thus—which is the purpose
of the enterprise—develop a strategic political grasp of the phenomenon.

The common denominator of these three historical criticisms of
Poulantzas' study is, therefore, that by failing to delve sufficiently
deeply into his historical material, Poulantzas missed successive instances of contradiction; and cumulatively these omissions led to a
major misunderstanding of fascism. Poulantzas failed, in effect, to act
out his own stated commitment to concrete research.

I have not, however, wanted to launch an attack on Poulantzas' work as such—as if, by bagging each school of theorists as it appeared, one could aim at exterminating the breed and making the world safe for history. On the contrary, it is precisely because of the constitutive relation between history and theory that I hope this essay will be read as a critique and not as an attack. In subjecting one of Poulantzas' ostensibly most historical texts to a deliberately historical critique, I hope to have indicated some of the problems of constructing an adequately based theorization, without implying that the purpose as a whole is worthless.

The generic historical weakness of *Fascism and Dictatorship* derives from a pervasive deficiency of method. There is an assumption, nowhere queried in the book, that at any given moment all the empirical knowledge required for the full expression of a theorized problem does, in fact, exist. But the only sense in which this can be true is a tautologous one, and this does not appear to be the position adopted by Poulantzas. Yet that his writing implies a total confidence in facts as they stand is a failing of some importance: it is not just a question of a superficial arrogance of style, but suggests a failure to grasp the writing of history as a refraction of current and past practice, a practice by which we in the present constitute the objects of our enquiry in the past.

On the simplest level, Poulantzas' theoretical constructions frequently make substantial promises that are then thrown away by a careless use of historical data. Moreover, if, as this critique has suggested, some significant information is likely to be unknown at any given time of writing, then what we write ought to respond to this absence—not in any sentimental sense of humility before history, but for the ordinary and concrete reasons that we are always engaged in a progressive articulation of knowledge.

A more serious objection to *Fascism and Dictatorship*, as both an interpretation of a phenomenon and an example of method, is that it seems able to offer only an analysis of a problem that is specifically given, that is, established by a cursorily defined prior situation, and emptied of its relation to later conjunctures. The isolation of a concrete moment from the succession of moments in which it is buried is, of course, a constant methodological problem for historians, and Poulantzas is far from being the only writer to fail to meet this challenge. Yet an effective awareness of this problem and its implications seems to be absent from his work: hence his rather uncritical treatment of the pre-history of the era he discusses, and the virtual impossibility, as we have seen, of deducing the next steps from his study. For historical enquiry this form of quarantine is the reverse of healthy, for, in this case, it bars Poulantzas from establishing the relationship between contradiction and collapse.

Nevertheless, though Poulantzas' study of fascism ultimately reveals a combination of historical and methodological weakness, it is still a work of great richness and value, as I hope I have made clear. A work of this provocative power and subtlety deserves a critique that tries to take the argument forward, rather than throwing it back; anything less would be a disservice to Poulantzas' project—a political project that Marxists cannot ignore or brush aside. Not to take Poulantzas' history seriously would also merely confirm the bankruptcy of the historical profession; too many of us are still bound to a level of sophistication little more demanding than that represented by the supposed distinction between facts and theories. If we must learn to elaborate a problematic that will not turn history into a prolonged tautology, we must also realize that history conceived unproblematically is reduced to the category of the factitious. Though the later fate is often unthinkingly embraced by historians, no Marxist should be satisfied to be numbered in their company.

Notes

This essay is dedicated to the memory of Jane Kendrick, from whose criticism and advice the original benefited. It was first published in *History Workshop Journal* 3, Spring 1977.

1. Nicos Poulantzas, *Pouvoir politique et classes sociales* (Paris: Maspero, 1968); translated as *Political Power and Social Classes* (London: NLB, 1973); citations here are from the English edition; and Ralph Miliband, *The State in Capitalist Society* (London: Weidenfeld and Nicolson, 1969).
2. Nicos Poulantzas, "The Problem of the Capitalist State," *New Left Review* 58 (November/December 1969); Ralph Miliband, "Reply to Nicos Poulantzas," *New Left Review* 59 (January/February 1970). Both articles are reprinted in Robin Blackburn, ed., *Ideology in Social Science* (London: NLB, 1972). Debate continued in Miliband, "Poulantzas and the Capitalist State," *NLR* 82 (November/December 1973); Ernesto Laclau, "The Specificity of the Political: The Poulantzas-Miliband Debate," *Economy and Society* 5, no. 1 (February 1975); and Poulantzas, "The Capitalist State: A Reply to Miliband and Laclau," *New Left Review* 95 (January/February 1976).
3. Miliband, "Poulantzas and the Capitalist State," pp. 84, 85–86.
4. Poulantzas, "Capitalist State," pp. 65, 68, 72.
5. Laclau, "Poulantzas-Miliband Debate," p. 94.
6. Nicos Poulantzas, *Fascisme et dictature* (Paris: Maspero, 1970); translated as *Fascism and Dictatorship* (London: NLB, 1974). Citations here are from the English edition. Cf. Poulantzas, "Capitalist State," p. 67.
7. Poulantzas, *Fascism and Dictatorship*, p. 12.
8. Ibid., p. 13.

9. Poulantzas, "Capitalist State," p. 65.

10. For Poulantzas' methodology, see the Introduction to his *Political Power and Social Classes*, pp. 18–19 and 24–25, where he warns against the tendency to construct theory "in the void, before proceeding to a sufficient amount of concrete research."

11. Ultimately, Poulantzas' full texts as cited, with the addition of *Classes in Contemporary Capitalism* (London: NLB, 1975), are necessary to an understanding of any part of his theory, since they are constructed in deliberate relation to each other, with the later texts correcting the earlier. However, as a brief introduction, see Poulantzas' "On Social Classes," *NLR* 78 (March/April 1973); and Laclau, "Poulantzas-Miliband Debate."

12. Poulantzas analyzes "non-exceptional" capitalist states in *Political Power and Social Classes* (London: NLB, 1973).

13. Poulantzas, *Fascism and Dictatorship*, pp. 85–86.

14. For a full exposition of the concept of the state apparatus(es), see initially *Fascism and Dictatorship*, pp. 299–309. Poulantzas distinguishes between "repressive state apparatuses" (roughly, the conventional organs of government) and "ideological state apparatuses," which include trade unions, political parties, the church, and so forth. In the context here, however, Poulantzas seems to be using the term in the former sense only, though this is not wholly clear; see pp. 111–12.

15. For a discussion of the terms *ruling class* and *class in charge of the state*, see *Political Power and Social Classes*, pp. 249–51; also "On Social Classes."

16. This resumé is drawn principally from pp. 86–88, 108–13, and 336–49.

17. Poulantzas, *Fascism and Dictatorship*, p. 112.

18. K. D. Bracher, *The German Dictatorship* (Harmondsworth, Middlesex: Penguin, 1971). Bracher's major researches were carried out in connection with his contribution to one of the first fully researched monographs on the early years of the regime, *Die nationalsozialistische Machtergreifung*, by K. D. Bracher, Wolfgang Sauer, and Gerhard Schultz (Cologne/Opladen: Westdeutscher Verlag, 1960).

19. See, for example, Martin Broszat, *The Hitler State* (London: Longman, 1981), originally published in 1966; Peter Diehl-Thiele, *Partei und Staat im Dritten Reich* (Munich: Beck, 1969); and E. N. Peterson, *The Limits of Hitler's Power* (Princeton: Princeton University Press, 1969). Some of the older writers on the regime, such as Hugh Trevor-Roper and Hannah Arendt, emphasized its extreme lack of coherence, though this view did not fully penetrate later writing. The assumption that terror depends on a coherent and systematic structure of government would seem to be misconceived, though it is easily suggested by the ring of the word *totalitarian* (and obviously encouraged by the political value in the cold war period of assimilating fascist and communist regimes under one title). But as the German experience shows, a regime of terror may derive its effect precisely from the absence of structure and central political control, in that this leaves so many interstices open for the invasion of prerogative power, as well as radicalizing the political process (though this is not to suggest that individual units within the general structure will not be organizationally "rational").

20. Poulantzas, *Fascism and Dictatorship*, pp. 237 ff.

21. See Poulantzas, *Political Power and Social Classes*, pp. 77–85.

22. Poulantzas, *Fascism and Dictatorship*, p. 239.

23. See Poulantzas, *Political Power and Social Classes*, pp. 325–59.

24. Poulantzas, *Fascism and Dictatorship*, p. 111.

25. Ibid., p. 264.

26. Ibid., p. 345.

27. Ibid., p. 63.

28. Ibid., p. 112.

29. See T. W. Mason, "The Primacy of Politics—Politics and Economics in National Socialist Germany," in S. J. Woolf, ed., *The Nature of Fascism* (London: Weidenfeld and Nicolson, 1968), an essay to which this discussion owes a great deal. The term *primacy of politics* may perhaps be slightly misleading, in that it implies a primacy *over* the economic sphere, as in a hierarchy. For this reason, the concept of *autonomy* seems preferable, with its clear connotation of detachment rather than paramountcy.
30. See Poulantzas, *Fascism and Dictatorship,* pp. 85ff., 111–13, and 340, where each of these definitions is implied, without clarification.
31. Ibid., pp. 111–13.
32. On pp. 344–45 Poulantzas notes the displacement of the class struggle into the state apparatuses, but then consigns it to the title of a "secondary contradiction" between social categories—a term that, as we have seen, is not sufficiently specified in relation to class in this concrete instance. The designation of this field as "secondary" is thus precarious. On pp. 250 and 254 the contradictions between capital and the petty bourgeoisie are mentioned but not investigated.
33. Ibid., p. 252.

Economy and Politics in the Destruction of the Weimar Republic

Kurt Gossweiler

The Marxist view regarding the relationship of economy and politics has often been presented in a distorted manner in Western publications. This is presumably due to either ignorance or bias, even though the basic writings of Marx, Engels, and Lenin are extremely precise in this respect.

One of the latest examples of such distortion can be found in Henry A. Turner's extensive work, *German Big Business and the Rise of Hitler.*[1]

Turner's comments regarding the "primacy of economy" or the "primacy of politics" reproduce the misleading usage of these terms within the framework of a controversy featured in the 1960s in the West Berlin journal *Das Argument.* The English historian Tim Mason there maintained that within the context of the entire history of bourgeois society the domestic and foreign policy of the Nazi state from 1936 onward was no longer determined by the primacy of economy but by the primacy of politics.[2] Thereby Mason wanted to uphold the viewpoint that during the fascist dictatorship it was not the economic power-wielders, as is generally understood, who determined politics but the Nazi politicians who allowed themselves to be guided by ideological conceptions and prejudices instead of by economic interests.

Translated by Michael N. Dobkowski and Isidor Wallimann

The use of the pair of there "economy" and "politics" therefore had nothing in common with the relationship usually brought forward in this connection by Marxists. Opposing Mason, Eberhard Czichon advocated the thesis of the "primacy of industry with the cartel of National-Socialist power" in a bid to defend an assumed Marxist position.[3] The facts he introduced to counter Mason were by and large excellently suited to contradict Mason's assertion that it was very difficult to prove even an indirect involvement of the economic leaders in state-political opinion-molding during the Third Reich. However, his usage of the term "primacy of industry" only served to complicate the terminological confusion because, first, he seemed to corroborate those who, like Mason, held and still hold the view that Marxism is characterized by its postulation of the primacy of economy and, second, because Czichon restricts the sphere of influence of the decisive economic circle to *industry.*

The main reason for the terminological confusion stems from the fact that within the scope of this controversy two different, albeit closely linked, questions have not been clearly differentiated: namely, the question pertaining to the foundation, that is to say, the basis of society, that sphere of the social organism which provides keynote stimuli for the sustained further development of society and, second, the consideration of which factors—economic or political—have priority in deciding practical politics.

A reply to the first question was strikingly given by Karl Marx in the famous sentences of his "Preface to a Critic of Political Economy":

> In the social production of their existence men inevitably enter in definite relations, which are independent of their will, namely relations of production appropriate to a given stage in the development of their material forces of production. The totality of these relations of production constitutes the economic structure of society, the real foundation, on which arises a legal and political super-structure and to which correspond definite forms of social consciousness. The mode of production of material life, conditions the general process of social, political and intellectual life. It is not the consciousness of men that determines their existence, but their social existence that determines their consciousness.[4]

Friedrich Engels in his late letters gave a number of additions and explanations concerning these fundamental stipulations in regard to the basis and superstructure of human society, directed against a simplified, undialectical interpretation. In his letter of July 14, 1893, to Franz Mehring, Engels explains why such additions became necessary:

That is to say we all laid, and *were bound* to lay, the main emphasis, in the first place, on the *derivation* of political, juridical and other ideological notions, and of actions arising through the med um of these notions, from basic economic facts. But in so doing we neglected the formal side—the ways and means by which these notions, etc., come about—for the sake of the content. This has given our adversaries a welcome opportunity for misunderstanding and distortions.[5]

The briefest summary of Engels' expositions is found in a letter sent to W. Borgius on January 25, 1894: Noting that "economic conditions [are those] which ultimately condition historical development," Engels states:

> political, juridical, philosophical, religious, literary, artistic, etc., development is based on economic development. But all these react upon one another and also upon the economic basis. It is not that economic situation is the cause, solely active, while everything else is only passive effect. There is, rather, interaction on the basis of economic necessity, which ultimately always asserts itself.[6]

In 1920, the third year of young Soviet power, V. I. Lenin was confronted with the need to reply in a fundamental manner to the second question, namely, the primacy of economy or politics in solving burning practical political issues. In the context of an inner-party dispute regarding the role and tasks of the trade unions, Trotsky and others criticized Lenin for seeking to solve this question *politically*, maintaining the correct approach was an *economic* one.[7] They thus also advocated the primacy of economy.

Lenin, in rejecting such a viewpoint, responded with an extensive reply that might, at first glance, appear contradictory.

> I said again in my speech, that politics is a concentrated expression of economics, because I had earlier heard my "political" approach rebuked in a manner which is inconsistent and inadmissable for a Marxist. Politics must take precedence over economics. To argue otherwise is to forget the ABC of Marxism. . . . Without a correct political approach to the matter the given class will be unable to stay on top, and consequently, will be incapable of solving its production problem either.[8]

The apparent inconsistency of this assertion, when considered carefully in detail, turns out to be a precise description of a dialectical relationship. Classes with counteracting economic and political interests emerge from an economic basis characterized by the private ownership of the means of production. In a narrow sense *economic interests* relate to the distribution of the national product, in a wider sense to the constellation of conditions of ownership of the means of production. *Political interests* are geared to attaining and holding such a share of political power for the fullest possible implementation of one's economic interests. This interrelationship is expressed in Lenin's formula: politics are concentrated economics.

The respectively ruling economic class requires political power in order to defend, to consolidate, and to extend its economic supremacy as on the other hand the nonpossessing, exploited class will have the means of freeing itself forever from its economic exploiters only by seizing political power and ensuring its consolidation. In the final analysis, for both classes political power and political struggle are the decisive means of implementing and ensuring their economic interests. This objectively given interrelationship was postulated by Lenin in his thesis on the primacy of politics. Indeed, from a Marxist-Leninist viewpoint, contrasting the economic with the political approach as completely counterposed, as done by Lenin's opponents, is impermissible because politics are the concentrated expression of the economy. However, by necessity, politics possesses primacy vis-à-vis the economy because all decisions, even those relating to "purely economic" questions, must be taken from a *political* standpoint, from the standpoint of attaining and legitimately preserving political power.

Thus, the facts hitherto presented clearly make plain that the struggle waged by Turner and others against an alleged Marxist thesis of primacy of economy is nothing other than a quixotic battle. (In order to rule out false interpretations, I should like to expressly indicate that this naturally does not signify that *all* political struggle pursued *only* economic goals. Needless to say, the political struggle comprehends the implementation of interests in respect to *all* other spheres of life.)

Economy and Politics in the Creation of the Weimar Republic

Following World War I, the economic situation facing German imperialism was catastrophic. Striking features included an economy dismembered and whittled down through the war costs. In addition, there were the inestimable costs stemming from the defeat, which in turn required a raising of the accumulation rate to a hitherto unknown level as a precondition for the economic survival of German capitalism, to a level leaving no freedom of movement whatsoever for social concessions to the wage earners.

Nonetheless, as the Weimar Republic dawned, an Arbeitgemeinschaft agreement was signed by Hugo Stinnes and Carl Legien, representing powerful capital interests, and the trade unions. Within this framework the employers made concessions to the workers that, even during the economic boom years before the war, they had rigorously rejected as unacceptable and ruinous. However, now not only were the economic bases for perpetuating the capitalist mode of production endangered, but political power as a whole, the very continued existence of capitalism in Germany, was at stake.

The imperative of the primacy of politics was implemented because, otherwise, survival would not have been possible. In order to retain political power and thereby the preconditions for subsequently restoring the supremacy vis-à-vis the contracting party, the German big bourgeoisie found itself compelled to accede to economic concessions that wholly contradicted the prerequisites for reestablishing a properly functioning capitalist reproduction process under the given economic conditions.

The German upper bourgeoisie (*Grossbourgeoisie*), who, as Lenin wrote, had "learned from the Russian example," implemented "an excellent strategy" as their power was being most seriously threatened.[9] Abraham Frowein, a presidium member of the League of German Industry (RDI) strikingly characterized this approach when, reviewing the past, he declared on June 12, 1919: "Gentlemen, in Russia events took the wrong turn and, right from the start, industry found itself rejecting the revolution. If we—and this would have been feasible—had taken up a stance of non-cooperation, then I am sure that by today we would have the same conditions as prevail in Russia."[10]

However, such a strategy was assured success only because the German "economic leaders" found partners in the form of trade union and Social Democratic party (SPD) leaders who were willing to guarantee the survival of capitalism in Germany in return for making economic, social, and political concessions that, in 1913, were seen as sensational, whereas in November 1918 they could be likened to a reward for having renounced the programmatic goals of Social Democracy for a bowl of soup. Moreover, these leaders, when confronting the German upper bourgeoisie and the former Kaiser's generals, behaved in the same manner as the liberal bourgeoisie had responded in 1848–49 when faced with the Prussian monarchy, and in the wake of Bismarck's successful blood-and-iron politics. They established an alliance with the representatives of old power to combat the forces of revolution. This behavior, which in Germany's past had brought about a complete counterrevolution for each semi-completed revolution, permitted the hitherto existing basis of German society to remain in almost unchanged form also during the Weimar Republic.

Indeed, not only were the most outspoken enemies of the German working-class movement, the coal and steel barons of the Ruhr, able to steer their empires undeterred by the turbulence of revolution, but also the most anachronistic element of this modern industrial country, the powerful Junker landowners, remained unchallenged because of the alliance between the social-democratic leaders and the generals, who primarily came from Junkerdom.

Thus, from the outset the Weimar Republic was afflicted by a most striking contradiction—the anomaly of an economic structure that was only insignificantly modified in comparison to the Empire and that was characterized above all by its continuity and similarity to it as well as a state domination apparatus that remained virtually untouched except for the very top levels. On the other hand, there was a bourgeois-parliamentary state form that, due to pressure from the revolutionary masses, was able to leave far behind the rights and the Constitution inherited from Bismarck.

This contradiction was so acute that merely sticking to it unchangeably was bound to give rise to constant, severe conflicts as neither of the two poles in society was prepared to accept limitations imposed by the other. The conditions for the realization of capital necessitated a political order in postwar Germany permitting a still greater exploitation of labor power than had been the case in the Empire. However, ensuring and realizing the democratic rights for the popular masses, as embodied in the Constitution, required, *as a minimum*, the elimination of the economic and political positions of power of the most entrenched enemies of parliamentary democracy, namely, the Junkerdom and the mighty Ruhr industrialists, as well as the nationalization of the big banks.

This fundamental contradiction explains the great number of class clashes between 1919 and 1923, with the short-lived rightist conspiracy in Berlin known as the Kapp putsch as the most prominent. A further result and at the same time also a significant piece of evidence of this contradiction was the Stinnes Plan of Autumn 1923, a plan for subjugating the German workers to a dictatorship motivated by the needs of capital realization.[11] It was drawn up by the same man who, four years earlier, had signed the agreement establishing the Arbeitsgemeinschaft.

Due to the unfavorable class-power relationship for the employers, between 1919 and 1923 high finance was not in a position to establish a political order in line with the realization needs of capital. Consequently, these needs had to be met in a different manner, namely, in a way that appeared to be independent of political conditions and not influenced by political bodies. *Inflation* proved just as brutal a means of fostering the exploitation of the wage recipients as would have been the case with an extensive increase of the work day—and that is precisely what happened.[12]

The short phase of "normal" development between 1924 and 1929 is no argument against the assertion regarding the absence of a foundation for a stable development of the Weimar Republic. For, whereas Social Democratic party and trade-union leaders hurriedly considered this phase a new beginning for a crisis-free economy that would subsequently grow into socialism along peaceful lines via "organized capitalism," in reality, as far as the big-capital opponents of the Weimar democracy were concerned, this period merely represented an armistice phase. Moreover, this phase had been accepted only after the SPD and the trade unions had actually renounced the eight-hour day, one of the principle revolutionary gains of the period, and only after the French waiver in respect to the priority rating of German reparation payments led to a situation in which other liabilities of American finance capital displayed an ostensible inclination to bolster up the capital-formation process in Germany by providing loans. The contradictions between capital and labor was therefore, during the normality phase, minutely less pronounced because of the partial abandonment of the revolutionary gains and particularly because of the external temporary capital inflow. That is why the stabilization of capitalism in Germany could be only very relative and had to be more fragile than was the case in the other developed capitalist industrial countries.

The Establishment of the Fascist Dictatorship: Economic Compulsion or the Implementation of Political Will?

The outbreak of the world economic crisis, coupled with its unexpected duration and severity and occurring at a time when many German economic leaders did not expect it, necessarily brought forth again the temporarily submerged contradiction. Big capital's need for an authoritarian (that is, a dictatorial) state and the need on the part of a broad section of the population, particularly organized labor, for expanded and secure democratic rights and social advances became again fully pronounced, although they had never totally disappeared.

One might conclude that the world economic crisis had been the development that triggered off the ever more resolute struggle of broader sections of the ruling class against the Weimar Republic.

Attentive observers, however, have been quick to note a keynote feature, namely that the offensive against the Weimar Republic began toward the end of 1927 and early 1928, that is to say, the temporary armistice initiated by capital came to an end considerably *before* the outbreak of the world economic crisis.[13] Singularly significant evidence in this context was the forming early in 1928 of the Association for the Renewal of the Reich, which, in rejecting the Weimar Republic, echoed the clarion call for establishing a Third Reich.[14] Further symptoms along similar lines were the right-wing seizure of leadership posts both in the German National People's party (DNVP) and the Center party, namely, Alfred Hugenberg and the Prelate Kaas; the lockout of some 250,000 metalworkers by the Ruhr trusts in November 1928, and the memorandum of the Reichsverband der Deutschen Industrie entitled "Ascent or Demise" in December 1929.[15]

All these facts run counter to the viewpoint that the outbreak of the world economic crisis sparked the employers' onslaught against the Weimar Republic. No doubt the said crisis clearly had a strengthening but by no means a causal effect. The real reasons lie deeper. In essence, they reside in a closely intermeshed combination of economic, domestic, and foreign policy forces. Moreover, it is by no means accidental that the end of the "armistice" coincides with the point at which Germany again regained its number-one position as an imperial power in Europe and number two in the capitalist world at large. Indeed, by 1927–28 the first stage was reached—namely, the restoration of prior economic power. Once this had been achieved, sights were set on further objectives. These included the liquidation of the political consequences of the defeat and the revolution, that is to say, the brushing aside of the Treaty of Versailles and parliamentary democracy, the "multiparty state" *(Parteienstaat).*[16]

Coupled with the regained economic power there developed an avid interest in a "fair" participation in the appropriation of the world's resources—in the urge to carve up the world once again in favor of German imperialism. As in 1914, German imperialism, feeling "left out in the cold," again demanded a "place in the sun," or—coining the rightist phraseology during the Weimar Republic—the "people without space" demanded "Lebensraum." If one is anxious to peddle "power politics" abroad then—according to Wilhelm Groener—it is essential to remain "firm and unrelenting" at home. An orientation to external expansion requires an orientation toward repression at home.[17]

The fate of the Weimar Republic was, however, by no means exclusively in the hands of hostile big-business interests. The counterforce was to be seen in the successful extension and defense of democracy, provided it took up a resolute and united stance in pursuit of these goals. This possibility had been demonstrated by the campaign for the expropriation of the princes waged in 1926, as well as by the Reichstag elections in spring 1928. Jointly the workers' parties along with the left-bourgeois German Democratic party gained a total of 13.9 million votes while the rightist bloc ranging from the National Socialist German Workers party (NSDAP) to the German People's party (DVP) garnered just over 10.2 million votes. Between these two blocs was the Center and the Bavarian People's party, which together drew 5.2 million votes. Of these, a considerable number, namely the Catholic workers, should in fact be included in the left-wing potential.[18]

The dreadfully fateful contradiction between the social structure of the Weimar Republic, with its semi-feudal residues, and the bourgeois-democratic state form needed to be overcome. Moreover, in order to beat back the offensive of high finance and the Junker enemies of the Weimar Republic, it was necessary to mobilize and bring fully into play this powerful left-potential for attainable goals.

As the expropriation campaign of the princes had shown, the first and the most politically urgent and popular agenda should have been the destruction of the East Elbe landed aristocracy in favor of a land reform that partitioned the Junker land among the land-impoverished peasants and agricultural workers. Naturally it was not sufficient to raise the issue in petitions brought to parliament; what was needed above all was backing by extraparliamentary forces, especially through trade-union actions, thereby spearheading mass pressure to the fullest possible extent. Indeed, such actions could safely have counted on sympathy and even support among elements of the powerful big bourgeoisie.[19]

Thus a program aimed at dividing up the Junker landed estates could have been a point of departure for creating a powerful, campaigning democratic front alongside it, thereby seriously weakening the most reactionary wing or the ruling elite.

The principal force of such a front could only be the working-class movement. A commensurate initiative along these lines would have had the chance to bring about a decisive shift in the balance of power in favor of bolstering up and consolidating the democratic content of the Weimar Republic. If the SPD and the allied Free Trade Unions had taken such an initiative following the overwhelming social-democratic electoral success in May 1928, this would most probably have resulted in a series of positive effects.

The first and most important commensurate outcome would have been the prevention of the disastrous further division of the working-class movement. The unity of action so aptly displayed during the expropriation campaign of the princes would have been given new impetus in the struggle for agrarian reform. As long as the Weimar Republic existed, even though its formation did not completely reflect the overall demands of the German Communist party (KPD), the party had backed every real move in defense of democracy notwithstanding the fact that the Communist party never once relinquished its goal, namely the aim of Karl Liebknecht and Rosa Luxemburg to establish a socialist German republic. Moreover, the Communist party would never have hesitated to back to the hilt any initiative for the elimination of the hotbed of reaction, namely the East Elbe Junkerdom as, indeed, such action would have been fully consistent with the agrarian program of the KPD.[20]

Second, a united campaign of struggle of the two workers' parties for such a popular goal would, undoubtedly, have drawn broad sections of the democratically minded bourgeoisie and petty bourgeoisie into the orbit of the overall working-class movement.

Third, by engaging in this struggle, the working-class movement would have proved itself the most resolute advocate of peasant interests and, thereby, real possibilities would have emerged for dismembering the grip of the most reactionary forces on the land.

Fourth, if such policies had been pursued, severe restrictions and obstacles would have been imposed, in particular, on the possibility of fascism's developing into a mass movement. Fascism would have been denied one of its main arguments (namely, that Marxism in the guise of the SPD ruined the middle classes and the peasantry) and, moreover, would have faced a united working-class movement. As a result, fascism would not have found itself in a position of merely having to combat a powerless, divided working-class movement, engaged in constant bickering.

Fifth, such an attack on the Junkers would have brought out the differences within the big bourgeoisie and weakened—for both political and economic reasons—that element within the heavy-industry faction which tended to form coalitions with the Junkers and was the major enemy of the Weimar Republic. The political reasons include the still widespread and deeply entrenched "Kapp putsch trauma," that is, the fear of provoking the regeneration of a united defense by the working class (as in 1920 against the Kapp putsch) which would have to be challenged and opposed by die-hard policies. Economically, large parts of the industrial and banking sections were interested in eliminating the Junkerdom and replacing it with a healthy peasant agriculture that would expand the domestic market, particularly for agricultural machinery and fertilizers. Thereby, subsidies to the parasitical, crisis-ridden, and semi-feudal Junker agriculture could have been avoided.

However, such considerations should not be taken to characterize the agrarian reform as the key issue for the survival of the Weimar Republic but are intended merely to rebuff the widespread concept that the Weimar Republic never had the slightest chance of escaping its subsequent fate. On the contrary, one should emphatically underline the following: a policy would have been possible that decidedly aimed at healing the recognized structural defects of German society. Furthermore, a policy for fostering the union of the left forces would have made it possible for them not only to ward off the rightist onslaughts on the Weimar Republic but to extend democratic rights in both the state and the economy at large. The chances that such a policy could have succeeded were still considerable in 1928 and had not completely disappeared even as late as 1932.

However, as is known after its electoral gains and victory, German social democracy took no initiative whatsoever in implementing a program to promote and consolidate democracy. Moreover, the SPD did not even revert to its own agrarian program, the draft of which, adopted on January 12, 1927, proclaims that for reasons of both production and population politics the SPD advocates a fundamental change in basic property ownership conditions and, therefore, a "planned land reform." According to this program, in the eastern part of the country, agrarian units were not to exceed 750 hectares, with additional areas being returned to the Reich without compensation.[21]

In reality, SPD policies were not geared to changes and reforms but solely to retaining what had been achieved through the alliance with that wing of the big bourgeoisie which had displayed a willingness to enter into an alliance with social democracy on conditions decreed by the big bourgeoisie. This had been succinctly expounded by Paul Silverberg, who, on September 4, 1926, when addressing the members' meeting of the RDI, declared that social democracy should "return to reality" and should "renounce radical doctrinarism along with the ever destructive never constructive policy of the streets and force" and cooperate in a responsible manner "with the employers and *under their direction*."[22]

In practice this meant that the Hermann Müller government, in defiance of the SPD's electoral promises, had to follow (and indeed followed) the basic policies of the preceding bourgeois bloc parties, that is, to step up the struggle against the Communist party and to continue the armaments program of German imperialism. This led to the Bloody May of 1929 with the subsequent banning of the Red Front Union (while the fascist SA and SS terror groupings could legally continue to exist!) and to the decision to build the armored cruiser, a project that was clearly rejected prior to the elections. Basically, this was a suicidal policy. It even more profoundly widened the divisions within the working-class movement, weakened the reputation and standing of social democracy with large segments of the population, undermined the confidence SPD members had in their own party, and thereby decidedly weakened the entire left. The counterforces on the right, however, in particular the Nazi fascists, gained ground as a direct consequence. Adhering to a policy that renounced positive political change was bound to pave the way for successive decline: from a policy that defended the status quo to a policy that tolerated the "lesser evil" to the final capitulation to the greatest evil without even a semblance of a fight. Weimar democracy could have been salvaged only by taking the initiative and inflicting ever new setbacks against its enemies, thereby deepening and consolidating it in every possible manner. Since the SPD as the left party with the greatest mass influence renounced such a policy, the shameful capitulation of the Prussian Braun-Severing government—facing the coup d'état initiated by Chancellor von Papen on July 20, 1932—was the unavoidable consequence.

The division of the left forces, coupled with the role of the social-democratic Hermann Müller government as executive organ in implementing a national policy dominated by big capital and hostile to the middle class, and an identical role of the Braun-Severing government in Prussia, created favorable preconditions for the successful development of a rightist offensive, although the electoral result of 1928 and the subsequent formation of the Grand Coalition compelled these forces to alter both tactics and timing.

The tactical goal, especially of Hugenberg's DNVP, was now to discredit the SPD in the eyes of the electorate by holding the party responsible for as many unpopular measures as possible. Even the signing of the Young Plan, which determined and regulated the size and mode of payment of reparations and which directly served the interests of German finance capital, was seized on by the German nationalists, along with the Nazis, to unleash an unrestrained hate campaign and to accuse the SPD of high treason.

The basic strategy for the attack on the Weimar Republic, as thought up inter alia by the Union for the Renewal of the Reich, sought the transformation of the Weimar Republic from a parliamentary democracy to a presidential dictatorship. Furthermore, this was to be undertaken *in a legal manner* by means of an extensive interpretation of all relevantly suitable articles of the Weimar Constitution.[23]

However, this approach alone could not ensure a lasting solution and a final break with the Constitution. For this to occur, an enabling act was required, for which, however, a two-thirds majority was necessary. This gave the illusion that the throttling of the Weimar Republic, outwardly at least, was to proceed nicely along constitutional lines.

The transformation of the Weimar Republic into a presidential dictatorship proved possible with relatively little friction not the least because of the social-democratic leadership's policy of tolerance toward the Brüning government, formed in the spring of 1930 following the dismantling of the Hermann Müller cabinet.[24]

The greatest difficulties arose in the attempt to obtain a parliamentary two-thirds majority for abolishing the Weimar Constitution, that is, through the Enabling Act. Over a long period, bourgeois party politicians and their allies in industry sought to set up a single, large bourgeois coalition or even party as a counterweight to social democracy. Backed by a sizable bourgeois parliamentary majority, they thus hoped to govern without and against the SPD and to implement the desired constitutional changes. However, all these efforts were unsuccessful, indeed were destined to remain so. First, there was considerable rivalry and jealousy-motivated bickering among party politicians. Second, the opposing interests of the diverse factions of the dominant class backing the different bourgeois parties were too great to overcome. Finally, because all these parties, with the exception of the Center party, had been deserted by a majority of their voters on account of their support for the emergency decrees, they gradually wasted away. In this manner, they lost ever more significance with regard to the aspired parliamentary majority necessary for a "legal" transition to the desired dictatorship.

Hugenberg's DNVP had been particularly outspoken against a fusion with the other bourgeois parties. The reasons for this stance were the substantial differences of interests that existed between decisive circles of heavy industry, especially in the Ruhr mining area, and the East Elbe landed aristocracy, represented by Hugenberg and his party on the one hand, and the export industry, certain sections of banking capital, and the wholesale sector (which partly backed the German People's party [DVP], the Center party, and the German Democratic party [DDP]), on the other.

Instead of cooperating with the bourgeois middle-of-the-road parties, Hugenberg opted for an alliance with the NSDAP. Although it was still (in 1928) rather unimportant, the NSDAP was in Hugenberg's sense at least radically antidemocratic. In this arrangement, analogous to the relationship between the Center party and the SPD, he hoped to gain an alliance partner that would provide the DNVP with the necessary mass basis for the unchallenged leadership of the bourgeois camp. For this reason he generously placed his extensive propaganda apparatus at the disposal of the NSDAP along with financial means from the heavy-industry-backed electoral fund he administered. This sponsorship of the NSDAP proved exceptionally fortunate for Hitler but not for Hugenberg. In September 1930, the NSDAP achieved a sensational electoral victory. Instead of weakening the workers' parties by attracting its electors, as Hugenberg had hoped, this victory came almost exclusively at the expense of the bourgeois parties, above all Hugenberg's own party. Its loss to the NSDAP amounted to 2 million voters.[25]

The September 1930 electoral result immediately created a hitherto unprecedented situation. Both the leaders of the bourgeois parties and important "captains of the economy" were suddenly confronted with a party that had mushroomed from an 800,000 voter organization to a 6 million one, thus turning the NSDAP into a powerful political force and the second most powerful party. The NSDAP had thus become a force that could no longer be overlooked, but equally as important, a power that opened up quite new, surprising, and welcome possibilities for overcoming the parliamentary obstacles for the "legal" transition to a dictatorial form of domination.

All bourgeois parties, along with other groups and factions of the ruling class, quickly realized that the NSDAP would have to be directly involved in government.[26] However, its possible role and the leadership under which this was to happen became a matter of contention, resurrecting old rivalries and competitive bickering. Hereby, as time passed and situations changed ever more, new considerations and combinations were brought into play. To simplify matters the following four major groups and strategies can be observed:

1. Alfred Hugenberg and his party, as well as the circles from heavy industry and the landed aristocracy behind this party, relying on Reich President Paul von Hindenberg, resolutely pressed for an alliance with the NSDAP, with the NSDAP in the role of junior partner, attracting the masses—in other words, an alliance that would assure the Hugenberg party of supremacy in the bourgeois camp and leadership in the desired "National Dictatorship," the culmination of which should in due course be the restoration of the monarchy.

2. The Center party (Brüning) and those circles in heavy industry, chemicals, the electrical industry, the export sector, and the bankers behind it, wanted to win over the NSDAP for a government alliance. With the assistance of the NSDAP it thereby hoped to move from the Weimar democracy to an authoritarian regime that in the long run would similarly culminate in the restoration of the monarchy.[27]

3. In contrast to these strategies, Hjalmar Schacht and Fritz Thyssen—both principal spokesmen of a group of industrialists and bankers particularly strongly linked to U.S. finance capital—were not anxious to subordinate the Hitler party to one of the old bourgeois parties. Instead, using Hermann Göring, whom they backed very generously as their go-between to the NSDAP, they pressed Adolf Hitler to stake a claim to the chancellorship as a precondition for the NSDAP's joining the government. Moreover, they advised Hitler to make his bid with utmost persistence and without the slightest concessions. Thereby they hoped that a Hitler government would allow them to triumph over all contenders and to pursue a foreign policy bent on expansion solely in the East in alliance with the West.

4. General Kurt von Schleicher cooperated with NSDAP organiza-

tion head Gregor Strasser, the second most powerful NSDAP figure after Hitler, until his demise early in December 1932, in attempting to set up a military dictatorship. He sought to anchor this in the working class by means of his "trade union axis" project ranging from the Free Trade Unions (Theodor Leipart) to the Christian trade unions to the NSDAP.[28]

Schleicher tried to implement his project under the Papen government, but Chancellor Franz von Papen swung toward the Hugenberg line and tried to "soften Hitler" and to cause him to relent by dissolving the Reichstag during a period of deep crisis in the NSDAP. He thereby compelled the Nazi party to enter a further costly electoral campaign. This maneuver proved to be a serious mistake, ending in von Papen's forced resignation.

By means of his September emergency decrees, von Papen brought about savage wage cuts and simultaneously put the tariff system out of order. Through this approach he gained for himself the enthusiastic support of large segments of the entrepreneurial community.[29] However this enthusiasm soon waned as he proved incapable of handling the unexpected resistance by the working people, which was highlighted by the Berlin transport workers strike in early November 1932. Moreover, as von Papen had anticipated, Hitler's popularity fell sharply in the elections, with the NSDAP losing some 2 million voters. The Nazis did not become more submissive as a consequence, and so he found himself being increasingly pressured by the industrial forces behind him, above all the leading figures of the "Langnamverein," Paul Reusch and Fritz Springorum, who urged him ever more vehemently now to establish the new, strong state by changing the Constitution, thereby making short play of all resistance. In the face of this pressure, plans were concocted in the von Papen cabinet to attain a change in the Constitution by means of a coup d'état, namely, by imposing a new constitution making the parliament powerless. However, these plans quickly provoked alarm among virtually all bourgeois party leaders as well as the majority of "economic leaders" and, above all, the Reichswehr leadership. They all agreed that the legal path should not be shelved, so as not to provoke unforeseeable reactions by the working people.[30]

Under these circumstances, the Hugenberg–von Papen variant, which got its strongest support from Reich President Hindenburg, had to be given up together with von Papen's chancellorship, and negotiations about the NSDAP participation in government had to be taken up again. The necessary breathing space and the domestic appeasement was achieved by bequeathing to General Schleicher the chancellorship and by revoking the most provocative stipulations of the emergency decrees enacted by von Papen in September.

Thus, one of two remaining possibilities for attaining the dictatorship had to be chosen: either the risky coup d'état backed solely by the army or the legal formation of a government for establishing a national dictatorship on the conditions demanded by the Nazi party, namely, Hitler's chancellorship. In this situation the key ruling-class circles opted for the path of (at least) formal legality, thereby revealing that Schacht and Thyssen were indeed the better strategists. They had foreseen that, provided Hitler remained steadfast and did not lose his nerve, all other variants would surely fail. For sound reasons, a coup d'état bid had to be avoided, yet the legal path was feasible only with the cooperation of the NSDAP, which now had more leverage and, being the most powerful government party, was in a position to insist on its claim to head the government. Both Schacht and Thyssen still feared that Hitler, given the signs of decline in his party, might be influenceable and agree to the compromise solutions as suggested, for example, by Schleicher and Strasser. Therefore, during these very weeks Schacht wrote several rallying letters to Hitler and in collusion with Hermann Göring, Schacht and Thyssen did everything possible to periodically prop up Hitler's confidence in the final, successful outcome.[31] Ironically, it was von Papen's mediation that set into motion these complicated and intrigue-ridden negotiations held during the weeks of December and January and that brought forth on January 30, 1933, that very government which was destined to plunge Germany and the world at large into the worst catastrophe ever recorded.

However, the ruling class was not only confronted with having to select between two paths to a *dictatorship*. It also had the opportunity to choose between destroying the Weimar Republic and reverting to a properly functioning parliamentary system. Commensurate possibilities existed, for as prominent economists and politicians correctly pointed out in the autumn of 1932, the most profound depths of the crisis had been overcome. The November elections had demonstrated that the antiparliamentary NSDAP showed strong signs of decline, characteristics that were bound to manifest themselves still more sharply and rapidly the longer the NSDAP was kept out of the government. The elections had also revealed that sizable chunks of the Nazi voters had reverted to their old parties, the DNVP and the DVP, a process that certainly would have continued. Probably quite a sizable number of disillusioned proletarian Nazi electors would have found their way to the extreme left, the KPD, and the SPD would also have gained from an NSDAP collapse. It should be noted that the Communist party did not pose a danger to the bourgeois order. The party was still, as always, advocating the establishment of socialism in Germany but was not planning a putsch; indeed, the party hoped to win over the majority of the working class through the ripening of a revolutionary situation in the future. The ruling class, as well as the KPD leadership, realized that the KDP—with the bulk of its supporters out of work—was not even in a position to spark a general strike without the SPD and the trade unions. The ruling circles were also convinced that the leading echelons of both the SPD and the trade unions would do everything in their power to avoid a general strike.

In a nutshell, if the ruling circles had renounced the establishment of the dictatorship, this would by no stretch of the imagination have denoted the demise of the bourgeois order in Germany but rather the possibility of a return to parliamentary democracy, albeit under conditions of a weakened right wing due to the collapse of the NSDAP and due to the larger KDP that would have spearheaded a struggle-imbued left. The rejuvenated left would have been in a position, given the next economic upsurge, to attain through sustained struggle far greater concessions than had been possible between 1924 and 1929—possibly even greater than those obtained in the Arbeitsgemeinschaft agreement. Moreover, under such conditions, an armaments and expansionist drive would never have become possible in the foreign policy arena.

This was exactly what the ruling circles feared most of all. A renunciation of the dictatorship would have denoted the loss to capital of all those valuable gains that resulted from the crisis, namely, the sacrifice of the low-wage policy so important for world market competition, the forfeiture of the benefits attained through the destruction of the tariff contract system, and the radical cutbacks exacted on social services. German big capital was not willing to accept such losses.[32] Consequently it opted for Hitler and persistently pressed for the initiation of the next stage in the restoration of the old power structure and German predominance in Europe. To this end it needed the fascist dictatorship. Therefore, the worst nightmare that could have happened as far as German monopoly capital was concerned was the collapse of the Nazi party and a return to parliamentary conditions. Indeed, this apprehension accelerated the delegation of power to the Nazi party.[33]

What does all this mean with respect to the relationship between economics and politics in the destruction of the Weimar Republic?

1. There was no economic compulsion for establishing a fascist dictatorship in Germany. A renunciation of the dictatorship would by no means have denoted the ultimate economic "death" of German capitalism, as Alfred Sohn-Rethel had purported.[34] Opting for the dictatorship constituted a political decision that had *also* been economically motivated—it promised far higher profits than a return to parliamentarism.

2. This decision was taken above all by the top levels of the most

important German companies, the leaders of the landed aristocracy, and the Reichswehr generals. They were joined by most of the big bourgeoisie politicians—except where the latter had already been commensurately active—as evidenced by their approval of the Enabling Act.

3. Attempts by certain historians, above all Henry A. Turner, to absolve economic leaders from responsibility for this decision are in sharp contradiction to historical truth and have nothing whatsoever to do with scholarship.[35]

4. The reason the Hitler variant succeeded in the face of other dictatorship possibilities lay in the commitment of the elites to rigorously retain the legislative course for fear that the "illegality from above" would give an inestimable impetus to "illegality from below."[36]

The reason was not primarily, as David Abraham argued, that "German capitalism could not surmount its own internal contradictions" and that fascism thereby came to power as "the outcome of the inability of fragmented dominant groups to organize and unify their interests."[37] It was rather the inverse: the Hitler solution was accepted by most important representatives of the ruling class because they agreed, despite their internal conflicts, not to allow a return to the parliamentary system, and because they also agreed that transition to the dictatorial regime was to proceed "constitutionally."

In sum, the motives of the ruling class for the destruction of the Weimar Republic and the establishment of the fascist dictatorship were, in the final analysis, economically substantiated but by no means economically determined. The decision to exclude the subjugated classes from a share in state power and concentrate this very state power in the hands of the executive, in effect handing over power to the fascists, was a *political* decision—indeed, an expression of the *primacy of politics*.

Notes

1. Henry A. Turner, Jr., *Die GroBunternehmer und der Aufstieg Hitlers* (West Berlin: Siedler Verlag, 1985), pp. 420–22.
2. Tim Mason, "Der Primat der Politik—Politik und Wirtschaft im Nationalsozialismus," *Das Argument* 6, no. 41 (December 1966): 474.
3. Eberhard Czichon, "Der Primat der Industrie im Kartell der nationalsozialistischen Macht," *Das Argument* 3, no. 47 (July 1968): 163–92.
4. Karl Marx, *A Contribution to the Critique of Political Economy* (New York: International Publishers, 1970), pp. 20–21.
5. Karl Marx and Frederick Engels, *Selected Correspondence* (Moscow: Foreign Languages Publishing House), pp. 540–41.
6. Ibid., p. 549.

7. V. I. Lenin, *Collected Works*, Vol. 32 (Moscow: Progress Publishers, 1975), p. 83.
8. Ibid., pp. 83–84. This same idea was formulated thirty years later by Friedrich Engels with the words: "Why are we struggling for the political dictatorship of the proletariat if political power is powerless in economic terms? The power (namely state power) is also an economic potential!" (Letter to Conrad Schmidt, 27.10.1890 in *Marx Engels Weilse*, Vol. 37 (Berlin: Dietz Verlag, 1967), p. 493.
9. Lenin, *Collected Works*, Vol. 32, p. 547.
10. Quoted in Kurt Gossweiler, *GroBbanken, Industrie-Monopole, Staat: Ökonomie und Politik des staatsmonopolist-ischen Kapitalismus in Deutschland 1914–1932* (Berlin: VEB Deutscher Verlag der Wissenschaften, 1971), p. 63.
11. George W. F. Hallgarten, *Hitler, Reichswehr und Industrie: Zur Geschichte der Jahre 1918–1933* (Frankfurt: Europäische Verlagsanstalt, 1955), Doc. 5, pp. 65–66.
12. For more details refer to Gossweiler, *GroBbanken*, pp. 143–55.
13. David Abraham, *The Collapse of the Weimar Republic: Political Economy and Crisis* (New York: Holmes & Meier, 1986), p. 111. See also Wolfgang Ruge, *Das Ende von Weimar: Monopolkapital und Hitler* (Berlin: Dietz Verlag, 1983), pp. 153–56.
14. Dieter Fricke et al., eds., *Lexikon zur Parteiengeschichte: Die bürgerlichen und kleinbürgerlichen Parteien und Verbände im Deutschland* (1789–1945), Vol. 1 (Leipzig: Bibliographisches Institut Leipzig, 1983), article "Bund zur Erneuerung des Reiches (BER) 1928–1933, pp. 374–82. The call for the "Third Reich" was common to most rightist groups and circles. In their jargon the First Reich was the Holy Roman Empire and the Second Reich was the "Kaiserreich" from 1871–1918. The Third Reich was to come after overcoming the weak, odious, and only provisional Weimar Republic.
15. On the lockout see Ludwig Preller, *Sozialpolitik in der Weimarer Republik* (Stuttgart: Franz Mittelbach Verlag, 1949), pp. 402–3. Refer also to Wolfgang Ruge, *Deutschland 1917–1933* (Berlin: VEB Deutscher Verlag der Wissenschaften, 1974), 2d rev. and exp. ed., p. 325. The memorandum appeared in Veröffentlichungen (publications) des Reichsverbandes der Deutschen Industrie No. 49, December 1929, *Aufstieg oder Niedergang* (Ascent or Demise)? Deutsche Wirtschafts-und Finanzreform 1929. Eine Denkschrift des Präsidiums des Reichsverbandes der Deutschen Industrie (Selbstverlag des Reichsverbandes der Deutschen Industrie Berlin).
16. From a secret memorandum of the Truppenamt des Reichswehrministeriums "Die Abrüstungsfrage nach real-politischen Gesichtspunkten betrachtet," March 1926: "The next goal of German policy must be the recovery of the full sovereignty pertaining to those territories remaining to Germany, the rigorous fusion into the German territories which had been taken away, areas essential for sound German economic life. In the coming stage the main political development will be only to regain her European position and only must later will the restoration of her position in the world find itself on the agenda" (*Akten zur deutschen auswärtigen Politik 1918–1945. Aus dem Archiv des Auswärtigen Amtes*, series B, vol. I/1, [Göttingen: Vandenhoeck & Ruprecht], pp. 343ff.) As David Abraham in *Collapse* leaves aside the expansionist goals as one of the keynote motives for establishing the fascist dictatorship in Germany, he is bound to attain an unsatisfactory result in his research work on the causes of the destruction of the Weimar Republic.
17. Only one example is given from a considerable number of evidential sources: in May 1919, addressing officers of the Supreme Command, Lieutenant-General Groener said: "If one wants to struggle for world supremacy this must be prepared looking well ahead and with unrelenting consequence. One cannot afford to move backwards and forwards whilst implementing a peace policy but must resolutely press ahead a power policy. This, however, presupposes that one's ground both at home and abroad

remains firm and unassailable" (Wilhelm Groener, *Lebenserinnerungen. Jugend-Generalität-Weltkrieg* published by Friedrich Frhr Hiller von Gaertringen [Gottingen: Vandenhoeck & Ruprecht, 1957], p. 495; taken from: *Weltherrschaft im Visier: Dokumente zu den Europa-und Weltherrschaftsplänen des deutschen Imperialismus von der Jahrhundertwende bis Mai 1945,* published and introduced by Wolfgang Schumann and Wolfgang Ruge [Berlin: VEB Deutscher Verlag der Wissenschaften, 1975], p. 165).

18. See Alfred Milatz, *Wähler und Wahlen in der Weimarer Republik, Schriftenreihe der Bundeszentrale für politische Bildung* 66 (Bonn, 1965), 151.
19. See Kurt Gossweiler, *Aufsätze zum Faschismus, Mit einem Vorwort von Rolf Richter* (Berlin: Akademie-Verlag, 1986), pp. 262–65.
20. See the call of the KPD "Das Gesicht dem Dorfe zu," which appeared in the *Rote Fahne* of February 2, 1926, equally the peasants aid program of the KPD (Bauernhilfeprogramm der Kommunistischen Partei Deutschlands), which appeared in the *Rote Fahne* on May 22, 1931.
21. See *Vorwärts,* January 1, 1927.
22. See *Veröffentlichungen des Reichsverbandes der Deutschen Industrie,* no. 32 (Berlin: 1926), pp. 62–65.
23. As a consequence of the failure of all attempts to eliminate the Weimar Republic by force, the former royal-Prussian Minister of the Interior, F. W. v. Loebell, reached the conclusion in July 1924 that all this had demonstrated that power could only be attained through lengthy political activity, but, "and that is its only good side, the Weimar Constitution embodies parliamentary and constitutional modes of behavior which permit the restoration of a firm state structure without civil war, street battles, dictatorial force if one understands how to operate using to the full all existing constitutional possibilities" (taken from Gossweiler, *Großbanken,* pp. 262–3).
24. On October 4, 1931, an editorial in the haute bourgeois newspaper *Deutsche Allgemeine Zeitung* reached the following conclusion regarding the role of the Brüning government: "Brüning's political activity can only be summarized as constituting the advance thrust of national dictatorial, that is to say his policies accustom the people to the dictatorship making it possible for its successors to uphold their position by referring back to their predecessors."
25. Milatz, "Wähler und Wahlen," p. 151.
26. In the *DAZ* (25.12.1930) a variety of political voices of various hues such as Hjalmar Schacht, General v. Seeckt, and the arch-reactionary junker Oldenburg-Januschau could be heard advocating already at that time the involvement of the NSDAP in the government. See also Wolfgang Ruge, *Weimar-Republik auf Zeit* (Berlin: VEB Deutscher Verlag der Wissenschaften, 1969), pp. 251–62.
27. Heinrich Brüning, *Memoiren 1918–1934* (Stuttgart: Deutsche Verlags-Anstalt, 1970), p. 378.
28. For full details consult Axel Schildt, *Militärdiktatur mit Massenbasis: Die Querfrontkonzeption der Reichswehrführung um General von Schleicher am Ende der Weimarer Republik* (Frankfurt: Campus Verlag, 1981).
29. See Reinhard Neebe, *Großindustrie, Staat und NSDAP 1930–1933* (Gottingen: Vandenhoeck & Ruprecht, 1981), pp. 127–30.
30. Resistance to relinquishing the "constitutional path" also became very evident during the sixtieth members' meeting of the so-called Langnamverein, the association for the preservation of common economic interests in the Rhineland and Westphalia, in remarks made by Carl Schmitt, the crown lawyer of German big business and leading constitutional expert who opposed demands by Fritz Springorum "to move from the stage of advance notifications and preliminaries" and to implement the necessary, basic reforms "without consideration," whereby Spring-

orum perceived as particularly urgent changing the electoral law and introducing a second chamber. See *Mitteilungen des Vereins zur Wahrung der gemeinsamen wirtschaftlichen Interessen im Rheinland und Westfalen,* 1932 annual, no. 1, vol. 21.

31. See Kurt Gossweiler, *Die Röhm-Affaire: Hintergründe-Zusammenhänge-Auswirkungen* (Cologne: Pahl-Rugenstein Verlag, 1983), pp. 285–89, 561–62.

32. The *Deutsche Führerbriefe* influenced above all by the industrial magnate Paul Silverberg in November 1932 carried an article in two parts headed "Jena or Sedan?" which expressed the fear that the "state wages system—after the ebbing of the crisis waters—will again operate with a plus omen "as in May of the system period." The journal continues: "Sedan or Jena? . . . Utilizing to the full the crisis for cleansing and reorientating or muddling along from one day to the next quite certain that the same trouble will, after a longer period, crop up all over again. This is the epochal question facing the economy." See also Gossweiler, *Aufsätze,* pp. 140–41.

33. Kurt von Schröder, co-owner of the Cologne bank J. H. Stein and a close, influential friend of Himmler, declared during the Nürnberg Tribunal proceedings against IG-Farben in 1947: "After the NSDAP had incurred its first rebuff on November 6, 1932, and thereby surpassed its pinnacle of success, backing by the German economy became particularly urgent" (taken from Gossweiler, *Aufsätze,* p. 559).

34. See Alfred Sohn-Rethel, *Ökonomie und Klassenstruktur des deutschen Faschismus: Aufzeichnungen und Analysen;* published and introduced by Johannes Agnoli, Berhnard Blanke, and Niels Kadritzke (Frankfurt: Suhrkamp Verlag, 1973), pp. 126, 188. See also criticism of Sohn-Rethel in Gossweiler, *Aufsätze,* pp. 636–43. The objection against Sohn-Rethel is also valid against Knut Borchardt's thesis that the Great Depression (and thus the collapse of the Weimar Republic) was due to the unbearably (for capital) high wages (see Knut Borchardt, *Wachstum, Krisen, Handlungsspielräume der Wirtschaftspolitik.* (Gottingen: Vandenhoeck & Ruprecht, 1982). Among others, the economic development of the Federal Republic of Germany (FRG) does not substantiate this view. For the past forty years, the wage level in the FRG has (in real terms) far exceeded that of the Weimar Republic without any threat to the bourgeois parliamentary system. Rather, as a comparison between the Weimar Republic and the FRG shows, monopoly capital in the FRG is no longer politically compelled to maintain a parasitic social segment like the Junkers. The FRG has been free of this financial burden, which so heavily bore on the entire Weimar society. This difference surely contributed significantly to the FRG's steep economic upswing and to the much larger political stability vis-à-vis the Weimar Republic.

35. H. A. Turner, Jr. maintained that the above-cited work by D. Abraham possessed no proper scholarly relevance because of errors in the footnotes and sources of reference. Although it is of course appropriate to criticize such negligence, it is not appropriate to elevate such errors as the sole criterion of a sound scholarly approach. A scholarly treatment of a topic can be discerned first and foremost by examining whether the historical process had been examined in line with its true motivating forces or merely exploited for the sake of its examples in point—whether historical research hinges on a scientific conception (method) or solely on pure empiricism. A comparison along such lines between the works of Abraham and Turner would decisively favor the former. Abraham's work can be justifiably regarded as a serious analysis of German society and the driving forces of its economic and political development during the years of the Weimar Republic. Moreover, Abraham uses sound methodological and theoretical techniques. Indeed, even if one cannot agree with his findings, the nature of his analyses must cause all impartial readers to treat them with commensurate respect. The thick volume by Turner, conversely, recalls to

mind—just like the earlier, smaller collection entitled *Faschismus und Kapitalismus in Deutschland*—the work of an attorney who delves into history for but one reason, namely to find exonerating arguments for his client. In Turner's case the client is German big business. All facts considered suitable are unbelievably exaggerated; conversely, everything countering the client's interests is either completely concealed or, at best, depicted by means of an intensely extreme presentation, as wholly insignificant or invalid in the final analysis.

36. Thus the substantiation of the Center leader Kaas in a letter to Schleicher, January 26, 1933. See also Gossweiler, *Aufsätze*, p. 59.
37. Abraham, *The Collapse*, pp. 35 and 316.

Regional Elites and the Rise of National Socialism, 1920–33

Brian Peterson

In the past decade, historians have actively debated the social composition of the Nazi party's membership and electorate during the Weimar years. Most now generally agree that the social class most inclined to join and vote for the National Socialists was the petty bourgeoisie, including artisans, shopkeepers, and peasants.[1] Substantial support, however, has been shown to have come from higher social strata. Recent studies have demonstrated that residents of affluent neighborhoods, vacationers, cruise ship passengers, civil servants, and rentiers—all arguably elite—supported the National Socialist German Workers party (NSDAP).[2] On the other hand, big business and Junkers—the core groups of the ruling class in Weimar Germany—were generally disinclined to join or vote for the Nazis, although some of them gave various other kinds of direct and indirect support.[3]

The present study is primarily interested in elite support manifested by membership in and voting for the Nazi party. The thesis here is that "peripheral elites", that is, provincial aristocratic and bourgeois elements that lacked control of the central machinery of the government and economy, were the main upper-class groups giving active support to Nazism. Nazism represented to these peripheral elites an aspiration to remove control over the machinery of the national government from the hands of the large corporations and the Junker class, as well as to free the government from influence by the organized working class. They desired government policies more favorable for small-to-medium-size industrial firms, banks, and commercial enterprises.

172

Table 1
Shifts from Election to Election in Correlations
Between Percentage of Domestic Servants and Percentage Nazi Vote

Region	1924A*	1924B	1928	1930
Urban	−.08x	.06x	−.12x	.13x
Rural	.04x	.12	−.24	.27
Protestant	.09	−.08	−.09	.16
Catholic	.24	.02x	.03x	.08x
Northeast	.16x	−.09x	.20	−.30
Silesia	−.07x	.24	.17x	−.19x
Northwest	.15x	.01x	−.13x	−.05x
Central	.22	−.14x	.19	.22
Rhineland	.22	.01x	.03x	−.04x
Southwest	.62	−.07x	−.69	.37
Bavaria	.22	.02x	.02x	.04x

	1932A	1932B	1933	Number of Localities
Urban	.00x	−.08x	.16	187
Rural	−.13	−.05x	−.06x	968
Protestant	−.30	−.03x	.00x	631
Catholic	−.19	−.08x	−.18	393
Northeast	−.17	−.06x	−.02x	150
Silesia	−.21x	.02x	−.06x	78
Northwest	−.15x	.06x	−.04x	179
Central	−.15x	−.09x	−.17	169
Rhineland	−.27	.00x	−.23	194
Southwest	−.17	−.11x	−.07x	169
Bavaria	−.31	−.02x	−.09x	211

Underlining: Significant, positive initial correlation or significant shift in direction of overall party vote shift.
Initial correlation, not shift.
x: Not significant at .05 level.

These peripheral elites never became the central decision-making group within the Nazi party, a part played by "military-political-intellectuals" of a statist and totalitarian orientation. The peripheral elites, however, played a very important role as a bridge between the party's ideologues and the petty-bourgeois masses. As seen in Table 1, peripheral elites contributed to the voting surges of the NSDAP in May 1924 and again in 1930. This elite support represented an assurance to the core elites that Nazism was not truly a socialist movement and thus served to ease Hitler's accession to power in 1933.

In distinguishing peripheral elites from core elites, geography and class position were closely related, for all regions were not equal. Core regions obviously included the great metropolises, especially Berlin,

Hamburg, and Düsseldorf, the home cities of many top industrial corporations, banks, and commercial enterprises, as well as government centers. Also included would be the heavy-industry centers of the Ruhr and Upper Silesia, home to some of the wealthiest people in Germany and headquarters to the great iron, steel, and coal companies. Likewise, Protestant Prussia, the region around which Germany was unified and the home of the Junkers, the aristocratic landowners of East Elbia, must be considered a core region, in spite of its predominantly agricultural composition. The rural elite of Protestant Prussia was accustomed down to the revolution in 1918 to exercising disproportionate influence over the political and economic life of Germany as a whole. This power continued to a lesser degree in the Weimar period through Junker influence in the military and civil service and through Junker control over the dominant national farm organization—the National Rural League (Reichslandbund—RLB). The political party of the Junkers in the Weimar period was the German National People's party—DNVP.

Peripheral regions, Catholic and/or non-Prussian, including Bavaria, Rhineland-Westphalia outside the Ruhr, and southwest and central Germany, lacked the political power of Protestant Prussia and were generally areas of peasant, rather than estate, agriculture and small to medium-sized industrial firms. Elites in these areas were less wealthy than the core elite and also lacked a tradition of service to the national state.

The consciousness of elites in core and periphery was historical as well as economic. Politics in Germany in the 1920s still reflected displacement of peripheral elites in the unification process of the 1860s, and old resentments lingered. Below the surface of the large national parties that appeared dominant in 1919, many regional and sectoral parties were waiting to break out and did so in 1920–28.

Within this constellation of class forces, the Junkers were in many respects the most volatile. Until 1918 Junkers obviously were an important component of the ruling class because of their close association with the Hohenzollern state machine. After 1918 their position became less dominant. The Kaiser had always seen himself as the natural leader of the Junkers, but Friedrich Ebert, the Social Democratic president of Germany from 1918 to 1925, in spite of his role in creating the Free Corps (right-wing paramilitary organizations, many of whose members later became Nazis), was despised by the estate owners. The election as president of Germany in 1925 of Field Marshal Paul von Hindenburg partially remedied this problem for the Junkers, and Hindenburg would play a vital role both in providing special government assistance for East Elbian agriculture and in brokering the deal between the Nazis and the DNVP that brought Hitler to power.

The revolution of 1918 cost the Junkers the dominance in Prussia given them by the three-class suffrage system, where the bottom 80 percent of the taxpayers could vote for only one-third of the state parliament seats. With their loss of control over Prussia, Junkers lost their leveraged position of dominance over the German federation. The ultimate indignity of the revolution for the Junkers was witnessing the support their agricultural workers gave to radical proposals such as dividing up the estates. With the support of the Social Democratic government, the Junkers smashed the revolutionary movement in both urban and rural areas, using army and the Free Corps. Finally, after a viable independent labor movement in rural East Elbia had been destroyed, the Junkers set about convincing peasants and agricultural workers to favor the DNVP and RLB, by involving them in cooperatives for credit, marketing, and purchases, protecting the workers from inflation through in-kind wages, and fighting for higher agricultural prices and an end to government restrictions on farming.[4] The success of the estate owners in winning special protection for the purported agricultural interests of all sections of the East Elbian population brought many in the lower classes to respect Junker hegemony during the early 1920s.

In the period from 1919 to 1923, an important group of Junkers aligned themselves with Erich Ludendorff, the quartermaster general of the German army in World War I and the effective dictator of Germany from 1916 to 1918, who set up a movement to overturn the Weimar state, rule by military dictatorship, and resume the war.[5] Hitler and the early Nazis were allied with the Ludendorff Circle in a subordinate capacity. The Junkers saw Hitler as a "drummer" with the task of stirring up the Bavarian masses on behalf of a nationalist counterrevolution. The failure of this plot in Berlin in the autumn of 1923 did not prevent the outbreak of the Beerhall Putsch in Munich, but the Reichswehr (German army), which had been arming, equipping, training, and providing officers for the Sturmabteilung (SA—the paramilitary wing of the Nazi party, which was actually more important and powerful than the party itself during this early period) now pulled away. There was a breach between the traditional Junker conservatives in the DNVP and the Ludendorff-Hitler movement, and the Junkers briefly moved toward cooperation with the Weimar regime.

From 1926 on, however, the Junkers entered a profound economic crisis that eventually cost them their leadership over the peasants and agricultural workers of East Elbia and Germany generally. As their estates became less and less profitable due to falling agricultural prices and rising industrial prices, they were under pressure to increase the exploitation of their workers.[6] In the agricultural crisis of the 1870s autonomous peasant cooperatives developed in western and southern

Germany because noble landlords were unable to provide traditional types of individual assistance to nearby peasants, but in the late 1920s many Junker-dominated agricultural cooperatives in northeastern Germany collapsed, damaging the ability of the Junkers to tie the peasants to themselves through co-op loans, marketing, and other assistance.[7] Junkers demanded special government assistance for themselves through the Osthilfe (Eastern Aid) program, and this angered many west and south German peasants who felt that they also deserved aid.[8]

The result was that peasant support for the DNVP greatly diminished in 1928, particularly in western, southern, and central Germany, where peasants switched to the Country People's party (*Landvolkpartei*) based on anti-Junker elements within the RLB. After 1928 the Nazis were able to recruit many *Landvolk* voters. Nazi meetings in East Elbia were filled with workers, small peasants, and agricultural workers, with high school students, teachers, or ministers usually the only representatives of the local elite present.[9] Junkers seldom attended. Nazism spread in the Northeast as an anti-Junker, as well as anti-urban-worker and anti-Jewish, movement.

The alliance between Hitler and the Junkers was renewed, however, in the joint DNVP-NSDAP referenda against the Young Plan—an arrangement for reparations payments on loans to Germany—in 1929 and against the Social Democratic-dominated Prussian government in 1931. Many areas of complete agreement between the Nazis and Junkers did, of course, exist. Both supported militarism and expansion in the East and opposed the workers' movement. Reports of Junker agricultural congresses from the early 1920s reveal a surprisingly crude anti-Semitism.[10] Junkers supported many aspects of the Nazi economic program: autarky through high tariff barriers for agricultural products; German self-sufficiency in grain; and compulsory mixing of alcohol made from distilled fermented potatoes with gasoline to keep up farm prices and make Germany more self-reliant in energy resources.[11]

Nazis and Junkers differed sharply on the questions both of settling peasants and agricultural workers on bankrupt estates and the use of imported Polish agricultural labor.[12] Speaking at a Silesian Nazi party school, von Reibnitz asserted, "In the German East there is not the correct, healthy mixture of small and large farms." He wished to restrict large estates to only 7 to 10 percent of the agricultural land in East Elbia, comparable to the percentage in Württemberg.[13] Harwig von Rheden-Rheden, writing in the agricultural supplement of the Nazi daily, called it "shameful" that foreign migratory workers were brought in for the sugar beet harvest.[14]

In any case, Junkers were not willing to concede a leadership role to Hitler. A Nazi estimate in January 1933 was that only one Junker in ten supported the Nazis in the Frankfurt/Oder electoral district, with the remaining nine supporting the DNVP.[15] Junkers always saw themselves as the natural rulers of Germany and regarded the Hohenzollern kaiser as the crowned symbol of Junker supremacy. They saw Nazis as plebeian, South German, and, perhaps worst of all, Catholic. Wilhelm Henning, the chairman of the Association of Nationalistic Soldiers, stated: "Our preference for the Hohenzollerns will not allow us to aid in the establishment of a one-sided party domination which at least in its practical consequences might aid Roman strivings to replace this party dictatorship through an empire of a South German Catholic prince."[16] Junkers could not rid themselves of nineteenth-century categories in evaluating the Nazis. For them, Nazis were always agents of rival monarchs in Bavaria and Austria.

Junkers saw the Nazi party as inclined toward socialism and aiming to tear down traditional leadership strata. This critique certainly seemed to have considerble local justification with reference to East Elbian Nazis, although their leftism was the consequence of the anti-Nazi stance of the Junkers. Northeast German Nazis were radical by default, since the local upper classes could not be recruited to the Nazi movement in large numbers. With an almost exclusively plebeian base, Nazis in Protestant Prussia adopted a "socialist" line.[17] The radical SA was larger in proportion to total Nazi party membership in the Northeast than elsewhere in Germany, while the more elite Schutzstaffel (SS) organization was delayed in establishing itself in East Elbia.[18]

North German "radicals" and South German "conservatives" within the NSDAP had in common an anti-Junker stance. Both opposed "Kaiser fetishists": "the men of the eternal yesterday, the stubborn dogmatists of Old Prussian-conservative tradition and pigtailed privy councillors and courtier circles of the Wilhelmian epoch are still today the leaders of the German Nationalists."[19]

In the contest between the plebeian NSDAP and the Junker-dominated DNVP for political control of East Elbian agriculture, estate owners defended their hegemony by refusing to allow members of the Stahlhelm to attend Nazi meetings, coercing local newspaper owners into refusing Nazi ads, and pressuring local innkeepers to refuse to rent meeting halls to the Nazis.[20] The conservative Junker newspaper, the *Kreuz-Zeitung*, criticized at length Nazi economic and agricultural programs as "socialist," "utopian," and dangerous to the autonomy of the farmer.[21] In turn, the *Völkischer Beobachter* accused DNVP estate owners of firing Nazi agricultural workers and hiring Communists in their stead.[22]

The Nazis quickly took away the mass following of the Junkers in the rural Northeast in 1930–31. Junker control over the Stahlhelm and

RLB was shaken. New Nazi or proto-Nazi elements ousted the previous DNVP-oriented leaders and gave greater attention to peasant and agricultural worker interests.[23] Nazi agitators aroused small peasants against the "moral serfdom" involved in the traditional custom of making deep bows to estate owners.[24]

The class composition of Nazi support among farm owners in East Elbia is shown by the occupations of the NSDAP representatives elected to the Brandenburg Chamber of Agriculture in 1931: thirteen peasants and one gardener on the plebeian side, and one estate renter, two estate owners, and three owners of knights' estates on the elite side, or fourteen to six in favor of the plebeians. Only one of the elite representatives of the Nazis had an aristocratic name, suggesting that big landlords who backed the Nazis were more likely to be commoners than noblemen.[25] By contrast, DNVP-RLB slates typically had a preponderance of aristocrats.

Hostility between Junkers and Nazis was particularly acute in the Reichstag campaign of November 1932, when Hitler said of the Herrenklub, a Berlin society of 300–400 nobles and capitalists to which many ministers in von Papen's cabinet belonged: "You speak against Marxism as a class phenomenon, and you yourselves are the worst sort of class phenomenon."[26] National Socialists were even worried in October 1932 that Junkers might engage in an anti-Nazi putsch with support from Franz von Papen and Paul von Hindenburg. Nazis feared that if they did well in the November 1932 elections, reactionaries could make a coup d'état, abolish the Constitution, and rule by means of a military dictatorship that could eventually restore the Hohenzollerns to power.[27] Nazis need not have worried because they did poorly in this election, and the reactionaries instead became anxious about the large increase in the Communist vote and decided that the best thing after all would be to make Hitler chancellor in a coalition government with the DNVP, Stahlhelm, and von Papen.

In this coalition government, formed at the end of January 1933, Alfred Hugenberg, head of the DNVP, was made minister of economics and also minister of agriculture, the two ministries that most affected core elites in big business and estate agriculture.[28] Hugenberg's job was to protect core elites, who had not backed Hitler, from peripheral elites and the petty-bourgeois masses, who had. Junkers had helped to oust General Kurt von Schleicher as chancellor in January 1933 because Schleicher favored dividing up bankrupt Junker estates among workers and peasants, and Junkers knew that this was also the Nazi program. In the event, their fears came true, but not in the manner they feared. Junker estates were divided up, not by Nazis in 1933, but with the arrival of the Red Army in 1945, as a logical consequence of Junker short-sightedness in giving power to Hitler.

Junker culpability in the Nazi accession to power, however, is not the same thing as direct Junker support for Nazism. The Junkers had resisted the Hitler movement for as long as they could. Only after they had lost their mass support to the Nazis and the only alternative seemed to be a leftist government did they agree to support a cabinet in which Hitler was chancellor. By contrast, outside Protestant Prussia, National Socialists were more successful in elite recruitment. In Catholic and/or non-Prussian regions, including central and southwest Germany, Rhineland-Westphalia, and Bavaria, members of local elites more frequently joined and voted for the Nazis.

One very common practice in these peripheral regions was for aristocrats who were leaders of local peasant organizations to join the NSDAP. Over and over again, one notes the presence of Nazis with names beginning with "von" or Nazis who farmed large estates as heads of state, provincial, or county branches of the RLB or the Chamber of Agriculture.[29] Aristocratic farm leaders in peripheral regions who joined the Nazis were much less inclined to quit the party over policy disputes than were Junkers.

Of all the peripheral regions, the Southwest—the most democratic and egalitarian area of Germany—surprisingly became the area of strongest elite support for Nazism. In Baden, members of the upper classes conversed casually with newspaper vendors, saleswomen, and waiters in cafes.[30] In Württemberg, "after a good supper, a man of office and worth will sit and drink wine with a modest artisan."[31] These could be regarded as matters of style, rather than substance, since there was no accompanying willingness to give up real privileges to the masses. Nevertheless, these expressions of democratic spirit had political consequences and served to differentiate the southwestern elite from the Junkers and North Germans generally. Their democratic traditions prepared them for the mass politics of National Socialism and, unlike North German elites, they had no inbred prejudices against associating with the masses. In many respects, the Nazi movement was a continuation of the *Grossdeutsch*—Greater German—democratic movement of 1848, with its aspirations to create a Germany inclusive of Austria and other eastern territories, which had great appeal in Catholic areas of the Southwest.

Another factor in the politics of southwestern elites was the many resorts and spas in the region. Rentiers and retired people living in these spa towns had suffered greatly in the inflation of 1923 and blamed Weimar democracy for their plight. They often voted Nazi in consequence. These people were geographically marginalized as a function of their generational marginalization. Many of them had lived and worked in core sectors of Protestant Prussia, but now no longer ran companies, estates, military units, or government departments. Unlike those actively running the institutions of society, they were under no constraint in the expression of their political beliefs. They had nothing to lose by radicalism. In this, they strongly resembled the young. High school and university age children of Junkers and big businessmen also frequently joined and supported the Nazis, even while their parents remained loyal to the DNVP.[32] Thus, Nazi support came from the generational—as well as geographic and power/wealth—periphery of the elite.

Central Germany shared with the Southwest an economy based on small factories and a political structure of autonomous states *(Länder)*. The Chemnitz-Zwickau electoral district of Saxony included the Erzgebirge and the Vogtland, a region of much domestic industry and many small lace, embroidery, silk-weaving, and toy factories, and was a prime locale for support by the local elite for the Nazis.[33] Here employers felt ignored by the national government, which they accused of favoring the interests of big business.[34] The prosperity of the rest of Germany seemingly had permanently left behind the Erzgebirge-Vogtland, where the poor still sometimes ate dog meat.[35] Thuringia was similar, only somewhat less impoverished, with no city over 100,000 population and generally small factories whose owners heavily favored the Nazis.[36] Throughout central Germany, then, a high elite vote for National Socialism was produced by the relatively small size of factories and by a regional pattern of political loyalites.

In Bavaria, the homeland of National Socialism, much more elite support for Nazism existed than in Protestant Prussia, but this Bavarian elite support was restricted in scope by religion. Certainly the core groups of the Bavarian upper class—the Catholic aristocracy, not very politically influential, and the large industrialists—did not desire Hitler in power.[37] The Catholic aristocracy supported the Bavarian People's party (BVP) and hoped for a restoration of the Wittelsbachs, the former ruling family of Bavaria, and the larger industrialists mostly moved from the German People's party (DVP) to the DNVP. The BVP attacked the Nazis as favoring a "Greater Prussia," just as the Prussian loyalists attacked the Nazis for wanting a Bavarian or an Austrian to rule all of Germany.[38] In general, Nazis in Bavaria received support from elite members who had formerly voted for the liberal parties, the DNVP, or the anti-clerical peasant movement, the Bavarian Peasant Association (BBB), rather than those who had supported the Catholic and particularist Bavarian People's party.

Upper-class Bavarians gave less support to the Nazis in towns where the Catholic church held a particularly dominating position, for instance, diocesan seats such as Eichstätt. In strongly clerical towns, the middle class tended to dominate the local Nazi group, while the upper class remained aloof and loyal to the church.[39] Anticlericalism distinguished Catholic elite support for the Nazis in Bavarian peasant villages.[40] In larger towns, the Nazis were more likely to have many supporters among the stratum of notables than in smaller towns where the local elite was more traditionalist. In Catholic agricultural areas in Bavaria, elite support for the Nazis came especially from individuals who were not well-established local residents, but rather less religious and less socially conservative newcomers. Civil servants, teachers, and educated professionals represented the Nazi elite in Catholic Bavaria, rather than large property owners, who remained true to the BVP.[41] In Protestant areas of Bavaria, wealthy estate owners, industrialists, and bankers quite frequently joined the Nazis.[42]

The class structure of Rhineland-Westphalia differed markedly from that of Bavaria. The heads of huge coal and steel corporations at the summit in the Ruhr, men of strong national political influence and international economic power, suspected Nazi social radicalism. Two leading heavy industrialists, however, Fritz Thyssen and Emil Kirdorf, were members of the Nazi party for a period, although both were suspicious of its anti-big business rhetoric.[43] In the German regional structure, the Ruhr counted as metropolitan, while the rest of the Rhineland and Westphalia was merely provincial and was typified by small and medium-size business. Thus, Nazism in the Ruhr, as in Protestant Prussia, was plebeian, although not proletarian.[44] Elsewhere in the Rhineland and Westphalia, however, National Socialism often had strong support from the same types of small-factory owners who backed it in central Germany.[45]

Elite members in peripheral regions who became Nazis often were former particularists and separatists, the supporters of local dynasties that had ruled before German unification. Many had been advocates of a local state separate from the rest of Germany in the turbulent period from 1918 to 1923 when the French sponsored such movements in western and southern Germany. The thwarted will to provincial sovereignty became transformed into a desire to oust the core elites from control over the central government.

The decline of particularism was simultaneously the death of monarchism. After the 1926 referendum to expropriate the former princely houses—a referendum sponsored by the Social Democratic party (SPD) and the German Communist party (KPD) that failed but, in the process, revealed extensive antimonarchical sentiment among non-

Marxist voters—the decline of monarchism was marked among the plebeian supporters of the pro-Hohenzollern DNVP as well as among particularists backing various regional dynasties.[46]

In Hanover the turning point away from particularism was the referendum of May 18, 1924, on separate state status. Hanover had been absorbed by Prussia as a result of the Austro-Prussian War of 1866, and the supporters of the dispossessed Guelph dynasty of Hanover formed their own political party, the German Hanoverian party (DHP), known as the Guelph party. The May 1924 referendum was a failure for the Guelphs.[47] This failure had been anticipated two weeks earlier by urban elite voters for the German Hanoverian party who switched to the Nazis in the May 4 Reichstag election.[48] Losses to the DHP between 1920 and May 1924 seem to have been concentrated in towns with a strong local elite population. Movement of Guelph peasants to the Nazis was much slower, and it was only in 1932 that the Nazis finally decimated the Guelph party among the deeply conservative and localist peasant masses.[49] As the Guelph movement disintegrated, its local units urged supporters to switch to the Nazis.[50]

Similar particularist movements in the northwest German regions of Schleswig-Holstein, Schaumburg-Lippe, and Oldenburg also eventually produced an important vote for the Nazis. Schleswig-Holstein and Hanover had been absorbed by Prussia in 1866, while Oldenburg retained its independence but remained in clear danger of being swallowed by Prussia as part of the movement of government rationalization. Particularist elites wanted to be controlled neither by the Junkers of Old Prussia nor by the Socialists of New Prussia, and the Nazis advocated continued independence for Mecklenburg-Strelitz, Oldenburg, and Schaumburg-Lippe and respect for local autonomy within Prussia elsewhere. For example, in Hanover, the Nazis criticized liberal peasant leaders who supported organizations devoted to centralizing the Reich government with greater Prussian dominance.[51]

In Bavaria, separatism and particularism were gradually exhausted by a long series of rebuffs. In the immediate postwar period, numerous consultations between BVP leaders and the French with a view toward establishing a separate Bavarian or Catholic monarchy in the south of Germany came to naught. Many in the BVP had separatist aims in the events leading up to the Beerhall Putsch in November 1923. However, the most decisive demonstration of public sentiment on the issue of separatism and particularism was the vote in April 1924 on a proposal of the BVP that was backed also by the DVP and DNVP. This referendum called for a separate Bavarian state president, an upper house to the state parliament, and a simplified form by which the Constitution could be revised. The purpose of the referendum was to establish a state structure for Bavaria as much like the prewar structure as possible, which would make it a simple matter to restore the local monarchy. This referendum was held simultaneously with the Landtag election in which the Nazis first showed substantial strength in Bavaria, and the referendum failed. In deciding against particularism, many Bavarian voters also decided in favor of Nazism and switched from the parties supporting the referendum.[52]

Bavaria also had its own internal particularism. The dominant region, Upper Bavaria, centered on Munich, gave strong support to the Wittelsbachs. Other regions of Bavaria were less supportive of the Wittelsbachs. The least favorable region was predominantly Protestant Franconia, where the most intense cluster of aristocratic support for National Socialism in Germany could be found. Franconian aristocrats felt alienated from the Catholic aristocracy of South Bavaria and the Wittelsbachs, yet not, of course, integrated into the Prussian aristocracy.[53] These aristocrats had no hope of restoring a favorable position for themselves merely by returning to the past, and support for the Nazis appeared to be the best way to create an authoritarian society. Franconia was unusual as well in the level of support the Nazis had among sections of the elite other than the aristocracy, including police officials, government administrators, and small factory owners.[54] Franconian localities had given the highest votes of any localities in Germany to the DNVP in 1920, but in 1924 they became the strongest localities for the Nazis.[55]

The key center for Nazi strength in Franconia—Coburg—had belonged to Thuringia until after the war and never quite fit into Bavaria. As the *Kreuz–Zeitung* drolly put it, Bavaria was so reactionary that it did not allow Coburgers to grill their beloved Bratwürste.[56] Dominated by a castle dating from the twelfth century, Coburg was a city in thrall to the past. The streets were filled with signs indicating "Suppliers to the Duke," including jewelers, barbers, druggists, and bookdealers. The local dukes had deliberately retarded the development of transportation and industry in the area so that their hunting grounds and castles would be peaceful. The townspeople felt grateful to their duke for supplying them with wide avenues, parks, and especially theaters, for Coburgers were famous for their love of plays, opera, and music. In June 1929 Coburg became the first of many "Residence Cities"—cities of residence for a territorial ruler—across Germany's small states to elect a Nazi government. The former duke, Karl Eduard, lived in Coburg and led the movement toward the Nazis.[57] The Nazi slogans in this election formed a revealing mélange of nationalism, particularism, and anti-Semitism: "Germany for the Germans! Coburg for the Coburgers! And to Palestine with those who belong there!"[58] At the end of 1929, Duke Karl Eduard appeared at the Nazi rally and in April 1932 endorsed Hitler for president.[59] Thus, the multiple levels of particularism in Coburg—against Thuringia, Bavaria, and the national government—made this a stronghold of Nazism.

Other areas of Bavaria also showed centrifugal tendencies. The Palatinate, geographically separated from the rest of Bavaria, was under Allied occupation, and the French and Belgians encouraged a local separatist movement designed to set up a buffer state they could permanently dominate. Conflicts here between the occupation troops and separatists, on the one hand, and loyal Germans, on the other, contributed to radicalization in Pirmasens, and in the winter of 1924 a group of separatists was lynched by the local population.[60] Pirmasens, a center for shoe manufacture with many small factories, served both as a locus of separatism in the 1920–23 period and one of the strongest cities for the Nazis from 1929 on.[61] There is a likelihood that both separatists and antiseparatists ended up in the Nazi camp.

Particularism and separatism also promoted elite support for National Socialism in other areas of the Southwest. Nazi voting totals were often highest in university towns and former residence cities, usually nonindustrial and nostalgic for the glories of their independent past. A disproportionate number of the well-to-do, especially professors, civil servants, professionals, and military officers, lived in such towns.[62] Examples of cities in the Southwest where the Nazis won a strong elite support included Marburg, a reactionary university town in Hesse, with a long history of conservative and anti-Semitic voting, and an educated Nazi local leadership;[63] Kassel, a residence city in Hesse, where the Nazi vote increased dramatically in 1924;[64] and Heidelberg, Baden, where in 1930, out of thirty-one Nazis on the city council, fourteen were educated professionals, including judges, doctors, architects, and engineers.[65] In Hesse, the Nazis attracted the "Old Nassauers," loyal to the dynasty displaced by the Prussians in 1866, just as these individuals had also flocked to separatism during the period of French occupation. During 1923, some Nazi party members in Frankfurt am Main simultaneously were active in the "Blücher Association," a paramilitary organization that sought an independent South German state under Wittelsbach rule and received funding from the French.[66] Of course, these separatist activities were not part of Hitler's program; they illustrate instead the confused ideological world of National Socialism on the periphery.

Microparticularism—loyalty to a single town or a tiny region—was a factor in support for Nazism by local elites in Thurginia. Because merger meant losing their status as capitals, cities that had been capitals of very small states resisted being merged into the larger state of Thuringia in 1920. Weimar became the capital of the united Thuringian state, but other former ducal capitals lost their function. This brought with it a loss of court patronage for local merchants, an end to the flow of tax moneys into the city's infrastructure, and a decline in such cultural amenities as ducal theaters and libraries. Gotha, for example, lost its Grand Duke's Court, garrison, and government ministries.[67]

Central German particularism was agitated again in 1928 when the governments of Saxony and Thuringia began exploratory steps toward merger with each other, and in 1929 when the German Democratic party (DDP) and SPD urged fusion with Prussia.[68] By an odd dialectic, the most parochial areas of Germany became the strongest bases of support for the movement that, once in power, would institute the most extreme policy of centralization—*Gleichschaltung*, the subordination of states to the national government.

Particularist support for National Socialism resulted from a complex process of "deprovincialization" that had economic, social, and political roots. Particularism was grounded in a localist economy, especially agrarian, with support from artisans, professionals, and banks serving local clients. As the German economy increasingly focused on national and international markets, the strength of economic localism declined. Another blow to provincialism was World War I. The experience of serving in military units with men from all over Germany, the growth of national consciousness both on the battlefield and on the home front, and the shared deprivation as a result of the peace settlement all served to undermine localism.

The loss of the war, to be sure, discredited Junker, Prussian, and Hohenzollern leadership, and during the 1919–23 period caused an upsurge of separatism. Once separatism irrevocably failed with Gustav Stresemann's restoration of effective central government in 1923–24, localist elites turned their attention back to the problem of controlling the national government in their own interest. The Weimar Republic, simply by abolishing all German monarchies, helped to delegitimate monarchism. All of these factors combined to send many particularists to the Nazis in the crisis elections of 1924 and 1930.

Besides particularists, Nazism received much support from liberal members of peripheral elites who had supported the DDP and DVP and always favored a strong central government. Liberals who became Nazis hearkened back to the *grossdeutsch* tradition of the German unification movement and welcomed any steps that would bring Austria and Germany together. These formerly liberal Nazis had several traits in common with former particularists who became Nazis. Both liberals and particularists were hostile to the power of Junkers and big business, and both were willing to join a *völkisch*—populist-racialist—movement and associate fraternally with the masses. These qualities allowed them to unite with one another and with the huge Nazi following among the lower middle class in order to reshape Germany. The grandsons of the Guelphs and the 48ers joined ranks to contest Bismarck's legacy with the grandsons of the Junkers and the Krupps.

Precedents existed in other countries for the kind of regional restructuring represented by the Nazi movement. In spite of the enormous differences in ideology, organization, and the human costs of the outcomes, structural similarities existed between the electoral coalition of National Socialism and that of Jacksonian Democracy in America from the 1820s to the 1840s. In both cases, the new movement represented a significant regional broadening of the traditional base of national power coming two generations after the founding of the new state. In both cases, peripheral elites (westerners in the American case) united with plebeian elements of the core regions to transform traditional political alignments. In both cases, core elites were divided into two major factions that had, at least temporarily, exhausted their potential for political leadership, industrialists and Junkers in Germany and northern merchants and Tidewater planters in America. In both cases, also, the agrarian and traditionalist half of the core elite was more willing to give support to the new movement than was the urban and modernist half.[69]

While Nazi supporters among the provincial elites hoped to create a truly national ruling class for Germany in which they could play a leading role, instead, by placing power in the hands of an irresponsible dictatorship, they brought calamity. Their banal political aim of broadening the regional basis of power was incommensurable with the consequences that ensued.

Methodological Appendix

County (*Kreis*) level analysis serves as the statistical base for this study, with material from 1,155 counties and towns. The percentage of domestic servants in the population is used as a substitute indicator for the percentage of affluent. For purposes of regional analysis, Germany has been broken up into seven areas. Three regions of Protestant Prussia are considered as the core: the Northeast, the heart of Old Prussia, and the preeminent Junker region, including Brandenburg, Pomerania, East Prussia, Grenzmark Posen-West Prussia, and the non-Prussian states of Mecklenburg-Schwerin and Mecklenburg-Strelitz; Silesia, with a predominance of estate agriculture, but the complicating factor of Catholic and industrial Upper Silesia; and the Northwest, including the Prussian provinces of Hanover and Schleswig-Holstein and the autonomous states of Brunswick, Oldenburg, Schaumburg-Lippe, Hamburg, Bremen, and Lübeck. Four regions formed the periphery: Central Germany, a Protestant, industrialized area consisting of Saxony, Thuringia, Anhalt, and the Prussian province of Saxony; Rhineland-Westphalia, Catholic, industrial provinces of Prussia; the Southwest, a region of mixed religion and light industry, including Baden, Württemberg, Hesse, Waldeck, Hohenzollern, and the Bavarian province of the Palatinate and the Prussian province of Hesse-Nassau; and Bavaria, the heavily Catholic and particularist homeland of the National Socialist movement. The election and census data used in this essay are from the Inter-University Consortium for Political Research at the University of Michigan.[70]

Domestic servants are a valid indicator of elite presence, since only one German family in ten could afford to employ a servant.[71] Of the 1.4 million domestic servants in Germany in 1925, three-fourths lived in the homes of their employers. Young women under the voting age comprised a majority of domestic servants, and those who qualified to vote seldom actually voted or else voted as their employers indicated. The rate of voting of domestic servants was the lowest of any major occupational group. Domestic servants could form independent political opinions only with difficulty simply because they seldom spent much time outside their employers' homes. They were expected to work fourteen hours a day, with only a half day off on Sundays. Servants had less free time than any other workers.[72] A good example of a Nazi domestic servant was Frau Friederike Brzoska of Wollin, East Prussia, who was eighty years old in 1932 and had been working for a Nazi physician since 1922. She accompanied him to party meetings in all weather and knit socks for the SA.[73] Her support for the Nazis was an aspect of her servility, rather than representing an independent class consciousness. This argues that these statistical correlations show not the direct impact of domestic servant voting so much as an indication of the voting pattern of the elite that employed the servants.

Correlations used in this essay are Pearson's r, generated by the DSTAT-2 program. Correlation shifts show the change from election to election. Rules of interpretation are simple. In order to be significant, the correlation shift should be statistically significant at the .05 level and should be moving in the same direction as the overall vote for that particular party. For instance, in rural localities between May and December 1924, the Nazi correlation with domestic servants went up .12, a statistically significant shift, but the overall Nazi vote was declining from 6.9 percent to 3.2 percent. This means that it was not likely that the affluent vote for the Nazis was increasing, but simply that the affluent were not deserting the Nazis in such large proportions as other groups in the population. However, the significant shift from December 1924 to 1928 of -.28 took place as the overall Nazi vote was declining from 3.2 percent to 2.8 percent, indicating that in this election affluent voters were deserting the Nazis faster than voters generally. Thus, this correlation shift is underlined.

Notes

1. Thomas Childers, *The Nazi Voter: The Social Foundations of Fascism in Germany, 1919–1933* (Chapel Hill: University of North Carolina Press, 1983); Rudolf Heberle, *From Democracy to Nazism: A Regional Case Study on Political Parties in Germany* (Baton Rouge: Louisiana State University Press, 1945); Jerzy Holzer, *Parteien und Massen: Die politische Krise in Deutschland, 1928–1930* (Wiesbaden: Franz Steiner Verlag, 1975); Michael H. Kater, *The Nazi Party: A Social Profile of Members and Leaders, 1919–1945* (Cambridge, MA: Harvard University Press, 1983); Claus-Dieter Krohn and Dirk Stegmann, "Kleingewerbe und National-Sozialismus in einer agrarisch-mittelständischen Region: Das Beispiel Lüneburg 1930–1939," *Archiv für Sozialgeschichte* 17 (1977): 41–98; Klaus Schaap, *Die Endphase der Weimarer Republik im Freistaat Oldenburg 1928–1933* (Dusseldorf: Droste Verlag, 1978); Gerhard Stoltenberg, *Politische Strömungen im schleswig-holsteinischen Landvolk 1918–1933* (Dusseldorf: Droste Verlag, 1962); Heinrich August Winkler, *Mittelstand, Demokratie und Nationalsozialismus: Die politische Entwicklung von Handwerk und Kleinhandel in der Weimarer Republik* (Cologne: Verlang Kiepenheuer & Witsch, 1972); "From Social Protectionism to National Socialism: The German Small-Business Movement in Comparative Pespective," *Journal of Modern History* 48, no. 1 (March 1976), and "Mittelstandsbewegung oder Volkspartei? Zur sozialen Basis der NSDAP," in Wolfgang Schieder, ed., *Faschismus als soziale Bewegung: Deutschland und Italien im Vergleich* (Hamburg: Hoffmann and Campe Verlag, 1976); Peter Wulf, *Die politische Haltung des schleswig-holsteinischen Handwerks 1928–1932* (Cologne: Westdeutsche Verlag, 1969); Wolfgang Zapf, *Wandlungen der deutschen Elite: Ein Zirkulationsmodell deutscher Führungsgruppen 1919–1961* (Munich: R. Piper Verlag, 1965); Hansjörg Zimmermann, *Wählerverhalten und Sozialstruktur im Kreis Herzogtum Lauenberg 1918–1933* (Neumünster: Karl Wachholtz Verlag, 1978); Zdenek Zofka, *Die Ausbreitung des Nationalsozialismus auf dem Lande: Eine regionale Fallstudie zur politischen Einstellung der Landbevölkerung in der Zeit des Aufstiegs und der Machtergreifung der NSDAP 1928–1936* (Munich: Stadtarchiv, 1979).

2. Richard F. Hamilton, *Who Voted for Hitler?* (Princeton: Princeton University Press, 1982); see also Childers, *Nazi Voter,* regarding civil servants and rentiers.

3. Henry Ashby Turner, Jr., *German Big Business and the Rise of Hitler* (New York: Oxford University Press, 1985). Older works indicating some of the kinds of support given to Nazism by big business include George W. F. Hallgarten, *Hitler, Reichswehr und Industrie* (Frankfurt: Europäische Verlagsanstalt, 1955); Eberhard Czichon, *Wer verhalf Hitler zur Macht? Zum Anteil der deutschen Industrie an der Zerstörung der Weimarer Republik* (Cologne, 1967); Arthur Schweitzer, *Big Business in the Third Reich* (Bloomington: Indiana University Press, 1964); Nicos Poulantzas, *Fascism and Dictatorship: The Third International and the Problem of Fascism* (London: NLB, 1974).

4. *Germania*, March 29, 1922, evening ed.; *Frankfurter Zeitung*, October 19, 1924, first morning ed. and May 11, 1928, first morning ed.; *Die rote Fahne*, December 21, 1924; *Vorwärts*, May 16, 1924, evening ed. and January 27, 1927, evening ed.; *Leipziger Volkszeitung*, April 9, 1920; Fritz Brehmer, "Die Landarbeiterbewegung in der Provinz Pommern," Inaug. diss., Greifswald University, 1923, p. 99; and Richard N. Hunt, *German Social Democracy, 1918–1933* (Chicago: Quadrangle, 1970), p. 121.

5. Bruno Thoss, *Der Ludendorff-Kreis 1919–1923* (Munich: Stadtarchiv, 1978); Gerst Borst, "Die Ludendorffbewegung 1914–1961," Inaug. diss., University of Munich, 1969; Andreas Werner, "SA and NSDAP. SA: 'Wehrverband,' 'Parteitruppe' oder 'Revolutionsarmee'? Studien zur Geschichte der SA und der NSDAP 1920–1933," Inaug. diss., University of Nuremberg, 1964; Heinrich Bennecke, *Hitler und die SA* (Munich: Günter Olzog Verlag, 1962); Dietrich Orlow, *The History of the Nazi Party: 1919–1933* (Pittsburgh: University of Pittsburgh Press, 1969); F. L. Carsten, *The Reichswehr and Politics, 1918 to 1933* (Oxford: Clarendon Press, 1966); Harold J. Gordon, Jr., *Hitler and the Beerhall Putsch* (Princeton: Princeton University Press, 1972); and Robert G. L. Waite, *Vanguard of Nazism: The Free Corps Movement in Postwar Germany, 1918–1923* (New York: Norton, 1969).

6. *Frankfurter Zeitung*, July 25, 1928, first morning ed.; Max Sering, *Die deutsche Landwirtschaft (unter volks- und weltwirtschaftlichen Gesichtspunkten)* (Berlin: Paul Parey, 1932), pp. 46, 49.

7. Allan Stanley Kovan, "The Reichs-Landbund and the Resurgence of Germany's Agrarian Conservatives, 1919–1923," Ph.D. diss., University of California-Berkeley, 1972, p. 145; Pankraz Fried, "Die Sozialentwicklung im Bauerntum und Landvolk," in *Handbuch der bayerischen Geschichte*, vol. 2, part 2 (Munich: C. H. Beck'sche Verlag, 1973), p. 753; *Die rote Fahne*, January 30, 1926; *Frankfurter Zeitung*, February 2, 1927, first morning ed.; and *Vorwärts*, March 1, 1930.

8. Bruno Buchta, *Die Junker und die Weimarer Republik: Charakter und Bedeutung der Osthilfe in den Jahren 1928–1933* (East Berlin: VEB Deutscher Verlag der Wissenschaft, 1959); Herman Lebovics, *Social Conservatism and the Middle Classes in Germany, 1914–1933* (Princeton: Princeton University Press, 1969), p. 41; Dieter Gessner, "The Dilemma of German Agriculture during the Weimar Republic," in Richard Bessel and E. J. Feuchtwanger, eds., *Social Change and Political Development in Weimar Germany* (Totowa, NJ: Barnes & Noble, 1981), pp. 142–43; Alexander Gerschenkron, *Bread and Democracy in Germany* (New York: Howard Fertig, 1966; reprint of 1943 original), p. 145; *Vorwärts*, May 17, 1930; and *Frankfurter Zeitung*, March 16, 1931, evening ed.

9. *Völkischer Beobachter*, January 24, 1928, February 9, 1928, June 6, 1928, June 15, 1928, and October 14/15, 1928; and *Frankfurter Zeitung*, September 9, 1930, evening ed.

10. *Kreuz-Zeitung*, February 18, 1920, morning ed.; and *Vorwärts*, February 18, 1920, morning ed.

11. *Völkischer Beobachter*, February 26, 1932.

12. *Kreuz-Zeitung*, January 28, 1929, evening ed.; *Völkischer Beobachter*, September 13, 1932, and December 18/19, 1932, and *Vorwärts*, July 27, 1927, evening ed.

13. Quoted in *Völkischer Beobachter*, February 12, 1932.

14. *Völkischer Beobachter*, February 16, 1932.

15. *Völkischer Beobachter*, January 4, 1933.

16. Quoted in *Kreuz-Zeitung*, February 21, 1933.

17. *Völkischer Beobachter*, July 7, 1929, February 15, 1930, and April 4, 1931; *Vorwärts*, July 4, 1930; *Frankfurter Zeitung*, April 3, 1931; second morning ed. See also Childers, *Nazi Voter*, p. 120; Orlow, *Nazi Party*, pp. 56–88; Jeremy Noakes, *The Nazi Party in Lower Saxony, 1921–1933* (London: Oxford University Press, 1971), pp. 71–

81; and Reinhard Kühnl, *Die national-sozialistische Linke 1925–1930* (Meisenheim am Glan: Verlag Anton Hain, 1966).

18. SA membership in proportion to party membership was highest in the following provinces as of January 1, 1930: East Prussia, Brandenburg, Hessen-Nord, Pomerania. See *Völkischer Beobachter*, February 15, 1930. On the late start of the SS in the northeast: Robert Lewis Koehl, *The Black Corps: The Structure and Power Struggles of the Nazi SS* (Madison: University of Wisconsin Press, 1983), p. 54.

19. *Völkischer Beobachter*, July 7, 1928.

20. Ibid., August 13, 1927, March 30, 1928, July 13/14, 1928, July 16, 1928, and October 26, 1932.

21. *Kreuz Zeitung*, March 22, 1930; July 11, 1930, second ed. and July 27, 1930.

22. *Völkischer Beobachter*, October 26, 1932.

23. *Frankfurter Zeitung*, December 31, 1931, evening/first morning ed.

24. *Völkischer Beobachter*, January 23, 1932.

25. Ibid., November 28, 1931.

26. Quoted in ibid., October 13, 1932.

27. Ibid., October 1, 1932.

28. Turner, *Big Business*, p. 313.

29. Such individuals were mentioned in the *Völkischer Beobachter* for the following regions: Palatinate, February 16, 1932; Eschwege, Hesse, February 11, 1932; Rhineland, April 10/11, 1932; Saxony, February 6, 1932; and Magdeburg-Anhalt, December 8, 1931.

30. *Frankfurter Zeitung*, November 28, 1924, first morning ed.; and November 29, 1924, first morning ed.

31. Ibid., November 12, 1924, first morning ed.

32. Nazis received strong support among fraternity members in East Elbian universities (*Völkischer Beobachter*, July 28/29, 1929). It was even said that Hugenberg's son in Munich supported the NSDAP (*Frankfurter Zeitung*, December 19, 1929, evening ed.). Many sons of members of the Building and Landowners' Association—a group tightly affiliated with the Economic Party— supported the Nazis (*Frankfurter Zeitung*, August 18, 1930, morning ed.).

33. *Kreuz Zeitung*, June 24, 1930; Heinrich Brandler, *Die Aktion gegen den Kapp-Putsch in Westsachsen* (Kommunistische Partei Deutschlands, 1920), p. 55; Ernst Heilmann, *Geschichte der Arbeiterbewegung in Chemnitz und dem Erzgebirge* (Chemnitz: Landgrat, n.d. [1910?]), p. 59.

34. *Frankfurter Zeitung*, April 22, 1932, evening/first morning ed.

35. *Vorwärts*, February 14, 1920, morning ed.; May 7, 1925, morning ed.; November 24, 1929, morning ed.

36. Turner, *Big Business*, pp. 194–95.

37. Axel Schnorbus, "Wirtschaft and Gesellschaft in Bayern vor dem Ersten Weltkrieg (1890–1914)," in *Bayern im Umbruch: Die Revolution von 1918, ihre Voraussetzungen, ihr Verlauf und ihre Folgen*, ed. Karl Bosl (Munich: R. Oldenbourg, 1969), p. 148.

38. Geoffrey Pridham, *Hitler's Rise to Power: The Nazi Movement in Bavaria, 1923–1933* (New York: Harper, 1973), p. 82.

39. In the 1930 Reichstag election, Nazis won 18 percent in Eichstätt, but in another diocesan seat, Passau, where the population was 95 percent Catholic, the Nazis won 31 percent. One difference was that Passau was close to the Austrian border and hence more nationalistic and *Grossdeutsch* in its attitudes (Pridham, *Bavaria*, pp. 140, 159); Elke Fröhlich, "Die Partei auf lokale Ebene. Zwischen gesellschaftlicher Assimilation und Veränderungsdynamik," in Gerhard Hirschfeld and Lothar Ket-

tenacker, eds., *Der "Führerstaat": Mythos und Realität. Studien zur Struktur und Politik des Dritten Reichs* (Stuttgart: Klett-Cotta, 1981), p. 262.

40. Oskar Maria Graf, *Unruhe um einen Friedfertigen* (Munich: Süddeutscher Verlag, 1975, first edition 1947), p. 309.

41. Zofka, *Ausbreitung*, p. 104.

42. Frölich, "Die Partei," p. 263.

43. Turner, *Big Business*, pp. 91, 95, 145.

44. Wilfried Bühnke, *Die NSDAP im Ruhrgebiet, 1920–1933* (Bonn: Verlag Neue Gesellschaft, 1974), pp. 174, 179, 199; and Herbert Kühr, *Parteien und Wahlen im Stadt- und Landkreis Essen in der Zeit der Weimarer Republik* (Dusseldorf: Droste Verlag, 1973), pp. 152, 155.

45. Turner, *Big Business*, pp. 198–201.

46. Ulrich Schüren, *Der Volksentscheid zur Fürstenenteignung 1926* (Dusseldorf, Droste Verlag, 1978).

47. *Germania*, May 14, 1924, morning ed.; and Noakes, *Lower Saxony*, p. 118.

48. Noakes, *Lower Saxony*, p. 117.

49. *Völkischer Beobachter*, May 26/27, 1929, and May 18, 1932; Noakes, *Lower Saxony*, p. 154.

50. On the dissolution of the Guelph party in the city of Braunschweig in late 1930, see *Vorwärts*, March 3, 1931.

51. *Völkischer Beobachter*, March 2, 1928; and *Kreuz Zeitung*, August 8, 1928, evening ed.

52. *Germania*, April 8, 1924, evening ed.

53. Rainer Hambrecht, *Der Aufstieg der NSDAP in Mittel- und Oberfranken (1925–1933)* (Nuremberg: Stadtarchiv, 1976), pp. 256, 537.

54. Hambrecht, *Mittel- und Oberfranken*, pp. 256, 258, 308.

55. Jürgen Falter, Thomas Lindenberger, and Siegfried Schumann, *Wahlen und Abstimmungen in der Weimarer Republik: Materialien zum Wahlverhalten 1919–1933* (Munich: C. H. Beck, 1986), pp. 132–33.

56. *Kreuz-Zeitung*, October 14, 1921, evening ed.

57. *Frankfurter Zeitung*, August 28, 1932, evening/first morning ed.; and *Völkischer Beobachter*, June 25, 1929, and September 8, 1929.

58. Hambrecht, *Mittel- und Oberfranken*, p. 349.

59. Ibid., p. 537; and *Kreuz-Zeitung*, April 2, 1932.

60. Hans Hartmann, "Die Pirmasenser Schuhindustrie in der Kriegs- und Nachkriegszeit," Ph.D. diss., University of Munich, 1935, pp. 12, 37–39, 43, 48, 50, 53; *Frankfurter Zeitung*, January 15, 1924, first morning ed.; February 13, 1924, first morning ed.; and February 24, 1924, first morning ed.

61. *Statistik des Deutschen Reichs*, vol. 315, part 2, *Die Wahlen zum Reichstag am 4. Mai 1924 und am 7. Dez. 1924* (Berlin: Verlag Reimar Hobbing, 1928), p. 60.

62. *Frankfurter Zeitung*, November 12, 1924, first morning ed.

63. Eberhart Schön, *Die Entstehung des Nationalsozialismus in Hessen* (Meisenheim am Glan: Verlag Anton Hain, 1972), p. 82.

64. Schön, *Hessen*, p. 161; *Frankfurter Zeitung*, July 20, 1928, evening ed.

65. Johnpeter Horst Grill, *The Nazi Movement in Baden, 1920–1945* (Chapel Hill: University of North Carolina Press, 1983), p. 196.

66. Schön, *Hessen*, pp. 39, 76; and *Frankfurter Zeitung*, July 4, 1930, evening ed.

67. *Kreuz Zeitung*, October 14, 1921, evening ed.; Donald R. Tracey, "The Development of the National Socialist Party in Thuringia, 1924–1930," *Central European History* 7, no. 1 (March 1975): 24.

68. *Germania*, June 15, 1928, morning ed.; and *Kreuz Zeitung*, April 30, 1928, evening ed.

69. Obviously, the differences between Jacksonian Democracy and National Socialism are qualitatively more important than the similarities. Jackson was for states' rights and limited government, while Hitler favored *Gleichschaltung* and totalitarianism. Whereas Jackson idly wished for the death penalty for Abolitionist writers, Hitler actually imposed concentration camps, torture, and execution on Marxists.

Both Jacksonian Democracy and National Socialism represented movement away from Honoratiorenparteien—parties of notables, dominated by the traditional elite—to modern, mass parties with a professional party leadership and more organized linkages to the rank-and-file party membership and electorate, and both brought with them a substantial increase in voting participation.

Just as National Socialism served to protect capitalism by creating a new pattern of electoral forces, so Jacksonian Democracy served to perpetuate slavery by bringing northern plebeians into a coalition with southern planters. Just as National Socialism rallied the petty-bourgeois masses around a program of anti-Semitism, so Jacksonian Democracy used antiblack measures to win the support of northern urban Irish immigrants.

Both movements appealed to younger, rather than older, men, and, among the elites, to the less established rather than to the better established. Both movements were heartily opposed, at least in rhetoric, to the power of "finance capital." Neither movement was particularly strong among urban industrial workers, and both played on male chauvinist, militarist, and antimodern themes. Just as National Socialism sought expansion in the East at the expense of the Slavic peoples, so too the Jacksonians promoted Indian Removal for the sake of white settlement.

A revealing distinction between the two movements was their relationship to Freemasonry. Jackson was a Mason and the target of agitation by the Antimasonic party, which was strong in some areas of the United States in 1828, while the Nazis were themselves devoted anti-Masons.

Arthur M. Schlesinger, Jr., *The Age of Jackson* (Boston: Little, Brown, 1953); Robert V. Remini, *The Election of Andrew Jackson* (Philadelphia: Lippincott, 1963); Edward Pessen, *Jacksonian America: Society, Personality, and Politics* (Homewood, IL: Greenwood Press, 1978); Harry L. Watson, *Jacksonian Politics and Community Conflict: The Emergence of the Second American Party System in Cumberland County, North Carolina* (Baton Rouge: Louisiana State University Press, 1981); Arthur W. Thompson, *Jacksonian Democracy on the Florida Frontier* (Gainesville: Florida State University Press, 1961); Donald B. Cole, *Jacksonian Democracy in New Hampshire, 1800–1851* (Cambridge, MA: Harvard University Press, 1970); Sean Wilentz, *Chants Democratic: New York City and the Rise of the American Working Class, 1788–1850* (New York: Oxford University Press, 1984), pp. 172–216; Alvin Kass, *Politics in New York State, 1800–1830* (Syracuse: Syracuse University Press, 1965); and Lee Benson, *The Concept of Jacksonian Democracy: New York as a Test Case* (Princeton: Princeton University Press, 1961).

70. Inter-University Consortium for Political Research, University of Michigan. These statistics come from: *Statistik des Deutschen Reichs*, vols. 402–12, *Volks-, Berufs-, und Betriebszählung vom 16. Juni 1925* (Berlin: Verlag Reimar Hobbing, 1927–29).

71. For another study that uses the presence of servants as an indicator of the elite status of the household, see Emmanuel LeRoy Ladurie, *Carnival in Romans* (New York: George Braziller, 1979), p. 5.

72. *Statistik des Deutschen Reichs*, vol. 402, part 2, p. 224; Herbert Tingsten, *Political Behavior: Studies in Election Statistics* (Totowa, NJ: Bedminster Press, 1963), p. 163; Eberhard Schultz, ed., *Dokumente und Materialien zur Geschichte der Arbeiterbewegung im Bezirk Halle*, Vol. 1 (Halle: Mitteldeutsche Druckerei Freiheit, 1965),

p. 87; *Deutsche Tagezeitung*, July 12, 1925; Seymour Martin Lipset, *Political Man* (Garden City, NY: Doubleday, 1963), p. 263; *Vorwärts*, March 10, 1929, morning ed., and September 9, 1931, morning ed.

73. *Völkischer Beobachter*, December 11/12, 1932.

The NSDAP as an Alternative Elite for Capitalism in Crisis

John D. Nagle

The rise of German fascism presents a question common to most fascist movements that have eventually achieved state power: namely, how is it that an extremist political elite is able to evolve from a political position of marginality, distrust, and disinterest vis-à-vis established social elites to a position in which political entrepreneurs from established elites are able to hand over state power to this same extremist elite?

Three Developmental Hurdles

This is a problem of general interest for the study of fascism, since most capitalist democracies have fascist "pretenders" as a more or less standard feature of the political landscape. From Louis Bonaparte and his Society of December 10 in the Second French Republic through the Moseley and Quisling movements of the 1930s to the current National Front in Britain, Jean-Marie Le Pen's National Front in France, and the Lyndon Larouche sect in the United States, fascist leadership groups have presented themselves as an alternative political elite and offered their services to established centers of power in business, state, and military sectors.[1]

Fascism as a political-elite alternative for a capitalist society faces several developmental or evolutionary hurdles before it can achieve state power. Of the many fascist pretenders, only a few have succeeded in achieving this goal. Only some have evolved beyond political marginality; fewer still have convinced established elites within society or elites representing foreign powers that they are useful and/or necessary for dealing with some crisis those established centers of power are unable or insufficiently able to deal with using their own resources. This could be called the recognition problem, the necessity for fascism to make its services attractive or even vital to the interests of important established centers of power.

A second problem for fascist pretender movements can be called the assurance (or reassurance) issue: a fascist elite must be able to assure established elites that in collaborating with this radical alternative political elite, or in helping it to achieve state power, the main interests of these established elites will themselves not be attacked. This is a problem not to be taken lightly, since the fascist movement has differentiated itself in various ways from the norms and rhetoric of mainstream elites, and the fascist elite may be viewed as insufficiently reliable or as potentially revolutionary, certainly as less calculable than more familiar political vehicles for safeguarding the established social order.

A third hurdle might be termed the normalization issue: established elites must have adequate reason to believe that, after some initial period of extraordinary service by the fascist movement, to accomplish certain critical tasks, the fascist political elite will over time "settle down" or transform its behavior to conform to more "normal" standards for a political elite in capitalist society.[2] This is a longer term expectation, and may be subordinated to the more immediate needs for short-term crisis solving and reassurance described above, but it is important that existing elites, if they are to undertake actions that support the gaining of state power by a fascist pretender elite, have some plausible reasons for thinking that in the long run the fascist leadership will "mature" into a more normal governing elite, meeting the more normal definitions of leadership recruitment, style, and career. Although these evolutionary hurdles may generally be sequenced as suggested here, there may be considerable overlap in time and some of these issues may reappear at rather separated critical points in the development of the antidemocratic political project that brings fascism to power, as well as within the period of fascist rule.

The Recognition Problem

The clearest element of the development character of the National Socialist German Workers party (NSDAP) in Weimar rests with its breakthrough as a mass mobilization vehicle after 1928, and its defeat of the Protestant bourgeois parties (The German Democratic party— DDP, the German People's party—DVP, the German National People's party—DNVP, and the Wirtschaftspartei—WP or Economy party) as political rivals. This also put the NSDAP in position to play a necessary and indispensable role in the anti-democracy projects proposed by established political elites.

With the decline in strength of the liberal DDP and the moderate-conservative DVP even before the economic collapse of 1929, certain bourgeois political elites were becoming more and more hostile to the continuation of the Weimar system, which is to say parliamentary democracy.

The rise in the mid-1920s of the WP party at the expense of the German Democratic party was an early signal of growing dissatisfaction among middle-class voters. It offered opportunities for political elites who represented these voters to take positions more openly hostile to Weimar democracy (the Weimar system), and to engage in political strategies intended to undermine the functioning of the democratically elected Reichstag. The Wirtschaftspartei drew heavily from former Democrats, and made its early gains at their expense, attacking the Democratic party as a party of big business, big banks, Jews, and collaborators of the Social Democrats.[3]

The 1926 Görlitz program of the WP called for a revision of the constitution, which would enable a strong central government to rule independently of Reichstag majority support, a more aggressive foreign policy toward eastern Europe, the regaining of German colonies overseas, and the resurrection of borders "matching the honor and greatness of the German Volk."[4] Even in advance of the depression, therefore, among the Protestant middle-class parties there was a shift underway from those political elites most favorable to Weimar democracy to those openly hostile to the Weimar system. Yet once the economic collapse hit, these "half-way house" parties, as Knauerhase has termed them, were unable to provide a credible basis for either mass antidemocratic mobilization or elite-level action to destroy the Republic.[5] Profoundly antidemocratic and an additional burden to the Weimar democracy, the small Wirtschaftspartei was an early symptom of the political weakness of the liberal and moderate political elites as supports for the Republic, and later for the pathetic attempts by class-based interest-group elites to provide mass support vehicles for smashing the Weimar system.

By 1928, the most liberal leadership groupings in the Democrat party were losing ground and were already rethinking their political allegiance to and identification with the Weimar democracy. After the

1928 Reichstag elections, which again brought a Social Democrat into the chancellor's office, the Democrats' leadership took a sharp turn to the right, in a forlorn attempt to compete with other Protestant political elites already staking out more hostile anti-Weimar positions.[6] Within the DNVP a decisive shift in leadership from the more moderate Count Kuno von Westarp to the vehemently antidemocratic architect of the Harzburg Front, Alfred Hugenberg, also reflected a shift over to the anti-system right. In 1928 the Catholic Center (Zentrum) party also chose a new and more right-wing chairman, Prelate Kaas, who would in the depression years be less supportive of the Weimar system.[7]

After 1929, among the bourgeois parties, both Protestant and Catholic, there was a further progressive shift to the right, what Hamilton has called a "competition in toughness," to which we must add a competition for a leading position to undermine or overthrow the parliamentary democratic system.[8] In this political environment, none of the bourgeois parties took a line of strong defense of the system, or renewed their commitment to work with the moderate Social Democrats to keep the system functioning. They opted instead to compete through projects that would in substance destroy the Weimar system, and in this competition they were no match for the NSDAP as an alternative political elite.

But why did the NSDAP win this struggle with the bourgeois parties, and why therefore did German fascism make this critical breakthrough as an increasingly recognized and appealing element in the antidemocratic projects that finally came to fruition in January 1933? First and foremost, the NSDAP was in many ways a "modern" party organization, able to rely on its own manpower and financial resources in order to function. It was also, in Hamilton's phrase, a "virtuous organization" in its fighting and work capabilities, resting on the bonding and war-fighting skills of the front generation that populated its units.[9] In many respects, the NSDAP was an extremist forerunner of the modern Volkspartei or "catch-all" party, able and willing to project political slogans and policy outlines toward the most diverse segments of the population, with differential effect, of course, but without much concern for the contradictory nature of its total package of appeals.[10]

Second, recent studies have emphasized the role of the newspapers and election-campaign speeches and posters in spreading the message of the NSDAP, and in making the party a known factor in the political landscape for voters. In this regard, special attention should be paid to Hamilton's findings about the role of leading bourgeois newspapers in their favorable and highly biased reporting of the activities of the

NSDAP, especially in respect to the street-fighting clashes with the Marxist parties. Hamilton points out that this reportage in newspapers widely read in the best upper- and upper-middle-class neighborhoods portrayed the Brownshirt fighters as defenders of these neighborhoods against the asserted growing threat of leftist violence and revolutionary upsurge.[11] This research has shown more specifically how the NSDAP built its huge and contradictory voter following, from upper-class neighborhoods to "Tory" working-class voters to rural farming communities. Of special interest here is the evidence that the highest level of voter support for the NSDAP on the scale of social class was to be found in the upper-class neighborhoods of the largest Protestant cities.[12] In the "best" neighborhoods of Berlin and Hamburg, for example, 60 to 70 percent of the upper- and upper-middle-class Protestant voters cast their votes for the NSDAP in the July 1932 elections. This indicates the overwhelming effectiveness of the NSDAP appeals, mediated by certain elements of the press, precisely among the families of established social elites, which could not have failed to have an effect on these elites' own perceptions of the Nazis as useful—even necessary—allies in any anti-Weimar political project. In fact, although Hamilton does not want to explore this line of reasoning, one might assert that there was something approaching a consensus among upper-class Protestants that the NSDAP represented their salvation as a social class.

Hamilton makes good points about the cleavage between Catholic and Protestant voting patterns, but his research actually supports the argument that in the Protestant big cities, where modern class relations and modern class struggle in the midst of the economic crisis would be expected to be most clear-cut and most bitterly fought, the socially advantaged classes were the greatest electoral supporters of the NSDAP, in proportions approaching what could reasonably be called a class consensus. Whether the bourgeois press played a planned or an unintended role in this process is an interesting question. The newspapers owned by Alfred Hugenberg certainly played a rather conscious role in legitimating the NSDAP to social elites, but the main point is that these social "betters" were not in any way bastions of resistance to Nazi appeals. Rather these social elites and their families were in fact voting for the NSDAP in higher percentages than was the lower middle class, on whom earlier theories of disproportionately high electoral support for the NSDAP had focused. One of Hamilton's additions to our understanding of this period is precisely that it was not the lower middle class that was most "panicked," or most susceptible to Nazi appeals, but rather the social milieu of the dominant Protestant urban establishment.

The NSDAP leadership was able to portray itself more credibly as an alternative political elite, an alternative to those bourgeois political

Table 1
Generational Composition of Reichstag Deputies

Birth decade	NSDAP 1928	NSDAP 1932	DNVP 1928	DNVP 1932	DVP 1928	DVP 1932	DDP 1928	DDP 1932	Zentrum 1928	Zentrum 1932
	%	%	%	%	%	%	%	%	%	%
pre-1870	15	2	20	8	19	—	14	—	19	9
1870s	15	8	49	42	47	46	68	50	39	30
1880s	23	21	30	37	35	46	14	50	37	42
1890s	46	42	7	14	—	9	5	—	5	16
1900s	—	27	—	—	—	—	—	—	—	3

elites that had participated in the Weimar system, even though they were increasingly more hostile to that system since they no longer seemed able to make it work in their interests. The NSDAP had developed a leadership profile that set it apart from its bourgeois rivals, both generationally and occupationally.[13] The bourgeois political elites that in the last years had denounced the Republic were overwhelmingly the same leaders who had sat in the Reichstag and participated in government coalitions before 1928; their verbal distancing from their own past behavior was not as convincing as was the Nazi leadership assertion of itself as a young, more diversely representative and physically aggressive, violent opponent of parliamentary democracy. From Reichstag parliamentary almanacs of the Weimar period, containing photos and short autobiographical sketches of each deputy, one can see the differences between the NSDAP Reichstag faction, with its emphasis on uniforms, fierce poses, war records, and fighting ability, and its bourgeois political opposition, older men of conventional upper-class credentials, even for the most notorious antidemocratic conspirators such as Hugenberg and Franz von Papen. (See Table 1).

Between 1928 and 1932 the old leadership groupings of the bourgeois parties did not give way to a younger, more vigorous cohort, nor did younger leaders in those parties succeed in ousting or overthrowing the old guard. Instead, there was a shift to the right within the old-guard leadership generation, and the plotting and playing out of a series of political projects by these bourgeois political elites, each designed in its way to undermine the Reichstag and to destroy the electoral process. After 1929, however, these antidemocratic political scenarios had to deal with the recognition that the NSDAP was a necessary and useful element in any plan to destroy Weimar.

The Reassurance Issue

There were many reasons for established elites in politics, business, the military, and elsewhere to be distrustful of the Nazi leadership as a possible alternative political leadership. The NSDAP since its revamping in the early 1920s had attempted to market its putschist skills to the antidemocratic right-wing establishment elites. Indeed, one of Hitler's steady goals had been to secure elite backing for his party and its activities.[14] For the most part, however, these early attempts to build bridges to established elites received little interest and only occasional financial support. Turner is probably correct in his assessment that business elites who regularly funded political organizations continued until 1933 "to bestow the bulk of their funds on opponents or rivals of the Nazis."[15] What Turner does not mention, however, is that these big-business political funds in the early 1930s were funneled to more respectable bourgeois political elites, such as von Papen and Hugenberg, who were engaged in their own schemes to destroy the Republic, utilizing Nazi strength but trying to maintain political control for themselves. Naturally big business was more comfortable with this type of prospect, but it does not make the big-business elites into supporters of democracy or excuse them from their support of von Papen and Hugenberg, who played such key roles in handing state power over to Hitler.

Several issues raised the anxiety level of elites about the NSDAP leadership. Most important perhaps was the Nazi economic program, which under the rubric of "national socialism" raised the suspicion that the Nazis might be, after all, "national Bolsheviks." The Nazi attacks on banking and finance circles, the glorification of village and peasant life exemplified by Walter Darre's *Blut und Boden* (Blood and Soul) *völkisch* philosophy, the call for the breaking up of department store chains, and the strength of the Strasser (Otto and Gregor) "left" wing of the party presented considerable difficulties for established elites. Precisely the contradictory appeals of the NSDAP, necessary to win support from farmers, rural and small-town residents, owners of small businesses, and "Tory" or anti-Marxist workers, also stirred some doubts about the NSDAP as the ultimate weapon for the salvation of German capitalism.

Hitler tried to resolve this problem by following a conscious two-pronged strategy.[16] In a series of private talks, he attempted to reassure business and banking elites that he had no intention of attacking private property or the private banking system (except for Jewish businesses and banks), and in June 1930 he threw Otto Strasser and his more serious left followers out of the party.[17] Yet the influence of

Gregor Strasser remained strong until the end of 1932, when Strasser lost influence after his discussions with General Kurt von Schleicher on the possible formation of some sort of militarist-populist dictatorship. Through the series of 1932 elections, including the November Reichstag elections, the Nazis continued to deploy their full array of anticapitalist slogans to their intended audiences to keep their massive but very diverse voter following together.

A second source of distrust of the Nazi leadership stemmed from the fact that it was different, socially and behaviorally, from conventional elite standards, and was proud of that difference. This social distance was more bothersome to business elites than to Reichswehr elites, who generally had a more positive attitude toward Hitler and his party's militarist organization, cultural values, and foreign policy goals. Turner takes this relative difference to mean that it was the military elite that bears an institutional guilt for the rise of Hitler, whereas the business elite was largely innocent.[18] Turner does not consider the overlapping economic interests and inter-elite social ties between big business and the Reichswehr leadership as important factors in the antidemocratic projects to destroy the Weimar system.

Many young NSDAP militants had indeed destroyed whatever business and professional careers they might have developed in the mid-1920s through their combative, often violent, behavior. By committing "economic suicide" in advance of the Depression they broke with normal bourgeois society and cemented a commitment to the militarized and continuous political activism of the NSDAP.[19] The NSDAP had also proven its capacity to build up a tough and competent party organization and street-fighting army that was largely self-supporting and beyond the control of established elites. This organization was on the one hand attractive for its antiunion and antileft coercive potential, but was also more independent of manipulation by financing, or by socializing, than elites of the bourgeois parties.[20] Yet at the same time these social elites were drawn to Hitler's appeals for national renewal, for overturning Versailles, and for smashing the unions, the Marxist parties, and the Weimar democracy. These appeals, combined with the apparent power and aggressive nature of the NSDAP, had a wide resonance and produced great enthusiasm among individuals of the established elite. Many observers have noted the simultaneous mixture of expressions of dizzying adulation, suspicion, and distrust with which leading businesspeople, military, and bourgeois party leaders described Hitler.[21] This sense of often messianic support mixed with anxieties of social distance was in part mirrored in the discrepancy between very high levels of upper-class voting support for the Nazis, and relative reluctance—before January 1933—to join the party.

Still another element of distrust revolved around the role of the street-fighting army (Sturmabteilung, or SA) which in the early 1930s under Ernst Röhm was claiming to be not only the military arm of the NSDAP but its political arm as well. While the bourgeois elites applauded the SA attacks on the Social Democratic party (SPD) and the German Communist party (KPD), and increasingly viewed SA violence as a useful asset that the Nazis would bring into any coalition of forces to undermine the democracy, it was also true that the Nazis had employed their thug tactics against bourgeois political parties as well.[22] These attacks started with Jewish candidates of the liberal Democrats as the targets, but grew to include non-Jewish candidates of the DDP and the moderate conservative DVP as well. With the "revolutionary" rhetoric and antibourgeois polemics of the SA, this use of coercion and violence against bourgeois party candidates and meetings might well have given pause to many established elites as to the reliability of the Nazi leadership as an ally, and about its true intentions if brought to state power with the help of established elites. Taken together, these doubts about Hitler and the NSDAP leadership constituted a second evolutionary hurdle for the party, and for those among the established bourgeois political and military elites who most wanted to utilize the Nazis as a weapon to bring down the Weimar Republic.

The empirical analysis of the process by which these anxieties were quieted has been enhanced by recent research. Kater has detailed the role of the Protestant church, through its clergy and church elders, between 1929 and 1932, in legitimizing the Nazi elite as a political alternative for executives, business people, professionals, and intellectuals.[23] Hamilton has stressed the biased, even hysterical, reporting of leading bourgeois newspapers, in heightening the fear of Red revolution, in defending and glorifying Nazi street-fighting actions, and in picturing NSDAP leaders as well-intentioned and honorable, if somewhat brash and overly idealistic. Other reassuring messages transmitted through leading bourgeois newspapers included statements from high-status individuals such as that of Prince August Wilhelm that Hitler was "sent by God to the German people," and reports from Italy on the merits of Italian fascism. The presentation of Italian fascism as a political model acceptable to the upper classes represents another avenue of reassurance "learning."[24] This process of selective communication networking and elite "vouching" for the legitimacy and reliability of the NSDAP as an alternative political elite, as well as the massive voting percentages for the Nazis among the families of Protestant urban elites, it can be argued, served to reduce elite anxieties, to facilitate the work of the leading bourgeois political anti-democratic schemers in negotiating an alliance with the NSDAP, and to head off the possibility of specifically anti-Nazi political projects led by more moderate elites.

What took place, therefore, from early 1930 to January 1933 was a series of political projects, undertaken by "political entrepreneur" groups from within the ranks of the antidemocratic bourgeois political elites, Reichswehr officers, business representatives, and Hindenburg advisers, to fashion a coalition of forces that could undermine the Weimar system as a functioning parliamentary democracy, and put in place a strong right-wing government not responsible to a freely elected Reichstag and not responsive to left or liberal parties or trade-union interests.

This process had begun in 1930, with the removal of the SPD from government and the elevation of Heinrich Brüning from the right wing of the Catholic Center party to reich Chancellor, permitted to govern under emergency powers of President Hindenburg under Article 48 of the Weimar Constitution, without heeding Reichstag majority support.[25] During the entire year of 1932, the development of projects to bring the NSDAP into some political project to destroy Weimar democracy and to smash organized labor and the political left intensified as the NSDAP reached the heights of its electoral support (37 percent in the July Reichstag elections) and even more after the Nazis showed signs of weakening in the November elections, losing over 2 million votes and dropping to 33 percent of the total vote. Hörster-Philipps has described the series of measures undertaken by the government of Franz von Papen in the course of 1932 aimed at putting in place the elements of a rightist coalition, which would be able to utilize the power of the NSDAP as a part of government.[26] Von Papen's government initiated actions that first tested the level of resistance that might be expected from the workers' movement and the Social Democrats in case a fascist government should come to power in Germany, and then engaged the NSDAP leadership in protracted negotiations over the role Hitler would be willing to accept in a new governing alliance of von Papen, Hugenberg's DNVP, and the NSDAP.

The von Papen government, from its first day in office on June 4, 1932, undertook measures that decreed major cuts in spending for pensions, jobless benefits, and war veterans. Ten days later it readmitted the Nazi street-fighting and paramilitary SA and SS organizations, while turning police and judicial forces against liberal and socialist self-defense organizations. The major test provocation of democratic forces, however, came with the deposing by Reich authorities of the elected SPD-Catholic Center government of Prussia, which in 1932 was the last great stronghold of democratic political strength in the Reich.

The next stage, according to Hörster-Philipps, was to bring the

NSDAP into negotiations that would include the Nazi leadership in a new Reich government.[27] These discussions came up against Hitler's demand that he be named chancellor, and despite advice from Fritz Thyssen and Hjalmar Schacht that he accept von Papen's offer, Hitler refused to join a reconstituted von Papen government as a junior partner.

After this setback, von Papen attempted to put through a new economic program favoring big business, and to engineer a constitutional reform project designed to legitimate a presidial-presidential central government; the latter in practice would have ended parliamentary democracy, while keeping the facade of an elected but ineffectual Reichstag. Von Papen's government was heavily supported in this attempt by members of leading big-business and military circles, and big business in particular put its political funding weight behind von Papen's allies in the November Reichstag elections. The result was a disaster for von Papen; his political allies garnered only 10.7 percent of the vote, and it was clear that without the NSDAP, there was no mass base of support behind his efforts to destroy the Republic.

The November elections, however, also demonstrated the possibly weak staying power of the NSDAP. In fear that the Nazi party might decline as rapidly as it had grown, the pressure to bring Hitler into the government actually increased. The signs of Communist electoral strength (nearly 18 percent of the vote) and increased strike activity added to fears that the political momentum might be swinging to the left, and that by waiting the right might miss its historic moment. Recent research by David Abraham on the Deutsche Führerbriefe, the internal political correspondence of German industry, shows the turnaround in the political thinking by the leading export sectors of German industry from support of Weimar in the mid-1920s to both support for Nazi participation in government and enthusiastic backing, by November and December of 1932, for Hitler to be named chancellor.[28] An analysis of the election results by the NSDAP's Reich Propaganda Leadership also concluded that the Nazi coalition was beginning to come unstuck, and that further free elections could be disastrous for the party; Childers concludes that had the NSDAP not come to power very quickly, it might well have declined rapidly in electoral strength, and Goebbels' RPL analysis made clear that there must be no more elections.[29] The Cologne banker Kurt von Schröder, who hosted a decisive round of negotiations in early January, stated to Allied authorities in 1945: "When the NSDAP suffered its first defeat on November 6, and had thus passed its peak, the support by the German business community became especially urgent."[30]

One last alternative project was undertaken by von Papen's former defense minister, General Schleicher. Schleicher attempted in December, during his brief interregnum, to put together an alliance of military (Reichswehr) and paramilitary (SA, Stahlhelm) forces, along with the left wing of the NSDAP (led by Gregor Strasser), and hopefully some worker support from both nonsocialist and socialist unions. Schleicher's scheming was viewed by many business elites as representing some sort of reparliamentarization process with further elections; this fear, voiced openly in the Führerbriefe, added all the greater critical importance to the immediate success of von Papen's project.[31] Schleicher's attempt to split the NSDAP as well as the working-class followings of several parties and give a mass basis to a military-led dictatorship not only failed but forced Strasser to resign his party offices, giving another "reassurance" message to established elites that a Hitler government would not be dominated by the Strasser wing of the party.

By January, the political environment again favored the antidemocratic political entrepreneur grouping of von Papen, Hugenberg, and Hindenburg's adviser circle. Turner details the remaining opposition to a Hitler-led government among big-business leaders, but his studies show that their line of preference fell mainly between a rightist coalition including Hitler but led by von Papen, and a coalition including von Papen but led by Hitler. Naturally, most big-business elites felt more comfortable with the Herrenklub-personage of Franz von Papen, but this hardly makes the case for their innocence in the whole process of destroying Weimar and shaping the rise of German fascism.[32] Despite understandable remaining anxieties and jitters, which were expressed in these fateful moments, business elites, like military and bureaucratic elites, were disposed to work with the new regime from its first days in office, to continue to seek reassurances, and to influence the unfolding of government policies in their favor. Big-business leaders who really feel threatened by a regime know how to express their opposition: investment boycott, decapitalization, capital flight, and emigration of families abroad. With the obvious exception of Jewish capitalists, these classic signs were remarkably absent in the first months and years of the Nazi regime. Turner, following Schumpeter, calls this "adapative" behavior on the part of big business, but at the same time notes all the overlapping areas of policy agreement with the NSDAP.[33] In these areas, no adaptation was necessary; the political understandings were broadly mutualistic, and the end effect synergistic, for the evolution of German fascism as a political elite alternative for capitalist interests.

The Normalization Issue

What expectations did established elites have about the longer term evolution of a governing fascist political elite? Beyond the immediate jubilation over the SA terror directed against the KPD, SPD, and trade-union organizations in the first months of the Nazi regime, how did social elites imagine that this new governing elite would develop? In particular, would the Nazi elite gradually conform to standards expected by social elites, becoming a more "normal" political leadership? Most scholars of German fascism have emphasized the belief among many bourgeois leaders that the Nazi elite could be tamed, or that it would mature with proper tutelage from bourgeois circles. Some, like von Papen and Hugenberg, believed that the Nazis could be used for their own reactionary, antidemocratic, and antileft purposes and later dismissed.[34] More moderate elites, who had opposed the Nazi rise to power, hoped that the Nazi movement would quickly burn itself out in office, and that by cooperating with the NSDAP (for example, in supporting the granting of emergency powers to Hitler in March of 1933) they might pave the way for a moderation in its behavior and a return to a more civil politics. Generally, these hopes and expectations of bourgeois leaders have been treated as evidence of political myopia, self-delusion, and incompetence, which on the personal level may be quite accurate. Certainly the Nazi leadership immediately used its newly acquired state power to suppress its left opponents and to scatter the organizations of its bourgeois party rivals.

On the other hand, despite the absence of bourgeois political liberty and bourgeois parties, the NSDAP elite did evolve in ways that represented a kind of normalization to established elite standards. Most often cited here are the defeat and bloody purge of both the Strasser left wing of the party and the Röhm SA leadership on June 30, 1934. Bracher also reports that by the end of 1934, nearly 80 percent of the political leadership consisted of newcomers who had joined the party since the beginning of 1933, and that only the Gauleiter ranks were predominantly still from the "old fighter" cohort.[35]

Likewise, the Nazi regime, while still paying lip service to Walter Darré's villagization plans and the protection of small business and small farms, pursued an economic policy, starting in June 1934, that was most favorable to big business and detrimental to small business.[36]

Certainly the share of national income going to capital rose each year from 1932 to 1939, as did retained earnings of corporations.[37] By comparison with the pre-Depression year 1928, property-entrepreneurial income rose from 29.2 percent of national income to 33.8 percent in 1939 and retained corporate earnings from 1.8 percent to

5.4 percent, while wages and salaries dropped from 65.1 percent to
58.8 percent. Nazi rhetoric about strengthening small enterprise and
artisans was an empty promise in actual practice.[38] Private investment
had risen by 267 percent in the 1932–38 period in steady progression,
and armaments investment had risen by 2400 percent; government
nonarmaments investment had risen too, but by only 180 percent, and
was in 1938 still 12 percent below the 1928 figure.[39]

The actual beneficiaries of Nazi economic policy, therefore, were
those elite sectors in big business and the military whose interests, far
from being threatened by the NSDAP regime, were in fact stregthened
by the changes within the NSDAP elite, resulting in closer working
collaboration and wide-ranging mutualism of interests. Looking at the
evolving social composition of the NSDAP leadership, established
elites had reason to believe that that leadership was not a revolutionary
elite, but rather one which might reasonbly be expected to gradually
adjust to standards of established power centers. Careful scholarship
has for some time now largely disproven Lerner's earlier notion of the
Nazi leaders as a collection of "marginal men" or social outsiders, and
recent research indicates that at the top levels of the NSDAP hierarchy,
leaders were themselves predominantly from elite backgrounds.[40] This
elite class in Weimar society, which represented only 2.8 percent of the
population, accounts for 14 of 17 NSDAP Reichsleiters, 46.3 percent of
Gauleiters (1925–28), and 36 percent of 1933 NSDAP Reichstag deputies. By contrast, in 1933, when social elites were joining the party in
relatively higher proportions, still only 12.2 percent of new Nazi party
members were from elite social backgrounds.[41]

Kater shows that during the Third Reich, the NSDAP elite also aged
in office, becoming far less a generation of "angry young men" distinct
from the expected age of a political elite in noncrisis times. The Nazi
leadership had been notable for its youth during Weimar; once in
power, this elite generation became quickly entrenched in office (see
Table 2).

The NSDAP Reichstag deputy contingent, already quite young in
1928 in comparison with other parties (except the KPD), and even
more radically rejuvenated by 1932, underwent a gradual aging
through 1938. Nearly 60 percent of Nazi Reichstag deputies in 1938
were over forty years of age, compared with only 43 percent in 1932
(November). In the five years from 1933 to 1938, despite the tremendous influx of first-time deputies to the all-Nazi Reichstags of 1933(II),
1936, and 1938, the average age rose by more than three years. The
average age of Reichleiters rose from forty-three in 1933 to fifty-four by
1944, and of Gauleiters from forty to forty-eight over the same
period.[42] At lower levels of the NSDAP organization, the Nazi lead-

Table 2
NSDAP Reichstag Deputies, 1932–38

Birth decade	NSDAP only	NSDAP only	all-NSDAP Reichstags		
	1932II %	1933I %	1933II %	1936 %	1938 %
pre-1870	2	1	1	1	1
1870s	8	6	5	5	5
1880s	21	23	19	17	16
1890s	42	44	46	44	42
1900s	27	25	29	32	34
1910s	—	—	—	1	2

Note: Roman numerals following 1932 and 1933 reflect the fact that there were two Reichstag elections in those years.

ership was also stagnant, entering middle age in office. The NSDAP did not represent a fundamentally different, innovative, or revolutionary type of political elite in this respect. While affirming in part the lower-middle-class values of the majority of the party leadership, Kater concludes:

> This judgment, however, requires three reservations, all of which emphasize the importance of elite elements in the leadership. First, the relative proportion of elite elements was higher among the leaders than in the party or in the Reich population. Second, the elite portion tended to increase with rank. And third, the elite element was particularly influential when extraordinary leadership was called for, as in the period between 1932 and 1934. These three points show that even the monopolistic party of the Nazi regime, whose corporate behavior has been described as impulsive, disorderly, and confused, was affected by the elite's rules of rationality, performance, and efficiency.[43]

The Nazi leadership, as an alternative political elite, was torn between the old fighter (lower-middle-class) mentality and the establishment "upper-class consciousness." Once in power, the NSDAP elite did not revolutionize the social order, nor did it undermine established elite social values, despite its pre-1933 antibourgeois rhetoric.

> Can it be deduced that the NSDAP leadership constituted a new elite in German society, as has been argued by a score of writers? No, that was not the case. . . . To classify as a counter-elite, the leaders would have had to bring about the completion of the National Socialist revolution, but this they were not able to do. And, coming after and aping in various respects their austere Prussian pre-cursors, they retained far too many epigonal

characteristics to be considered a new species. . . . There were too many elements of accommodation, of fusion, of absorption. In social composition alone, the pattern of mutual interactions and interlockings between the two groups was nearer to collusion than to collision.[44]

The mutual penetration of party elite and social elite (already considerable before 1933), the purging of SA and Strasser leadership factions, and the aging in office throughout the entire Third Reich era all indicate that the German fascist leadership was undergoing a normalization process; established elites were not foolish or myopic in their belief that the NSDAP would be critically useful, as an alternative political elite: safe, and ultimately unable to revolutionize the social order.[45]

The Debate on the NSDAP as an Alternative Elite

In recent years, various scholars have attempted to exonerate established elites, and in particular big business, from responsibility for the rise of German fascism. The line of defense has been that big business and other elements of the established elite did not favor handing over state power to the Nazis, and were surprised and outflanked by a small group of conspirators around von Papen, Hugenberg, and Hindenburg. The later collaboration with the NSDAP is either not dealt with, or is seen as an accidental by-product of Nazi policies, not as a preexisting mutuality of interests or as the fruits of a mutually sought political coalition.

It is ironic that the research findings of these scholars in fact provide additional evidence for the thesis of a bourgeois-fascist coalition-building process, a process with several hurdles, to be sure, but one of conscious political projects designed to bring down the Weimar democracy, to utilize the NSDAP mass support and street-fighting army, and to bring about a decisive shift in economic and military policy in favor of elites in big business and the military. Several entrepreneurial efforts were undertaken to accomplish these goals, and the offers to the NSDAP started at a lower level than Hitler would accept. In the end, the bidding included the acceptance of Hitler as chancellor, and the effective handing over of state power to the fascist elite. This was not the first choice of established elites for solving their problems with the Weimar system, but it was a conscious choice, an opportunity they did not let slip through their fingers.

Notes

1. Reinhard Kühnl, *Faschismustheorien* (Hamburg: Rowohlt, 1979), esp. section 3. Also John Nagle, *The National Democratic Party of Germany* (Berkeley: University of California Press, 1970); Reinhard Kühnl, "The Rise of Fascism in Germany and its Causes" in M. Dobkowksi and I. Wallimann, eds., *Towards the Holocaust* (Westport, CN: Greenwood, 1983); and Karl Marx, "The Eighteenth Brumaire of Louis Bonaparte" in R. Tucker, ed., *The Marx-Engels Reader* (New York: Norton, 1972).
2. Cf. Richard Hamilton, *Who Voted for Hitler?* (Princeton: Princeton University Press, 1982); and Reinhard Kühnl, *Die Weimarer Republik* (Hamburg: Rowohlt, 1985), for contrasting views on this point.
3. See Bruce Frye, *Liberal Democrats in the Weimar Republic* (Carbondale: Southern Illinois University Press, 1985), p. 106.
4. Cf. Martin Schumacher, *Mittelstandsfront und Republik* (Dusseldorf: Droste, 1972), pp. 51–52.
5. Ramon Knauerhase, *An Introduction to National Socialism, 1920 to 1939* (Columbus, Ohio: Merrill, 1972), p. 38.
6. See Frye, *Liberal Democrats in the Weimar Republic*, esp. ch. 7 and conclusion.
7. Fritz Fischer, *Bündnis der Eliten* (Dusseldorf: Droste, 1979), pp. 66–68.
8. Cf. Hamilton, *Who Voted for Hitler?* p. 264.
9. See ibid. for a well-documented accounting of this "virtuousity," especially compared with its competition, both on the left and among the bourgeois parties.
10. See especially here Thomas Childers, *The Nazi Voter* (Chapel Hill, NC: University of North Carolina Press, 1983), for a good analysis of the group-specific appeals of the NSDAP.
11. Hamilton fails to give a credible explanation for this pro-Nazi bias in reportage, instead attributing it and its effects to unintended consequences and political myopia (Hamilton, *Who Voted For Hitler?*, pp. 414–19, 436–37).
12. Cf. Hamilton, *Who Voted for Hitler?* pp. 85–86, 118–19, and Childers, *The Nazi Voter*, esp. pp. 264–65.
13. See John D. Nagle, *System and Succession* (Austin: University of Texas Press, 1977), ch. 7; and "Composition and Evolution of the Nazi Elite," in Dobkowski and Wallimann, eds., *Towards the Holocaust*.
14. Kühnl, *Weimarer Republik*, pp. 215ff.; see Karl Bracher, *The German Dictatorship* (New York: Praeger, 1970), pp. 84–91, for early contacts between Hitler and potential elite backers.
15. Henry A. Turner, *German Big Business and the Rise of Hitler* (New York: Oxford University Press, 1985), p. 346.
16. See Childers, *The Nazi Voter*, pp. 268–69; and Fischer, *Bündnis*, p. 71.
17. Bracher, *The German Dictatorship*, pp. 180–81.
18. Turner, *German Big Business*, pp. 341–46.
19. Peter Merkl, "Notes on the Psychology of Extremism: 581 pre-1933 Nazis," APSA paper presented in New Orleans, 1973.
20. Hamilton and Turner both make the point that big business consistently overestimated its manipulative capabilities through political funding even for bourgeois parties. Still, the relative difference with respect to the Nazis is important, and was probably recognized as a different situation by business elites involved in political funding.
21. Cf. Hamilton, *Who Voted for Hitler?* pp. 460, 640 (note); and Michael Kater, *The Nazi Party* (Cambridge, MA: Harvard University Press, 1983), pp. 62–71.
22. See Frye, *Liberal Democrats*, p. 170; Bracher, *The German Dictatorship*, pp. 187ff.; Hamilton, *Who Voted for Hitler?* pp. 353–34; and Kater, *The Nazi Party*, pp. 70–71.

However, Goebbels specifically reduced the violence of attacks on Hugenberg's Conservatives for the November 1932 elections. Cf. Childers, *The Nazi Voter*, pp. 209–10.

23. Kater, *The Nazi Party*, pp. 65–70.
24. Cf. Hamilton, *Who Voted for Hitler?* pp. 168, 413–19.
25. Cf. Bracher, *The German Dictatorship*, pp. 170ff.
26. Ulrike Hörster-Philipps, "Conservative Concepts of Dictatorship in the Final Phase of the Weimar Republic," in Dobkoswki and Wallimann, eds., *Towards the Holocaust*, pp. 115–30.
27. Ibid., p. 122.
28. David Abraham, *The Collapse of the Weimar Republic*, 2d ed. (New York: Holmes & Meier, 1986), pp. xxxviiiff.
29. Thomas Childers, "The Limits of National Socialist Mobilization," in T. Childers, ed., *Formation of the Nazi Constituency 1919–1933* (Totawa, NJ: Barnes & Noble, 1986).
30. Quoted in Küéhnl, *Die Weimarer Republik*, p. 219.
31. Abraham, *Collapse*, p. xxxix; see also Bracher, *The German Dictatorship*, pp. 177–78.
32. Turner, *German Big Business*, ch. 5.
33. Ibid., p. 349.
34. Cf. Bracher, *The German Dictatorship*, pp. 194ff.; Frye, *Liberal Democrats*, pp. 187–94; Childers, *The Nazi Voter*, p. 267; and Turner, *German Big Business*, p. 348.
35. Bracher, *The German Dictatorship*, p. 235.
36. For a good analysis, see esp. David Schoenbrun, *Hitler's Social Revolution* (Garden City, NY: Doubleday, 1967); Knauerhase, *Introduction to National Socialism*, pp. 96–98; and Arthur Schweitzer, *Big Business and the Third Reich* (Bloomington: Indiana University Press, 1964), for a detailed description of the evolving alliance of big business with the Nazi regime after 1933.
37. Knauerhase, *Introduction to National Socialism*, p. 129.
38. Ibid., p. 130.
39. Ibid., p. 133. Even Hamilton, in a buried footnote, recognizes the benefits to big business of Nazi policy (cf. Hamilton, *Who Voted for Hitler?* p. 626). See also A. R. L. Gurland, Otto Kirchheimer, and Franz Neumann, *The Fate of Small Business in Nazi Germany* (New York: Fertig, 1975; first published in 1943).
40. Kater, *The Nazi Party*, esp. pp. 194–95. See also Daniel Lerner, *The Nazi Elite* (Stanford: Hoover Institute, 1951); and Nagle, "Composition and Evolution of the Nazi Elite." Max Knight, even in the earliest Hoover studies, disputes Lerner's "marginal men" thesis, in his study of German cabinet members from 1890–1945, finding that within the cabinet, the Nazi regime represented a restoration of military, and aristocratic, backgrounds, and for the first time a sizable contingent from business, banking, engineering, and insurance backgrounds (cf. Max Knight, *The German Executive* [Stanford: Hoover Institute, 1952], p. 41).
41. Ibid., p. 252.
42. Kater, *The Nazi Party*, p. 200. The Reichstag calculations are from Reichstag almanac data. Cf. also Nagle, *System and Succession*, p. 208.
43. Ibid., p. 229.
44. Ibid., pp. 232–33.
45. Kater argues that the July 1944 putsch revived, too late, Hitler's hatred for the old elite (ibid., pp. 237–40).

Part II

Confronting the Past: Lessons from History

The Destruction of the Workers' Mass Movements in Nazi Germany

Gunter W. Remmling

Since its appearance on the political scene of Weimar Germany the National Socialist German Workers party (NSDAP), had been bitterly opposed by the workers' mass movements. Berlin, a stronghold of workers' organizations, was the Rote Festung, the Red Fortress, in Nazi jargon. And there were many other red fortresses in Weimar Germany. The Nazis thus viewed the destruction of the workers' mass movements as a prerequisite for the establishment of absolute power. Adolf Hitler was obsessed by the idea of annihilating the workers' movements—an obsession that was equaled only by his pathological preoccupation with the destruction of the Jews. Flagrant misuse of the law and secret-police terror constituted Hitler's chief weapons in his attack on the Jews and workers. Hitler, the cunning demagogue, also knew that many Germans either shared his hatreds or believed them to operate to their advantage.

When Hitler ordered the destruction of the workers' mass movements, he certainly fulfilled the wishes of the German ruling class. As far as the large landowners, industrialists, generals, and top administrators were concerned, workers existed to be exploited, and rebellious workers belonged at the end of a rope or in front of a firing squad. Most middle-class Germans aped the attitude of the ruling class and admired the Freikorps mercenaries who were murdering thousands of German workers when Hitler was still an obscure fanatic. As long as the workers were impoverished and powerless the solid burghers had nothing but loathing and contempt for them. When the workers rebelled against their oppressors the middle-class citizens applauded the most brutal methods of ruling-class repression.

Class-conscious workers were fully aware of their situation in the "fatherland." Their experience had made quite clear the truth of Marx's observation that the capitalists view the person who, without capital or ground rent lives entirely by his labor, in other words the proletarian, as a mere worker, but not as a human being.[1] They also recognized fully that the modern working class consists of laborers who live only so long as they have work, and who have work only "so long as their work increases capital."[2] The consequences cut deeply into the workers' lives: capitalist laws of the market rendered the price of labor equal to its cost of production, limited to "the cost of the means of subsistence he needs for his upkeep and for the propagation of his race."[3] The workers knew one thing for sure: the capitalist laws of the market forced them to live in slums and eat garbage. In the Kaiser's Germany the workers sang the imperial anthem with their own lyrics describing their customary dinner of Pellkartoffeln und Heringschwanz (boiled potatoes and herring tail).

But the German workers did more than ridicule the emperor's fatherland. They fought back against their oppressors and created powerful proletarian mass movements, whose growing strength was reflected in working-class participation in government. In the first of the nine national legislative elections in the Weimar Republic, which took place on January 19, 1919, the combined left vote amounted to 45.5 percent of the total. The Social Democratic party (SPD), took 37.9 percent of the vote; 7.6 percent of the voters supported the radical Independent Social Democratic party (USPD). On January 19, 1919, voting participation was 82.7 percent.[4] During the last free Reichstag elections of November 6, 1932, the SPD polled 7,248,000 votes with 121 seats in the German parliament; the German Communist party (KPD) polled close to 6 million votes with 100 seats in the Reichstag.[5] In other words, the SPD took 20.4 percent of the total vote; 16.9 percent of the voters supported the KPD. Together the two disunited Marxist parties had 37.3 percent of the total vote. On the other side of the trenches lurked the NSDAP; the Nazis received 33.1 percent of all the votes. On November 6, 1932, voting participation was 80.6 percent. These elections brought gains for the Communists and losses for the Socialists and Nazis. In the preceding election of July 31, 1932, the NSDAP had received 37.3 percent of the total, the highest percentage the party ever won before its assumption of power on January 30, 1933. On July 31, 1932, the German people gave 21.6 percent of the vote to the SPD and 14.3 percent to the KDP—a combined left vote of 35.9 percent. The voting participation was 84 percent.[6]

The KPD, the most powerful Communist party in Europe, was founded in December 1918, growing out of the revolutionary Spartakusbund. The KPD originated within the left wing of the pre-world War I Social Democratic party. The KPD achieved a mass basis in 1920, when the party reported some 380,000 members, and Communist party membership held steady until March 1922. During the period of relative stabilization in Weimar Germany, Communist party membership declined. In September 1930, in the first year of the Depression, the KPD had some 120,000 members.[7] The Communists also led the 100,000 workers who in 1924 had joined together in an organization called Roter Frontkämpferbund, or League of Red War Veterans. Half of the membership consisted of workers who were not members of the KPD or any other political party.[8] Many of the men gave their lives in the street battles which they fought against the Nazi's Sturmabteilung (SA), or Storm Detachment. The stormtroopers killed or tortured many red fighters in the basements of their Nazi party strongholds (Braune Haus).

The KPD represented the workers' mass movement as a revolutionary party.[9] The majority of the workers supported the SPD—a party strongly committed to social reform. The Social Democratic party, founded in 1891, has its roots in the political activities of German workers which date back to 1790, gaining momentum in the 1830s and 1840s. In 1869, August Bebel and Wilhelm Liebknecht—the father of Karl Liebknecht, leader of the Spartakusbund—founded the Social Democratic Workers' party, which was the immediate Marxist predecessor of the SPD.[10] In 1912, the SPD had 110 seats in the Reichstag and was the strongest parliamentary group in Germany. During the nationalistic fever dance of World War I, the SPD lost almost three-fourths of its members, dropping from 1 million to 250,000. By 1921, the SPD had regained its character as a mass movement, numbering 1.2 million members. During the period of relative stabilization the SPD suffered numerical losses, but by 1930 it again had over 1 million members.[11] On February 22, 1924, the Reichsbanner Schwarz-Rot-Gold was founded in Magdeburg. The Reichsbanner, a paramilitary organization of war veterans dedicated to the protection of the Weimar Republic, eventually numbered over 1 million members—most of them recruited from the ranks of the SPD and the free trade unions.[12]

In the second half of the nineteenth century German workers formed trade unions to protect their social and economic interests. After World War I, the union movement achieved great strength, and the free trade unions with their social democratic orientation came together to establish the powerful German Trade Union Federation (ADGB), which grew during the years 1920–22 into an organization of

7.9 million members. During the period of relative stabilization the ADGB lost members, dropping to 4.1 million in 1925. The German population in 1925 numbered 63,178,619. By 1929, membership had increased to 4.9 million. Membership began to decline again in 1930 as the world economic crisis made its impact on Germany.[13]

During the last years of the Weimar Republic the deadliest enemy of the workers, the Nazi Party, grew in strength. As the depression year of 1929 drew to a close the NSDAP had about 178,000 members. A total of 129,563 Germans belonged to the Nazi party on September 14, 1930. At the beginning of 1932 the NSDAP probably had 450,000 members. The party's membership stood at 719,446 at the end of January 1933. By the end of 1933, 4 million Germans had jumped on the bandwagon, and 750,000 of them were workers.[14] In 1930, there were approximately 100,000 SA stormtroopers who clashed in street battles with Red Front fighters and the Reichsbanner. In these confrontations the SA could usually count on the support of the German police who shot down many Communist and Socialist workers.[15]

Despite their partial self-definition as a socialist workers' party the Nazis were not successful in mobilizing the working class and their "radical rhetoric about socialism remained nothing but rhetoric."[16] The Nazis' rise to power was made possible by the support of large numbers of middle-class voters who saw their economic position and social status threatened by the social and economic changes in Weimar Germany. The Nazis were especially successful in rural and small-town areas, where they "gave the most blatant expression to the fears and prejudices of the middle and particularly the lower middle classes."[17] During the 1930s the Nazis also operated with the consent and backing of the ruling class. Many generals, big businessmen, bankers, top civil servants, and landowning aristocrats supported the NSDAP. Hitler's destruction of the workers' mass movements was in keeping with ruling-class wishes and expectations. His suppression of the workers also laid the fears of many middle-class Germans to rest.

As the NSDAP rose to political prominence in Weimar Germany, the party began to receive political nad financial support from influential representatives of banking and big business. Hitler repeatedly made speeches to leading capitalists, including "industrial magnates such as Vögler of the United Steelworks and Springorum of Hoesch," persuading them to become Nazi supporters.[18] On January 27, 1932, Hitler spoke to the Dusseldorf Industry Club, an organization of the industrial leaders of the city and surrounding area. Fritz Thyssen, the steel baron, championed Hitler's political career and had made the arrangements for the Nazi leader's speech which took place in the exclusive Park Hotel. This meeting brought the NSDAP "increased support from industrialists in the Ruhr district," who by the summer of 1932 wanted to include the NSDAP in the government.[19] Fritz Thyssen and Hjalmar Schacht, who had been president of the Reichsbank until April 1930, went a step further—they wanted to have Hitler as the next German chancellor.[20]

In the spring of 1932, Nazis and industrialists worked together in a circle organized by the chemical engineer and corporate executive Wilhelm Keppler. The group mapped out the details of a promise made by leading Nazis that they would fulfill and safeguard "the wishes and interests of big industrialists," and in November 1932, thirty-eight German industrialists recommended the Nazi cause in a letter to President Hindenburg. Signatories included Cuno, Schacht, Vögler, Thyssen, Krupp, Siemens, Springorum, and Bosch.[21] Industrial and business leaders who opposed the Nazis favored traditional conservative causes; their opposition was guided by pragmatic reasoning rather than political principles.[22]

Shortly after the accession of the Nazis on January 30, 1933, the Schutzstaffel (SS) found new recruits among German aristocrats. A number of industrialists accepted membership in the circle of Friends of the Reichsführer-SS; Heinrich Himmler's new pals who paid money into the coffers of the SS included Dr. Heinrich Buetefisch of I. G. Farben, Hans Waltz, a director of Robert Bosch, Friedrich Flick and representatives of the Deutsche Bank, Norddeutscher Lloyd and Hamburg-Amerika shipping lines, the Dresdner Bank, the Dr. Oetker food company, Siemens-Schuckert, and Mitteldeutsche Stahlwerke.[23]

If the destruction of all workers' organizations constituted the immediate payoff which the Nazis made to the rural aristocracy and the leaders of German industry and commerce, the Nazis made another payoff in the form of slave labor. The National Socialist government forced the inmates of concentration camps, foreign workers, and prisoners of war to perform slave labor, allowing large landowners and industrialists—as well as the Nazis themselves—to reap enormous profits. Some industrial moguls, such as Alfried Krupp von Bohlen und Halbach, operated their own slave labor camps near their factories. Krupp's profit-making inferno included Buschmannshof, the German capitalist's concentration camp for children. In 1944 Krupp exploited about 100,000 slave workers in Germany, other Nazi-dominated countries, and in concentration camps.[24] Other industrialists opened factories inside the concentration camps. The giant chemical combine I. G. Farben used camp labor after 1941 in its Buna synthetic rubber plant at Auschwitz concentration camp and operated its own concentration camp in nearby Monowitz.[25] And other companies in Germany that exploited concentration camp prisoners included AEG, Telefunken, Siemens, BMW, and Rheinmetall.[26]

The business relationship between the SS and German capitalists was not one-sided, however. The SS also realized profits from the forced labor system, both in its own enterprises and from monetary contributions which German corporations and banks made to the organization.[27]

The millions of political prisoners, Jews, and other victims of race hatred which the SS had collected worked under hellish conditions and were fed a starvation diet. Camp workers usually died after four months or became unfit for work. Those who could no longer work were put to death in the gas chambers. At Auschwitz prisoners were tortured in "medical experiments conducted by the Bayer division of I. G. Farben."[28]

Hitler's destruction of the workers' mass movements satisfied the expectations of the ruling class; but the dictator had another, more important reason for his campaign of swift annihilation. Hitler and his gang realized that Marxist working-class organizations were a potential threat to the consideration of Nazi dictatorship, making their destruction inevitable. The seeds of dictatorship were cast upon the land during the final phase of the Weimar Republic, when German politics drifted into extraconstitutionality. The Reich President's Emergency Decree for the Protection of the People and the State of February 28, 1933, obviously revoking the basic constitutional rights of the citizens, hastened these developments.[29] Then the enabling law of March 24, 1933, gave the Hitler government unquestioned authority to issue any kind of dictatorial edict.[30]

The chief weapons the Nazis used to destroy the workers' movements were secret-police terror and a perverted legal system called National Socialist battle law, or Kampfrecht. The wide ranging attack included the arrest, torture, and murder of proletarian leaders and activist workers, the theft of all properties and funds belonging to trade unions, workers' organizations, the KPD and the SPD, and the prohibition of all working-class activities.[31]

The first blow against the KPD fell on February 2, 1933—the fourth day of Nazi rule—when the Communists were denied the right to hold demonstrations.[32] Two days later the Nazis initiated what soon became recurrent practice: invoking article 48 of the Weimar Constitution to issue a Decree for the Protection of the German People, they spread a threadbare mantle of legality over their dictatorial rule. This measure made it impossible for opponents of the Nazi regime to hold meetings, engage in demonstrations, or publish their views.[33] On February 17, 1933, Hermann Göring, in his capacity as Reichskommissar for the Prussian Ministry of the Interior, ordered all police officers to use their firearms against Communists without mercy.[34] Göring's decree, euphemistically entitled Furtherance of the National Movement, represented another aspect of what became standard practice in Nazi Germany: the combination of repressive legislation with police terror. On February 24, 1933, Berlin's Political Police closed Karl-Liebknecht-Haus, the Communist party's headquarters. On the evening of February 27, Göring sneaked an SA squad into the Reichstag, the seat of Germany's national parliament. The stormtroopers set the building on fire, but the Nazis blamed the Communists for the destruction. The National Socialists made the Reichstag fire a pretext to step up the brutal violence which they employed to suppress the KPD. On February 28, the day after the blaze, the Nazis prompted the senile Hindenburg to sign the Emergency Decree for the Protection of the People and the State, which again invoked article 48 of the Weimar Constitution and threatened "to repulse Communist acts of violence endangering the State."[35] With one stroke of his pen Hindenburg had suspended all constitutional provisions for individual and civil liberties; he had also put his legal seal of approval on Hitler's establishment of the German dictatorship. On the same day came the sweeping mass arrests of Communist Reichstag deputies, party officials, workers, and Communist and pacifist writers, journalists, lawyers, and physicians. The SA occupied the Karl-Liebknecht-Haus in Berlin and changed its name to Horst-Wessel-Haus.

On March 1, Reichsminister Göring delivered an interminable radio address and told his listeners: "We do not only want to repulse the Communist danger . . . rather . . . it will be my noblest task . . . to exterminate Communism in our people"[36] One day later Hitler endorsed his fat henchman's attack on the KPD in an election speech which he gave in Berlin's Sportpalast. But the newly anointed chancellor widened Göring's offensive, reviling Marxism in general and the "destructive" idea of democracy. The Nazi leader also revealed his Social Darwinist frame of mind as he went on to assail the ideal of human equality and to glorify the superior personality and the productive strength of capitalism.[37] While Hitler raved in the Sport Palace the German police kept on arresting thousands of Communists. On March 3, Ernst Thälmann, chairman of the KPD's Central Committee, was arrested in Berlin-Charlottenburg in the apartment of a lathe operator.[38] On March 8, the Political Police moved its department for the "fight against bolshevism" into the KPD's former Karl-Liebknecht-Haus.[39]

On March 9, Wilhelm Frick, minister of the interior, declared in a speech that Communists and their "red allies" from the SPD must be taught "productive work" in the concentration camps.[40] On March 15, the Reich Cabinet echoed the minister when its members recom-

mended that Communists should be punished with special brutality—
"*mit ganz brutalen Strafen.*"[41]

The official announcement of the SS state came on March 20, 1933,
when Heinrich Himmler, acting police president of Munich and leader
of the SS, told journalists at a press conference that the concentration
camp at Dachau was about to open.[42]

On March 23, the Nazi government carried out the second major
legal maneuver in support of Hitler's establishment of the German
dictatorship. By a vote of 441 the Nazi-dominated Reichstag adopted
the Law for the Removal of Distress of People and Reich, transferring
the legislative powers of the Reichstag to the Cabinet and thereby
giving Hitler the power to enact laws deviating from the Constitution.
The incarceration of all Communist deputies had forced the KPD out of
the Reichstag, and this left only the Socialist deputies, who cast their
ninety-four votes courageously against the enabling law.[43]

Under their newly tailored legal mantle the Nazis intensified their
terror campaign; with increasing regularity the never-ending reports of
arrests of Communist and Socialist functionaries included the news that
the victim had been shot while "trying to escape."[44]

At the beginning of their third month in power the Nazi leaders
knew that most Communist political activists were either dead, in
prison, on their way to a concentration camp, or in exile. Therefore the
Nazis widened the attack which came to include people suspected of
harboring left-wing or other anti-Nazi feelings. Consequently the Law
for the Restoration of the Professional Civil Service was promulgated on
April 7, 1933. Paragraph four of the law was sufficiently vague to fit the
dictator's purposes, stating that all civil servants who were suspect
because of their "former political activity" could be dismissed. Paragraph three decreed the immediate dismissal of civil servants who were
not of "Aryan descent." The National Socialists used this infamous
"Aryan paragraph" as their big "legal" canon in their relentless attack
on "the economic underpinnings of the Jewish community: a tidal wave
of discriminatory legislation followed the attack on Jewish civil servants."[45]

The First Decree to the Law for the Restoration of the Professional
Civil Service of April 11, 1933, ordered in section one the immediate
dismissal of all civil servants with Communist affiliations. In section
two the decree extended the firing to civil servants who had only one
Jewish grandparent.[46] The Third Decree of May 6 extended the expulsion to *former* members of the Communist party and its affiliated
organizations, including the national-communist movement *Schwarze
Front.* The Third Decree furthermore extended the definition of civil
servants to judges, notaries, school and university teachers, and mem-

bers of the Schutzpolizei, or police.[47] Professional proscription continued until Communists, Socialists, Jews, and other politically "undesirable" people had been economically ruined. With the growth of the concentration camp population and the unfolding of the Holocaust the economic destruction of these people was followed by their physical annihilation. When the smoke swirled around the ruins which were the only legacy of Hitler's Third Reich over 10 million concentration camp prisoners had been murdered—among them were 6 million European Jews.

On April 7, 1933, the Nazi government decreed that Communists and Jews could no longer practice law. A decree of April 22 forced Communists and Jews out of the medical profession. On April 30 professional proscription victimized Jewish and Marxist journalists. On May 6 the Nazi government promulgated a law prohibiting Communists and Jews from working as tax consultants. A decree of July 27 expelled Communists and Jews from the ranks of dentists and dental technicians, while other laws and decrees reached into other types of professional activity.[48]

On May 1, 1933, Joseph Goebbels published an article carried by all German newspapers; the Minister for Popular Enlightenment and Propaganda boasted that Marxism had been smashed. With typical insolence he declared: "Marxism had to die so that a road to freedom could be opened up for German work."[49]

The Social Democratic party and the trade unions suffered the same fate as the Communists. The SPD and the KPD had failed to establish a united front against the National Socialists. The Nazis, however, made no distinctions in their attack on the German workers: Communists and Socialists who had not fought side by side eventually perished together.

During the first month of their rule the Nazis had concentrated their attack on the German Communists, and within a few weeks they had destroyed the most powerful Communist party in Europe. In the second month of their dictatorship the Nazis directed the full force of their onslaught against the Social Democratic party and the trade unions.

On March 8, 1933, SA and SS units occupied SPD and trade union offices and the buildings housing Socialist newspapers. These artibrary and unlawful acts occurred all over Germany. On the same day the Nazis arrested thousands of Social Democratic functionaries.[50]

The attacks continued. On May 10, the Nazis began their campaign against Social Democratic leaders, leading to the removal and arrest of all Socialist deputies, politicians, administrators, and mayors. To forestall the resistance of paramilitary units the Nazis moved against the

Reichsbanner occupying their headquarters in Magdeburg on March 11.[51]

On March 31, the Reich government promulgated a law that brought back the death penalty by hanging, targeting "crimes against public security" for this barbaric punishment. In this way the Nazis fused their perverted "battle law" with their political terrorism. This law was followed by the Anti-Terror Law of April 4, which introduced the death penalty for "political crimes."[52] Always quick to add insult to injury Göring announced to a Berlin audience on April 9, that he was "especially happy that also German socialism has been victorious."[53] On May 2, at 10 A.M. the Nazis occupied by surprise all buildings and firms belonging to the Free Trade Unions, including the Arbeiterbank, or Workers' Bank. Robert Ley, president of the Prussian Privy Council, who ordered this gigantic robbery of the German working class, used the occasion to declare: "The devil's doctrine of Marxism must croak miserably on the battlefield of the National Socialist revolution."[54] The payoff came on the next day, when Hitler ordered his mouthpiece Rudolf Hess to elevate Ley to the rank of Reichsleiter of the Deutsche Arbeitsfront, or German Labor Front.[55] This totalitarian apparatus run by Nazis for the benefit of Nazis replaced all German labor unions. The relationship between the Nazi Labor Front and the Free Trade Unions exhibited the same nightmarish unreality shrouding the ghastly performances of concentration camp orchestras that played under the SS whip in front of the gas chambers. The Nazi attack on the German labor unions triggered mass arrests of union leaders. And the population living behind barbed wire kept on growing—by April 1939, Nazi concentration camps were crowded with more than 300,000 Germans.[56]

Hitler opened the first congress of the Arbeitsfront on May 10, 1933, with a speech declaring that the fight against Marxism would never end. He vowed to destroy Marxism, "to exterminate [it] down to the last root, ruthlessly and mercilessly."[57] On the same day the Nazis literally kicked the Social Democratic deputies out of the Munich town council, and in Berlin and many other German cities Nazi students burned so-called un-German books.[58] The book burning happened shortly after the publication of a "first list" of forbidden authors which had appeared on April 23, outlawing all significant writers from Bertolt Brecht to Stefan Zweig. Nazi proscription of creative activity silenced about eight hundred authors and banned all major artists and thinkers.[59] In the concentration camps the Nazis murdered many artists, writers, and intellectuals along with activist workers and other political foes of the German dictatorship.

On May 19 the working people became subject to the Law About

Trustees of Labor which empowered the chancellor to appoint such trustees. By filling the posts with high-ranking Nazis, including lawyers, administrators, and managers, Hitler greatly expanded their power to maintain the Arbeitsfrieden, or labor peace, including the determination of wage scales, working conditions, vacations, and dismissals.[60] From then on, these lackeys ruled the workers' lives, always to the benefit of employers. The stormtrooper and Minister of Labor Franz Seldte addressed the entire gang of trustees on June 20. Seldte, who would soon be promoted to the rank of SA-Obergruppenführer, parroted the authoritarian nature of the law ordained by his master and declared that collective bargaining and arbitration based on the "Marxist principle of the class struggle" had ceased to exist.[61] The minister's speech announced to the workers that the entire organizational structure erected by the trade unions since the dawn of the labor movement had been buried in the graveyard of the Labor Front. One June 22, Ley, the führer of the Labor Front, ordered the Nazi thugs in the National Socialist Organization of Industrial Cells (NSBO) to "clean out" the Arbeitsfront "down to the last cell." Ley told his minions to "brutally remove" all former Marxists, followers of the Catholic Center party, and members of middle-class organizations from the Labor Front. With this pronouncement the Nazis declared war on the Christian labor unions: On June 24, members of the NSBO occupied all offices of the Christian labor unions and terminated their existence.[62]

The destruction of the SPD was officially announced on June 22, 1933, with the declaration by the minister of the interior that the Social Democratic party was an enemy of the state and the people, deserving the same treatment that had been used against the Communist party. The Nazi government prohibited all functions performed by the SPD including parliamentary representation, meetings, and publications. The Nazis confiscated all assets belonging to the SPD and its affiliated organizations and arrested the remaining Socialist leaders including Paul Löbe.[63] Löbe, who had been president of the Reichstag from 1925 to 1932, later joined the German resistance group Goerdeler-Leuschner to carry on the fight against the Nazis. During the Nazi regime the 120 seats of the SPD in the Reichstag remained vacant.[64]

After the final destruction of the workers' mass movements on June 22, 1933, the Nazis began their attack on the other political parties. On June 25, Goebbels gave a speech in the Rhineland town of Rheydt, where he was born, and declared that the German people must be "unified" in one political party, the NSDAP, and denied that any other political party had the right to exist.[65] On the same day the Nazis arrested the deputies and functionaries of the Bavarian People's party. On the evening of June 27, representatives of the conservative German

Nationalist Front, got together with Chancellor Hitler and signed a pact of friendship; then the German Nationalist Front "decided" to dissolve itself.[66] On June 28, Goebbels spoke in Stuttgart and demanded self-dissolution from the leading Catholic political party, the Catholic Center party, and on July 1, the Staatspolizei closed the offices of the entire complex of organizations affiliated with the Center party. The Gestapo also confiscated all the assets owned by the organizations of the party.[67]

On July 4, the Bavarian People's party and the German People's party ceased to exist. The leaders used the occasion of their parties' "voluntary" dissolution to make subservient noises in the direction of the Nazis. On July 5, the leaders of the Catholic Center party addressed their subservient utterances to Herrn Reichskanzler Hitler and declared the Center party's "self-dissolution."[68] This day marked the end of political parties in Germany. On July 5 the Nazi-dominated press celebrated the National Socialist Totalitätsanspruch, or "totality claim." As Kriegk, the editor of a popular Berlin newspaper, put it in the incredible neo-German of the Third Reich: "Now the work of destruction of the party state has been completed."[69]

On July 11, Hitler's mouthpiece Reich Minister Frick officially declared the completion of the "German revolution" and proclaimed: "The National Socialist German Workers' party has herewith become the sole carrier of the state."[70] On July 14, a law was passed which declared that the NSDAP was the only political party in Germany, making all attempts to maintain or form other political parties a crime subject to severe punishment. The law concerning the Unity of Party and State of December 1, 1933, completely and irrevocably handed the state over to Hitler's National Socialist party.[71]

For the Nazis the destruction of the workers' mass movements and democratic politics was not only a political maneuver on the road to genocide and total war; it was also a gigantic heist foreshadowing the colossal plunder of the Jews and many European peoples. On May 9, 1933, the Nazis set the Prussian criminal justice system in motion to engineer the confiscation of all assets belonging to the SPD, the Socialist press, and the Reichsbanner. On May 12, all assets belonging to the Free Trade Unions were confiscated and handed over to the leader of the Nazi Labor Front, while the confiscation of SPD assets was carried out in all parts of Germany.[72] On May 15, the Labor Front took over the consumers' cooperative societies thereby giving the Nazis a fortune in hard-earned savings which millions of workers had entrusted to the cooperatives. On May 26, the Reich government passed a law based on paragraph 40 of the penal code concerning high treason which led to the confiscation of all Communist assets. On June 22, the

Nazis confiscated all remaining SPD assets and those of organizations affiliated with the Socialists.[73]

On July 11, 1933, the Nazi government officially declared that the "German revolution" had been completed. The official circular, signed by Frick as minister of the interior, also celebrated the establishment of the one-party system.[74]

Meanwhile the National Socialist leaders reviled the other political parties as collections of miserable cowards who had deserted their colors without a fight. On June 16, 1933, Goebbels spoke at a Nazi party rally in Hamburg and expressed his astonishment over the swift disappearance of the Nazis' enemies.[75]

Long after the destruction of Nazism by the Allied armies of World War II, many problematic questions continue to haunt us. Did the anti-Nazi forces underestimate Hitler's will and ability to rule? Did they assume Nazism was doomed to quick failure and disintegration? Did German leftists believe that the Nazis were a necessary evil needed to hasten the collapse of capitalism, thereby opening the road to socialism? Did the hostile feelings separating the KPD from the SPD run deep enough to forestall the formation of a proletarian United Front? Did the workers' leaders fear that high unemployment would turn the call for a general strike into an empty gesture? Were the workers' leaders out of touch with the rank and file? Did the leftists fear the Reichswehr, believing that the army would come out shooting to prop up the Nazis? Were the proletarian leaders rooted too deeply in the parliamentary-legal process to force the fast-moving Nazis out of the political arena? Did the Nazis' gangster methods stun their opponents to such an extent that they could not defend themselves? Had the world economic crisis paralyzed the workers' will to resist?

These questions and others have remained part of the debate surrounding the destruction of the workers' mass movements. Writing in late May 1933, Leon Trotsky called "the unparalleled defeat of the German proletariat the most important event in modern history since the assumption of power by the Russian proletariat."[76]

Notes

1. See Karl Marx, "Ökonomisch-Philosophische Manuskripte aus dem Jahre 1844," in Marx and Engels, *Historisch-Kritische Gesamtausgabe*, Vol. I/3, ed. V. Adoratskij (Berlin: Marx-Engels-Verlag, 1932), pp. 45–46.
2. Karl Marx and Friedrich Engels, "Manifesto of the Communist Party," in *The Communist Manifesto of Karl Marx and Friedrich Engels*, ed. D. Ryazanoff, trans. Eden and Cedar Paul (New York: Russell & Russell, 1963), p. 34.
3. Marx and Engels, "Manifesto of the Communist Party," p. 34.

4. See Richard F. Hamilton, *Who Voted for Hitler?* (Princeton: Princeton University Press, 1982), p. 476.
5. Cuno Horkenbach, ed., *Das Deutsche Reich von 1918 bis heute* (hereafter cited as *Reich*) (Berlin: Presse- und Wirtschafts-Verlag, 1935), p. 84.
6. Hamilton, *Who Voted for Hitler?* p. 476.
7. Walter Rist, "Die KPD in der Krise," *Neue Blätter für den Sozialismus* 2 (1931): 440. For the different periods of the Weimar Republic see Gunter W. Remmling, "Prologue: Weimar Society in Retrospect," in Michael N. Dobkowski and Isidor Wallimann, eds., *Towards the Holocaust: The Social and Economic Collapse of the Weimar Republic* (hereafter cited as *Holocaust*) (Westport, CT: Greenwood Press, 1983), pp. 3–14.
8. Reinhard Kühnl, *Die Weimarer Republik: Errichtung, Machtstruktur und Zerstörung einer Demokratie* (Reinbek bei Hamburg: Rowohlt Taschenbuch Verlag, 1985), p. 172.
9. See Ossip K. Flechtheim, *Die KPD in der Weimarer Republik* (Frankfurt: Europäische Verlagsanstalt, 1969). See also Siegfried Bahne, *Die KPD und das Ende von Weimar* (Frankfurt: Campus-Verlag, 1976); Hermann Weber, *Die Wandlung des deutschen Kommunismus: Die Stalinisierung der KPD in der Weimarer Republik*, 2 vol. (Frankfurt: Europäische Verlagsanstalt, 1969).
10. See Richard Breitman, *German Socialism and Weimar Democracy* (Chapel Hill: University of North Carolina Press, 1981); Richard N. Hunt, *German Social Democracy, 1918–1933* (New Haven: Yale University Press, 1964); Carl Landauer, *European Socialism: A History of Ideas and Movements from the Industrial Revolution to Hitler's Seizure of Power* (Berkeley: University of California Press, 1959).
11. See Kühnl, *Die Weimarer Republik*, p. 163.
12. See ibid., p. 172. See also Karl Rohe, *Das Reichsbanner Schwarz Rot Gold: Ein Beitrag zur Geschichte und Struktur der politischen Kampfverbände zur Zeit der Weimarer Republik* (Dusseldorf: Droste Verlag, 1966).
13. See Kühnl, *Die Weimarer Republik*, pp. 155, 159. See also Cuno Horkenbach, ed., *Das Deutsche Reich von 1918 bis heute* (Berlin: Verlag für Presse, Wirtschaft und Politik, 1930), p. 598.
14. See Karl Dietrich Bracher, *Die Deutsche Diktatur: Entstehung, Struktur, Folgen des Nationalsozialismus* (Cologne and Berlin: Kiepenheuer & Witsch, 1969), p. 183; Dietrich Orlow, *The History of the Nazi Party: 1919–1933* (Pittsburgh: University of Pittsburgh Press, 1969), p. 239; Fritz Bolle, ed., *Knaurs Lexikon* (Munich: Th. Knaur Nachf. Verlag, 1954), p. 1113; David Schoenbaum, *Hitler's Social Revolution: Class and Status in Nazi Germany, 1933–1939* (New York: Doubleday, 1966), p. 74; Michael H. Kater, *The Nazi Party: A Social Profile of Members and Leaders, 1919–1945* (Cambridge, MA: Harvard University Press, 1983).
15. See G. S. Graber, *History of the SS* (New York: David McKay, 1978), p. 40. For reports on police brutality see *Reich*, pp. 23, 24, 28.
16. Dobkowski and Wallimann, "Introduction," *Holocaust*, p. 18.
17. Orlow, *The History of the Nazi Party*, p. 153.
18. Ulrike Hörster-Philipps, "Conservative Concepts of Dictatorship in the Final Phase of the Weimar Republic," in *Holocaust*, p. 120.
19. Ibid. See also Alan Bullock, *Hitler: A Study in Tyranny*, rev. ed. (New York: Harper & Row, 1962), pp. 196–99.
20. *Holocaust*, p. 120.
21. Ibid., p. 121, and IMG, Bd. 33, Dok. 3901–PS. Cited in Helmut Eschwege, ed., *Kennzeichen J: Bilder, Dokumente, Berichte zur Geschichte der Verbrechen des Hitlerfaschismus an den deutschen Juden, 1933–1945* (Frankfurt: Röderberg-Verlag, 1979), pp. 29–31.

22. See George Hallgarten and Joachim Radkau, *Deutsche Industrie und Politik von Bismarck bis Heute* (Cologne: Europäische Verlagsanstalt, 1974).
23. Graber, *History of the SS*, p. 66.
24. See William Manchester, *The Arms of Krupp, 1587–1968* (Boston: Little, Brown and Company, 1968), pp. 470, 471, 612.
25. See Eschwege, ed., *Kennzeichen J*, pp. 264–65.
26. *Holocaust*, p. 32.
27. For a list of corporations, banks, and their contributions to Himmler's special account see Eschwege, ed. *Kennzeichen J*, p. 267.
28. *Holocaust*, p. 32.
29. The decree of February 28, 1933, based on Article 48, paragraph 2 of the Weimar Constitution was the basis of the Nazis' totalitarian police state. See *Verordnung des Reichspräsidenten zum Schutze von Volk und Staat, Reichsgesetzblatt* (hereafter cited as RGBI) I, 1933, p. 83.
30. *Gesetz zur Behebung der Not von Volk und Reich (Ermächtigungsgesetz)*, RGBI I, 1933, p. 141. Article 3 of this enabling law empowered the chancellor to engross and promulgate the laws of the Reich.
31. See Gunter W. Remmling, "Discrimination, Persecution, Theft, and Murder under Color of Law: The Totalitarian Corruption of the German Legal System, 1933–1945," in Isidor Wallimann and Michael Dobkowski, eds., *Genocide and the Modern Age: Etiology and Case Studies of Mass Death* (Westport, CT: Greenwood Press, 1987), p. 189.
32. *Reich*, p. 41.
33. See *Verordnung des Reichspräsidenten zum Schutze des deutschen Volkes*, RGBI I, 1933, pp. 35–37.
34. For Göring's *Runderlass, Förderung der nationalen Bewegung*, see *Reich*, p. 61. See also *Reich*, p. 104.
35. RGBI I, 1933, p. 83.
36. *Reich*, p. 75. See also Hermann Göring, *Reden und Aufsätze*, ed. Erich Gritzbach (Munich: Zentralverlag der NSDAP, Franz Eher Nachf., 1938), pp. 27–28.
37. See *Reich*, p. 79–81. See also *Reich*, p. 108.
38. See ibid., p. 83. In 1944 Thälmann died in a Nazi concentration camp.
39. See ibid., p. 103.
40. Ibid., p. 106.
41. Ibid., p. 115.
42. See ibid., p. 123. Oranienburg concentration camp opened on March 21, 1933.
43. See ibid., p. 140; RGBI I, 1933, p. 141.
44. See *Reich*, p. 155.
45. Gunter W. Remmling, "Discrimination, Persecution, Theft, and Murder Under Color of Law," Wallimann and Dobkowski, eds., *Genocide and the Modern Age*, p. 191. See also RGBI I, 1933, p. 175.
46. See RGBI. I, 1933, p. 195.
47. Ibid., p. 245.
48. Ibid., pp. 188, 222, 257, 542. See also *Reich*, p. 191.
49. *Reich*, p. 182. See also Joseph Goebbels, *Signale der neuen Zeit*, 2nd ed. (Munich: Zentralverlag der NSDAP., Franz Eher Nachf., 1934), pp. 151–52.
50. See *Reich*, pp. 105–6.
51. See ibid., p. 109.
52. See ibid., pp. 150, 156.
53. Hermann Göring, *Reden und Aufsätze*, p. 37.
54. *Reich*, p. 197.
55. See ibid., p. 198.

56. See *Reich,* pp. 202, 216, 238, 255, 261, 268, 284, 304. See also Schoenbaum, *Hitler's Social Revolution,* p. xiii.
57. *Reich,* p. 211.
58. See ibid., p. 212.
59. See Richard Drews and Alfred Kantorowicz, eds., *Verboten und Verbrannt: Deutsche Literatur 12 Jahre unterdrückt* (Berlin and Munich: Heinz Ullstein-Helmut Kindler Verlag, 1947).
60. See *Gesetz über Treuhänder der Arbeit,* RGBI I, 1933, p. 285.
61. *Reich,* p. 258.
62. See ibid., p. 260.
63. See ibid., pp. 260–61.
64. See *Reich,* p. 277.
65. See ibid., p. 263. See also Joseph Goebbels, *Goebbels-Reden,* vol. 1: 1932–1939, ed. Helmut Heiber (Dusseldorf: Droste Verlag, 1971), p. 116.
66. See *Reich,* p. 264.
67. See ibid., p. 271. The organizations included Friedensbund Deutscher Katholiken, Kreuzschar, Sturmschar, Volksverein, Katholischer Jungmännerverband.
68. Ibid., p. 275.
69. *Berliner Lokal-Anzeiger,* July 5, 1933.
70. *Reich,* p. 280.
71. See *Gesetz über die Neubildung von Parteien,* RGBI I, 1933, pp. 479, 1016.
72. See *Reich,* pp. 209, 216.
73. See ibid., pp. 220, 236, 261.
74. See ibid., p. 280.
75. See Goebbels, *Goebbels-Reden,* p. 114.
76. Leon Trotsky, "Die deutsche Katastrophe," *Die Neue Weltbühne* (June 8, 1933): 699. Cited in Istvan Deak, *Weimar Germany's Left-Wing Intellectuals: A Political History of the Weltbühne and Its Circle* (Berkeley: University of California Press, 1968), p. 217.

Terror and Demagoguery in the Consolidation of the Fascist Dictatorship in Germany, 1933–34

Kurt Pätzold

The question of how the fascist politicians succeeded in winning power over millions upon millions of Germans and mobilizing them against their own basic interests is still one of the most exciting historical themes that engages historians in both German states as well as in the West generally. There are obvious reasons for this attraction: there has not been another state system in recent German history that could temporarily rely on such a broad popular basis and there has not been another system that plunged its followers into such a disastrous situation.

For decades, this question has been attractive in its many aspects: economic, ideological, cultural, historical, philosophical, anthropological, even religious. A generalizing question raised in this connection is the issue of what people are capable of, what can be done to them or what they would tolerate to be done to them. The fact that such a savage regime as Nazism was able to recruit so many followers is considered by many to be a source of skepticism and pessimism concerning the human condition. This is all the more reason why historians should feel challenged to develop their theories.

Furthermore, this seems to be advisable in view of the many simplistic conceptions of history that are extant concerning this extremely

Translated by Michael N. Dobkowski and Isidor Wallimann

complex problem. In fact, in terms of the fascist dictatorship in Germany, there may be no other historical issue where there is a deeper gulf between the specialists' understanding of history and the interpretations held by many lay people. This gap is due not so much to the work of historians as to the misconceptions spread by magazines and illustrated history books, motion pictures, and, above all, television. Time and again the images of propagandizing Nazi leaders and their followers are presented in magazines, on film, and on television screens and they take on the character of a commercialized commodity. We see the demagogues who talk and gesticulate in a way that hardly impresses anyone today and may even make people laugh. In contrast, we view the masses deeply stirred and enthusiastic for reasons that are obscure, trustfully looking up to these leaders or applauding them hysterically. A world is re-created that is completely alien to our times, and is not understood by the average person, even if informed. Frequently one has the sense that the fascist leaders of the past were somehow very clever and manipulative, whereas their followers were foolish and unthinking. Presented in this fashion, the history of how German fascism won over millions of people is a matter that dazzles and amazes many, inducing them to be astonished or even making them shake their heads in disbelief. The information embodied in experience is lost, and the notion that this could happen again also ceases to be taken seriously, whereas in reality similar processes in character happen every day, wherever popular masses are aligned against their own interests.

The Rise of the Fascist Dictatorship

The leaders of German fascism did not come to power through the votes of the majority of the people. Under the conditions of the bourgeois-parliamentary system of the Weimar Republic they received somewhat more than one-third of the electoral vote. Late in 1932 the National Socialist German Workers party (NSDAP) was faced with a dramatic loss of voters. All efforts taken to make good the loss on the occasion of a state parliament election in a miniature landslide early in 1933 were not fully successful. The Nazis did not win the same number of votes as they had in the summer of 1932. In terms of mobilizing the voters, they had arrived at a hiatus they were unable to breach so long as their rivals and opponents were allowed to act unrestrictedly. If the NSDAP had intensified national demagoguery, they probably would have won over more voters from the right wing but would have lost "leftist" followers. The process would have taken a reverse course if the Nazis had stressed social demagoguery. This tension meant that the fascist politicians had little chance of coming into state power through observing the parliamentary rules of forming a government, but they could entertain hope because the Constitution was being increasingly invalidated under the Heinrich Brüning and Franz von Papen administrations.

Once the situation had fundamentally changed through Hitler's being appointed chancellor of the Reich, which made it possible to combine the power of the Nazi organizations with the power of the state, the fascist politicians thought it possible to win over the majority of the people during a Reichstag election. They did not fully succeed in subsequently legitimizing the undemocratic formation of a government on January 30, 1933, that was repugnant to the letter and spirit of the law. No doubt, the NSDAP won votes on the wave of their success— two out of five voters gave their support to the Nazi party—but the government could surpass the 50 percent mark only due to the fact that the union of the German nationalist allies of Nazi fascism provided the margin and that narrowly. The elections of March 5, 1933, reflect a fatally tragic decision by half of the electorate in the German Reich. Organization of the majority of the people under the swastika still lay ahead. When did it in fact occur? There are no election returns or opinion polls available to answer this question. It is not appropriate to consider those votes given in November 1933, on the occasion of the German Reich's provocative withdrawal from the League of Nations, to be a general declaration for the fascist regime. It is also difficult for contemporary observers to understand the actual attitude of the masses toward the regime. There are many possibilities to speculate about, at that time and later. It was the antifascist forces who especially hoped that the followers of the regime would soon be brought down to earth, thus initiating its isolation from the masses.

What then can the historian focus on? An obvious area of examination is the changing environment under which the Nazi leaders could manipulate the people. Another is the drift in methods and tactics used in canvassing for more followers. It is obvious—but not frequently enough noted—that the Nazis' success in canvassing for more followers was by no means due only to their own efforts and activities. The new economic and other living conditions created by the regime for sections of the population can be referred to but their effect is difficult to assess. To summarize: the historian can only analyze the factors that fostered the consolidation process and helped the rulers to achieve more influence in the domestic sphere. With this focus, it is possible for the trend of development and its causes to become recognizable.

Long before January 30, 1933, the fascist politicians had, time and again, declared their intention to "reunite" the German people, to overcome the—allegedly artifically developed—polarity of the classes and strata, and to create a "national socialist popular community." This is also what Hitler and other leaders of the Nazi party offered the industrial and land-owning aristocracy, the Junkers, when they met with them. The community and system they proposed was not to be an end in itself. On the one hand, it sought to directly improve the situation of capital's rule and its conditions of realilzation; on the other hand, it aimed at facilitating the preparation and waging of a war for world domination in the course of which there would "never again be November 9th" (1918). This meant, simply, that the people under fascist rule would have to be willing to sacrifice until the victorious end of the coming war. The fascists held (and so did all other deadly enemies of the working-class movement) that it was, above all but not alone, the political parties of the working class and the trade unions that stood in the way of the popular community. German fascism also came out as an avowed and unqualified opponent of democracy and liberalism and undertook to turn back history not only to before 1917 but even before 1789. These unpopular goals could be reached only through force escalated up to terror because the working-class movement would not disappear voluntarily and there were also unswerving people among democrats and liberals who would use any opportunity to act against Nazism as long as they were not deprived of this option. The fascist politicians made no apologies for their determination to resort to terror. Even before they came to power they had already mentioned concentration camps as a final destination for their political opponents.

The first stage in the consolidation phase of the fascist dictatorship, which lasted from late January to approximately mid-July 1933, was marked above all by the attempt of the Nazi leadership to manipulate public opinion through terrorism and brutality. Consequently, they severely punished any basic opposition toward the regime. The political scene in Germany changed in those months, in a fashion and at a rate that surely had been unimaginable for contemporaries at the beginning of the year. All parties other than the Nazi party were made illegal. The trade unions were smashed. Many other more-or-less political organizations, federations, and associations disappeared. Some were eliminated through the intimidation and violence of the paramilitary formations of the Nazis and the state; others quit of their own free will and declared themselves dissolved. In each case it was the use of force, the threat of violence, or, at the very least, the fear of force and violence that created the desired situation for the fascist rulers, namely, the end of an effective legal opposition. This meant that the opposition was pushed underground, thereby severely reducing its impact from the outset.

The methods of terrorist deterrence were used openly and pointedly in the course of this first stage of the consolidation process. Political opponents were murdered in public places. The Communists, Social Democrats, and other opponents of Hitler, bearing the marks of the tortures to which they had been exposed in the "brown houses" and other meeting places of the fascist storm troops, were sent back to their homes, to the employment offices, and to the factories to be a living warning. In most cases, the first concentration camps were located in or near towns and industrial districts so that what occurred within these camps would become more well known than would be the case in the concentration camps built later whose names have become notorious. The first Communists executed, for example, were sentenced to death by a court even before the Reichstag fire trial.

Briefly, force and its most extreme manifestation, terror, was from the very beginning the basic factor that made the manipulation of the masses in the fascist state possible. It was the precondition and basis of everything else. A graphic representation of the three factors that most influenced the population could be made in the form of a triangle, the foundation of which is the terror, from which emanates the demagoguery; a third factor could be called corruption through success.

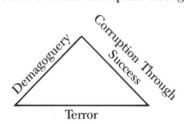

Terror

The respective influence of these factors in the overall thrust of fascist alignment and mobilization of the popular masses did not remain unchanged during the years of Nazi rule. The proportions varied. It is evident that for the consolidation phase the corruption through success in domestic and foreign policies (real or imagined) still had a very limited effect. Terror remained the fundamental element even when the regime dazzled large sections of the population through its successes in implementing its foreign policy without war. The major fascist leaders understood that fact and offered resistance against all proposals—which were also made from their own ranks—to restrict its arbitrary application and to grant some of the prisoners in the concentration camps the legal instrument to force reconsideration of the reasons for their detention. The direct effect of the terror, which included murder, put the opponents of fascism to the most severe test as early as the first months of 1933, and it influenced the decisions of Hitler's opponents in terms of how they would face the regime. The German Communist party (KPD), in particular, but other opponents of fascism as well, resolved to wage the illegal fight although they knew they could be cast into concentration camps or guillotined, whereas others remained antifascists by conviction but refrained from action.

The terror did not only act as a deterrent. It also had a propagandizing effect. Some people, often those from the socially weak middle class, were opposed to the use of extreme force whereas others assessed it as a sign of the regime's durability and hence to be expected and began adapting themselves to its demands. Thus the demonstration of violence in itself had a demagogical effect. Certain preconditions for this tendency had already been set. Many Germans had learned to overrate the role of force, even to admire it. They interpreted the use of terror in the establishment of the fascist state as proof of the fact that now Germany had strong-willed leaders who would be able to maintain "order." It is in this tendency that we see a close connection between terror and demagoguery.

In order to judge the effects of demagoguery in the initial phase of fascist rule, it is necessary to examine carefully the situation of the masses to whom the Nazi politicians addressed their promises, for it was not intrinsically the programs promised and the slogans issued that brought the rulers new followers and sympathizers. During the years of the international economic crisis, the NSDAP fomenters and particularly Hitler himself had developed a particular appreciation for the methods that would be most useful in the exploitation of the miserable conditions of the masses for their own fascist purposes. They had long since become aware of the fact that, due to increasing levels of despair, it was possible to win over not only the middle class but also fringe groups of the proletariat, provided these people received promises that the situations they found unbearable would change drastically and rapidly. Furthermore, the low educational standard of these strata made it possible to promote simplistic solutions revolving around the notion that Hitler was the savior who would rescue Germany from the depths of economic and political despair.

After January 30, 1933, the NSDAP was faced with the problem, which they had created themselves, of meeting the high expectations of their followers. Since they were unable to meet these expectations, they had to mollify the masses by the claim that the first signs of change were harbingers of more fundamental transformations coming later. After seizing power, when clocks began running differently, the fascist policy had a twofold agenda. It had to keep the existing followers fine-tuned and, at the same time, recruit new followers. It is a well-known fact that the Nazis lost a few followers in the early months of power, but won many more who became supporters of the NSDAP again or joined the party for the first time. Before the elections in March, Hitler had demanded that he be given four years' time so that he could realize his plan "for the rescue of workers" and a parallel plan "for the rescue of farmers." This modulated approach indicated that his tactic now was to restrain the high expectations of the German people. As to the more extremist demands of his own followers regarding the need for prompt social measures, the fascist leadership at once declared that the first order of business was to correct policy before they could deal with "the economy." This approach was very different from the promises made in 1932. The divergence inevitably produced disappointment, which sometimes intensified because the ordinary Nazis saw how rapidly their leaders managed to feather their own nests. Social demagoguery was not abandoned but the timetable was extended. Moreover, this was justified by the fascist politicians with the claim that they had to reverse the dreadful Marxist legacy of the "System Period," as they disparagingly called the Weimar Republic. This legacy was unfairly described as being the result of Marxist policy, although Brüning and von Papen during the crisis had clearly supported the interests of capitalist rule and exploitation. The new rulers were also aware of the fact that using terror and making demagogic excuses was not enough to consolidate the fascist regime but that it was necessary for them to be able to show results, and the sooner the better. The reduction of mass unemployment was considered the decisive policy that would keep millions of people loyal to the party. This would improve the living conditions of proletarians and indirectly alleviate the situation of the middle classes.

In fact, the campaign aimed at creating jobs was the Nazis' propaganda coup as early as 1933. The leaders produced the impression that all their efforts were concentrated on doing away with unemployment and they tried to make people believe that this program was for them. In truth, the economic status of the masses was of less importance to Hitler, Joseph Goebbels, and Robert Ley, who only pretended solidarity with the people, than to any other group of politicians in recent German history. In their search for shortcuts to war, they considered job-providing measures that stepped up the process of armament and that were likely to promote Germany's war preparations to be preferable. Of course, it was impossible to immediately adopt and implement this course because jobs in the war industry were expensive and there were only limited state funds that could be used to subsidize them. Yet, each step toward the reduction of the unemployment figures had to be highly appreciated by the regime for its political benefits.

As early as the summer of 1933, the Nazi newspapers started to report triumphantly about rural districts where unemployment was said to have been done away with completely. These were remote agrarian regions where there had been a low unemployment rate to begin with and a high rate of rural exodus because of the monotony and dullness of life without any prospect of change. A greater advantage for the regime was the fact that it established itself at a time when there was a gradual and slow upswing in economic activity. Work-providing measures, particularly in the building trades—already planned by the last cabinets of the Weimar Republic and now realized and passed off as an indication of the new policy—additionally reduced the unemployment rate. In this regard, the spectacularly staged start of the construction of the autobahn in the autumn of 1933, which was the implementation of another technological idea the fascists had adopted, showed Hitler himself as a worker, as a very new type of German politician.

In view of the fact that the unemployment rate rapidly increased again by the end of 1933 and soon exceeded the 4 million mark, references to full employment alone would have placed the fascists' demagoguery on too weak a foundation. The notion that the "New Germany" was a community in which everybody extended active solidarity toward the poorest in their midst was also exploited. In that state the "national socialist people's community" would not leave anybody to his fate. The attention Goebbels aroused in the winter aid campaign (Winterhiltswerk) in 1933–34 even exceeded that called forth in the struggle against unemployment. The campaigns in which charity donations in the form of money and goods were collected from the people in order to be distributed again among the very needy, preferably the old and the sick and among large families, proved to be very effective in terms of propaganda.

Other campaigns were less effective than these two drives. This, for example, is true of the organization "Vigor Through Joy" (*Kraft durch Freude*), launched in the autumn of 1933, and it is true of its initial activity aimed at demonstrating a new attitude toward work and performance by providing recreation and holidays for working people. It was Nazi followers in the first stages of the program who were provided with inexpensive or gratuitous holiday trips and who received them as a reward for their "work," which they had carried out within the ranks of the Sturmabteilung (SA) or Schutzstaffel (SS) in the early years of the struggle. The fascist politicians pointedly showed their solicitude for the war-disabled of World War I and claimed that they were defamed through the work of such painters as Otto Dix or George Grosz, who had in fact accused not victims but profiteers of war in their paintings and drawings.

The essence of Nazi demagoguery was the description of economic and social measures as policies that would make Germany a flourishing country once again, inhabited by contented people. This is a critical point that helps explain the rush of followers fascism could register. War was not discussed; none of the ruling politicians trifled with the idea of unleashing a war. The Nazi propaganda itself used Goethe's picture of a people resembling Faust making deserts accessible for mankind. This was another ruse to deflect any suspicions that might be raised concerning the intensifying preparations for a war aimed at achieving revenge for Versailles and realizing the conquest plans that German imperialism had striven for in 1914 plus additional territorial ambitions. In fact, these activities were carried out energetically despite Nazi denials.

The peace demagoguery played a central role in creating the mass foundation of the regime as early as the consolidation phase. In 1933–34 it was easier than in the following years to deceive the people through false pretensions for peace, because the measures taken for armament and the extension of the Reichswehr (German armed forces) could hardly be noticed by the public. Those who would have been able to draw the people's attention to this fact and warn against these attempts had already been largely deprived of their influence. Thus it was even possible for the Nazis to describe the withdrawal from the League of Nations largely without let or hindrance as a sign of national self-esteem, although in reality it was a step toward unhindered and unchecked armament.

The pretense of the pursuit of peace would not have been accepted by so many credulous people if the fascist rulers had not been able to supplement the demagoguery of their words with the demagoguery of their deeds. The diplomatic isolation of the regime was at no time complete, even though the capitalist governments were rather inhibited in their dealings with the Nazis, particularly at times when the proletarian and middle-class opponents of the Nazis in their own countries took concerted action to jointly accuse the fascists—as for example on the occasion of the first persecutions of the Jews. The negotiations concerning the Four-Power Pact, which was never effective; the conclusion of the concordate between the Vatican and the German Reich; and above all the signing of the German-Polish nonaggression pact in January 1934 could be used by the fascist leaders and declared voluntary corroboration on the part of foreign powers of their readiness to cooperate with the "new" Germany. Furthermore, the agreement made with Warsaw provided the Nazis with an opportunity to exhibit their readiness to pursue a policy of rapprochement toward the neighboring countries in the East, a policy that—the fascists asserted—had broken with the anti-Polish policy of the Weimar Republic.

Fascist demagoguery found its greatest success in the willingness of the masses to accept deceit and to exploit a national myth. Here it was possible for the Nazi politicians not only to act on the basis of the fruits of their own policies but to take advantage of the unintentional concessions provided by the activities of all other bourgeois parties, and that was more effective than the social hypocrisy connecting Nazism with a national "socialism." All politicians from the center to the right had inveighed against the "infamy," the "shame," the "chains" of Versailles for nearly one and a half decades. There had been endless discussions of Germany's "utmost humiliation" and "enslavement." This mythology averted consideration of the fact that German imperialism was responsible for the unleashing and the aftermath of World War I and the exporting of internal causes of social misery and it kept alive the idea of the total revision of the 1919 treaty and the determination to avenge it, both very popular ideas with the German people.

When the Nazis came into power, they knew how to arouse national enthusiasm among old and new followers. Still, they did not escalate it into a chauvinist frenzy in 1933–34 because they were forced to use certain moderating tactics in their foreign policy for some years. The refrain "Germany awaken" issued time and again showed clearly enough, however, which trend was envisaged for the mobilization of the masses. In fact, there was nobody in Germany who had not encountered at school those pictures of sleeping giants and warriors who had been awakened and had risen to perform new great deeds. Who did not know the legend of the Emperor Frederick I Barbarossa, who had vanished in a mountain and was said to return one day in order to make the empire great again? Of course, Hitler was not naively considered the resurrected member of the Hohenstaufen dynasty, but broad elements of the middle classes and the petty bourgeoisie were seized by the rescuer/savior sentiment, the desire to win new glamor and glory.

The fascist demagogues endlessly reiterated that they were only interested in acting for "Germany" and their "fellow Germans." Concord and harmony were described in a simple but effective way as the original nature of the Germans, which had been destroyed by their enemies, the Jews, striving for world domination, and those Germans depraved by them. The awareness of the existence of social classes and class struggle seemed to be arbitrarily created by the enemies of the people. It was alleged that the subjugation, elimination, or, at best, reeducation of those enemies would reunite the Germans and put an end to discord among them once and for all. The internal purpose of this national demagoguery was quite obvious. It served to justify the persecution of all opponents and, particularly, the terrorizing of the working-class movement. That is, the policy aimed at "wiping Marxism off the map." What seemed to be the necessary precondition for the emergence of a new community of all Germans, the "national socialist" community of the people, was the belief that the opponents of fascism, which was propagated as the actual embodiment of the national idea, be subjugated or exiled, that they be made to vanish in penitentiaries and prisons. This national socialist community of the people, in turn, was considered to be the guarantor of the rise of the new Germany. From the first months of 1933, high national and world-historic importance was attributed to the victory of the fascist counterrevolution by the use of such terms as "national uprising," "Third Reich," and "millennium." The prophetic term was not used later on.

This national demagoguery, the core of which was to serve the mobilization of national ideas and feelings for reactionary and, finally, aggressive-warmongering purposes, formed a unity with a demagoguery of action, and the same is true of the social demagoguery. It found its expression in the policy of persecuting the Jews. To put it bluntly, this shameless policy was not only aimed at aligning the "Aryan" Germans along fascist principles and for adventurous-imperialist purposes. Particularly in the early phase of practical anti-Semitism, it aimed at the internal consolidaiton of the system. What were the benefits of that tide of Nazi slogans such as "Germans, only buy from Germans"; "Germans, only allow Germans to judge you"; "Germans, do not let anybody but Germans teach you"; "Germans, only allow Germans to medically treat you"; "Germans, only read German literature, only enjoy German art"; and so forth? All these slogans obviously showed anti-Semitism in its classical diverting function. Attempts were made to use them—now as before—to muddle the causes of all social grievances, to brand guilty those who were not. The Jew-baiting not only had the function of reducing the focus of the "national socialist revolution" to the persecution, expropriation, and expulsion of German Jews, thus being conducive to feigning a revolution where only vulgar and purposive nationalism and racism spent themselves. Anti-Semitism and persecution of Jews in 1933, which mainly used the arbitrary contrast of "German" and "Jewish" and flatly denied that Jews could assimilate, had an integrating function: uniting the approximately 99 percent of the Germans declared to be Aryans, isolating them from the "aliens" and "enemies," and committing them to the allegedly national government, and thus, in the last analysis, to fascist rule.

The German Jews were the obvious victims of practical anti-Semitism, but those who were intended to be disciplined were the non-Jewish Germans. This policy was successful, and not only within the strata of the social petty bourgeoisie. It was very easy, for example, to commence the implementation of anti-Semitic laws and regulations in the field of higher education even as early as a few weeks after the establishment of a fascist dictatorship. It was not even fascist special superintendents who did so but, initially, rectors and deans already elected before January 30, 1933, who were assisted in implementing the mendacious principle according to which "Jewish" tenets were no longer allowed to be disseminated at "German" universities and colleges. Indeed, it was the holders of the traditional elected posts who saw to it that the questionnaires searching for "Jews" were distributed and filled in and then handed over to the fascist authorities. These professors, often erudite but committed to anti-Semitism—as a rule, not fascist anti-Semitism—started to collaborate with the fascist racists in March/April 1933. German-Jewish scholars were suspended from office, pensioned off, or divested of their lectureships.

These early events at the universities and colleges are only one example of a multitide of events that took place, only slightly modified—in supervisory boards of corporations, banks, industry, the executive boards of world-famous companies, and management boards of hospitals, theaters, and orchestras. They all demonstrated that the consolidation process of the fascist dictatorship was stimulated and directed by members of the administration but that it was by no means their work alone. The speed by which the regime was established was possible only because a rapidly increasing number of persons volunteered for Nazi leadership although they were not fascists themselves, but mistook the new government for a force of national awakening, and accepted and supported it. The aspects of the regime they did not like were rationalized away by the excuse that you cannot make an omelette without breaking eggs. The German-Jewish colleague who was formerly treated as an integral part of German society was now sacrificed for a greater cause. How can a dismissed Jew plunged into misfortune and misery be compared with the imaginary importance of national events?

The national demogoguery became the ideological cement of collaboration: it mobilized collaborators, and served to justify their doing the fascists' dirty work although they had not been forced to do so and although fascism had not yet established itself. I am not denying the fact that some followers of fascism were very uneasy about this nor am I minimizing the psychic pressures to which they were exposed. No doubt, much personal energy and courage was necessary to set oneself against this wave of "national awakening" that was running so high and not allow oneself to be swept away with it. This was a type of strength that mostly characterized those who were able to oppose fascism on the basis of fundamental alternative ideological and political creeds and conceptions. Even those sections of the German middle classes and petty bourgeoisie who as yet had resisted Nazi propaganda were still influenced by many of the ideas and views regarding Germany's present and future that were kindred or very similar to fascism and, in the changed circumstances of 1933, were no more resilient than cracks in a dam bound to break once the pressure increased.

What added to this pressure was the collapse of the non-Nazi bourgeois parties and organizations and the concomitant circumstances around their retreat. They did not simply quit without comment. The last papers issued by those parties announcing their self-disbandment used the national phrase and even included strict orders to their own cadres and members to volunteer for the "national government." What else could the fascist rulers actually desire? They had already been able to take advantage of other decisions prior to these statements. The bourgeois parties, rivals so far but in part already partners of the NSDAP (e.g., in some state governments before 1933), had repeatedly stooped to provide surety for cabinets headed by Hitler. Their behavior on the occasion of the vote regarding the Enabling Act in March and the government's foreign-affairs declaration in May 1933 had to be considered votes of confidence and provided excellent opportunities to overcome the reservations that had been entertained against the NSDAP and its leaders by members of the Catholic parties, the Center party, and the Bavarian People's party, as well as the German People's party and the State party. The very last actions of all these parties called on their followers to give their allegiance to the rulers. What must also be mentioned in this connection is the vote of the remaining fraction of the Social Democratic party of Germany on the occasion of the ballot in May 1933.

There is a long list of organizations and institutions that called on the people to rally around the Hitler administration or at least demanded subordination to the government. They were not all equally important or influential. The Christian churches figured prominently. Their call to the faithful to apply to the fascist power the appeal quoted from the Bible, to render unto Caesar the things that are Caesar's, was most significant. As early as March 28, 1933, the leadership of the Catholic church of Germany removed most of the obstacles they had set up and maintained to prevent priests and laypeople from going over to the NSDAP. The penalties for siding and affiliating with Nazi fascism that had been pronounced and executed before that date were no longer effective.

There was a wide range of motives for this support of the fascist government. Some were of an intellectual or material nature; others were marked by economic, political, and personal interests. For many, it was pure opportunism. From time to time the structure of the motives varied because in most cases there was not only one operative motive. In capitalist circles, for example, a mixture of political and economic interests was decisive for those large and small employers' associations that "backed the government" and called on the people to follow their example because it made good business sense. Similarly, the most powerful economic forces used their relations and contacts with foreign countries to assure their business partners that the Hitler administration would not resort to anticapitalist measures and would not obstruct the turnover of capital and foreign trade. In the episcopate, it was a mixture of intellectual-political motives influenced primarily by committed anitcommunism that led to sympathy for a fascism that had come to power.

No doubt, it is one of the tasks of historiography to shed light on the motives of the historical actors but it is also very obvious that the course of historic events is not determined by motives, but by political behavior. Creeds as such are of little historic relevance. They become significant in terms of history only if they give rise to action. The consolidation phase of fascism in Germany also demonstrates that action resulted from very different inducements, all of which, irrespective of their causes, contributed to consolidating the dictatorship through their creation of a broader mass basis for fascism. For this support did not only contribute to the rapidly deteriorating balance between fascism and antifascism to the disadvantage of the latter. The ability of the fascist administration to consolidate itself so rapidly led to subsequent developments. The fact that the fascist dictatorship in Germany fulfilled domestic objectives within months rather than the years it had taken the Mussolini regime, and the conclusion of an agreement between the state and the Catholic church, just to mention two examples, accelerated the speed of the fascist system. There is also a causal connection between the depth and speed of the consolidation process in 1933–34 and the fact that it took the German Reich no longer than six and a half years to be prepared for the total war that was to begin in 1939, a war they had striven for and unleashed. Developments would have been quite different if fascism, after having come to power, had been forced to maintain it in an open battle or had been faced with stronger resistance in its initial phase. Taking this into account, one can state that the subsequent evil was not only determined by the victory of fascism but by the way in which it was reached.

At the end of its consolidation phase, which is felt to coincide with the murder of Ernst Röhm, the SA chief of staff, in 1934, the regime obviously had a relatively stable group of followers that included more than half of the population. There had not been any essential change in its social composition compared with the crowd of partisans of the NSDAP before January 30, 1933. The bulk of the followers was recruited from the middle class, although the first year of the fascist dictatorship had not met their expectations. Even the demagogues themselves confessed that they had not decisively succeeded in winning over sections of blue-collar workers. This was achieved in the two or three years immediately preceding the outbreak of the war. The composition of the group of followers did not remain fully stable in the subsequent period. There were more or less significant movements at the fringes of the mass basis of the fascist dictatorship, mostly depending on the attractiveness or unattractiveness of particular steps and measures taken by the rulers as they impacted on individual social groups.

Thus the partisans did not follow in an unquestioning way. As the subsequent years showed, they responded very sensitively to two factors: the drastic deterioration of the working and living conditions they were faced with in the second half of 1935, in connection with shortages of mass consumption goods, and foreign-policy decisions of the government that could lead to war, such as the so-called Sudeten crises in May and September 1938. The frequently used picture of the people blindly following fascism is not completely true, although there were masses who were fanatic champions of the regime. For the course of history it was of decisive significance that the temporary dips in support of the policy of the fascist leadership never reached such an extent that it would have forced them to change their policy or to essentially decrease the pace of their efforts to accomplish imperialist objects.

This also shows that the opponents of fascism, in spite of all their activities and spirit of sacrifice, could not favorably alter the relationship of forces between themselves and the rulers as it had developed during the consolidation phase. It was impossible to set off sweeping antifascist actions, even during times when the regime lost popularity with sections of the population. The political police, gradually united throughout the Reich in 1933–34 to form the Secret State Police (Gestapo), functioned effectively and hardly made it possible for broader stable contacts to be established between the organized opponents of the regime and the dissatisfied people. The method of brutally persecuting certain persons and thus disciplining, frightening off, and discouraging others so they would give up was successfully practiced.

Between January 30 and June 30, 1933, when fascism established itself as state power and gained in stability, preliminary decisions were made that turned out to be of grave consequence to German and European history. There is no deterministic relationship between these preliminary decisions and September 1–3, 1939. Alternatives were still possible in 1933, but they can only be thought of as an interplay of internal and external factors. Since none were realized, it was possible for German imperialism to largely dominate developments in Europe for a short but disastrous period. Looking on history in the early phase of fascist rule strikingly corroborates the truth of Goethe's warning to learn to be wiser early enough. The battles between humanism and barbarism once lost by those championing the cause of humanity, the chance to determine the course of history to the favor of human interests once given away, may result in the initiative being taken by destructive forces for a relatively long period. Now that the turn of the century is drawing near, historians in many countries surely will more and more reflect that, on the one hand, those twelve years of fascist rule were a very short period—less than one-eighth of this century— but that, on the other hand, they played a significant role in this century. There is an international urge to continue reflecting on the questions raised in this connection and to decline any offers to turn away from them and direct one's attention to "more welcome" events and processes.

Defense of Democracy or Advance to Socialism? Arguments Within German Social Democracy in the mid-1920s

Ben Fowkes

It might well be thought that the antithesis stated in the title of this essay is somewhat unreal, given the closeness of the connection between democracy and socialism. It gains meaning, however, when one counterposes the defense of existing democracy, "bourgeois democracy," "political democracy," "formal democracy," to the advance to a deeper, more consistent, more all-embracing democracy, the extension of democracy from the narrowly political and technically electoral field to society, the economy, and the various institutions of the state (bureaucracy, army, judiciary), all of which is one part of the "advance to socialism." The other part is of course the conversion of the means of production into social or national property: "socialization" or "nationalization."

The conflict over the defense of bourgeois democracy and its extension was thus central to the debates within the noncommunist left parties in the mid-1920s. In addition, there were secondary disagreements over whether bourgeois democracy was itself in such imminent danger that the advance to socialism would have to be postponed to a more distant future; or whether the material interests of the workers (sometimes wrongly identified with socialism) were more important than either aspect of the advance to socialism; or whether local and partial achievements (as exemplified by the measures of the Social Democratic party [SPD] in the Prussian government) were possible while the commanding heights of the state were in capitalist hands.[1]

Eventually, a less ambitious dispute centered around whether a more specialized and technical version of the advance to socialism could be achieved ("economic democracy," as in the German Trade Union Federation [ADGB] plan of 1928) on the basis not of political action but of the inherent suitability of such plans to the given stage of capitalist development, as well as the employers' assumed need to maintain a partnership with the other side of industry.[2]

While these debates went on both before 1924 and after 1930, the period between 1924 and 1930 has been chosen because it possesses a conjunctural unity in terms of political economy: this is true for the German, the European, and perhaps even the world economy. Before 1924 one sees economic instability, difficulties of postwar adjustment,and in Germany, an inflationary crisis; after 1929 there is the onset of the Great Depression. The intervening period is marked by relative stabilization, based on the integration of Germany into the world economy through the Dawes Plan, and its social and political concomitants, namely, the defeat of the working-class struggles of the early 1920s, the restoration of middle-class domination over German politics, and the reestablishment of industrial peace on a new basis, the main features of which were industrial rationalization, an export-led boom, and a readiness by some sections of industrial capital to compromise with the more "reasonable" demands of the workers and accept the democratic foundations of the Weimar Republic. The repercussions of this readiness to compromise extended to the sphere of bourgeois politics and therefore opened the way to broad and potentially stable coalitions. My purpose here is to examine the reaction of the noncommunist left to this situation.

Not surprisingly, most of the basic issues had already been raised before 1924, but in connection with urgent developments in critical political situations that did not allow a leisurely examination of possible strategies.[3] After 1924, on the other hand, the issues could be argued through. The official position of the SPD had been clear since 1918: it was possible to achieve long-term socialist advance through the parliamentary system. In the shorter term, the aim was a democratic reconstruction of state and society by evolutionary means. These conceptions implied a fundamental optimism, but already by 1920 (after the fiasco of the Workers' Government proposal in the aftermath of the Kapp putsch*) most Social Democrats had considerably lowered

---

*A rightist conspiracy headed by Wolfgang Kapp that assumed power in Berlin for a few days.

their sights. It appeared that there was a permanent antisocialist majority under the Weimar Constitution, and that the only (parliamentary) way forward was through coalition with parties to the right of Social Democracy.

Moreover, the defense, rather than the extension, of the achievements of the November revolution, the movement that toppled the Prussian military monarchy and replaced it with a parliamentary-democratic state, was by 1920 the explicit aim. When Hermann Müller, the outgoing German chancellor and a leading figure in the Majority Social Democratic party (MSPD), approached the Independent Social Democratic party (USPD) in June 1920 it was for a defensive not an offensive coalition: "Only through a coalition strengthened by the inclusion of the left" (i.e., the USPD) "would it be possible to defend republican institutions against all attacks from the right and to maintain social gains, especially the eight hour day."[4]

The USPD rejected these overtures, and the SPD withdrew from government; the moment for a coalition of working-class parties passed, not to return. From then on the problem was the kind of conditions the noncommunist left parties should lay down for collaborating with the nonsocialist parties. The SPD Congress of October 1920 in Kassel—greatly influenced by SPD disillusionment with the previous coalition, and its demise—set some conditions that sounded very stringent: "Re-entry to the government would only be possible if urgently demanded by the interests of the proletariat, which require above all the democratisation of the administration, the republicanisation of the *Reichswehr,* the socialisation of those branches of the economy ripe for this, and a peaceful foreign policy."[5] A further requirement was added subsequently: "Cooperation with a party which does not in principle and in practice stand on the ground of the Republican form of state cannot come into consideration."[6]

These conditions would have made coalition with the nonsocialist parties impossible, and in fact only a peaceful foreign policy and a practical commitment to the Republic were insisted on. Nevertheless, the conditions were reaffirmed by the Görlitz program of 1921, which proclaimed the democratic republic to be "the form of state irrevocably brought about by historical development," a form of state in which Social Democracy could not realistically expect to take sole power. The SPD must therefore "throw its political power into the scales on behalf of the republican, democratic form of state" while making certain conditions.[7]

One condition not explicitly made was the defense of workers' material interests, but in fact this exerted a powerful pull. Coalition with the influential German People's party (DVP) was rejected not so much on the grounds of its essential monarchism as because it represented capitalist interests against the workers. This was why the SPD refused to join the DVP in the Wirth Cabinet on November 14, 1922, and why it left Gustav Stresemann's first Grand Coalition cabinet on October 3, 1923, the issue in this case being the preservation of the eight-hour working day.[8] The SPD's withdrawal from the second Stresemann coalition (November 2, 1923), on the other hand, was a reaction to the use of Article 48 of the Weimar Constitution to remove the Social Democratic government in the state of Saxony. This undemocratic act made SPD participation in a coalition meaningless.[9]

The SPD remained outside the government between 1923 and 1928. Although Erich Matthias has criticized the party leaders for having "no political plan, either in power or for opposition," the fact is that there was no shortage of strategic conceptions, merely an inability to agree on applying them.[10] The division between the "activists," such as Otto Braun, Carl Severing, and the revisionists around *Sozialistische Monatshefte,* and the "passivists," such as Hermann Müller, Rudolf Hilferding, and everyone to their left, already apparent in October 1923, continued to bedevil Social Democratic policymaking.

The activists (or, to use David Abraham's typology, the "social-liberal integrationists") were prepared to accept the Weimar system as it stood.[11] Philipp Scheidemann put this view energetically at the party congress held in Berlin in 1924: "We are committed to this republican state which with all its shortcomings is our creation. . . . Our most important duty, on which all our forces should be concentrated, is to save the republic, cost what it may."[12]

Carl Severing, himself continuously involved in the Grand Coalition in Prussia, often used the columns of *Sozialistische Monatshefte* to argue in favor of this position.[13] His main points were (1) given the need to pursue a consistent foreign policy on the lines of Locarno, which would be jeopardized by the entry of the German National People's party (DNVP) into a coalition because they did not accept the German renunciation of Alsace-Lorraine; the SPD should keep out the DNVP by joining the coalition themselves; (2) the experience of the Prussian coalition had shown that it was possible to cooperate with the DVP despite disagreements with it; (3) the struggle between capital and labor needed to be robbed of its hateful and poisonous character (an authentic revisionist note); and (4) the presence of the SDP in the government helped to prevent the reemergence of the Black Reichswehr (i.e., the secret military formations that had sprung up in defiance of the Versailles Treaty in 1923). Further advice of a similar character came from Karl Hildenbrand, Heinrich Peus, and Wally Zepler, who condemned "a large group of comrades" for "fearing to go over from the comfortable defensive of political opposition to the offensive [of coalition]."[14]

The majority of the party held very different views, as was shown in early 1926. On January 11, President Hindenburg asked Fehrenbach (Center) and Koch-Weser (German Democratic party—DDP) to try to form a new edition of the Grand Coalition. There was a sharp conflict within the SPD parliamentary party over the question. The activists, who might almost be called "the Prussians" in view of the predominance among them of people with Prussian ministerial experience, favored entering negotiations with the Center, the DDP, and the DVP. Otto Braun called on the party to find "the courage to take responsibility," adding that "if they were to continue to let their actions be determined by the fear of responsibility, it would deliver a devastating blow to the parliamentary system and smooth the path for the reaction."[15] The passivists argued that "the interests of the working masses should alone be decisive here," and they won the day (by 85 votes to 33). The three reasons the party put forward eventually for its refusal to enter negotiations reflected the "passivist'" position: (1) the importance of returning to the eight-hour day, which the DVP had rejected; (2) the urgent need for unemployment insurance, SPD proposals which the DVP had rejected; and (3) the persistent efforts of the DVP to get compensation for the former German princes.[16] As Hermann Müller (who must at this stage be counted a passivist) wrote in April 1926: "The views of the DVP on the restoration of the German economy at the expense of the German workers and the practical abolition of the eight hour day are incompatible with the views of Social Democracy."[17]

There was, however, a middle way between coalition and opposition: toleration. For much of this period the issue was whether to tolerate the government of the day or to help overturn it. The December 1924 elections confirmed the situation brought about in May of that year: a government opposed by both the extreme left (German Communist party—KPD) and the Monarchist and fascist right (i.e., the DNVP and the National Socialist German Workers party—NSDAP) could retain its majority only with SPD toleration. The activists and the passivists could agree on the necessity of tolerating the cabinets of this period for foreign policy reasons. Hence the government formed in January 1926 owed its survival to Social Democratic abstention in a vote of confidence. Shortly afterward Müller wrote an article in *Die Gesellschaft* defending the principle of tolerating a government the party was not prepared actually to join: "An opposition party, which does not itself want to enter the government, may in some circumstances have the duty to give a government over which it has no influence the chance to begin its legislative work, if that government itself stands on the ground of the parliamentary system."[18]

The policy of toleration bore considerable fruit in the years 1926 and 1927. It could be argued that the SPD achieved more for the workers when out of office than when in it. The list of gains is impressive: establishment of compulsory arbitration by the ministry of labor; the 1927 law on working hours, restoring the eight-hour day in large firms; the Labour Courts Law of 1926; and the Employment Facilitation and Unemployment Insurance Law of July 1927 (AVAVG), which established insurance paid for by contributions from employers, employees, and the state.[19]

Despite these achievements, opinion within the SPD moved away from mere toleration toward active participation in bourgeois governments in this period. There were several reasons for this. First, the Prussian experience seemed to show that coalitions could be fruitful; second, the increasing division within the conservative camp between the DVP, which was moving away from its anti-working-class position, and the DNVP seemed to indicate the possibility of a coalition with the former (though this was hardly a new development); third, and perhaps most important, Paul Silverberg's speech of September 1926 to the League of German Industry (RDI) seemed to be an olive branch from the industrialists to labor. It provided coalition with the necessary social basis, in the sense of the readiness of an important section of German industry (Abraham's "dynamic-export fraction") to take the SPD into partnership. The gains of the years 1926 and 1927 were in part a reflection of this situation. Rudolf Hilferding in particular, as the major theorist of the SPD leadership, provided a Marxist justification for entering a coalition government, based on his perception of a contradiction between the "finished goods industries and the raw materials industries." He saw the former attaining leadership in German capitalism, a fact that should benefit the German working class since they did not "stand in such a direct contradiction to the working class as heavy industry."[20] Hilferding's article of October 1926 in *Die Gesellschaft* is the first presentation of ideas he was to put forward with success at the Kiel Party Congress of 1927. They were adopted by the party, and Hermann Müller tried to put them into practice in his coalition government of 1928 to 1930.

Political Power and Economic Democracy

The Kiel Party Congress of 1927 was dominated by Rudolf Hilferding's defense of coalitions. His basic theoretical justification for coalitions between the SPD and bourgeois parties was that the state was not inevitably an instrument of the ruling class. The ruling class under the Weimar Republic was the capitalist class, but the parliamentary democracy set up in 1919 was not its instrument. It was rather a special form of state that the workers should support. The way forward was to reassert the supremacy of the state—now under threat from the monarchist reaction—by intervening politically. This could be done by participating in governments alongside nonsocialist parties. Coalition was therefore justified in principle.[21]

Participation in government, in Hilferding's view, could serve one of two purposes: it was "either a means of warding off the danger of reaction or of achieving advances in the interests of the workers' movement." His keynote speech at the congress dwelt much more on the first goal, the protection of democracy against the danger of monarchist reaction.[22] "Viewed historically, *democracy* has always been the *cause of the proletariat. . . . The preservation of democracy and the republic* is the most important interest of the party."[23] The left-wing opposition, on the other hand, argued that the interests of the workers were not served by coalition. The resolution moved by the left in 1927 made this very plain:

> The task of Social Democracy in the German republic is to represent proletarian class interests in opposition to the class rule of capitalism, and to fight for social demands and socialism. In comparison with this task the fight for the preservation of the republic which the bourgeoisie has decided to put up with is of lesser significance. . . . The tactics of the SPD must be: *opposition instead of coalition*. This opposition must be conducted in the spirit of proletarian class struggle with all appropriate parliamentary and extra-parliamentary means.[24]

In her eloquent speech in support of this resolution, Toni Sender concentrated her fire on the question of power. Mere entry into a coalition, she said, did not bring power. Power could be achieved only if "strong, active social forces stand behind the government, if we have conquered a position of power in society as well." She was all in favor of a united will to power on the part of Social Democracy, but "not a will to the semblance of power." The second point was one that has been made repeatedly by left-oppositions since the late nineteenth century: cooperation with the bourgeoisie would mislead the workers. "How can we educate the workers to class-consciousness? Not by co-operating with the bourgeoisie in a coalition government."[25]

The second major speaker for the left was Siegfried Aufhäuser. He brought out another constant theme of the left's arguments: the impossibility of separating out the issues, or, to put this another way, the presence behind the Monarchist agitation against the republic of a hidden capitalist agenda. To stress the danger from the developing capitalist offensive was not to deny the importance of republican institutions, but to penetrate to a deeper level of analysis. "This government" (i.e., the *Bürgerblock* government headed by Wilhelm Marx) "is a sign that the capitalists rule the state more than ever." (This point was intended as a rebuttal of Hilferding's argument about the role of the state.) "The content of our resolution is that this government represents less a move against the republic than an anti-social move against the working class. . . . The present bourgeois government does not want the form of state to be the decisive factor, but the desires of the economic interests that stand behind the state."[26]

The left's resolution received 83 votes at the congress, as against 255 for the executive: a minority, therefore, but a substantial one. The party went forward to the 1928 elections, and to eventual coalition, with Hilferding's resolution to guide it:

> The participation of Social Democracy in the government of the *Reich* depends solely on its judgement as to whether its strength among the people and the *Reichstag* gives the guarantee that it can achieve certain specific goals in the interests of the workers' movement, or ward off reactionary dangers by participating in the government in a given situation. The decision is a tactical question and cannot be answered by applying definite formulas laid down once and for all.[27]

The absence from this resolution of any mention of structural change or the achievement of economic democracy is striking. The revisionist wing of the party saw the decision of the Kiel Congress as a complete vindication of their attitude over the previous thirty years. Paul Kampffmeyer described their pre-war slogan, "More Power," as identical with Hilferding's call at Kiel for "the conquest of state power." In each case the aim was the "gradual democratic conquest of power and the advance of constitutionalism."[28] Carl Severing was equally satisfied by the Kiel Congress. The Kiel debates, he said, had removed the impression of hesitancy that had grown since 1923. "We want political power, we want to conquer the state," he added, encouraging the party with the words "Push forward step by step! . . . The fight for power in the republic is ultimately a fight for the republic itself."[29]

While the party went forward from the Kiel Congress with an agenda of the conquest of (shared) political power, the question of economic democracy was left to be raised by the trade unions. This corresponded to the formal division of tasks that was upheld by both sides, but it was nonetheless unrealistic. The proposals for economic democracy, worked out by Hilferding and others and presented by Fritz Naphtali in 1928 at the Hamburg Congress of the ADGB, could not fail to have an effect on the attitude of the SPD's potential coalition partners: the latter regarded these proposals as dangerous nonsense, even though they were explicitly meant to be inserted into the given capitalist system and to correspond to the stage of "monopoly capitalism" reached in the interwar years.[30]

Naphtali distinguished economic democracy specifically from socialization: economic democracy was not meant to affect power over industry, but was rather aimed at restricting "the autocratic management of industry."[31] This could be achieved through "trade union participation in the communal-economic institutions of self-government"—a reference to the National Economic Council, an advisory body that was the sole relic of the hopes of 1919 for codetermination in industry through factory councils.[32] Despite Naphtali's statement that "the Free Trade Unions and the SPD are in complete agreement about the present tasks of economic policy," the SPD took no steps to implement the trade unions' plans politically.[33] Economic democracy did not, for instance, figure in the SPD 1928 election program despite the stress laid on it by Hilferding at the Kiel Congress.[34]

Things might have been different if the developing left-opposition within the party had had trade-union connections (apart from Siegfried Aufhäuser, leader of the clerical unions). It did not, and when it began to take shape it defined itself above all negatively: against the behavior of the Saxon *Land* fraction, against coalition, against the theory of the neutral state, against pocket battleships. The *raison d'être* of the left's journal, *Der Klassenkampf,* was to attack the practical steps taken by the SPD in coalition, to call for its withdrawal from government, and to undermine the theoretical defense of coalition provided by the party majority. This entailed a running battle between the Austro-Marxist theorist Max Adler and Rudolf Hilferding over the correct Marxist analysis of the state, with Adler reaffirming the idea that the state could not be neutral as between the classes and that therefore the Weimar state must be the state of the capitalist class. Given these overwhelmingly political preoccupations it was not surprising that steps toward economic democracy did not form a part of either the opposition's election program or the (already impossibly stringent) conditions for coalition with the bourgeois parties advocated by *Der Klassenkampf* in 1928.[35]

The favorable showing of the SPD in the 1928 elections (29.8 percent of the votes, and 153 out of 491 seats in the Reichstag) was followed by Hermann Müller's attempt to form a grand coalition, in line with the green light for such an endeavor given by the 1927 congress. It was not an easy task. In view of the refusal of the DVP to agree on a common program with the other parties, Müller had to form a "cabinet of heads," selecting leaders from each of the five parties to serve in a personal capacity. This curious arrangement continued until April 1929, when the parties finally agreed to support the Müller government in an organized manner. This did not improve matters. In both cases the only issues where agreement could be reached within the cabinet were in the realm of foreign affairs, where support for Stresemann's policy of fulfillment was noncontentious. Otherwise there was constant conflict, and constant retreat by the SPD in order to save the cabinet. There was the failure to get the ninth of November accepted as an official celebration of the anniversary of the November 1918 workers' revolution; there was the surrender of the SPD ministers to blackmail over the decision to build Pocket Battleship A, opposed in favor of expanding social programs; there was the defeat of Labour Minister Rudolf Wissell over the 1928 Ruhr Iron Company lockouts, when management refused to abide by the decision of his appointed arbitrator; there were disappointments over fiscal policy, with the abandonment of Hilferding's budget proposal of March 1929 to raise the tax on beer due to the opposition of the Bavarian People's party (BVP); finally, and most significantly for the future, there was the running battle over financing unemployment benefits.

The resources provided under the Unemployment Insurance Law of 1927 were already inadequate to meet the lowest Weimar unemployment level of 1 million (they were meant to cover 800,000); and the number of registered unemployed (annual average) went up from 1.4 million in 1928 to 1.9 million in 1929, leaping to 3.3 million in 1930. The conflict over this eventually broke up the Grand Coalition, but the issue was already smoldering in 1928. The view of the trade unions, which they impressed strongly on the SPD, was that contributions should be raised from 3 percent to 3.5 percent; the DVP was entirely opposed to this, calling instead for a reduction in unemployment benefits and a means test, plus a campaign to weed out scroungers (March 1929). In saying this they were accurately reflecting the views of their supporters in big business.[36]

It was in this situation, with a crumbling coalition government in which the SPD ministers seemed captives to anti-working-class policies, that the next national congress of the SPD met, the Magdeburg Congress of May 1929. The "passivist" or "left" arguments against coalition had now gained added weight. Even Rudolf Breitscheid, reporting on behalf of the parliamentary party, had to admit that after a year of government "there is still a tremendous amount left to be desired." "We have neither fulfilled nor brought close to fulfillment what we demanded in the years of opposition," he added.[37]

The complaints of the left were manifold. In the first place, the party had entered the coalition in 1928 without a program. The Party Committee had simply met (June 6, 1928) after the successful elections and resolved to empower the parliamentary party to undertake negotiations with a view to forming a government under SPD chancellorship.[38] No prior conditions were set. As Hans Vogel put it, on behalf of the executive, "With coalition governments every party has to come down a peg or two with its demands of basic principle," otherwise no government could ever come into existence.[39] There were no guarantees therefore that the SPD would achieve anything; but there were certain expectations raised in the course of the election campaign in the minds of the voters: the major positive slogan had been "Food for the children not pocket battleships," implying a simultaneous rejection of naval expansion and commitment to social politics. These hopes were disappointed. Naval expansion went ahead; social politics were put in question, first, by the Ruhr lockouts and the succcessful defiance of arbitration, then by threats to the financing of the unemployment insurance fund. Hence two points dominated the proceedings of the Magdeburg Congress: the way to prevent the building of Pocket Battleship A and the way to defend the social achievements of the late 1920s.[40]

The SPD had fought the elections of 1928 in part against the building of pocket battleships; the SPD ministers promptly voted in favor of Pocket Battleship A once they had entered the cabinet (August 10, 1928). Müller justified this by saying: "If the SPD were to take a negative attitude on questions of defence it could never participate in the national government at all."[41] A storm of indignation arose in the party at large, and the parliamentary party disavowed the decision of its own ministers, subsequently introducing into the Reichstag the resolution that "the building of Pocket Battleship A should cease."[42] The SPD ministers were compelled under party discipline to vote in favor of the resolution and against their own cabinet (November 16, 1928). The naval building program went ahead anyway, since there was a center-right majority in support of it.

There was nothing the SPD could do at Magdeburg to reverse this decision; what they could do was work out an overall defense program. A party commission was set up for this purpose, and it produced a program that accepted the need for national defense but made ten proposals directed at increasing parliamentary control over the Reichswehr and restraining it from violating the armaments limitations laid down by the Treaty of Versailles.[43] The necessity of giving ground to the SPD's coalition partners was not mentioned in this context; the party's leaders favored national defense for its own sake. The resolution was pushed through by 242 to 147 votes.[44] The left-opposition, which had been going from strength to strength in its campaign against the compromises forced on the SPD by its participation in a coalition government, was in the most favorable possible situation to make its mark. The left objected in principle to providing the Weimar state with the means for conducting wars, and called for the removal of the army and navy altogether, as instruments of the ruling class, and their replacement by "the instruments of proletarian power needed by the coming socialist society for its defense." That was the long-term program; in the short term the left suggested the abolition of the navy, parliamentary control of the army, and a large number of measures of democratization.[45] The revisionist right of the party, in contrast, maintained that the German navy should be expanded. Max Cohen argued in *Sozialistische Monatshefte* that the building of Pocket Battleship A was justified in itself, and that the SPD had been "unforgiveably" wrong to base its agitation in the 1928 elections on opposition to this. The fleet was needed against Britain, he implied: "What was wrong with the pre-war naval policy of the *Reich* was that it lacked a guiding idea, which is to be found in securing our flanks by alliance with France and Russia."[46]

The party executive did not take this extreme view, of course, but argued that the pocket battleship affair should not be taken as a reason for leaving the coalition, since positive advances could still be made in social politics. It conceded, conversely, that a failure in that sphere would be much more serious. As Stampfer said: "If once the fateful situation came up that we had to decide, in a question of social politics like unemployment insurance, between the government on the one hand and the trade unions on the other, there could be no doubt about our decision. In such a case we should have to act according to the principle: party and goverment are two, but party and trade unions are one."[47] Rudolf Breitscheid underlined this: "We do not want a crisis [in the cabinet] but if it comes to serious disagreements, the unemployment insurance is a much more favourable battlefield than the battleship." No attack on the principle of unemployment insurance or any attempt to reduce the numbers qualifying would be permitted, he added.[48]

The matter of unemployment insurance was thus given a rather one-sided weighting by the party's leaders, and this was to provide the psychological background for their controversial decision to dig their heels in precisely on this issue.[49] Nevertheless, the general approach that emerged from the Magdeburg Congress was rather one of staying in the government at any cost. Breitscheid issued this remarkably accurate prophecy to the restless left: "Consider this! If this government falls what comes next? Dissolution. Fine. But do you think that democracy can survive in the long run if there is a dissolution every two years? Otherwise what? We might receive a kind of cabinet of officials which would in itself already be a concealed dictatorship."[50]

The End of the Coalition

The decision of March 27, 1930, to end the Grand Coalition, which is often regarded as the fatal turning point in the history of Weimar and of German Social Democracy between the wars, cannot be understood without reference to the increasing intransigence of the bourgeois coalition parties over at least the previous six months, in the context of the onset of the world economic depression, and reflecting industry's abandonment of the policy of concessions to the industrial working class, or, as Abraham puts it, the shift in the leadership of industry from the "dynamic-export fraction" (Silverberg, Duisberg) to the "heavy-domestic fraction" (Hugenberg),[51] followed by a joint onslaught on the social gains of the previous few years in the shape of the League of German Industry (RDI) manifesto of December 1929, entitled "Recovery or Collapse."[52]

Two major surrenders by the SPD ministers in face of this pressure on the cabinet—the October 2, 1929, compromise with the DVP over unemployment insurance, and the removal of Hilferding as finance minister after an ultimatum from both Schacht (at the Reichsbank) and the DVP—strengthened the left-opposition's case against coalition and led even some defenders of coalition to express doubts. By January 1930 George Decker, writing in *Die Gesellschaft*, had been driven to advocate posing an ultimatum to the other coalition parties: "The standpoint of Social Democracy must be this: we are not prepared to go along with a coalition as a party merely there on sufferance. . . . The task of Social Democracy is to force upon the bourgeois parties the stabilization of the government's position they themselves preach but don't practice."[53]

The last straw was the insistence of the DVP on meeting the growing economic crisis by reducing unemployment pay rather than increasing contributions, and the support of the Center party for that position. The decision of March 27, 1930, to break up the Grand Coalition was made by a majority of the SPD parliamentary party, who followed Wissell and the trade-union leaders in rejecting the advice of the other SPD ministers in the cabinet (Müller, Severing, and Robert Schmidt). This has been seen in retrospect as the great turning point for German democracy, and the fatal error of the interwar SPD. Julius Leber, in his influential memoir, concluded as follows: "27 March 1930 was a black day for Social Democracy and for German democracy altogether: for on that day German democracy refuted itself, and Social Democracy showed it was still incapable of directing the government of the state."[54] Stampfer's point of view is similar; he condemns the trade-union leaders in particular.[55] There is a considerable degree of hindsight in these judgments. The memoirs of the only person directly involved at the time (Severing) take a different line. Severing regrets only that Müller resigned precipitately, depriving himself of the opportunity of explaining to the Reichstag the impossibility of holding the coalition together any longer.[56] The decision is defended strongly in Wilhelm Keil's memoirs. He points out that "the party went to the uttermost limits to save the Müller government but social antagonisms were stronger than this endeavour."[57] Similarly Rudolf Breitscheid: "Perhaps a compromise tolerable to the working class might still have been arrived at that stage, but later developments have taught us that it would not have lasted long. The forces on the bourgeois side pressing towards a break were too strong."[58]

Seen in this light the decision of March 27, 1930, has an air of inevitability. It was not so much a "victory of Marxist ideological principles over a realism capable of compromise" as the *reductio ad absurdum* of the policy of defending the day-to-day interests of the working class conceived in a narrow material sense.[59] Once the SPD began to regard itself as an interest group and an extension of the trade-union movement, it was bound to be defeated by the much stronger interest group of the employers. The "Prussian strategy" of coalition was bound to fail once the SPD's coalition partners decided that the social conflicts were too strong for them to avoid the pull of their middle-class paymasters. The in itself rather minor dispute over a one-quarter percent reduction in the employers' unemployment contribution was only the culmination of a capitalist offensive that had been in progress since the Ruhr lockout of 1928.[60] In this context the departure of the SPD from the coalition seems like a foregone conclusion. The party did have a choice, but it was a choice between leaving the coalition and staying in it "to preside over the dismantling of the social programmes" of the late 1920s.[61]

In the course of 1930, under the impact of twin crises in the economy and the political system, the terms of the argument changed radically. The economic crisis meant that any genuine parliamentary coalition containing the SPD was deprived of its social basis through the unwillingness of any section of the capitalist class to accept measures favorable to the workers; this had after all been the lesson of March 1930 and it was underlined by Brüning's reliance on Article 48 of the Constitution to force through his deflationary fiscal policies. The political crisis took some time to ripen: in the summer of 1930 the SPD leadership continued to believe that the Brüning government was a temporary phenomenon and would be replaced by a new coalition after defeat at elections. The decision of the voters on September 14, 1930, made it plain that the situation had been transformed. From then on the choice was no longer "coalition or opposition" but "toleration or opposition." The new kind of toleration, of a government the SPD would normally have combatted fiercely, was something not envisaged in Hermann Müller's analysis of 1926 of the conditions for tolerating a government Social Democracy was not prepared to join. The alternative with which this essay began, "defense of democracy or advance to socialism," ceased to have any meaning, since the latter could now occur only within the context of the kind of radical overthrow of capitalism ruled out by the principles of Social Democracy.

Let us, finally, draw together some of the themes that have emerged in this discussion. First, it should be clear that the defense of existing democracy was always a very clear priority in the minds of the leading group in the SPD. Any steps liable to compromise this, even if they furthered or appeared to further the material interests of the workers, were always opposed. This applied even to the decision of March 1930, which was opposed by all the political leaders except one—Rudolf Wissell, with his strong bias toward giving priority to social politics. The left-opposition (which in March 1930 fortuitously had its way for the first and only time) was less concerned with the defense of existing democracy than with giving it some real content: this could not be done through parliamentary maneuvers. Even within the context of the mere maintenance of existing democracy, the left argued that once the economy was in crisis the only option was a far-reaching transformation of the economy during the crisis itself: for the political crisis could not be solved without solving the economic crisis. The second theme, raised repeatedly by the left-opposition, was the need to mobilize the working class, and, conversely, the danger of demobilization arising from participation in government or responsibility for it.

There were several subsidiary themes as well: the effectiveness of coalition at the local level, with the Prussian example to the forefront (the confused situation in Saxony, in contrast, was more a deterrent than an encouragement); and the possibility of somehow bypassing capitalism, first advanced by Hilferding in 1924 and taken up by the trade unions (the ADGB plan of 1928).[62] Hilferding represented a form of Marxist Fabianism. His proposals for economic democracy would be introduced, he thought, inevitably, since this necessarily followed from the concentration of capital, and the growth of organized capitalism, as outlined in his article of 1924 in *Die Gesellschaft* and his speech of 1927 to the Kiel Congress.[63] The ADGB, similarly, based their own 1928 proposals for economic democracy on an optimistic overestimate of the weight of trade-union advice. Fritz Tarnow, in introducing them, described capitalism as "malleable" and capable of being changed "without power being 100 per cent in our hands."[64] The capitalists themselves, on the other hand, regarded economic democracy as a serious threat.[65] There was an immense gulf in both cases between the radical nature of the proposals and the moderate means envisaged for their implementation.[66]

What was needed was a combination of the program for achieving economic democracy with political action designed to implement the program: it was necessary to explore the limits of bourgeois political democracy before the bourgeoisie itself began to close in those limits under the impact of the world economic crisis. The two halves of the equation were never fitted together: the defense of existing democracy became the obsession and sole *raison d'être* of the SPD leadership; the steps toward socialism proposed by the ADGB in 1928 and by some SPD theorists were developed in isolation as campaigns over single issues. Without the vitalizing effect of a militant mass movement there was no prospect that political and economic democracy could be combined.

Notes

1. See H. Schulze, *Otto Braun* (Frankfurt: Wiln, 1977), for a positive evaluation of the work of the Prussian SPD government, and H. P. Ehni, *Bollwerk Preussen?* (Bonn: Verlag Neue Gesellschaft, 1975), for a critical view.
2. In 1926 the ADGB refused to return to the partnership system of the early 1920s known as the *Zentralarbeitsgemeinschaft* unless the employers accepted trade-union plans for "economic democracy" (C. Erdmann, "Das Problem der Arbeitsgemeinschaft," *Die Arbeit* 3 [1926]: 674).
3. The evolution of the SPD's policies on these issues is treated in detail for the years up to 1924 by R. Breitman, *German Socialism and Weimar Democracy* (Chapel Hill: University of North Carolina Press, 1981).
4. F. Stampfer, *Die ersten vierzehn Jahre der Deutschen Republik* (Offenbach: Bollwerk-Verlag, 1947), pp. 188–89.
5. *Protokoll über die Verhandlungen des Parteitages der Sozialdemokratischen Partei Deutschlands, abgehalten in Kassel vom 10. bis 16.Oktober 1920* (Berlin, 1920; reprint, 1973), p. 319. Hereafter the titles of SPD congress reports are given in abbreviated form.
6. *Protokoll SPD Kassel 1920*, p. 321.
7. *Protokoll SPD Görlitz 1921*, p. 389.
8. H. Schulze, "Die SPD und der Staat von Weimar," in M. Stürmer, ed., *Die Weimarer Republik. Belagerte Civitas* 2d. ed. (Konigstein: Athenaum, 1985), p. 277. The term "Grand Coalition" refers to a coalition between the SPD, the DDP (German Democratic Party), the Center Party, and the DVP.
9. Breitman, *German Socialism*, p. 108.
10. E. Matthias, "Social Democracy and the Power in the State," in T. Eschenburg et al., eds., *The Road to Dictatorship: Germany 1918–1933* (London: O. Wolff, 1970), p. 62.

11. David Abraham, *The Collapse of the Weimar Republic: Political Economy and Crisis* (Princeton: Princeton University Press, 1981), p. 8.
12. *Protokoll SPD Berlin 1924*, pp. 106–7.
13. See *Sozialistische Monatshefte* [hereafter SM] 62 (1925): 1–3; SM 62 (1925): 729–31; SM 64 (1927): I, 1–5; SM 65 (1927): II, 697–701; SM 67 (1928): II, 563–6.
14. SM 66 (1928): I, 375–78; 472–75; SM 63 (1926): 175.
15. *Vorwärts* 17, January 12, 1926.
16. *Schulthess' Europäischer Geschichtskalender*, 1926, p. 6.
17. H. Müller-Franken, "Vom Deutschen Parlamentarismus," *Die Gesellschaft* 3, no. 4 (April 1926): 298.
18. Ibid., p. 299.
19. Gains summarized in *Jahrbuch des ADGB*, 1928, p. 34.
20. R. Hilferding, "Politische Probleme: Zum Aufruf Wirths und zur Rede Silverbergs," in *Die Gesellschaft* 3, no. 10 (Oct. 1926): 289–302.
21. *Protokoll SPD Kiel 1927*, p. 170.
22. Ibid., pp. 265–66.
23. Ibid., p. 173.
24. Ibid., p. 272.
25. Quoted in Ibid., pp. 184–88.
26. Quoted in Ibid., pp. 198–200.
27. Ibid., pp. 265–66.
28. Kampffmeyer, "Mehr Macht!" in SM 65 (1927): II, 783–88.
29. C. Severing, "Kiel: Ein Nachwort zum Parteitag," *Die Gesellschaft* 4, no. 7 (July 1927): 3–5.
30. E. Nölting, "Wirtschaftsdemokratie," in Wolfgang Luthardt, ed., *Sozialdemokratische Arbeiterbewegung und Weimarer Republik* (Frankfurt: Westdeutscher Verlag, 1978), vol. 1, p. 294.
31. F. Naphtali, in Luthardt, *Arbeiterbewegung*, vol. 1, p. 300.
32. F. Naphtali, *Wirtschaftsdemokratie: Ihr Wesen, Weg und Ziel* (Berlin: Verlagsgesellschaft des Allgemeinen Deutschen Gewerkschaftsbundes, 1928), pp. 61–62.
33. F. Naphtali, in Luthardt, *Arbeiterbewegung*, vol. 1, p. 304.
34. *Vorwärts* 191 (April 22, 1928): 1.
35. "Unsere Wahlkampfforderungen," in *Der Klassenkampf* (hereinafter KK) 2, no. 8 (April 15, 1928): 228–32; K. Rosenfeld, "Die 'grosse Koalition'?" KK 2, no. 11 (June 1, 1928): 328.
36. H. Timm, *Die deutsche Sozialpolitik und der Bruch der grossen Koalition im März 1930* (Dusseldorf: Droste Verlag, 1952), pp. 124–26.
37. *Protokoll SPD Magdeburg 1929*, p. 155.
38. Not unanimously; as Seydewitz pointed out, the Saxon delegates opposed this policy (*Protokoll SPD Magdeburg 1929*, p. 69).
39. *Protokoll SPD Magdeburg 1929*, p. 37.
40. B. Weisbrod, *Schwerindustrie in der Weimarer Republik: Industrielle Interessenpolitik zwischen Stabilisierung und Krise* (Wuppertal: Peter Hammer, 1978), p. 435.
41. Breitman, *German Socialism*, p. 149.
42. *Jahrbuch der SPD*, 1928, p. 124 .
43. *Protokoll SPD Magdeburg 1929*, pp. 288–89.
44. The vote was much closer in terms of elected as opposed to *ex officio* delegates: 154 to 142 (see KK 3 [1929]: 435).
45. The opposition's proposals were not printed in the official report of the congress. They were issued later as a pamphlet, which is printed in part in Luthardt, ed., *Sozialdemokratische Arbeiterbewegung*, vol. 2 (Frankfurt: Suhrkamp, 1978), pp. 165–66.

46. M. Cohen, "Agitation gegen Politik," SM 67 (1928): II, 737–41.

47. *Protokoll SPD Magdeburg 1929*, pp. 173–74.

48. Ibid., p. 165.

49. Timm, *Sozialpolitik*, p. 185.

50. *Protokoll SPD Magdeburg 1929*, p. 170.

51. Abraham, *Collapse*, p. 263.

52. Summarized in ibid., pp. 236–37.

53. G. Decker, "Koalitionskrämpfe," *Die Gesellschaft* 7 (January 1930): 3.

54. J. Leber, *Ein Mann geht seinen Weg*, p. 220.

55. Stampfer, *Die Ersten Jahre*, pp. 515–16.

56. C. Severing, *Mein Lebensweg*, vol. 2 (Cologne: Greuen Verlag, 1950), pp. 239–40.

57. W. Keil, *Erinnerungen*, vol. 2, pp. 371–72.

58. R. Breitscheid "Worum es ging und geht," *Die Gesellschaft* 7, no. 8 (August 1930): 98.

59. K. D. Bracher, *Die Auflösung der Weimarer Republik*, 5th ed. (Dusseldorf: Droste, 1978), p. 270.

60. A reduction, that is, from the 4 percent originally envisaged in the proposals rejected earlier in the month by the DVP, to 3.75 percent. See Wissell, writing in *Die Arbeit* 7 (1930): 217.

61. Abraham, *Collapse*, pp. 262–63.

62. I have deliberately excluded such important themes as the attempt to move from "class party" to "people's party," and the development of the SPD's agrarian program, as not being directly relevant to the problem under discussion here.

63. R. Hilferding, "Probleme der Zeit," in *Die Gesellschaft* 1, no. 1 (1924): 1–3.

64. U. Hüllbüsch, "Die deutschen Gewerkschaften in der Weltwirtschaftskrise," in W. Conze and H. Raupach, eds., *Die Staats- und Wirtschaftskrise des deutschen Reichs 1929–1933*, (Stuttgart: Klett, 1967), pp. 134–35.

65. Abraham, *Collapse*, p. 259.

66. This essay is restricted to analyzing the solutions worked out and applied by the German Social Democrats between 1924 and 1930, in the period of relative prosperity. After 1930 the locus of decision-making shifted irremediably. For the subsequent period see the thorough discussion by Erich Matthias "Die Sozialdemokratische Partei Deutschlands," in E. Matthias and R. Morsey, eds., *Das Ende der Parteien* (Dusseldorf: Droste, 1960).

Part III

Forgetting the Past:
Redoing History

From Denazification to the "Historiker-Debatte": Reckoning with the Past in the Federal Republic of Germany

Reinhard Kühnl

In the immediate wake of the destruction of the fascist regime in 1945 a relatively broad consensus existed among all Germans, from the Christian Democrats to the Communists, with regard at least to the basic issues involved in fascism and its consequences. This antifascist consensus was evident in the early party platforms, in the state constitutions established in the years 1946–47, and in the denazification and punishment of war criminals undertaken together with the Allied Forces. In these early postwar years, the demands for a thorough process of democratization of government and all aspects of public life, for effective guarantees of broad political and social civil rights—including the right of civil disobedience in the face of unconstitutional use of government powers—and for socialist measures allowing democratic control of economic forces, had considerable political significance.[1] It can be readily seen that these demands were based on definite views of the causes and beneficiaries of fascism. These demands were even incorporated into the Basic Law *(Grundgesetz)* of 1949, although by then in a weakened form, in Article 139 (Ban on Fascism), Article 26 (Peace Imperative), and Article 15 (Sanctioning Socialization), among others.[2]

The antifascist consensus was gradually destroyed, however, as

---

Translated by Martha Baker

the United States began to (1) move toward a policy of confrontation with the Soviet Union, (2) view the class of former leaders under the fascist regime as allies, and (3) reestablish those leaders in positions of power in government, the economy, and society on a large scale. At the same time, all those who were suspected of sympathy for communism were pushed into sideline positions. Already by 1950 members of the German Communist party (KPD), the Association of Persons Persecuted during the Nazi Regime (VVN), and many other organizations were barred from the civil service through a resolution by the German federal government. These were exactly the same groups of people who had been sorted out and persecuted under the fascist system and who had made the greatest sacrifices during the fight against fascism.

On the other hand, the process of denazification was completely halted. Approximately 150,000 civil servants and employees who at first had been fired from their positions because of their activities during the fascist regime were rehabilitated in their jobs through the so-called 131 Law of 1951, associations for persons expelled or evacuated from former German territories were organized largely under the leadership of former functionaries of the Nazi party; and neofascist organizations and publications were again tolerated. Since the policies of the North Atlantic Treaty Organization (NATO) and the "Policy of Strength," which according to Konrad Adenauer were aimed at the liberation of "all of the enslaved East European countries," considered the enemy, in terms of foreign policy, to be the same as in the war against the Soviet Union up to 1945, there was a strongly felt need to rehabilitate that war and those who had been its leaders—namely, the military and the Waffen-SS (armed special forces), even though the Waffen-SS had been condemned by the Military Tribunal in Nuremberg as a criminal organization.[3]

Thus the armed forces of the Federal Republic were built up under the leadership of Hitler's former generals. The Waffen-SS and the Gestapo were publicly rehabilitated through inclusion in the 131 Law. The SS veterans associations were thus not only accepted, but often even welcomed and lauded by representatives of the local authorities, the armed forces, and the Christian Democratic party when they held their meetings. Franz-Joseph Strauss praised the Battle of Stalingrad as a "meaningful sacrifice" and a "legitimate calculation" and emphatically rejected the thesis that Germany must shoulder the major portion of blame for World War II.[4] As early as the 1960s Strauss interspersed his remarks on this topic with the claim that in view of the reparations made by the Federal Republic, it had earned the right to hear nothing more about Auschwitz.

In view of the international constellation of powers, the ruling right could go no further. Those who adamantly claimed—quite correctly from their own point of view—that May 8, 1945, represented defeat and not liberation did not have an easy time of restoring their position of power at the outset, in spite of the prevailing hysteria of the cold war. The mistrust of the neighboring countries, even those in Western Europe that had suffered fascist occupation, was much too great. In order to achieve state sovereignty, freedom of economic development, and a new military power, certain concessions had to be made. The ruling classes had already experienced this after the defeat of 1918 and had successfully mastered the situation.[5] Now, after World War II, it was held that a disassociation from fascism and its crimes as well as an acknowledgment of a certain degree of blame (which was expressed, for example, in the financial reparations made to the state of Israel) were necessary prerequisities for a new rise to political power. These steps were the price of admission to the circle of "free nations" and the "Western cultural community."

These were things the "recalcitrants" on the extreme right did not comprehend. The ruling right was forced by its own sense of political realism to keep a certain distance between itself and right extremists. At the same time, they saw to it that neofascism was able to formulate new, far-reaching position statements and thus generate and preserve a certain consciousness, which was on the whole beneficial to the consolidation of right-wing ideology. Since the beginning of the 1950s, neofascists have spread the idea that all accusations against the Third Reich that claim that it planned and conducted a war of aggression and perpetrated war crimes and mass murder are unfounded and based on lies that have been invented only in order to keep Germans in a state of intellectual and political subservience. Whoever accepts such tales has become a stooge of the enemy and a betrayer of his own nation's interests. Measured against this position, the ruling right could in fact portray itself as being "moderate" and part of the political "middle," while in cases such as the Deutschland-Stiftung (German Foundation), the associations for displaced persons, and the right wing of the Christian Union parties, the borderline is indeed quite thin.[6]

Thus the conception of history that came to dominate political public opinion shows definite traces of revisionism. The methods used by this rightist form of revisionism have always been (and are still today) characterized by a combination of three factors. First, the crimes of fascism are made to appear innocuous and edged into the range of normality. Second, some of these crimes are portrayed as legitimate because they were committed for a good cause in a harsh but unavoidable set of circumstances. Finally, the causal structure of crimes that cannot be otherwise excused is shrouded to such an extent that, in the end, they can best be attributed to socialism and communism.

The ideas necessary for this kind of treatment of fascist crimes had to a large extent already been developed during the fascist era itself. Ways of rendering acts harmless or innocuous had already been incorporated into the offical vocabulary—with such terms as *Sonderbehandlung* (special treatment) and *Endlösung* (final solution). Ideological and rhetorical legitimation was characteristic of the overall policies of fascism. For instance, the machinery of terrorism was established in 1933 "to save the people and the state," war was conducted "to save Germany" and, in 1943, to "save Europe" from Bolshevism.[7] It goes without saying that others were responsible for terror, war, and mass murders. The Reichstag building was supposedly set ablaze by the Communists, and the Jewish people pushed Germany into war after actually declaring war on it in 1939. On January 30, 1939, Hitler made the following statement to this effect before the Reichstag: "Today I have another prophecy to make. If the international Jewish financiers in and beyond Europe should again succeed in plunging the nations into a world war, the result will not be the bolshevism of Europe and thereby a victory for Judaism, but rather the annihilation of the Jewish race throughout Europe."[8] The attack on the Soviet Union in June 1941 was naturally declared a war of prevention which only in the last minute prevented the Soviet aggression that had been imminent, just as the attack on Poland in 1939 had been declared a war of self-defense, during which, to quote Hitler's words before the Reichstag, Germany only "shot back."

This method of argumentation was taken up and developed further in 1945–46 by the politicians, military leaders, and economic leaders who were accused of war crimes. Since the beginning of the 1950s the country has been inundated by a flood of memoirs, neofascist brochures, pamphlets, and newspapers using such arguments. This defense has also been taken up, to some extent, by the right wing of such groups as the Christian Union parties, the associations of displaced persons, the Springer publishing conglomerate, the German armed forces, the German Foundation, and so forth.

This position is in marked contrast to the official image the Federal Republic has defined for itself. In order to be accepted into the Western European community, where the memory of fascist crimes was deeply ingrained, and to be able to acquire national sovereignty and new military power, it was essential to portray the Federal Republic as a country that had completely turned away from fascism: the Federal Republic stood in the tradition of resistance (civil and military) and opened itself unreservedly to "Western values" in its Basic Law (*Grundgesetz*).

Beyond this, the lessons to be learned from fascism encompassed nothing more than political institutions and ideology—the parliamentary and democratic form of government, the constitutional state, the disavowal of a racial ideology, and, above all, the reconciliation with the Jews and their state, Israel. The political segregation of Communists and Socialists corresponded to the methodological exclusion of social and economic causes from the analysis of fascism. The restoration of the former leading elite class was also methodologically consistent with foregoing the inquiry into the role of capital, the upper levels of civil service, and the military establishment in fascist systems. The main thrust of this "diminished" antifascist consensus was, of course, no longer still aimed at fascism, but was governed instead by the totalitarianism thesis, that is, against communism and socialism. As Rainer Barzel of the Christian Democratic party aptly put it in 1965 in a speech before the Bundestag: "Hitler is dead, but not Ulbricht" (Walter Ulbricht was at that time chairman of the Staatsrat of the German Democratic Republic).

The scholarly debate over fascism is naturally embedded in the general political and intellectual climate of its time, but it is not simply identical with the prevailing political course. It so happened, however, that the spirit of the cold war quite thoroughly coincided with the traditions and the view of life held by historians themselves. Ever since the time of the first German empire, history as the leading social science has played a decisive role in forming the views held by the educated elite. Historians legitimized the efforts to sidetrack the working-class movement, the socially privileged status of the bourgeois and titled classes, and the militarism and wars of conquest by the German empire. After 1918—since the revolution was not strong enough to democratize the higher schools of learning—historians made significant contributions to the conservative, reactionary, and militaristic climate of opinion that flourished and even became especially strong in the universities, and that in turn enabled fascism to prevail. Thus, under the fascist regime the historical sciences did not need to be subjected to purging measures; they were already clean of democratic and socialist ideas. In the following years historians for the most part were faithful, even enthusiastic adherents of fascism. Many even became members of the National Socialist German Workers Party (NSDAP).

The basic theoretical ideas on which the German historians founded their apologetic for a powerful nation-state were developed by Leopold von Ranke, and since the end of the nineteenth century, by proponents of what is often called "historicism."[9] Among the tenets of this theory is that the state is the determinant subject of the historical process, and its activities are therefore the focus of historical study. The essential nature of the state is power and the expansion of power, expressed above all in foreign policy and in war. Since striving for power is its instrinsic task, the state cannot be considered to be wronging anyone by following its existential purpose. The state is not only an instrument of power, however; it is at the same time the representative of morality, and thereby superior to individuals and their interests, which is to say it is an end in itself.

It is perfectly obvious that these ideas originate in an authoritarian state; that they are directed against the principles of enlightenment, sovereignty of the people, and democracy; and, furthermore, that they help to justify any form of a government's political power over its society and toward all others. Moreover, since another tenet is that all historical events and personalities are solitary and singular occurrences, adherents of this theory can claim that Hitler and fascism were such unique events in German history that one does not need to look for moments of continuity with preceding stages of history. Second, it could be deduced that with the defeat of the fascist regime and the death of Hitler the problem has been taken care of once and for all. Third, it follows that there is no coherent historical process, but rather a wealth of individual cases whose meaning is not discernible. As Karl Dietrich Erdmann, chairman of the Association of German Historians (1962–67) and chairman of the German Education Council (1966–70), wrote: "There is no scientific basis for statements which explain where history is coming from or where it is going."[10]

Naturally it was clear to these historians after 1945—just as it was in other branches of research—that one had to distance oneself from fascism in order to solidify one's own position and come out of isolation on the international level. Thus the portrayals of fascism within the history profession at that time coincided to a large extent with the official image of the Federal Republic itself.[11] The issue of totalitarianism dominated historical research. Racism, anti-Semitism, and concentration camps were condemned, as was the war of aggression the German Reich began in 1939. The interests of society that gave rise to these policies and the forces that supported and carried them out remained outside the range of investigation. That the working classes were deprived of their rights and that millions of foreign workers were made into slaves to be exploited by the German industrial economy was not even mentioned. One spoke of *Machtergreifung* (seizure of power) and by use of this concept from the arsenal of fascistic propaganda, the question of who had turned the power over to the NSDAP remained shrouded. In much the same way, one spoke of "Hitler's tyranny" as being the product of a single individual. Whenever the leading echelons of the corporate industry, the military, the higher civil service, and the church were mentioned, they were portrayed either as being all equally subjugated by the regime or as supporters of the resistance and representatives of the "better part of Germany." In this way they also acquired the moral qualities that were requisite for taking on leadership roles in the new German state. Responsibility for the victory of fascism and the success of its policies was shifted instead as much as possible to the new (and old) public enemy, the communists. The allegations ranged from the Weimar Republic's being throttled jointly by the National Socialists and the communists to the fascist movement's having a socialist or even proletarian character, from the suppression of a workers' resistance movement to a joint plotting of World War II by both "totalitarian dictators" via the Hitler-Stalin Pact.

Undoubtedly, this version of history contained some elements of historical fact. It admitted, above all, to those facts that corresponded to the images held by the Western Allies—namely concentration camps, war of aggression against Poland, racial discrimination, anti-Semitism, and dictatorship—and therefore acted, so to speak, as the admission ticket to the Western community of nations. These elements of fascist domination were described, but not given serious analysis. In other words, the causal interrelationships were not exposed. Thus the overall image that resulted did not allow fascism to be portrayed in terms of the conditions of its success, the underlying interest groups, and the forces that sustained it.[12] The Führer, Adolf Hitler, was presented as the only relevant subject—as the lone culprit.

The legend of German history as an otherwise unscathed tradition was not shaken until the beginning of the 1960s, when Fritz Fischer and his followers proved that the German Reich had carefully planned and intentionally precipitated World War I with the goal of subjugating half of Europe. In the following years they even demonstrated that it was at that time the same ruling echelons who ruined the Weimar democracy and joined ranks with the NSDAP in order to stage a new war.[13] Thus at the same time that the ruling forces were officially distancing themselves from fascism and attempting to legitimize their image of having been part of the bourgeois resistance, especially in connection with the failed attempt to assassinate Hitler on July 20, 1944, and the established academic circles were admitting and portraying selected aspects of Nazi crimes, the belittling portrayal of fascist crimes and the partial rehabilitation of fascism were already in full swing in wide sectors of day-to-day journalism and politics.

Nevertheless, the collapse of cold war politics led to significant changes in the political climate of the Federal Republic. The politics of detente and the social-liberal hopes for reform gave the left such a strong stimulus that it was not only able to hold back the spread of organized neofascism, but also to weaken the entire right altogether and keep it out of power for twelve years. Certain democratic improvements in the structures of the colleges and universities, an increase of entry paths to schools of higher education to the benefit of students from the lower classes, and a general liberalization of public discussions of political and intellectual topics served then to fortify antifascist modes of thought, particularly among the younger generation.

The historical sciences, still locked into conservatism, lost a considerable amount of prestige to the "new" political science, which had advanced considerably in the United States since 1945 and was being portrayed as the "science of democracy," and to sociology, which viewed itself as the science of emancipation par excellence.[14] Under these circumstances a social-liberal tendency was able to develop within the left wing of the historical sciences. As a result, some attention was given to social and structural dimensions of the historical process. This new political context enabled research to take a critical view of topics that had previously been treated apologetically or avoided entirely. In particular, this included the role of capital in the destruction of the Weimar Republic, the erection of a fascist dictatorship, and the role of the military establishment in conceiving and achieving fascist policies—including mass murder. The resistance efforts of the workers' movement—even the Communist component— were no longer barred from consideration.[15]

In the 1970s, however, the right again moved into the offensive. With considerable financial and propagandistic support, a campaign was started that has become known as the Hitlerwelle (Wave of Interest in Hitler). The entire country was flooded with brochures, newspaper articles, magazine articles, films, and television documentaries whose common message boiled down to the idea that Hitler and his regime also had their positive side—in particular in terms of achieving full employment and generating enthusiasm for collective causes—which indeed deserved reconsideration when looking for solutions for contemporary problems.[16]

Many of the central topics brought up then have since been consolidated into a new view of history by right-wing conservative historians. Joachim Fest developed the thesis that Hitler's error lay in his not mobilizing all his European forces in the war against the Soviet Union, instead of conducting war against the West too. Fest cast his vote for a new assessment of the war and for using anti-Bolshevism as the decisive criterion in judging Hitler's policies.[17] Sebastian Haffner described Hitler as *eine Leistungskanone größten Kalibers* (powerful mastermind of the highest caliber), who was able to abolish unemployment through his *Wirtschaftswunder* (economic miracles). As far as the war was concerned, this should be considered a perfectly natural event as long as there are so many sovereign nations and should in no case be considered a criminal act. War criminals ought to be treated as "phenomena which inevitably accompany those extraordinary circumstances, under which citizens and family men have accustomed themselves to killing."[18]

The positive reviews the Fest and Haffner books received from their colleagues and in various publications of right-wing conservative historians (such as Klaus Hildebrand and Andreas Hillgruber) reflected a trend toward the right within established historical scholarship that, in spite of sharp criticism from the left, was hardly noticed by liberal sectors of the general public. Ernst Nolte was even able to publish his thesis regarding the connection between political developments in Russia and Auschwitz in the face of the Bolshevik menace in the *Frankfurter Allgemeine Zeitung* (July 24, 1980), without a stir of protest. Disappointment over the abandonment of reform policies by the Social Democratic government, the economic crisis resulting in mass unemployment and the destruction of hopes and dreams for many young people, and the obvious inability of the governing politicians to deal with this crisis led to the dissipation of the potential for further reforms and prepared the way for the new and once again attractive version of a right-wing ideology as well as the formation of a conservative government.

New Qualities in the Government of the Wende (Turnabout)

Thus in many diverse ways the path had already been paved when conservative historians appeared on the scene in the summer of 1986. Nonetheless, since their opponents, as described above, had been able to garner a considerable measure of influence since the end of the 1960s, one could count on a stronger resistance.

Since the beginning of the 1980s there have been ever louder proclamations regarding the need for a new feeling of nationalism, of self-confidence, in order to stimulate the higher levels of performance required to participate in international competitive markets and to exercise a leadership role within Europe—including a new level of military preparedness. National self-confidence and stamina are also needed to keep open the unresolved question of the reunification of Germany. Since 1982 this version of national identity has been an essential characteristic of the "intellectual and moral turning-point," the slogan under which the Kohl government came into power.[19]

From the beginning the complaint was that the complete development of the economic and military capacity of the Federal Republic is heavily handicapped by the memory of fascism and its enormous crimes, which so deeply affected the peoples of this world and had such a great influence on the mentality of the citizens of the Federal Republic themselves. It was thus time for the Federal Republic to finally free itself from the "curse of the years 1933–1945," in the words of historian Michael Stürmer, and "step out from the shadow of Hitler," in those of Franz Joseph Strauss. These views were proclaimed by conservative historians and political scientists as well as the leading politicians of the right.[20]

Michael Stürmer, historian at the University of Erlangen, advisor to the chancellor, and editorial contributor to the *Frankfurter Allgemeine Zeitung,* has expressed the basic ideas of this new view of history in the following words: "If we do not succeed in agreeing on an elementary lesson plan for our culture, in setting forth our work with continuity and consensus throughout the land, and in rediscovering the moderate middle-path of patriotism, then it could just be that the best years of the Federal Republic of Germany have already gone by." The political effect of statements such as these is more important than the historical truth: "The future belongs to whoever supplies memory, shapes ideas, and interprets the past."[21] The Federal Republic needs "that high-minded insight, which next to religion, has only been achieved through national identity and patriotism."[22] To substitute history for religion as the means of achieving national political consensus—this is the platform on which the ideological offensive of the ruling forces was based. The historian takes on a primarily political, even quasi-military task: to occupy the battlefield and fill it with meaning—politically generated meaning.

A distinctively new step in the direction of *Vergangenheitsbewälti-gung* (coming to terms with the past) was taken during a widely publicized conference held in commemoration of the fiftieth anniversary of Hitler's appointment as imperial chancellor in the Reichstag building in West Berlin. One of the main addresses, which received considerable coverage in the German newspapers read by the upper classes, was given by Hermann Lübbe, now a professor of philosophy in Zurich, who had previously resigned his post as minister for cultural affairs in the state of North Rhein-Westphalia after a law allowing greater democracy in the affairs of the state's colleges and universities had been passed. Here he stated reasons for "communicative silence about the Nazi past as a citizen's duty." Keeping silent about fascism is a prerequisite for political consolidation and necessary for internal reconciliation within the Federal Republic; "a certain degree of still-ness was the social-psychological and politically necessary means of transforming our post-war population into citizens of the Federal Republic of Germany."[23]

Lübbe also made it clear that a certain ideological opponent was threatening the domestic peace, was preventing the lifting of the curse of the years 1933–45, which would enable Germany to achieve a more active political basis, and was getting in the way of a new national ascendency. The opponent is antifascism, whose precise task it is to keep awake the awareness of fascism and its crimes. At the same time, Lübbe set himself the task of really revising the current view of history and, in particular, of repainting the picture of fascism, which is still bound up with images of blood and terror, of war and mass murder, in lighter tones.

This is the point of departure for the "Historiker-Debatte." Such was the state of affairs when the fortieth anniversary of the liberation from fascism—May 8, 1985—drew closer and groups from every position in the political spectrum felt compelled to issue a statement concerning this event. The ritual ceremony performed by Chancellor Kohl and President Reagan in the German town of Bitburg was a public rehabilitation of the Wehrmacht forces and the Waffen-SS by the German government as well as by a leading member of NATO. They thus committed themselves to a position that was already being called for by Alfred Dregger and that fraction of the Christian Democrats known as the Stahlhelmflügel (Steel Helmeters). A direct connection was made between the battle of the fascist German army against the Soviet army at the end of World War II and the necessity of establishing defenses against the same enemy today. In other words, these fronts were considered identical.

This view of the significance of May 8, which although always held by the extreme right-wingers, had been supported in the past by only a small number of voices in the mainstream right, was now taken up by a strong fraction of the ruling right-wingers and aggressively advanced. May 8, 1945, was by no means the day of "liberation," but much more a "devastating defeat, almost a catastrophe" for Germany—if not indeed for Europe.[24] Thus, with this event all of the key views had been put forward, which were then taken up and consecrated as scientific findings a year later by conservative historians. In other words, all of the essential ideological statements had already been expounded. They only needed—and found—support from the scholarly world.

At first this path proved to be untenable. Even among the ruling forces there was apparently no consensus on these issues. The opposition was most clearly and impressively articulated by the president of the Federal Republic, Richard Weizsäcker, in his speech on May 8 in the Bundestag. Even the simple sentence "the 8th of May was a day of liberation" can be seen as a clear rejection of the right-wing views. The following statement was directed against the ideology of compensation: "The end of the war should not be viewed as the cause of evacuation, expulsion, and bondage. It is to be found at the beginning. We should not separate the 8th of May, 1945, from the 30th of January, 1933." Then, as the president counted up the victims of that regime and those who took part in the resistance, he also recalled the "innumerable citizens of the Soviet Union and Poland" and the "hostages who were executed"; among the resisters he specifically named "the resistance among the working classes and in the labor unions," the "resistance of the communists," and the "resistance in all of the countries which we occupied."

The Debate

This was the starting position for the next stage of the offensive venture which the conservative right began in the summer of 1986.[25] Once again the upper-middle-class newspapers served as a platform, and the leading politicians of the ruling right provided the general ideological backing in the form of ever more acrimonious statements. The demands for a revision of the current view of history were now indeed presented as the outcome of scientific research and endowed with the prestige of recognized historians.

The offensive concentrated on three main themes. Andreas Hillgruber, a Cologne historian who is often a guest at panels and interviews and supplies political catchwords for Strauss and Kohl, declared that a historian must identify with the battles of the German armies on the Eastern front in the years 1944–45.[26] Decisive for him was the fact that this was a "defensive" struggle against the Soviet Union and the chance to maintain Germany's position as a major power. In view of these dominating concerns, Hillgruber held that the oppressed peoples of Europe and the tortured and murdered victims of concentration camps should take a subsidiary position. Every form of antifascist resistance, even that of the upper-class military circles involved in the assassination attempt on July 20, 1944, was considered by Hillgruber as being actually in the interest of the Bolshevik enemy. The lesson to be learned for the present day from this interpretation of history was quite obviously that when it comes to erecting defenses against Bolshevik threats, certain things must be put up with—if need be, even fascist terror.

Gillessen, of the *Frankfurter Allgemeine Zeitung*, and Hoffmann, at the Research Office for Military History in Freiburg, attempted to make credible the idea that even by 1941 the war against the Soviet Union was at least understandable, because it was a war of prevention against Soviet aggression.[27] Just before this, the Christian Social Union (CSU) had given considerable publicity to a book by Ernst Topitsch, a social philosopher, in which Hitler and World War II were described as being tools of Stalin from the very beginning. The lesson to be learned from this thesis of a war of prevention was quite obviously that a war of aggression against the Soviet Union is then justified when signs of preparation for attack can be detected. What this thesis can lead to is not hard to imagine.

Finally, Ernst Nolte, a historian in West Berlin, defined Auschwitz as an "Asian act," as a reaction to the "Asian" Bolshevism that had made Hitler so afraid that he had to commit mass murder as a preventive measure, so to speak.[28] The Bonn historian Klaus Hildebrand, a member of the advisory board for Kohl's Bonn Museum, and Joachim Fest, co-editor of the *Frankfurter Allgemeine Zeitung*, gave the Hillgruber and Nolte theses flank protection in his paper and swept the critical objections that began to crop up resolutely under the carpet.[29]

With the adoption of these three theses the image of the Federal Republic that had been officially presented up to that time was in effect cast onto the rubbish heap. The new image no longer consisted of an aversion to fascism, of the tradition of a civil resistance and the unconditional allegiance to liberalism and democracy in the Western sense, but rather of a far-reaching justification of fascism and its policies. "The consensus was revoked from the right."[30] The new view of history is politically characterized by the assertion that the German Reich, on the whole, was already at that time oriented toward the correct foe, fighting the right war, and even defending the interests of all of Europe—in contrast to the Western Allies, who were at that time on the wrong side. In view of the danger coming from the East, the crimes of fascism appear to some extent reasonable and to some extent less serious. For these reasons, the Federal Republic has no reason to have scruples today about developing its full potential as a major power.

The themes developed by these historians did not go entirely unheralded. First of all, when German fascism and all of its political activities are viewed as deriving mainly from Hitler's ideas and intentions, and Hitler is made into the sole person responsible for all that happened, then it would seem obvious that all other parties involved must be found guiltless. This goes as well for the Wehrmacht, the fascist party and its branch organizations, and the Waffen-SS. In point of fact, this very *Führertheorie* has been one of the dominant approaches to explaining that period of history right up to today. Hillgruber and Hildebrand, in particular, have never tired of speaking of "Hitler's war" and "Hitler's regime." The only new development has been that Hillgruber now draws certain explicit conclusions that serious historians had not yet drawn, but that fit in well with current political trends. Hillgruber assures us, indeed, that he wants to identify himself not with Hitler, but with government and Nazi party officials and with the military establishment that organized the "defensive struggle."

Second, when it as been stated for decades that National Socialism and communism are essentially equivalent phenomena, and the totalitarianism thesis has been elevated to an official state ideology as well as to a major scientific tenet, then it is natural that all questions concerning the specific interests and power constellations that brought fascism into power and determined its policies will become negligible. Class struggle and racial struggle can be declared equivalent. When leading politicians are forever bringing up the idea that one form of totalitarianism is now part of the past, while the other is quite alive and extremely dangerous, historians have no reason not to consider the relationship between the two forms of totalitarianism and, wherever possible, to make the Soviet version, which is at present still a threat, responsible for Nazism, which belongs to the past but is still so burdensome. In this way the political enemy of German society can also be charged with the crimes that totalitarianism committed in Germany and in Europe forty years ago. Nolte has in fact emphasized that he intends to help bring the theory of totalitarianism again into the forefront and to determine more exactly just what kind of qualitative difference exists between the two forms of totalitarianism.[31]

Finally, when one views as given that all states attempt to expand their power beyond their own boundaries, then it is quite clear that the struggle of the fascist empire and the defense of its position as a great world power in 1944–45 be considered legitimate and the interests of those peoples who were oppressed or locked up in concentration camps be considered subordinate to the former. By following these tenets, one can also justify the new power politics in the Federal Republic. These conclusions, which the conservative-right historians have drawn on the basis of long-standing, academically influential theoretical approaches, are not imperative. Other historians whose research is based on the same types of approaches certainly have not made the same claims. It is possible to draw these conclusions, however, and it has happened now that the ideological climate has changed as a result of the political *Wende*.

Since these three historians are not concerned to exclude fascism from the continuity of German history, but rather to integrate fascist crimes into the normal course of historical process, they have gone to some trouble to obscure distinctions in political and historical phenomena. Not only has fascism taken its place within a series of tyrannical regimes from Stalin to Pol Pot, but modern history generally speaking can be seen—as in an article by Hildebrand of this title—as the "Age of Tyrants." In keeping with this new view of history, questions about the particulars of fascist crimes, not to mention questions about their perpetrators and beneficiaries, are merely bothersome.

Critics based their criticisms on political and moral considerations, although the debate often appeared to be a purely methodological one. Thus, it was asked whether or not it is meaningful to even talk of historical events as singular and whether or not historical comparisons are viable and meaningful in the case of fascist crimes. Significantly, the methods of argumentation used by the conservatives, when measured against all standards of the historian's craft, were exposed as unsound and absolutely untenable. Of course, it was primarily historians specializing in social and structural history, namely the leftist minority in the guild of historians, who voiced their views in this matter. Among such methodological critics, Jäckell—a Stuttgart historian—was most articulate. From his point of view, Hitler's ideas and aspirations were the most important factor in the political activities of German fascism.

All critics agreed, however, that this conservative revision of history was quite sufficient to reawaken the dangerous rightist traditions of Germany's past, thereby endangering the democratic tendencies within the Federal Republic itself and the development of peaceful relationships with other nations. United in this view were not only historians and social scientists connected with the Social Democrats, but also liberal editors (such as Rudolf Augstein of the weekly newsmagazine *Der Spiegel*), Marxist scholars in the Federal Republic and in the German Democratic Republic (such as Ulrike Hörster-Philipps, Georg Fülberth, and Kurt Pätzold), and Jewish intellectuals (such as Walter Grab, Michael Brumlik, and Dan Diner).[32] This broad spectrum shows clearly what it was and is all about: a controversy being debated with the tools of the historian's craft, but substantially political in nature. At stake is the political path to be taken by the Federal Republic, its internal political structure, and the direction of its foreign policy.

The Standards of Criticism

Critics in general object to the attempt by rightist historians (and politicians) to place fascist crimes among the events considered normal in the "Age of Tyrants," arguing that they can be shown to be of a singular nature. In reply these writers argue it is by all means valid to draw comparisons between evils and test the viability of these comparisons. Here is a remarkable reversal of fronts. It was precisely the thesis of singularity in the historicist school that for decades served to justify removal of the fascist period from the continuity of German history and to prevent the building of any social science concepts at all. Even today it is still an absolute requirement for any historian who wants to gain recognition among his peers to speak of "National Socialism," or better yet "Hitlerism," but not of "fascism." (Nolte developed the other variation of the apologetic in favor of using the term "fascism" by viewing it purely in intellectual terms as the idealistic product of the Führer, and then declaring the "Era of Fascism" as having ended with his death, but this view has not prevailed.)

Yet the concept of fascism does cover all of those essential features shared by the various movements and systems in different countries. It does not deny the existence of special national characteristics or the fact that these peculiarities can take on enormous proportions. It does open the way for viewing social-economic structures and interests, the connection between property and forms of political power—questions that historicism's thesis of singularity does not take into view.[33] It is therefore important to consider the insistence on the methods and the singular extent of the crimes committed during German fascism as absolutely justified. Additionally, only a social-scientific concept of fascism can clarify the conditions under which fascist developments can still exist or develop following the fall of the fascist regime in 1945. A second point of concern relates to the new direction taken by the Federal Republic after 1945. Liberal and social liberal critics (Jürgen Habermas, Jürgen Kocka, Kurt Sontheimer, Heinrich August Winkler, and others) have reproached conservative historians in particular for endangering that most singular historical achievement by the Federal Republic which has in fact given it a special role: the unrestricted opening toward the West.

The so-called *Öffnung zum Westen* after 1945 was, however, also connected with the restoration of capitalism, with rearmament, and with integration into the military alliance headed by the United States. The Kohl government reasons exactly along these lines whenever it makes reference to the commonality of values between the Federal Republic and the United States or the North Atlantic Treaty Organization (NATO). Habermas, on the other hand, wishes to make a distinction between the opening of the Federal Republic to "the political culture of the West," which he considers a major achievement, and to the "philosophy of NATO," from which he disassociates himself. In reply, Andreas Hillgruber asks whether one can separate culture and politics in this manner and whether the "aversion to NATO which the left loudly asserts does not usher in and accelerate exactly that political and cultural process which Habermas supposedly wants to prevent."[34]

Liberal historians and political scientists project, in fact, a certain idealism when speaking of the origins of the Federal Republic and its "opening to the West." This is evident when references are made to the structure and politics of Western powers, as well as to the conditions under which the Federal Republic was founded and the goals related to that process. By comparison, Hillgruber can really portray himself as a "realist" when he points to Britain's (imperialist) war plans or to the fact that the Federal Republic is militarily integrated with the West.

The fact that the objections of the liberal historians are much more pointedly aimed at Nolte, while Hillgruber's theses have been treated fairly benignly, may also be related to this idealistic *Westorietierung*. More specifically, Nolte broke the very taboo that has officially symbolized the Federal Republic's renunciation of fascism. He has portrayed Auschwitz as an insignificant matter and dispensed with any admission of guilt in connection with the genocide of the Jews. By doing so, he robbed the Federal Republic of a certain amount of the credibility it had gained in the West. Hillgruber, however, has turned his attention primarily toward the Soviet Union and declared the war conducted by the German Empire in 1944–45 to be legitimate and necessary. In this way, his thoughts, at least, are in principle in line with those of the postwar Western Allies. While Marxist historians have been quick to challenge Hillgruber's theses, sharp criticism among liberal historians has come only from Habermas; liberal historians for the most have been very guarded in their remarks.

So it is necessary to differentiate between various versions of the notion of an unreserved opening to the West. It is undoubtedly correct that this notion is implicitly distinct from all ideologies concerning the *deutsche Sonderweg* (Germany's unique course) or the conception that the Prussian-German tradition—with its code of virtue based on the belief in the authority of the state, military power, obedience to superiors, and willingness to work hard for the benefit of the whole—represents something especially valuable, relevant for the future, and even exemplary for other nations *(Modell Deutschland)*. In point of fact, the idea is again in vogue among conservative historians and politicians that the Federal Republic of Germany may acquire certain leadership functions (for instance, because of its location in middle Europe) that could be carried out only if "well-tried" German traditions are revived.

Another problem in the arguments of liberal critics relates to the question of who was responsible for the crimes of fascism. The idea that "we Germans" are responsible and therefore, even today, have every reason to be ashamed is the leitmotiv in their criticism. Morally this is an absolutely respectable position and, insofar as it refers to the overall responsibility of the German nation and its state as an object of international laws, it is no doubt correct. Nonetheless, I have my doubts whether this is in keeping with historical reality and whether it is sufficiently effective to counteract the ideological offensive from the right.

First of all, it must be made clear that the phrase "we Germans" is logically equivalent to phrases such as "the Germans" or "the French," and so forth. It supposes the existence of shared interests and a uniformity in thinking and doing that, in reality, does not exist, not even under fascism. This phrase ends up, explicitly or not, quite near the conservative ideology of *Volksgemeinschaft* (the distinctive identity of a people) and, more specifically, the thesis of collective guilt.

But who would contend that those who fought fascism from the underground or the antifascists who were condemned to prison and concentration camps share in this guilt? Who would expect them to be ashamed of their actions? Of course, they made political mistakes by not having found the right way to put a stop to fascism. In this sense one could also speak of a joint guilt (as did the appeal of the German Communist party on July 11, 1945). The joint guilt of the victims, however, is obviously on a different level from that of those who were actively involved in initiating and carrying out the policies of fascism. Thus it is necessary to name more precisely the forces and interest groups responsible for fascism. Even the thesis of collective guilt, which at first (for instance, in the American press) was an expression of the inability to grasp realistically the social characteristics of fascism, eventually became one of many ways in which the real power structure behind fascism became shrouded. With this thesis the entire period of fascism is viewed so nebulously that it is no longer possible to tell the difference among the fascists, the antifascists, the leading decision makers, those who followed their orders, and those who were hoodwinked by them.

From such a vantage point the thesis of collective guilt is hardly different from the Führer theory (although it is usually based on entirely different moral reasoning). Whether one claims that everyone has to carry the same amount of blame or that everyone is equally free of guilt (since only the Führer is guilty), there is no significant difference in these views. I would even dare to claim that the appeal to finally close the books on the past will prevail all the more easily if the right succeeds in convincing the general public that the question of guilt applies to "the Germans." Thus, to champion the thesis of collective guilt is likely to help further the right—even though the advocates of this thesis are acting with honorable intentions.

Second, one must take into account those who grew up after 1945 or were not even born until the 1950s or 1960s. These groups now comprise the majority of the population. They are encountering traces of the fascist past everywhere. There is hardly a town in the Federal Republic that did not have a field station of a concentration camp or a camp for forced labor, hardly a village where some inhabitants whom everyone knew were not murdered or deported. Local histories—often researched by volunteers or school classes—have uncovered many things the adult generation of that time had already pushed out of mind and believed forgotten. It was and is their own grandfathers and grandmothers who lived through those years and whom the students can consult as *Zeitzeugen* (contemporary witnesses).

We are dealing here not with crimes that are as distant to us as the crimes of Nebuchadnezzar or Genghis Khan, in spite of what the conservative ideologists would have us believe. The extent and the methods of these crimes are, by all means, so singular in character that they force us to make penetrating inquiries about how they could have happened. Yet the fact is that the effort of conservative historians to integrate fascism into the "normal" course of modern history is already part of the lesson plans in the schools of most of the federal states (by no means only in those governed by the Christian Union parties).

There has been a struggle over the correct view of history ever since the rise of class society and the consequent need to maintain the privileges of power by means of, among other things, ideology. This struggle has reached a new level since the ruling class has been confronted with organized forces in the form of a workers' movement, which represents not only a social-economic alternative, but also an intellectual and moral alternative that has developed its own world view, giving the struggle a goal and a sense of direction. The fact that it was possible for the ruling classes to defend their ideological hegemony over the correct interpretation of history until 1918, and then after 1919 gradually to win it back, contributed to fascism's ability to establish itself and achieve its political goals.

This struggle over historical questions did not, of course, come to an end in 1945. It has also represented for the history of the Federal Republic a significant impulse for the wide-ranging altercation over the interpretation of the world and humanity and over the path the Federal Republic should take. Conflict over history is thus a political conflict. It is taking place whether we are conscious of it or not. It is better to be conscious of it, because only they can we effectively intervene in it.

For anyone who is at all interested in historical questions—and there are many, not only in academic circles—the question as to which side of this *Historikerstreit* is correct is highly relevant. Here the conservative historians have obviously been unsuccessful. Their critics have been able to show conclusively that, for one thing, they have disregarded the most basic ground rules of historical craftsmanship in order to arrive at their results. Second, it is not the case that new scientific results are under examination; these are simply new assessments, which have been reached, in part, by means of abstruse speculation. Finally, these new assessments are in reality quite old, namely, the ones propagated by neofascism for decades.

While the untenability of its scientific claims has never been a reason for Germany's guild of historians to revise its position, the defeat of the conservative historians is nevertheless significant. Not only the established left, but also the liberal and perhaps even some of the conservative sectors of the general public will be much more skeptical from now on when "recognized historians" present their "scholarly" judgments about German fascism. Democratic and liberal historians must nevertheless confront the revisionists with ever more careful research and analysis of the past to enable a new generation to shape the present and the future to their own liking.

Notes

1. For this and following points, see Th. Doerry, *Antifaschismus in der Bundesrepublik* (Frankfurt: Roederberg, 1980), esp. pp. 5ff.
2. Cf. G. Stuby and U. Mayer, eds., *Die Entstehung des Grundgesetzes, Beiträge und Dokumente* (Cologne: Pahl-Rugenstein, 1976); and W. Abendroth, *Das Grundsetz*, 2nd ed., (Pfullingen: Neske, 1966).
3. See Adenauer's address on March 5, 1952 in Northwest German Radio; cf. *Bonner Bulletin* 27 (March 6, 1952): 262.
4. See *Bayernkurier*, July 4, 1970; and *Spiegel*, no. 32, 1969.
5. Described in detail in my book *Die Weimarer Republik* (Reinbek: Rowohlt TB, 1985).
6. Cf. in particular M. Imhof. "Die Vertriebenenverbände in der Bundesrepublik Deutschland," University of Marburg, 1975; and H.-D. Bamberg, *Die Deutschlandstiftung e.V.* (Meisenheim: Anton Hain, 1978). Regarding the further development of the transitional space between the ruling right and the extreme right refer to R. Kühnl, *Die von F. J. Strauß repräsentierten politischen Kräfte und ihr Verhältnis zum Faschismus* (Cologne: Pahl-Rugenstein, 1980); A. Meyer and K.-K Rabe, eds., *Einschlägige Beziehungen von Unionspolitikern* (Bornheim-Merten: Lamuv Verlag, 1980); K.-K Rabe, ed., *Von Oggersheim bis Oberschlesien. Union und Vertriebenenverbände im politischen Gleichklang. Eine Dokumentation* (Bornheim-Merten: Lamuv Verlag, 1985); and R. Opitz, *Faschismus und Neofaschismus* (Frankfurt: Verlag Marxistischer Blätter, 1984).
7. Cf. R. Kühnl, *Der deutsche Faschismus in Quellen und Dokumenten*, 6th ed. (Cologne: Pahl-Rugenstein, 1987), esp. chap. V. 2a.

8. Excerpts quoted in ibid., chap. V. 1b.

9. Cf. G. G. Iggers, *Deutsche Geschichtswissenschaft* (Munich: Deutsche Taschenbuch Verlag [dtv], 1971); *Neue Geschichtswissenschafat. Vom Historismus zur historischen Sozialwissenschaft* (Munich: Deutsche Taschenbuch Verlag [dtv], 1978); and H. Schleier, "Zum idealistischen Historismus in der bürgerlichen deutschen Geschichtswissenschaft," *Jahrbuch für Geschichte* 28 (1983): 133–54.

10. K. D. Erdmann, *Geschichte, Politik und Pädagogik* (Stuttgart: Klett-Cotta, 1970), p. 90.

11. Cf. R. Kühnl, *Faschismustheorien. Texte zur Faschismusdiskussion 2* (Reinbek: Rowohlt TB, 1979).

12. According to Gerhard Ritter it was "the masses in the modern industrial regions," and according to Röpke, "the proletariat proper," that formed the fascist masses. Cf. G. Ritter, *Europa und die deutsche Frage* (Munich: Munchener Verlag, 1948), p. 188 and p. 19; and W. Röpke, *Die deutsche Frage* (Erlenbach/Zurich: Rentsch, 1948), pp. 48 and 64.

13. Cf. in particular F. Fischer, *Griff nach der Weltmacht* (Dusseldorf: Droste, 1961); and F. Fischer, *Bündnis der Eliten. Zur Kontinuität der Machtstrukturen in Deutschland 1871 bis 1945* (Dusseldorf: Droste, 1979). See also W. Jäger, *Historische Forschung und politische Kultur in Deutschland. Die Debatte 1914–1980 über den Ausbruch des Ersten Weltkrieges* (Gottingen: Vandenhoeck & Ruprecht, 1984).

14. B. Blanke et al., *Kritik der Politischen Wissenschaft*, Bd. 1 (Frankfurt: Campus, 1975), pp. 52ff.

15. Cf. in particular B. Weisbrod, *Schwerindustrie in der Weimarer Republik* (Wuppertal: P. Hammer, 1978): Ch. Streit, *Keine Kameraden: Die Wehrmacht und die sowjetischen Kriegsgefangenen 1941–1945* (Stuttgart: Deutsche Verlags-Anstalt, 1978); H. Krausnick and H.-H Wilhelm, *Die Truppe des Weltanschauungskrieges: Die Einsatzgruppen der Sicherheitspolizei und des SD 1938–1942* (Stuttgart: Oldenbourg, 1981); and Ch. Kleßmann and F. Pingel, eds., *Gegner des Nationalsizialismus* (Frankfurt/New York: Campus, 1980).

16. Cf. A. Manzmann, ed., *Hitlerwelle und historische Fakten* (Konigstein: Scriptor, 1979).

17. J. C. Fest, *Hitler* (West Berlin: Ullstein TB, 1973); cf. J. Berlin et al., *Was verschweigt Fest? Analysen und Dokumente zum Hitler* (Cologne: Pahl-Rugenstein, 1978); and S. Haffner, *Anmerkungen zu Hitler* (Zurich/Munich: Fischer TB, 1978). See also my book review in *Politische Vierteljahresschrift—Literatur*, February 1980, pp. 136ff.

18. Haffner, *Anmerkungen zu Hitler*, note 18, pp. 41ff. and pp. 161ff.

19. I have described in detail the argumentation and the goals of this new nationalism, as well as the needs on which it capitalizes, in my book *Nation, Nationalismus, nationale Frage* (Cologne: Pahl-Rugenstein, 1986).

20. Documented in ibid.

21. Cf., in addition to the editorials by Stürmer in the *Frankfurter Allgemeine Zeitung*, his collection of essays *Dissonanzen des Fortschritts* (Munich: R. Piper, 1986).

22. Ibid.

23. Cf. *Frankfurter Allgemeine Zeitung*, January 24, 1983. A good analysis of this speech is to be found in the new edition of W. F. Haug, *Der hilflose Antifaschismus* (West Berlin: Pahl-Rugenstein, 1986).

24. According to Fest in an editorial in *Frankfurter Allgemeine Zeitung*, April 20, 1985. Similar sentiments found in *Rheinische Merkur/Christ und Welt*, February 16, 1985.

25. I present a thorough documentation and analysis of the debate in my book *Vergangenheit, die nicht vergeht* (Cologne: Pahl-Rugenstein, 1987).

26. A. Hillgruber, *Zweierlei Untergang: Die Zerschlagung des Deutschen Reiches und das Ende des europäischen Judentums* (West Berlin: Siedler, 1986). This also contains the text of his lecture "Der Zusammenbruch im Osten als Problem der deutschen Nationalgeschichte und der europäischen Geschichte," which Hillgruber had published in 1985.

27. *Frankfurter Allgemeine Zeitung*, August 20, 1986, and October 16, 1986.

28. *Frankfurter Allgemeine Zeitung*, June 6, 1986. Cf. *Frankfurter Allgemeine Zeitung*, July 24, 1980, as well as E. Nolte, "Der Faschismus in seiner Epoche und seine weltpolitischen Konsequenzen bis zur Gegenwart," in Peter Bergler et al., eds., *Deutsche Identität heute* with an introduction by Heinrich Windelen (Mainz-Laubenheim: Hase und Koehler, 1983), pp. 25–47, esp. pp. 43–46.

29. K. Hildebrand, "Das Zeitalter der Tyrannien," *Frankfurter Allgemeine Zeitung*, July 31, 1986; and J. C. Fest, *Frankfurter Allgemeine Zeitung*, August 29, 1986.

30. J. Habermas, "Eine Art Schadensabwicklung," *Die Zeit*, July 11, 1986; and "Vom öffentlichen Gebrauch der Historie," *Die Zeit*, November 7, 1986.

31. Nolte's comments at a conference sponsored by the Social Democratic party, "Erziehung—Aufklärung—Restauration," were cited in the German newspaper *Deutsche Volkszeitung/die Tat*, October 17, 1986. The degree to which government leaders of the right still feel obliged to employ totalitarianism as a value criterion is evidenced in the answer given by the chairman of the parliamentary group of Bavaria's Christian Social Unionist Party, Theo Waigel, to a question posed to a different prominent public figure every week in the *Frankfurter Allgemeine Zeitung*. To the question "Which historical figures do you despise most of all?" Waigel gave the straight stereotypical reply: "Hitler and Stalin." The U.S. ambassador to Germany, Richard Burt, could afford to be more ingenuous. He answered quite simply "Josef Stalin." See *FAZ-Magazin*, January 9, 1987, and January 23, 1987.

32. Cf. in particular W. J. Mommsen, "Weder Leugnen noch Vergessen: Befreit von der Vergangenheit," *Frankfurter Rundschau*, December 1, 1986; H. Mommsen, "Suche nach der verlorenen Geschichte?" *Merkur* 451, no. 2 (1986): 863ff; M. Broszat, "Wo sich die Geister scheiden," *Die Zeit*, October 3, 1986; J. Habermas, "Eine Art Schadensabwicklung," note 29; and K. Sontheimer, "Maskenbildner schminken eine neue Identität," *Rheinischer Merkur/Christ und Welt*, November 21, 1986. See also U. Hörster-Philipps "Kernfrage des bundesdeutschen Historikerstreits," *Deutsche Volkszeitung/die Tat*, December 12, 1986; G. Fülberth, "Ein Philosoph blamiert die Historiker," *Deutsche Volkszeitung/die Tat*, September 26, 1986; H. Pätzold, "Von Verlorenem, Gewonnenem und Erstrebtem: Zur Historikerdebatte," *Blätter für deutsche und internationale Politik*, 2 (1987): 160–72; W. Grab, "Kritische Bemerkungen zur nationalen Apologetik Joachim Fests, Ernst Noltes und Andreas Hillgrubers," *1999*, 2 (1987); M. Brumlik, "Neuer Staatsmythos Ostfront," *die Tageszeitung (taz)*, July 12, 1986; D. Diner, "Der Kern der Wende," *links*, November 1986; and reports in *Der Spiegel* 36 (1986): 66ff., and 41 (1986): 62.

33. I have discussed the question as to whether National Socialism was a form of fascism in my book *Der Faschismus: Ursachen, Herrschaftsstruktur, Aktualität* (Heilbronn: Distel, 1983), pp. 97–113.

34. Habermas, "Eine Art Schadensabwicklung," and Hillgruber, *Zweierlei Untergang*, p. 733.

After Nazism: Antifascism and Democracy in Dachau, 1945

Tony Barta

On May 8, 1945, World War II ended with Nationalist Socialist Germany's unconditional surrender to the Allies. That has not, until recently, been an occasion for commemoration in West Germany. But each year, in the last days of April or in early May, at a special site, a group of men with a special bond have met to commemorate a day of special significance for them. From Poland, from France, from Italy, from East Germany, from Czechoslovakia, from all the countries occupied by Hitler's armies, old men, in dwindling numbers, have come to Dachau, to the *Appellplatz* of the former concentration camp, to remember the day of liberation. Some of the men spent twelve years imprisoned in this camp or elsewhere in the system that spread out from Dachau. They, of course, and others arrested as the original opponents of the Nazis, did not come from Poland, or the Soviet Union, or from Austria: every person sent to a concentration camp before 1938 was a German citizen. Whether Communists (the largest group) or Social Democrats, they sustained themselves with the belief that the defeat of the Nazis would bring a new beginning in which the solidarity of the left would be the basis of a progressive democracy. The story I want to tell here concerns the hopes of these men on liberation day 1945 and what happened to them in the first year of the Allied victory over fascism.[1]

Most of those who spoke of the Hitler dictatorship in terms of "fascism" were Communists. Their belief that they had recognized more clearly than anyone else what fascism was, and against whom it was directed, was supported by the number of their comrades the regime had imprisoned. Anti-Nazis might oppose the dictatorship; "antifascists" were engaged in a more historic struggle. With the defeat of Hitler's Reich the dark night of reaction was over; everywhere in Europe the men of the left who had played leading roles in the resistance to the Nazis stood at the head of the liberators. Everywhere Communists expected, and for a time made, political gains. The situation in Germany after the war was different, however. The Germans were not liberated, they were conquered. In the eastern part of their truncated country that would mean the establishment of a Communist regime in a new state under Soviet protection. In the western zones of occupation there was also to be a new state, founded on liberal and democractic (as well as anti-Soviet) principles, and under American protection. Dachau, being in the zone originally occupied and governed by the U. S. Army, was a microcosm of this evolution. There we can see the principles of the conquerors of Nazism being converted into the practices of the successor West German state. It was talking about what happened there with those disappointed men who still call themselves antifascists that led me to reflect more closely on a transition they have long perceived as critical.

It is not a transition to which historians have paid a great deal of attention: we will probably always be more fascinated by what took place when the Nazis came into power than by what happened when they lost it. The aftermath as been discussed mainly in terms of Allied policy and the division of Germany into two states when the Allies fell out. In both East and West Germany the emphasis is on the opening of a new chapter rather than the closing of an old one. Or else it is assumed that the old one simply did close with the defeat of Nazism in 1945—as in very important respects it did. However, just as it is more illuminating to look at the Nazi "seizure of power" over a period of months, and perhaps best in one place (as W. S. Allen does), it is instructive to follow the Nazi fall from power over several months, and again in one place.[2] The place, Dachau, has become a symbol for what happened when the Nazis took over; that gives it a special interest after their fall, too. Just as we can see the seizure of power as "a coup d'état by installments" directed at eliminating the socialist threat from German life, it becomes evident that the liberation from Nazism entailed (at least in Dachau) a remarkably parallel elimination of the threat from the left, though this time by very different means.

The difference in means can hardly be overemphasised—democracy rather than violent dictatorship. But we should not lose sight of the ends. If the most important thing about National Socialism was its guarantee to remove the left threat to majority conceptions of social and individual interest—and it undoubtedly was—it makes sense not to close the campaign with Hitler's bullet in the bunker but to pursue it at least into the denouement of 1945–46. That places the question of the historical failure or success of National Socialism in a rather different perspective.[3]

No one in Germany was thinking of the historical success of National Socialism in April 1945. There had been more than five years of war, which ordinary people had continued only because they had no power to stop it and because they were constantly reminded of the terrible retribution advancing toward them from the East. The propaganda pictures of Soviet atrocities were stark. When so many men had died— fathers, husbands, brothers, sons—should it have been so that their families would end like this? There was no alternative but to continue, simply continue.

Rosel Kirchhoff had grown up in Dachau. In 1944 and 1945, as a student in Stuttgart, she helped serve meals to the survivors of the terrible Allied raids. She noticed that the people no longer cried as they took their food amid the rubble and watched the bodies of their sisters or their parents being dug out. They were no longer capable of responding with grief, and they did not care about defeat. When the Wehrmacht finally began to disintegrate at the end of April, Rosel hitched a ride home to Dachau. It looked, she remembers, just the same as it always did. Though Munich, only seventeen kilometers to the south, was almost as badly bombed as Stuttgart, in the old market town on the Amper river it could have been peace time.[4] The local newspaper no longer appeared but in the last issues life can be seen going on as usual, in the small print of personal notices under the large print rhetoric of the war:

> *Business notices:* Johann Fischer and son, farm equipment. Closed from 27.12.44 to 2.1.45 for stocktaking.

> *Employment:* Housemaid required for hotel-restaurant in Dachau. Opportunity to learn cooking. Factory seeks cook for foreigners' canteen.

> *Exchange:* Pram, ivory, good condition, for accordion, 3 or 4 chord.[5]

On April 29 the end was obviously near. American guns could be heard not very far away. The Schutzstaffel (SS), so prominent in Dachau for twelve years, had fled, leaving behind huge storehouses of almost every conceivable commodity—spirits, cosmetics, cigarette papers, leather, fabric, canned foods—things ordinary people had not seen in years. Many were still out on the streets with armloads of Italian cloth or oxcarts of French champagne when the first American soldiers appeared.

They came like cats, silently, on their rubber soles.[6] Strange creatures in their greenish overalls and curious helmets, they fanned out among the houses and started to requisition billets. Their armored vehicles rumbled through the town, down the hill, and across the river, in the direction of the concentration camp. From inside the camp the prisoners heard shooting. Their wait was tense. Many had already gone, forced into a "death march" to the south, and it was known by those remaining that Hitler wanted no concentration camp prisoner to fall into Allied hands alive. When the helmet of the first American soldier appeared over the gate there was cheering and immense relief. Before long the flags of all the imprisoned nationalities were flying over the camp.

It is significant that the euphoria of liberation was celebrated not in the town itself but largely by foreigners in that other Dachau which the local community had always felt was fastened on to it as an alien growth. It was assumed in the town that these foreigners, the liberators and the liberated, would now have the say in what was to happen. Only a few people, in the first days, had the presence of mind to sense that key moves in determining the political future of Bavaria—and these people were still as much Bavarian as German—would be made early in the rule of the outsiders. Whether the hitherto dominant community values of the conservative majority were reasserted or whether radical departures were allowed to get under way would depend (or so it was then thought) on this first struggle for influence. In Dachau the contending forces were to be represented by the American commandant, Captain Malcolm Vendig, his chief German administrative official, Landrat Heinrich Kneuer, and the leader of the antifascist resistance, Georg Scherer.

Everyone in Dachau said I must try to talk to Georg Scherer, though some thought he would not talk very willingly: "He doesn't have anything to do with politics these days." To members of his generation on the left he was clearly something of a folk hero and even conservative townspeople spoke of him with affection and respect. People who could never get themselves to utter the word "antifascist," and did not particularly admire him for spending six years in the concentration camp or for leading Dachau's only armed resistance against the SS, recalled his decency, energy, and fairness in the difficult days after the war. Nobody had a bad word to say about "der Scherer Schorsch." So when, on a weekday evening, I succeeded in seeing him—even in his seventies he was very busy running his clothing factory—he was very much as I expected to find him: shortish, vigorous, straight to the point, more comfortable in shirt sleeves than in his business suit. He thought he would complete the interview more efficiently in his office than in his home, so he led me through the back garden to the rear entrance of the big building, whose front facing the Münchener Strasse bears the name "Bardtke und Scherer, Kleiderfabrik." Under the harsh factory office lights, surrounded by fabric samples and racks of winter coats, he told me in a few sentences about his arrest, his release, the rising at the end of the war. He did not expect to be asked about his earlier life: that was not part of the history of which he was the recognized custodian. He was uncomfortable, outside his field, because at that time in his life there was nothing remarkable in his experience. He had gone hungry, he had worked hard just like everybody else. A childhood in Dachau meant severe and crowded schooling, a kind of poverty that was normal and therefore not unhappy in retrospect. You remembered things like being sent to buy beer—by the jugful, not by the bottle. You had a ten-minute run up to the pub to get what was called "three-quarters"—just short of a litre. On the way home you always drank a bit off the top and then ran water into it so your father did not notice. His early life, he insisted, was typical for working-class people of his generation.

Georg Scherer was eight when World War I broke out. It was the summer holidays and he had been sent to work for a farmer at Pippinsried, twenty-five kilometers away. On August 1, 1914, coming home from the fields at midday, the workers were met by people telling them to unhitch the horses and park their wagons across the road to hold up the French advance. The roadbock stayed there all through dinnertime, but at one o'clock the French still had not come so the horses were hitched up again and everyone went back to the fields. That was his last memory of summer. The four long years of war were years of grim struggle for most families. In his view, Dachauers who knew only World War II, when Germany could draw supplies from all of conquered Europe, had no idea of deprivation. Even the years of hardship afterward were luxury in comparison.

The euphoria of going off to fight for the Fatherland did not last long. When Georg's father went, immediately on the outbreak of the war, his mother was left alone with four small children. Georg was the eldest and became joint breadwinner with his mother. While she worked at the gunpowder factory down on the flat to the east of the town, Georg spent half of every day working for a farmer, half going to school. The farmer kept an ox in his barn where the family lived in Dachau, just off the Mittermayer Strasse, and had a field down on the Moos. Georg had to cart feed from the field to the ox every day and was paid with a loaf of bread. On Wednesdays, because that was the day the peasants ate noodles, he would put on a knapsack and go from farmhouse to farm-house, begging for bread. The pieces he brought home were cut up and dried out so that there would be something for soup in the winter. The other staple was potatoes found by picking over the fields after the crop had been harvested. Wheat fields also yielded a few gleanings, small ears of wheat that he would sometimes eat where he found them. In the evenings the children would climb over the walls of the convent to steal apples, which would also be stored for winter. Georg as a provider had to do what was necessary: "After all, I had four mouths to feed." What his mother earned in the powder factory and what she received as a war pension did not go far. Each morning she sent him off to school with a single slice of bread, leaving the loaf marked with a notch. When he came home he carefully cut himself another slice and marked the loaf off again with a ruler. After he finished his day's work for the farmer he cooked the evening meal—almost always bread, soup, and potatoes. There was never any question of meat: the family went right through the war without eating meat.

At the end of the war Georg had his first taste of the political violence that was to consume Germany in the aftermath and to fasten itself, as a very synonym, on Dachau. When the White Army arrived in 1919 to give the coup de grâce to the Bavarian *Räterepublik* (Soviet Republic), the twelve-year-old Georg was rather thoughtlessly wearing a red cockade. A White soldier hit him so hard in the face that he was knocked into the dirt. Georg's father came back from the war and found a job emptying powder from surplus shells in the explosives factory. One day there was an accident and he was blown to bits. The workers' factory committee decided the least they could do was to help the boy learn a trade so he too went into the factory—now called "Deutsche Werke"—apprenticed as a fitter and turner. When the Deutsche Werke closed down in 1923 (Himmler was to find another use for all those empty barracks ten years later) Scherer was forced to clear ditches, pick hops—anything to support the family through the infla-tion. Then in April 1925, when money was again worth something, he was taken on at the Bavarian Motor Works in Munich. He held his job, on good pay, through the depression. He bought a motorbike, got married, became a father. There was no need for him to rock the boat.

He was, however, a socialist. Even if his main interest was sport it was always, since 1922, *workers'* sport. The affairs of the Dachau Workers' Sports Association were his major interest: he was a commit-tee man and in 1928 he attended the Workers' Olympics in Frankfurt. In 1931, when the Socialist Workers' party (SAP) was founded, to the left of the Social Democractic party (SPD), he was attracted by its call for a united working-class front against the Nazi challenge. He was not the kind to give up either his sport or his politics just because the Nazis had taken over government, dissolved the unions, and closed down the Workers' Sports Association. Despite pressure at work he refused to join any party organization; in 1935 he even distributed some anti-Nazi pamphlets given to him by one of the foremen. He should, he said, have known better. He was taking some children for a gymnastics lesson, practicing for a Christmas show, when they came to arrest him.

He was interrogated, beaten, and finally thrown into the concentration camp—a world removed from the Dachau he had lived in up to now. For six years he knew only the society of imprisoned comrades and SS brutality. In 1940 he was appointed *Lagerältester*, responsible for all prisoners. In this time he not only learned what solidarity between comrades was; his name became virtually synonymous with it. Released in 1941 in order to be sent to the eastern front he found a job in a small munitions plant. He evaded an almost certain death by being able to stay in Dachau, but there was almost no one who would talk to him. He was now not a Dachauer, but a "KZler"—one of those from down there. By 1945, however, it was precisely this unique dual identity that was to give him his extraordinary role. Fearing that the SS might commit further atrocities before the Americans arrived, and determined also to show that not all Germans had to be liberated from fascism by foreign arms, he led an armed insurrection in Dachau on April 28. The rising, coordinated with resistance action in Munich, was at first successful—the Rathaus was taken, the Volkssturm sent home. It was then bloodily suppressed by the SS. Three Dachau workers and three concentration camp prisoners lost their lives.[7] Their bodies were left lying in the town square as a warning.

Scherer and others fled to the woods in the west. He watched, appalled, as the Americans rounded up the few Germans who attempted to make a fight of it and shot them down against the wall of a church. The next day someone came to fetch him. He was called before the American commandant and appointed deputy *Bürgermeister*. "I didn't especially want to do it," he told me, "but there was no-one else."

There were huge practical tasks to be accomplished. There were 6,000 dead from the camp to be buried; 27,000 survivors to be fed. A typhoid outbreak had to be contained by strict quarantine. Transport and labor had to be organized, food requisitioned, prisoners awaiting repatriation accommodated. For all these tasks the Americans relied on local organization. In the camp there was the discipline of the prisoners' national and international committees. They knew that to survive the liberation continued solidarity and patience were necessary.

Outside the camp there was chaos, and something like a "great fear." Forced laborers of many nationalities, but mainly Russians and Poles, were in the streets, along with concentration camp prisoners from outside work brigades. Not all the prisoners, as some people in Dachau still remind you rather too quickly, were political prisoners. There *were* common criminals. People in Dachau feared vengeance; in fact the worst crimes were thefts of radios and bicycles. The main hardship they suffered was the wholesale requisitioning of housing by the Americans.

Max Gorbach was one of the prisoners outside the camp. His experiences in the hotel trade in Switzerland and Canada had helped make him a Communist; he had smuggled anti-Nazi material across the border into Germany and he had fought fascism in the Spanish Civil War. After he was handed over by the Vichy French to the Gestapo in 1941, and sent to Dachau, he had been put to work in the Wülfert meat-canning factory in the town. Now, at the liberation, he immediately became one of the organizers of provisions and of labor.

Several times in the account Gorbach gave me (he supplied rather more detail than Scherer) the same phrase crops up: "Es war notwendig Ordnung zu schaffen." The first necessity was to create order. To stop plundering, restore essential services, create the basic conditions for the continuance of organized life. There is some irony in this: the Communists had often enough mocked the Majority Social Democratic party (MSPD) for keeping things going at the end of World War I. Ebert had said, "We were in the truest sense trustees in bankruptcy of the old regime." Were not men like Gorbach, disciplined Communists, becoming trustees in bankruptcy for the society that had produced National Socialism? Certainly at the time it was not the most pressing consideration: these men felt they simply had no choice but to step into the breach. They had to act. First of all they had to act out of solidarity for their comrades. The supplies, transport, and housing they organized were in the first instance for their fellow prisoners in the camp. Second, in the special case of Scherer, he had to act out of solidarity with his own community. He was a Dachauer, and even if many people in Dachau had not wanted to know him after he was released from the camp, there was now a job to be done and he was the only one who could do it. Someone had to organize fuel for the bakeries and hospitals in the coming winter, to find workers and provisions for turf-cutting brigades. Someone had to organize labor and transport for the burial parties if disease was going to be contained.

This emergency organization, of course, was never nonpolitical. Quite the contrary. These men had not spent twelve years in unflinching ideological opposition to National Socialism for nothing. They saw themselves as *Widerstandskämpfer,* resistance fighters. In fact they believed, not without some reason, that they were the only Germans who offered determined resistance to Hitler. Further, some among them were theoretically as well as experientally educated to understand the historical phenomenon of fascism and they had fairly clear-cut ideas about the political tactics to be adopted at the moment of fascism's defeat. These tactics they now put into effect.[8] They divided Dachau, then containing some 22,000 inhabitants, into seventeen districts. In open meetings on the streets they called on people to take part and everywhere committees of seven members were elected. This meant that all the things that had to be done could be organized on the broadest possible base. There was an attempt to establish the broadest political base as well. To coordinate the seventeen districts a committee of eight was chosen: two Communists, two Socialists, two from the former Bavarian Peoples' party—the populist Catholic conservative party of the majority—and two without party affiliation. To this committee they gave the name Anti-Fascist Action Committee (AFA).

Such committees—generally known as "Antifa"—sprang up almost everywhere in Germany when the Third Reich collapsed. They were purely local and uncoordinated creations that, as a U. S. intelligence report put it, set out "to mobilize all the politically healthy forces in the population so as to create the conditions for a new, democratic Germany." In the best early assessment of the antifascist initiatives, the report pointed out that under the circumstances it was naturally "the old working class, the group in German society most active in opposing the Nazis, which makes up the overwhelming majority and also most of the leaders." Whether the leaders were from the German Communist party (KPD) or the SPD depended mainly on the qualifications of available personnel. "The Communists have nevertheless taken over the leadership in the majority of groups because on the one hand their commitment is especially strong and on the other hand the idea of the united front accords exactly with their current programme." Many older Social Democratic leaders were suspicious of the Communists and more interested in their own party organization. They may also have doubted that antifascism could build on the social base the Communists thought had been created by the war, with sections of the middle class moving to the left. Whether the basically working-class antifascist organizations could win over the middle class remained to be seen. "At the moment," commented the report, "the mass of the middle class regards these groups constituted mainly of workers with traditional mistrust."[9]

In Dachau, of course, there was an additional reason for suspicion. The concentration camp gave extra strength to the antifascists—they were able, for instance, to issue a duplicated broadsheet almost daily—

but with regard to the local population it was not an advantage to belong to such a notorious concentration of Communists, or to be associated with the threatening horde of foreigners. The broadsheet, called "The Anti-Fascist," was subtitled "Voice of the Germans from Dachau," partly to identify it among the publications of all the other nationalities.[10] However, in Dachau town it was not enough to be German; even more than elsewhere people wanted reassurance that the voices listened to would be from their own community.

The AFA in Dachau was not a coterie of outsiders. The initiative and organizing energy came from men of the left, some of whom had been in the camp, and the presence of the camp undoubtedly strengthened their hand. The AFA itself was not made up of former prisoners; as in other towns it was set up as a citizens' organization across party and to some extent across class lines. Because "antifascist" was a term used mainly by Communists it was difficult for middle-class people, whether compromised with Nazism or not, to take the word into their mouths. Some Catholics believed their anti-Nazi credentials were as good as any Communist's; they believed cooperation was both necessary and politic. Such men as master glazier Syrius Eberle served both to reassure the conservative majority and to give them a voice.

The AFA was prominent and energetic. It could claim to be representative. However, it had no authority of its own. It started the post-Nazi reconstruction working, street-by-street, home-by-home: making lists of all Nazi party members, evicting them from houses, enrolling them for compulsory labor—"you put in the next three days with your oxcart shifting bodies; here's a gas mask"—but the AFA could issue orders only so long as it was permitted to do so by the U. S. Army.

The American army had fought its way across Europe in a crusade against Hitlerite evil. It took over responsibility for governing the largest part of occupied Germany with a basic prejudice that all Germans had more or less supported Hitler and that they should therefore be treated as a conquered rather than as a liberated people. Apart from the consequent "nonfraternization" order—a directive crying out for subversion by battle-weary soldiers—policy was still in the process of being formulated when the military government detachments took over the towns and districts assigned to them. They had the *Handbook of Military Government*, whose status was rather uncertain, and two general aims: to remove Nazis and to "get things going."[11] These aims, as they hardened into the twin pillars of American occupation policy, did not necessarily contradict each other but they did involve deciding which Germans really were Nazis, which groups should have influence on local policy, and who should have executive authority in administration. The obvious groups to turn to, in the first instance, were the antifascist committees.

In the first days there was agreement on priorities and effective cooperation. With regard to the first American objective, "denazification," the antifascists had already led the way. Even before the occupation authorities issued their 132-question *Fragebogen* to all people over eighteen, the AFA in Dachau had started compiling lists and distributing handwritten questionnaires. Their concern—and in this almost all Germans, as distinct from almost all Americans, agreed—was that the real Nazis, those who had promoted and profited from the regime, be identified. Nominal membership in a Nazi organization they saw as unimportant. Their realism about this, and the neighborhood structure that let people decide who was a real Nazi and who was not, did not impress the Americans; they persisted in an inflexible policy of excluding all party members from even minor official positions. When denazification, again on American insistence, was given over mainly to ad hoc German courts, the *Spruchkammern*, in which those with the right connections could produce exonerating testimonials *(Persilscheine)* while "little Nazis" were fined or deprived of their livelihood, most antifascists quit in disgust. Because it affected so many people personally, denazification was to remain one of the most resented consequences of Germany's defeat and few people distinguished the commonsense practice of the local antifascists from the rigid directives of the occupying power.[12]

Even as they attempted to purge every branch of administration of Nazis, the Americans knew they had no option but to rely on Germans as administrative personnel. Yet they never seriously considered basing the continuing operations of military government on the antifascist committees. Rather more curiously, in view of what had happened in the transition to the supposedly democratic and republican administration after 1918, the American practice of installing experienced civil servants was never seriously questioned by the antifascists. They seem to have recognized it (in perhaps a too-German way) as inevitable even though they knew that trained administrators were unlikely to be men of the left. The result, at least in Dachau, was an element of "dual power" that indeed had striking parallels with the situation in 1918–19.[13] There developed almost immediately a competition for influence between those who believed they were nurturing a new democracy in the cooperative effort of antifascism and those who regarded the experiment with deep suspicion.

The competition was not, in the first instance, for the allegiance of the German people, but for the ear of the sole authority, the occupying power. Captain Malcolm Vendig, its representative in Dachau, was described by one of the men who served under him, later a minister in the Bavarian government, as being "filled with what could only be called missionary zeal for the democratisation of Germany."[14] Working together with Georg Scherer and the Anti-Fascist Action Committee seems to have posed few problems for him in the beginning. But local administration was not to remain a matter for local decision. The military government, while not yet formally recognizing any Bavarian entity, decided to restore the pre-Nazi administrative system and on May 7, the day before Germany's unconditional capitulation, Vendig was given (or himself selected—the exact process is obscure) a German chief executive who immediately managed to make that surrender seem more conditional than it appeared. This man was Heinrich Kneuer, described by everyone who knew him as "a professional administrator of the old school." He had served in a lesser position in Dachau from 1921 to 1930; during the war he held an important post in the State Food Supply Office in Munich. As district administrator, or Landrat, he was now answerable for the entire Dachau district administration. His deputy, Josef Schwalber, the future minister, later called him "ein Mann des Rechtes"—a man of justice and right (not of "the right," though he was that, too), a man "for whom the principles of the rule of law had become second nature—a quality which, in a time when no one knew what rights and laws were still valid, could not be valued too highly."[15]

The Landrat was directly responsible to the commandant and was required to report every day. A full transcript of these meetings is preserved in the state archives in Munich.[16] It is a fascinating record not only for the information it contains about the turmoil of the immediate postwar situation but because it shows how in that situation two men with completely different ideas about politics and German history see themselves as deciding the direction of Germany's political development. In theory and in practice they thrash out whose conception of democracy should prevail; in the end, of course, it is the practice and not the theory that counts.

From the outset Landrat Kneuer took it as his duty to educate the American as to German realities. So from the first day he complained about the antifascist committee, which he considered not only a challenge to orthodox administration but a threat to the social order—and the political order he believed necessary to maintain it.

On May 14 Kneuer claimed he could not get on with registering the foreigners—the main object of local anxiety—and the farmers out in the villages were forming vigilante groups for their own security.[17]

LANDRAT: They have not been listed by their nationalities. Besides I
             am being held up too much by these antifascist people.

COMMANDANT: In what way?

LANDRAT: They simply undermine all authority, decide against everything that they think might be bourgeois.

COMMANDANT: Who are they?

LANDRAT: They are Communists. They want a Communist Bürgermeister.

COMMANDANT: But who would they put forward?

LANDRAT: Scherer. I had a talk with Dr. Linnmeier [the Bürgermeister] on Saturday and he told me he would make way for Scherer . . . I asked him not to rush matters, but to let me talk things over with you today, as I did not wish to be pushed into any decision. Since yesterday I have been informed that it is Scherer who is bringing confusion into the population, he being head of the antifascist movement, by making them work hard labor, worse than the Nazis ever did.

Kneuer is outraged because his own wife, his children, his servant, and his father (aged 70) have been asked to appear at 7:00 each morning to work as laborers. The commandant does not seem to think it would hurt them to put in some hours with a shovel but in the end he gives the Landrat authority over labor matters. "It is your affair to get the house in order—I want to see the results."

Some days later Kneuer tried to have the antifascists dissolved, as in Munich, on the grounds that they were a political party.

COMMANDANT: I have not looked at this antifascist movement we have here as a political party . . . they may be helpful in ferreting out people, that's why I have not taken action so far. I can't see any definite political direction there.

LANDRAT: But the name!

All through June, Kneuer was relentless in his attempts to have the antifascists suppressed. Though he did not say so in so many words, he seems to have seen the AFA structure as something not far removed from soviets and he was determined to end the situation of dual power. By the end of the month he was largely victorious. Though the commandant refused to veto the publication of antifascist propaganda in the *Amtsblatt*, the weekly official bulletin, he called in Herr Eberle, chairman of the AFA, and told him that he wanted the Landrat to have authority in all matters.

Still the Landrat's anxieties about political developments were not resolved. Some days later he managed to engage the commandant in discussion of fundamental political principles, on which he considered himself an authority. He perhaps got more of a debate than he expected.

LANDRAT: It won't do to listen too much to the people.
COMMANDANT: Well, we do in the United States.
LANDRAT: The voice of the street never determined any political convictions.
COMMANDANT: That is one of the reasons why Germany never had a good democracy. I maintain that the Nazi party came into power because the majority of the people wanted that government. It was a perfectly legal government.
LANDRAT: I believe that a certain class of intellectual men should run the government of the state.
COMMANDANT: Well, here you have it, you do not want democracy but what we would call autocracy.
LANDRAT: The mass is stupid and if it is permitted to run the government, nothing good would come from it. The government should educate the masses.
COMMANDANT: We don't look upon the people or the public as a mass, we look at him as an individual. We think that every individual has his rights and we think that the rights of the individual are as strong as the rights of the state.
LANDRAT: Oh no, this is not what I meant. I have written books on politics. I mean to indicate that there must be one body which represents the government.
COMMANDANT: That's Hegel's thesis on political philosophy. Hegel considers the supreme body the state, we don't. When did you ever have liberalism in Germany?
LANDRAT: In the Weimar Republic.
COMMANDANT: Look here: when does Germany's history start? Say from the year 500 to 1919. All right, you had a steady growth. That means 1,500 years against the 15 years of the Weimar Republic and most of that freedom was only on paper. I think that Dr. Kneuer is a perfect example for a German democracy. He has the theory, but in practice he does not even know what democracy really is. He wants democracy but as soon as people are to have something to say in politics he will maintain that they are incapable of governing themselves. We don't think that any group of people are that smart that they should tell other people what to do.
LANDRAT: My idea of democracy is different. I have studied democracy and I still believe that a certain class of clever men should run the government for the other masses. I am against all sorts of dictatorship.
COMMANDANT: Well, to me it seems your democracy will be a dictatorship of a certain group of persons. That's enough on democracy today.

The Landrat's most pressing concern was not with principles. His real worry was that under the cover of democratic principles the

Communists lurking within antifascism would take up positions from which it would be hard to shift them. A case in point was whether Communists would be eligible for appointment for the new gendarmerie.

COMMANDANT: If you keep Communists out of everything they are going to go against you. I think a man should not be barred from a position because he is a Communist. I do believe that we should not engage an undue proportion of Communists in the Gendarmerie, but they should not be excluded. The Communist party in the United States is perfectly legal, but they never can get too many votes.

LANDRAT: Communism in America or England is an altogether different thing than in Germany. Germany is a poor nation and open to Communism.

COMMANDANT: Well it wouldn't be so poor if it did not start a war every twenty years.

LANDRAT: Communism among the Gendarmerie won't do. We have had our reports coming in from the whole *Landkreis*. Now if we have men who are working against us [Communists] we can't rely on these reports.

COMMANDANT: I don't want communism to establish a dictatorship as you say in Germany. But understand me: if you put a cup of water on the stove and take away the lid it will never boil over. As soon as you put the lid on it will boil over. As far as appointing the new gendarmes goes, they should be picked as to whether they are good gendarmes and not as to whether they are Communists.

LANDRAT: Now we are clearing this country of National Socialism and bringing Communism in. Dictatorship again. National Socialism is no danger to us any more, it is dead. Communism is the future danger.

COMMANDANT: We won't have another dictatorship. Because you forget that we have a military government, you can afford these experiments in your government now, because you have the ultimate control of the military government.

LANDRAT: I am afraid that America will get tired of getting order into European affairs. They are liable to up and leave it to someone else who may be more interested.

COMMANDANT: Military government will stay here for a few more years to come. For a couple of years you do not have to worry.

In fact, Kneuer did not have to wait two years to have his mind put at rest. His speculation about America was shrewd, yet he turned out to be wrong. He turned out to be wrong about democracy too. On July 21 the Commandant read him a list of names. They were to constitute a new town council, which according to Vendig would be the first town council in postwar Bavaria. There were eight men of the right—mainly affiliated to the old Bavarian People's party (BVP)—and eight men of the left, five Social Democrats and three Communists.[18]

This signaled the end of the political moratorium the Americans had continued for twelve weeks after the collapse of twelve years of Nazi repression. The beginning of democratic politics, which Kneuer dreaded and Vendig was determined to establish, could not be far off. Already in July the Western powers had begun to authorize political parties—the German Communist party (KPD) was the first—and in September they began to organize in Dachau. In November the first party political statements—under the authority of the Landrat and the military government—appeared in the *Amtsblatt*. There were three equal columns: for the Social Democratic party, the Bavarian *Volksbund* or People's League, soon to merge with the new Christian Social Union (CSU), and the KPD.

The statements, as is the way with political platforms, offer few surprises. The SPD appealed to history, its credentials as the longest-standing democratic party in Germany; the KPD soldiered on with its strategy: "the firm unity of all antifascist, democratic, and progressive popular forces." Most interesting, though, is the pitch made by the Bavarian Volksbund:

1. The Bavarian Volksbund is the organization recognized by the Dachau military government which has made it its aim to embrace all those opponents of National Socialism who don't subscribe to the Socialist-Communist common action program.

2. It is a solely local organization of the town and district for, on the one hand, making preparations for the coming Bavarian *Landespartei* [the party that would express the particularist interest and special character of Bavaria] which will fulfil the basic principles below; on the other hand for representing these principles in public life in the locality until such time as that party is founded.

3. The fundamental principles of the Bavarian Volksbund are:

   (a) The building up of a state and social order out of the powers of Christianity which has been the foundation of Western civilization for two thousand years and which gave a large proportion of the active fighters against National Socialism the strength to reject its horrible and corrupting teachings and methods.

   (b) Attainment of a true democracy by rejecting all militarist and dictatorial efforts no matter of what kind or color.

   (c) Creation of a powerful Bavarian state as guarantor of the common good and cultural particularity of the Bavarian people.

(d) Setting up a social community life recognizing the worth of the human personality. The equal rights of all before the law, without difference as to status or property. Help for the economically weak.[19]

Everybody recognized the Bavarian Volksbund for what it was: the successor to the old Bavarian Volkspartei, which could not be directly refloated because in the end it, and its voters, had not resisted Nazism as firmly as its rhetoric implied. Catholicism was initially an effective inoculation. It wore off when economic interests were threatened and the very order of society appeared to be imperiled by the increase in Communist strength during the depression. Even though the Volksbund's political demands now included "cleansing Bavaria from National Socialism in every form," ordinary Nazi party members might be excused for thinking that "exclusion of all real National Socialists from political, economic and cultural life; punishment of the criminally guilty" did not apply to them. They might also have noted that though workers' interests as represented in unions would be recognized, the state would exercise economic leadership "according to the sole criterion of the interests of the *Volksgemeinschaft*"—a collectivity impossible to purge of its Nazi connotations. Not every former Nazi would vote for the party farthest to the right. Some turned to the SPD, a few even to the Communists, who consistently defended the "little Nazis" while demanding that the powerful and the profiteers be called to account. However, it could be expected that those whose strongest political instinct was for conservative stability would declare themselves as soon as they had the opportunity.

The American reports repeatedly referred to the apathy of the Germans, and without doubt many were now past caring what happened politically: their immediate preoccupations were food and shelter and the fate of missing husbands and sons. They were not, however, devoid of political opinions and when, at American insistence, they were asked to express them, they made completely clear where they stood. In the first turnout of the new democracy, a poll for an elected town council held on January 27, 1946, the people of Dachau voted 59 percent for the Bavarian Volksbund, the only party, as it proclaimed, for those who did not want to vote Socialist or Communist. The SPD got 29.4 percent, the KPD 11.6 percent. The Volksbund's vote was six percentage points higher than the combined BVP and National Socialist vote in March 1933 (29.2 and 24 percent respectively); the SPD's was almost exactly the same; the Communists' was down by a fifth from what they got under Hitler (14.7 percent).[20]

What had happened to antifascism? The short answer, one vigorously disputed by antifascists, is that it had been superseded by democracy. In a free expression of opinion the people had declared themselves firmly against taking any risks. They preferred known party loyalties. Because this result could have been foreseen, the Communists in particular had appealed against holding early elections. They needed time to negotiate their common-front program with the other parties, and to convince the electorate that their policy of cooperation and nonrevolutionary democratic consensus was genuine. Goldhammer, secretary of the Bavarian Communist party, was energetic in his efforts to set up a bloc of democratic parties after the model of the Russian zone and indeed would have preferred to participate in a Bavarian government under CSU founder Josef Müller, rather than under the socialist Wilhelm Hoegner.[21] The Communists, their ranks terribly thinned from the struggle with fascism, knew that their only chance of continuing political influence was inclusion in an alliance—a governing alliance—of all progressive parties. Elections were bound to drive the parties into contests that the Communists could not hope to win: they therefore had to be put off as long as possible. "Several of our people were ministers, and they made a good job of it, too," Max Gorbach told me. "But the Americans did the same here as in Greece; they scheduled elections too early, before the process of democratization had taken hold."

The military government definitely intended to thwart the left by insisting on early elections at a local level. From the beginning, as it reported in August 1945, it saw the antifascist committees as posing "something of a problem." On the one hand there was "their evident desire to play a part in denazification activities and local community self-help": they contained "democratic elements only too anxious to cooperate with MG" whose services in tracking down Nazis and getting things going locally were thoroughly useful. On the other hand the committees were "almost wholly of leftist orientation."[22] The responses of American authorities at the local level varied from the cooperative caution of Vendig in Dachau to the outright banning of the largest and most active committees on the grounds that they were contravening the prohibition on party political activity. Obviously, though, prohibition of party politics could only be an interim policy for the most ideologically democratic of the victors, especially when parties were permitted, under license, in the Soviet zone. Once parties were authorized (on a local level in August, on a statewide basis in November) it would be better to hold elections quickly before the left could organize the "alliance of progressive forces" that was the key to Communist hopes. Writing in 1950, at the height of the cold war, and with the West German government successfully established under Konrad Adenauer, General Lucius Clay was straightforward about why, as head of the American military government, he had pushed for early elections.

"The overthrow of the Nazi regime which had ruled Germany for twelve years left a political vacuum. This had to be filled promptly with democratic leadership while we were still there to prevent the growth of new totalitarian systems under different names. I was convinced that we could neither hesitate nor delay."[23]

Early elections, then, had a threefold purpose. First, they would encourage the silent majority, known to be conservative, to come out, as it were, after the debacle of conservatism Hitler had lured them into. Second, they would force the progressive parties to compete with each other before they had time to consolidate a bloc. Third, since such a grouping might give the Communists access to government office for an extended period it was important to isolate them from the outset.

The results of local council elections in Dachau showed that this never-quite-explicit purpose of the poll was a complete success. The Communists had worked successfully with Social Democrats and even conservative Catholics in the Anti-Fascist Action Committee. They were included in the Bavarian government headed by the Socialist Hoegner, and even though they knew of Schumacher's determination to keep the SPD in the western zones out of a merger with the KPD they had hopes for a united front at least in Bavaria. Now the parties had gone into the election not only separately but as rivals and the consequences of this were drawn dramatically at the first meeting of the newly elected town council. The Bavarian Volksbund had won twelve seats, the SPD five, and the Communists two. The new burgermeister was of course from the majority—Josef Schwalber, about to make his career in the CSU. Scherer, when he had been the center of antifascist inspiration and organization as deputy burgermeister, had not been thought of as a party man. For the election, though, he had to choose whether he would stand as a Socialist or a Communist. It was not a choice: he would stick with his comrades from the concentration camp resistance. The Communists tried to capitalize on his popularity—and no doubt to an extent succeeded—by running the slogan "Wählt die Liste Scherer": vote for the list headed by Scherer. Now, when his position of deputy burgermeister again had to be filled, the SPD decided not to support Scherer. They put up their own man and secured the numbers to have him elected. Subsequently they explained it was the democratic thing to do. If the people had wanted a Communist as deputy burgermeister they could have voted for his party in the first place.[24]

Failure to win the Socialists to an electoral alliance was the death blow to antifascism. In explaining why they did not vote for Comrade Scherer, the SPD made much of the fact that the parties were still separate at the national level; they could not move ahead of the national leadership. For another two months it was still possible to hope that the considerable rank-and-file sentiment in favor of closer cooperation between the working-class parties would have concrete results. In April 1946, a merger was achieved in the Soviet zone. The SPD in the West, however, chose as its leader Kurt Schumacher, a most vehement opponent of amalgamation. In the Soviet zone the Communists never contested an election on their own; at local and state elections held later in the year it was the new Socialist Unity party (SED) that represented the combined left.[25] The KPD, like the SPD, henceforth existed only in the western zones. It was not allowed by the occupation powers to use the name Socialist Unity party because, as the SPD pointed out, in the west the parties were not unified. An application by the Communists to change their name to "Sozialistische Volkspartei Deutschlands" was also disallowed. They had to face the electorate isolated as the same old KPD.

This outcome was everything the Communists had sought to avoid. The hope of both local antifascists and the party leadership had been that common programs and in effect consensus politics would secure them much more broadly based support. The line Walter Ulbricht brought back from Moscow in 1945 appealed for nothing more radical than "the completion of the bourgeois democratic revolution which was begun in 1848." Part of the aim was to give the working-class parties time to recover and organize in a more united way; there was also a genuine belief that "people from all sections of the population who jointly suffered in the prisons and concentration camps have become friends and will now, too, continue to stick together and work together." Ulbricht believed the Communists could form a progressive alliance even with people from the middle classes because "profound social changes have taken place as a result of Hitler's war. Men and women from bourgeois circles have been thrown out of their customary ways of life."[26]

This view—until elections reminded people that their customary ways of life went together with customary political allegiances—seemed to have some foundation in Dachau. Though basically a working-class initiative and the key organization of the radical left, the Anti-Fascist Action Committee clearly had strong middle-class representation at its meetings and as the Communists reminded voters at the time of the 1946 elections, they themselves had taken the lead in bringing in people like Eberle, in order to secure the cooperation of "positive antifascist elements" from among the middle classes. "Georg Scherer didn't ask, 'Are you a Communist, a Social Democrat, or from the Volkspartei?' He asked, "Are you an antifascist and willing to help clear up the *Scherbenhaufen* (heap of rubble) that the Nazis have left us?'"

That the middle classes—overwhelmingly Catholic, commercial, and conservative—might gain more from the cleanup and the return to normality than the left seems not to have been considered. As Scherer told the very first meeting of the AFA on May 8, 1945, what he proposed was simply a necessity: the bringing together of all positive antifascist forces in Dachau as the indispensable basis for forming policies that were both healthy and possible for Dachau; rooting out the remnants of fascism; and reestablishing a normal civilian life—"ein normales bürgerliches Leben."[27]

Bürgerlich does not only mean "civilian": in fact, only in the extraordinary circumstances of 1945 could it have that meaning. "Bourgeois," "civic," and "respectable" are all more important connotations of *bürgerlich*, though no one word translates this key term of German politics adequately. It denotes, in ways Scherer certainly did not have in mind, that large class sector of German society whose economic and social standing can be more or less affluent and status conscious, whose attitudes can vary between righteous philistinism and relatively relaxed liberalism, but whose politics have the reliable common ground of being conservative in an antisocialist sense. In Dachau, where even under the monarchy there had only been a couple of aristocrats, and where the ideology of the center and the right was cemented into Catholicism, *bürgerlich* denoted a political culture that embraced not only the genuine *Bürger*, the old-established craft and trading families clustered round the church, the Rathaus, and the marketplace on the top of the hill; it also linked naturally with the rural conservatism of the surrounding farmers. Since the beginning of the century this majority had been in passionate ideological combat with the incursions of socialism, spreading out from Munich through the unionized workers living down on the flat, and the insistent campaigning of the Social Democratic party.

Socialist electoral strength increased steadily in Dachau (though never in the outlying villages) and for a time after World War I the Socialists had a majority on the town council. They may have thought that this phase—their leader, Burgermeister Böck, could claim to come from one of the oldest settled Dachau families—integrated them into the dominant political culture. To an extent it did, but such a historic shift toward democratic norms could not be consolidated under the unfavorable conditions of the Weimar Republic. When the crisis came, the local Socialist majorities—whether in whole states such as Prussia or small towns such as Dachau—were overwhelmed by a radical reaction that exploited the values, norms, and rules of the old political culture to give Germany a revolution in political institutions. The old political system (in both monarchical and republican variants) had not been without its successes in representing social interests ideologically and in reconciling them pragmatically. Under the impact of successive disasters even its forms could not survive the long ideologized but now desperately polarized consciousness of interests.

With the ruinous inflation a fresh memory, and as the lines of unemployed and gains in Communist strength threatened further social upheaval in the depression, the political culture of conservativism found a place for Nazi radicalism.[28] More and more of those who saw themselves, and the society in which they wanted to continue living, as *bürgerlich* saw their political choice as being ever more starkly between socialism—not necessarily any longer Social Democracy—and National Socialism. Hitler persuaded an increasing number of Germans, many more than voted for his party, that the Communist threat demanded the most resolute action. "Fourteen years of Marxism have undermined Germany. One year of Bolshevism would destroy Germany." For Germany to experience political and economic revival, "a decisive act is required: *we must overcome Germany's demoralization by the Communists.*"[29] What Hitler's decisive action meant became clear after the Reichstag fire and his subsequent election victory. On March 20, 1933, Himmler announced the setting up of the first concentration camp, outside Dachau.

The anti-Communist majority in Dachau, and in similar towns throughout Germany, still felt beleaguered in 1945. The war was over, Hitler's twelve-year rule was ended, but they had not been delivered from their enemies. They were occupied by foreigners they had not been trained to regard as liberators: those who did regard the Americans as liberators were a highly suspect and threatening assortment. Some of them—Poles, Russians, and other "displaced persons" (DPs)—were an immediate danger. Others, notably the antifascists who had emerged from the camps together with the Poles and Russians, were bent on reordering their world in ways ordinary peaceable people had gone to extraordinary lengths to resist. For anti-Communists, as well as antifascists, should the awful sacrifices of the Hitler years have been in vain? Most people remembered vividly what had happened after the last war: the revolution born out of defeat seemed to be the start of all their troubles. Then too there had been workers' committees and eventually—if briefly—a "Council Republic" (*Räterepublik*) antithetical to their conceptions of social and political order. They had had to mobilize then, with much less equivocation than in 1933—the Nazis after all had not been the most savory allies— and now that the Nazis were out of the way they had no doubts at all about the kind of society they wanted to protect and the political institutions appropriate to it. They did not want antifascist committees; they wanted regular town councils. They wanted parties with which they could clearly identify their interests, not "alliances of all democratic and progressive forces" that would most likely be against their interests. They wanted things very much as they had been.

The Americans did not want things as they had been. They set out to effect a revolution in German history. Malcolm Vendig in Dachau was a very articulate spokesman of their cause. It may be true, as an Americn historian (Gimbel) who studied the experiment in another place (Marburg) has remarked, that they "proceeded without a conscious theory of artificial revolution:: they did not know how to turn a fascist society into a democratic one.[30] But then nobody else did, either. The two obvious policies were to remove fascists and to bring in democracy. Unfortunately, the first of these policies, denazification, was not altogether a satisfactory basis for the second. Niethammer has called denazification "the American surrogate for anti-fascist reform," and he shows why this purging of people rather than institutions was only a partial and contradictory success. It was radical enough to take the wind out of the sails of genuine antifascists; it was not radical enough to prevent the return of rehabilitated Nazis or those who had gone along with the Nazis *(Mitläufer)* into positions of authority in structures that continued to function as before. Its main effect was probably, as Niethammer says, to provide many West Germans with the idea that any possible responsibility they might have had for fascism and its consequences was more than compensated for—and disposed of—by what they were subjected to in the discriminatory and corrupt procedures of denazification.[31]

In the first years of the occupation many more people were concerned with clearing themselves through these proceedings than with political reconstructon. When those most actively interested in political reconstruction—the antifascists—were squeezed out, their disillusionment, as Gimbel says, "permitted the assumption of leadership, at the local level, by others whose political, social and economic views bear a striking similarity to those of the leaders of the same community who proved so ineffective in the face of the Nazi challenge."[32]

That is carefully worded—and dead right. It reminds us again that it was the occupying power alone that had authority in the situation and must therefore bear a large part of the responsibility for encouraging or thwarting political tendencies. It also reminds us that the tendencies themselves were not made in America; they were home grown, the product of communities with much more political experience than has generally been recognized. Though we can blame the Americans for cutting short the experiment in antifascist democracy, for reverting too speedily to the institutional forms of the established political culture—town councils locally, aligned with political parties nationally—it is difficult to imagine that any genuinely democratic reconstruction of post-Nazi Germany could have had a different result. Political cultures, especially those with a highly ideologized history in which the connection between social interests, societal conceptions, and political allegiance has been tested and reconfirmed, are not so easily dislodged. The terrible trials of violent political conflict and total war are as likely to strengthen them as subvert them. For most people the disaster of National Socialism would have become total only if it had ended in the Communist takeover that they had put their faith in Hitler to save them from in the first place.

The antifascists, who had experienced the worst that desperate majorities can do, never fully understood this. Toward the end of September 1945, when Communists and Socialists had been working for almost five months in close cooperation with their more conservative fellow townspeople both on the AFA and the appointed town council, they held their first political meeting. In the *Schlosssaal*, Dachau's largest and most prestigious location, 700 people applauded the speakers from both parties who spoke of the sacrifices their members had made in the fight against fascism, and the need for all to cooperate in removing the remnants of Nazism and in political renewal. Even those who shared responsibility for what had happened could atone by joining in the work of democratic reconstruction. The report in the *Amtsblatt* ended with an appeal: "Looking beyond the differences of opinion of differing world views we offer you our hand, for the building up of a new, antifascist, truly democratic Germany."[33]

For the antifascists, that was the only possible appeal; for those to whom it was addressed it said everything wrong. No one in the conservative majority believed that either Social Democrats or Communists had changed their own world views; even among Social Democrats there was suspicion of what, in a Communist world view, the "building up of a new, antifascist, truly democratic Germany" might mean.[34] Cooperation in practical matters, in what antifascists hoped was a radical political departure, had been possible precisely because politics had been suppressed. Once democracy allowed the expression of different world views, the world view of the majority, for whom all the connotations of antifascism would only invoke mistrust, would be bound to prevail. What the idealism, energy, and fairness of men like Gorbach and Scherer had achieved was the reconstitution of that political world that would unequivocally reject them.

It has often been said that Marxists have little conception of culture, that their phrases about consciousness and "false" consciousness obscure for them the real ways social values and individual expectancies form each other. I think however, that ordinary Communists in West Germany had and still have a strong sense, from their experience rather than from their theory, of how powerful a political culture can be. A majority *is* a majority because its values, expectations, conceptions of legitimate political order, are publically recognizable and privately shared. The antifascists, by the more heroic, historic qualities of their biographies, had demonstrated their distance from the majority; what makes them so impressive also made them politically ineffective. If the majority won again, and not more heroically than in 1933, it was because of a socially and culturally grounded political solidarity that antifascists had every reason to regard as formidable.

It was this previously mobilized, historically tested solidarity and not just ideology that Kneuer represented at every opportunity to Vendig. Vendig, with not much more enthusiasm than Scherer, had to recognize its power within the first few weeks. Scherer, representing an alternative solidarity, would also have to be the representative of its defeat. The victory of the Landrat in his dealings with the commandant, of the Bavarian Volksbund and then the CSU in one election after another, were all democratic victories. Those who had suffered and struggled for twelve years to bring democracy to Germany had to accept what they had won.

In 1949, with the Federal Republic established, the cold war mounting to its pitch, a few weeks before the explosion of the Soviet atomic bomb, the first elections for the new Bundestag were held in West Germany. In Dachau the Communist party, perhaps wanting to recall the hopeful days of 1945, again hired the *Schlosssaal* for an election meeting, but just before the meeting began a "troop" of 150 DPs, mostly from Hungary, arrived in a body. As soon as the chairman rose to speak he was shouted down, the stage was stormed, and the candidate, Egon Hermann, fled to the Rathaus, from where he was rescued only by the intervention of local police, state police,and American military police. Hermann declared that he would not speak in Dachau again and "freely," as the report says, accepted the offer to place himself in "protective custody"—"sich in Schutzhaft zu begeben."[35] The word must have had resonance for Hermann and others in Dachau: "Schutzhaft" was what the Gestapo placed you under when, without going through the courts, you were to be put away in a concentration camp. There were of course to be no more concentraton camps; that solution had been tried. Hermann was simply escorted into Munich, and in the election the KPD received only 5.7 percent of the vote anyway. Just to be sure, on November 22, 1951, the democratic government of West Germany began proceedings to have the Communist party banned.[36]

Former Landrat Kneuer, I do not doubt, was pleased. (His tenure of office had been cut short by the discovery that he had given misleading answers in his denazification questionnaire.) What Malcolm Vendig might have thought I can only guess. It has not been possible to trace him through the U. S. Army. Max Gorbach would have been angry but philosophical. At the end of 1945 he married the woman who had been his fiancée twenty years before. Burgermeister Scherer officiated. Scherer was also a realist. When he could not persuade the town of Dachau to use the sewing machines from the SS tailoring shop to start a municipal undertaking, he took them over himself. Down on the flat, beside the road to Munich, exactly, as he told me, where the last 1919 revolutionaries were shot down by the Whites, he built a factory. There, late at night, surrounded by the bolts of material and racks of winter coats, he recalled how long ago, on the eve of his departure, the American Commandant had said: "I've only known one genuine democrat in Dachau, Herr Scherer. And that is you."

If "Dachau" means anything in terms of Germany's political development it means the failure of the left to secure democracy between 1918 and 1930 and the determination of the right to have done with challenges to entrenched interests once and for all. Hitler pledged to be the destroyer of Marxism and Dachau was set up to put this final solution, not the more famous one, into effect. It was assumed in 1945 that he had failed. Later, people could point to the German Democratic Republic and say: so much for destroying Marxism. From where Georg Scherer looked back, half a lifetime after Hitler's defeat—well, he must have wondered.

Notes

A German version of this essay appeared in *Dachauer Hefte* 1. Jahrgang, Heft 1, *Die Befreiung* (Dachau: Verlag Dachauer Hefte, 1985).

The essay owes much to many people. I am particularly grateful to those who contributed generously in interviews and to friends who suggested improvements in the writing. My greatest debt is to my mother, Hedy Barta, for her many hours of work in turning often indistinct recordings into readily consultable transcripts.

1. According to Bruno Bettelheim's review of the various estimates, at least 11 million people and possibly twice that number died in the concentration camps; at best 530,000 survived at the time of Allied liberation. If, at the beginning of 1938, there were fewer than 30,000 prisoners, mainly in Dachau (6,000) and Sachsenhausen (8,000), the old political prisoners must have been a small proportion of the survivors. However their solidarity and the positions they established in the camp administrations enabled them to increase not only their own survival chances but

those of members of the resistance sent to the camps at later dates, often at the completion of jail sentences. See Bruno Bettelheim, "The German Concentration Camps," in *Surviving and Other Essays* (New York: Random House, 1980), pp. 46–67. Bettelheim's views of *how* people survived in the camps should be treated with great caution.

For new research and documentation on the National Socialist concentration camps see the continuing series edited by Barbara Distel and Wolfgang Benz, *Dachauer Hefte*, vol. 1 *Die Befreiung*; vol. 2 *Sklavenarbeit im KZ*; vol. 3 *Frauen: Verfolgung und Widerstand* (Dachau: Verlag Dachauer Hefte, 1985-). The best historical survey of the concentration camp system is by Martin Broszat, "The Concentration Camps 1933–45," in Helmut Krausnick, Hans Buchheim, Martin Broszat, and Hans-Adolf Jacobsen, eds., *Anatomy of the SS State*, (New York: Walker and Company, 1968). On Dachau see also Barbara Distel and Ruth Jakusch, *Concentration Camp Dachau* (Dachau, n.d.,), and P. Berben, *Dachau, 1933–1945* (London: Norfolk Press, 1975).

2. W. S. Allen, *The Nazi Seizure of Power: The Experience of a Single German Town 1922–1945*, rev. ed. (New York: Franklin Watts, 1984). The idea of the Nazi revolution as a "coup d'état by instalments" is Konrad Heiden's, quoted by Allen, p. 298.

3. This question is dealt with only by implication in even the best books on the post-Nazi transition. The three indispensable studies are Lutz Niethammer, *Entnazifizierung in Bayern* (Frankfurt: S. Fischer Verlag, 1972); Lutz Niethammer, Ulrich Borsdorf, and Peter Brandt, eds., *Arbeiterinitiative 1945* (Wuppertal: Hammer, 1976); and Ulrich Borsdorf and Lutz Niethammer, eds., *Zwischen Befreiung und Besatzung: Analysen des US-Geheimdienstes über Positionen und Strukturen deutscher Politik 1945* (Wuppertal: Hammer, 1976). See also Berndt Hüppauf, ed., *"Die Mühen der Ebenen." Kontinuität und Wandel in der deutschen Literatur und Gesellschaft 1945–1949* (Heidelberg: Carl Winter Universitätsverlag, 1981), especially the essays by Bernd Hüppauf, David Roberts, and Konrad Kwiet. For a full bibliography, including early studies of postwar Germany in English, see Niethammer, *Entnazifierung* and *Arbeiterinitiative*.

4. Interview with Rosel Kirchoff, Dachau, 1974. Stuttgart was about 55 percent destroyed, Munich about 45 percent (Hans Dollinger, *Deutschland unter den Besatzungsmächten 1945–1949* [Munich: Verlag Kurt Desch, 1967], p. 28). Between 5 and 6 million Germans were killed in World War II. Of the more than 40 million of all nationalities who died, 20 million were Soviet citizens, as compared with 386,000 British and 260,000 Americans. Cf. tables and notes in Karl Dietrich Erdmann, *Das Ende des Reiches und die Neubildung deutscher Staaten* (Munich: Deutscher Taschenbuch Verlag, 1980), p. 364.

5. *Amperbote*, Dachau, December 1944. Information on the arrival of the Americans from Rosel Kirchhoff and from "Vor 5 Jahren—Dachau am Tage der Befreiung," *Dachauer Anzeiger*, April 29, 1950.

6. The image is Rosel Kirchhoff's.

7. Interview with Georg Scherer, Dachau, 1974. Further information on the rising was supplied by another participant, Richard Titze, Dachau, 1974. On the Bavarian resistance see Heike Bretschneider, *Der Widerstand gegen den Nationalsozialismus in München 1933 bis 1945* (Munich: Stadtarchiv München, 1968).

8. Interview with Max Gorbach, Munich, 1974.

9. Written by emigré intellectuals sympathetic to the antifascist initiatives, this overview report of June 1945 appears to have had little influence on the American authorities, who by the middle of May had already banned most of the larger Antifas, including the one in Munich (*Arbeiterinitiative*, pp. 14, 636–38. and for a general assessment, 699–717). A German translation of the report is in *Zwischen Befreiung und Besatzung*, pp. 107–16.

10. Concentration Camp Museum Archive, Dachau. Cf. *Arbeiterinitiative*, p. 160, note 19.

11. Cf. John Gimbel, *A German Community under American Occupation: Marburg, 1945–52* (Stanford: Stanford University Press, 1968), p. 32. The instances recounted by Gimbel of anti-Nazi Germans being roughly treated by Americans were, it seems, typical. In Dachau Max Gorbach was twice threatened by American soldiers for trying to check the taking over of houses by Poles and other displaced nationals: "You goddam German son of a bitch, these people have lost everything because of you. You're lucky I don't shoot you."

12. On the evolution and application of denazification policy see Niethammer, *Entnazifierung*. One of the reasons Communists were outraged by the crudity of U. S. procedures was that their own members who had joined Nazi organizations as a cover for resistance work were now purged along with genuine Nazis (ibid., p. 207).

13. On the comparison with 1918–19 see *Arbeiterinitiative*, pp. 715–17.

14. Dr. Josef Schwalber, "Dachau in der Stunde Null," *Amperland* 4. Jahrgang, Heft 4, Dachau, 1968, pp. 83–87.

15. Ibid., p. 86. For comparison with larger centers see Rebecca Boehling, "German Municipal Self Government and the Personnel Policies of the Local U. S. Military Government in Three Major Cities of the Zone of Occupation: Frankfurt, Munich and Stuttgart," *Archiv für Sozialgeschichte* 25 (1985): 333–83.

16. Staatsarchiv, Munich, LRA 128075. The original transcript is in English.

17. Not all the foreigners were from the concentration camp. At the end of 1944 there were altogether almost 9 million forced laborers in Germany, approximately a quarter of the workforce. "Wastage" was very high; to achieve 2 million Russians actually working in Germany in 1944 perhaps 5 million were deported to the Reich (*Arbeiterinitiative*, pp. 145–50). There were several forced labor camps, for women as well as men, in the vicinity of Dachau.

18. *Amtsblatt für die Stadt und den Landkreis Dachau*, August 4, 1945. In terms of official status Vendig may have been right, though Neithammer suggests there were already similar bodies in the larger West German towns (*Arbeiterinitiative*, p. 659; *Entnazifizierung*, pp. 136–37, 203). Since party affiliations were not given they are not clear in every case.

19. *Amtsblatt*, November 17 and 24, 1945.

20. *Amtsblatt*, January 30, 1946. March 1933 election results for all electoral districts are in Karl Dietrich Bracher, Wolfgang Sauer, and Gerhard Schulz, *Die National-sozialistische Machtergreifung* (Cologne and Opladen: Westdeutscher Verlag, 1962), pp. 95–133.

21. Niethammer, *Entnazifizierung*, pp. 201–28. and Max Spindler, ed., *Handbuch der bayerischen Geschichte*, vol. 4 (Munich: C. H. Beck, 1974), pp. 556–86.

22. OMGUS Monthly Report, no. 1, 20.8.1945, quoted by Niethammer, *Entnazifizierung* p. 136.

23. Lucius D. Clay, *Decision in Germany* (London: Heinemann, 1950), pp. 87–88. There was strong resistance to Clay's drive for party politics and early elections from his advisers in the military government; Clay liked to tease them that a military man had to persuade the liberal professors to restore to the German people their right to vote. Cf. Niethammer, *Entnazifizierung*; pp. 201–02.

24. *Amtsblatt*, February 13, 1946. The Communists did not reply directly but noted that in Hamburg the SPD had voted 270–24 for closer cooperation between the left parties. However such expressions of solidarity did not mean the SPD rank and file were in favor of amalgamation with the Communists. A military government survey at this time showed that one out of three SPD supporters in the U. S. zone was prepared to support a unity party along the lines of the SED (OMGUS Opinion

Survey Reports, Series I, no. 3, March 15, 1946, cited by Lewis J. Edinger, *Kurt Schumacher* [Stanford: Stanford University Press, 1965], p. 100).

25. In the state *(Land)* elections held in the Soviet zone in October 1946 the SED won 47.8 percent in a three-way contest. The Christian Democrats won 26.5 percent and the Liberals 9.3 percent. In Berlin, where the four-power agreement allowed the SPD to contest the election as an independent party, it won 48.7 percent to the SED's 19.8 percent (Erdmann, *Das Ende*, p. 141). For more detailed election results, and the subsequent composition of *Land* governments, see J. P. Nettl, *The Eastern Zone and Soviet Policy in Germany* (London: Oxford University Press, 1951). For the formation of the SED and the attitude of the SPD in the West see Erdmann, *Das Ende*, pp. 132–45, Edinger, *Kurt Schumacher*, pp. 94–104; and Wolfgang Leonhard, *Child of the Revolution* (London: Collins, 1957), pp. 350–60.

26. Walter Ulbricht, "The Program of the Anti-Fascist Democratic Order," his speech to the first conference of officials of the KPD of Greater Berlin on June 25, 1945; and *On Questions of Socialist Construction in the GDR* (Dresden: Zeit im Bild Publishing House, 1968), p. 17. The Communist strategy of class cooperation within a progressive alliance did not mean that the antifascist committees fared any better in the East than they did in the West. If anything, they were even more cruelly disappointed. The Communist leadership wanted no potential rival to official authority and insisted that the Antifas be immediately disbanded. Ulbricht's own ruthless and apparently contemptuous attitude is described by Leonhard, pp. 318–26: "In this way ever initiative from below was nipped in the bud between the beginning of May and the middle of June" (see also *Arbeiterinitiative*, pp. 635–43).

27. "Vom Dachauer Aufstand bis zur ersten Stadratssitzung," Concentration Camp Museum Archive, Dachau.

28. I use the term "political culture" here in the sense outlined by Almond and Verba for purposes of comparative analysis: "When we speak of the political culture of a society we refer to the political system as internalized in the cognitions, feelings and evaluations of its population. People are inducted into it just as they are socialized into nonpolitical roles and social systems. Conflicts of political cultures have much in common with other culture conflicts and political acculturative processes are more understandable if we view them in terms of the resistances and the fusional and incorporative tendencies of cultural change in general" (Gabriel A. Almond and Sydney Verba, *The Civic Culture* [Princeton: Princeton University Press, 1963], p. 14).

For detailed historical accounts of how nonpolitical and political elements combined to the advantage of the Nazis compare Allen, *The Nazi Seizure of Power*, and Rudy Koshar, *Social Life, Local Politics and Nazism: Marburg 1880–1935* (Chapel Hill and London: University of North Carolina Press, 1986). On the further task, both important and difficult, of understanding the phenomenon of National Socialism in terms of a defined concept of fascism, see Reinhard Kühnl, "Problems of a Theory of German Fascism: A Critique of the Dominant Interpretations," *New German Critique* 4 (Winter 1975): 26–50. Kühnl's overall view is indicated by the title of his *Formen Bürgerlicher Herrschaft—Liberalismus and Faschismus* (Hamburg: Rowohlt, 1971). See also Anson G. Rabinbach, "Toward a Marxist Theory of Fascism and National Socialism: A Report on Developments in West Germany," *New German Critique,* 3 (Fall 1974).

29. Hitler's "Appeal to the German People" on becoming chancellor, January 31, 1933. This is the single italicized line in the statement (Jeremy Noakes and Geoffrey Pridham, eds., *Documents on Nazism* [London: Jonathan Cape, 1974], pp. 162–65). There is a yet more emphatic statement—to industrialists on February 20—on p. 168. For the relatively small electoral gains made by the Communists, as compared

with the huge increase in the Nazi vote during the depression (the Communist peak of almost 6 million votes, 16.9 percent of the electorate, in November 1932, can itself be seen as a response to the Nazis' winning 13.7 million votes, 37.4 percent, in the July election), see the table in Koppel S. Pinson, *Modern Germany* (New York: Macmillan, 1966), pp. 603–04.

On the Nazi effort to suppress the working class as a political force, see Tim Mason, "National Socialism and the Working Class, 1925–May 1933," *New German Critique* 11 (Spring 1977): 49–93; and "The Workers' Opposition in Nazi Germany," *History Workshop Journal*, 11 (Spring 1981): 120–37. Reinhard Kühnl, *Der Deutsche Faschismus in Quellen and Dokumenten* (Cologne: Pahl Rugenstein, 1977), chap. 6, p. 419, gives figure indicating the continued repression of working-class resistance even in the most settled years of the regime. In 1936, for instance, 11,687 Communists and 1,374 Social Democrats were arrested; in 1937 the numbers were 8,068 and 733. Antifascist declarations of the working-class party leadership in exile can also be found in this section (see esp. documents 276, 280, and 289).

30. Gimbel, *German Community*, p. 201; cf. the criticism of Hajo Droll, dissenting from his co-authors, that the antifascists also lacked a theory of revolutionary democracy and for that reason succumbed to conventional conceptions antithetical to their class interests (*Arbeiterinitiative*, pp. 628–31).

31. Niethammer, *Entnazifizierung*, pp. 653–54.

32. Gimbel, *German Community*, p. 1.

33. *Amtsblatt*, September 29, 1945.

34. The same report commented that some people "so smart that they think they can hear grass growing" claimed to have heard a dissonance between the Social Democratic and Communist speakers. They were reminded of the assurances given by both speakers that their parties had learned from the mistakes of 1918–33 and of the continuing common action *(Aktionsgemeinschaft)* that proved it. In fact, this first joint meeting under the antifascist banner was also the last.

35. *Dachauer Anzeiger*, August 12, 1949.

36. The Constitutional Court decided on August 17, 1956, that the principles of the KPD were incompatible with the "free and democratic basic order" (Alfred Grosser, *Germany in Our Time* [Harmondsworth, Middlesex: Penguin, 1974], p. 215).

Bibliographical Essay

Below is a working bibliography of the most important books and articles that have been particularly useful to the editors and that complement the essays contained in the volume. Since we focused on the structural, i.e., economic, class, and power dimensions that largely led to the collapse of the Weimar Republic and the successful ascension to power of the Nazi party, most of the items listed reflect that approach. Although not exhaustive, this list includes some of the most significant works in the field and those which have shaped our thinking.

For a discussion of the emergence of fascism and its relation to class, economics, and political development, see: Nicos Poulantzas, *Fascism and Dictatorship* (London: NLB, 1974); Renzo De Felice, *Fascism: An Informal Introduction to Its Theory and Practice* (New Brunswick, NJ: Transaction, 1976); Stanley Payne, *Fascism: Comparison and Definition* (Madison: University of Wisconsin Press, 1980); Stein Ugelvik Larsen, Bernt Hagtvet, Jan Petter Myklebust, eds., *Who Were the Fascists: Social Roots of European Fascism* (Bergen: Universitetsforlaget, 1980); Peter Stachura, ed., *The Shaping of the Nazi State* (London: Croom Helm, 1978); Walter Laqueur, *Fascism: A Reader's Guide* (London: Wildwood House, 1976); Ernst Nolte, *Three Faces of Fascism* (London: Weidenfeld and Nicholson, 1965); Barrington Moore, Jr., *Social Origins of Dictatorship and Democracy* (Boston: Beacon Press, 1966); Eugen Weber, *Varieties of Fascism* (New York: Van Nostrand Reinhold Co., 1964); Francis L. Carsten, *The Rise of Fascism* (London: Batsford, 1967); John Weiss, *The Fascist Tradition* (New York: Harper & Row, 1967); Hans Rogger and Eugen Weber, eds., *The European Right* (London: Weidenfeld and Nicholson, 1965); George L. Mosse, ed.,

International Fascism: New Thoughts and New Approaches (London: Sage Publications, 1979); Stuart Woolf, ed., *Fascism in Europe* (London: Methuen, 1981); Jürgen Kocka, *White Collar Workers in America 1890–1940* (London: Sage Publications, 1980); Martin Kitchen, *Fascism* (London: Macmillan, 1976); Jost Dülffer, "Bonapartism, Fascism and National Socialism," *Journal of Contemporary History* 11 (1976): 109–28; David Beetham, *Marxists in the Face of Fascism* (Totawa, NJ: Barnes & Noble, 1984); Theo Pirker, *Komintern und Faschismus* (Stuttgart: Deutsche Verlags-Anstalt, 1965); Pierre Aycoberry, *The Nazi Question* (New York: Random House, 1981); Martin Kitchen, "August Thalheimer's Theory of Fascism," *Journal of the History of Ideas* 34 (1974): 77–78; Wolfgang Abendroth, ed., *Faschismus und Kapitalismus* (Frankfurt: Europäische Verlag, 1967); Leon Trotsky, *The Struggle Against Fascism in Germany* (New York: Pathfinder Press, 1971); Robert S. Wistrich, "Leon Trotsky's Theory of Fascism," *Journal of Contemporary History* 11 (1976): 169–73; Reinhard Kühnl, *Formen bürgerlicher Herrschaft* (Reinbek: Rowohlt, 1971); Mihaly Vadja, *Fascism as a Mass Movement* (New York: St. Martin's, 1976); Reinhard Kühnl, *Faschismustheorien* (Hamburg: Rowohlt, 1979); Kühnl, *Die Weimarer Republik* (Hamburg: Rowohlt, 1985); Kühnl, "Problems of a Theory of German Fascism," *New German Critique* 4 (Winter 1975): 26–50; Michael N. Dobkowski, Isidor Wallimann, eds., *Towards the Holocaust* (Westport, CT: Greenwood Press, 1983); Kurt Gossweiler, *Aufsätze zum Faschismus, Mit einem Vorwort von Rolf Richter* (Berlin: Akademe-Verlag, 1986); Anson G. Rabinbach, "Toward a Marxist Theory of Fascism and National Socialism," *New German Critique* (Fall 1974); and Rabinbach, "Poulantzas and the Problem of Fascism," *New German Critique* (Spring 1976): 157–70.

For a discussion of the relationship among politics, economics, and Nazism, see: J. W. Angell, *The Recovery of Germany* (New Haven: Yale University Press, 1929); F. L. Carsten, *Reichswehr and Politics* (New York: Oxford University Press, 1966); A. Dorpalen, *Hindenburg and the Weimar Republic* (Princeton: Princeton University Press, 1966); Hans Gatzke, *Stresemann and the Rearmament of Germany* (Baltimore: Johns Hopkins University Press, 1954); R. H. Hunt, *Social Democracy 1918–33* (New Haven: Yale University Press, 1953); Henry A. Turner, Jr., *Stresemann and the Politics of the Weimar Republic* (Princeton: Princeton University Press, 1963); James Diehl, *Paramilitary Politics in Weimar Germany* (Bloomington: Indiana University Press, 1977); Medris Eksteins, *The Limits of Reason: The German Democratic Press and the Collapse of Weimar German Democracy* (Oxford: Oxford University Press, 1975); S. W. Halperin, *Germany*

Tried Democracy (New York: W. W. Norton, 1965); Ulrike, Hörster-Philipps, "Konservative Politik in der Weimarer Republik," Ph.d. diss., University of Marburg, 1980; Erick Matthias and Anthony Nicholls, eds., *German Democracy and the Triumph of Hitler* (London: Allen and Unwin, 1971); Hans Mommsen, Dietmar Petzina, and Bernard Weisbrod, eds., *Industrielles System und Politische Entwicklung in der Weimarer Republic* (Dusseldorf: Droste, 1974); Rudolf Morsey, *Die Deutsche Zentrumspartei 1917–1923* (Dusseldorf: Droste, 1966); John Nagle, *System and Succession* (Austin: University of Texas Press, 1977); Jeremy Noakes, *The Nazi Party in Lower Saxony 1921–1933* (Oxford: Oxford University Press, 1971); Dietrich Orlow, *The History of the Nazi Party 1919–1933* (Pittsburgh: University of Pittsburgh Press, 1969); Robert Pois, *The Bourgeois Democrats of Weimar Germany* (Philadelphia: American Philosophical Society, 1976); Geoffrey Pridham, *Hitler's Rise to Power* (New York: Harper & Row, 1973); James M. Rhodes, *The Hitler Movement. A Modern Millenarian Revolution* (Stanford: Stanford University Press, 1980); Peter Stachura, *Nazi Youth in the Weimar Republic* (Santa Barbara: ABC-Clio, 1975); Fritz Stern, *The Politics of Cultural Despair* (Berkeley: University of California Press, 1961); Walter Struve, *Elites Against Democracy* (Princeton: Princeton University Press, 1973); Timothy Tilton, *Nazism, Neo-Nazism and the Peasantry* (Bloomington: Indiana University Press, 1975); David Abraham, *The Collapse of the Weimar Republic* (Princeton: Princeton University Press, 1981); Abraham, *The Collapse of the Weimar Republic,* 2nd ed. (New York: Holmes & Meier, 1986); Wolfgang Ruge, *Das Ende von Weimar, Monopolkapital und Hitler* (Berlin: Dietz Verlag, 1983); Tim Mason, "Der Primat der Politik—Politick und Wirtschaft im Nationalsozialismus," *Das Argument* no. 41 (December 1966): 470–84; Kurt Gossweiler, *Die Röhm-Affaire* (Cologne: Pahl-Rugenstein Verlag, 1983); Reinhard Neebe, *Grosindustrie, Staat und NSDAP 1930–1933* (Gottingen: Vandenhoeck & Ruprecht, 1981); and Henry Turner, Jr., *German Big Business and the Rise of Hitler* (New York: Oxford University Press, 1985).

For a discussion of the issue of class and support of the Nazi party, see: Thomas Childers, *The Nazi Voter: The Social Foundations of Fascism in Germany, 1919–1933* (Chapel Hill: University of North Carolina Press, 1983); Jerzy Holzer, *Parteien und Massen* (Wiesbaden: Franz Steiner Verlag, 1975); Michael H. Kater, *The Nazi: A Social Profile of Members and Leaders, 1919–1945* (Cambridge, MA: Harvard University Press, 1983); Klaus Schaap, *Die Endphase der Weimarer Republik im Freistaat Oldenburg 1928–1933* (Dusseldorf: Droste Verlag, 1978); Winkler, "From Social Protectionism to National Socialism: The German Small-Business Movement in Comparative Perspective,"

Journal of Modern History 48, no. 1 (March 1976); Wolfgang Schieder, ed., *Faschismus als soziale Bewegung* (Hamburg: Hoffmann und Campe Verlag, 1976); Richard Hamilton, *Who Voted for Hitler?* (Princeton: Princeton University Press, 1982); Bruno Buchta, *Die Junker und die Weimarer Republic* (East Berlin: VEB Deutscher Verlag der Wissenschaft, 1959); Herman Lebovics, *Social Conservatism and the Middle Classes in Germany, 1914–1933* (Princeton: Princeton University Press, 1969); Richard Bessel and E. J. Feuchtwanger, eds., *Social Change and Political Development in Weimar Germany* (Totowa, NJ: Barnes & Noble, 1981); Robert Lewis Koehl, *The Black Corps* (Madison: University of Wisconsin Press, 1983); Johnpeter Horst Grill, *The Nazi Movement in Baden, 1920–1945* (Chapel Hill: University of North Carolina Press, 1983); Donald R. Tracey, "The Development of the National Socialist Party in Thuringia, 1924–1930," *Central European History* 7, no. 1 (March 1975); Bruce Frye, *Liberal Democrats in the Weimar Republic* (Carbondale, IL: Southern Illinois University Press, 1985); Martin Schumacher, *Mittelstandsfront und Republik* (Dusseldorf: Droste, 1972); Michael Kater, *The Nazi Party* (Cambridge, MA: Harvard University Press, 1983); Rudolf Herberle, *From Democracy to Nazism* (Baton Rouge: Louisiana State University Press, 1945); Ralf Dahrendorf, *Society and Democracy in Germany* (Garden City: Doubleday Anchor, 1967); F. L. Carsten, *The Reichswehr and Politics, 1918–1933* (London: Oxford University Press, 1966); Harold Gordon, *The Reichswehr and the German Republic 1919–1926* (Princeton: Princeton University Press, 1957); and Jürgen Falter, et al., *Wahlen und Abstimmungen in der Weimarer Republik* (Munich: Beck, 1986).

For a discussion of the left in the Weimar period, see: Werner Angress, *Stillborn Revolution. The Communist Bid for Power in Germany, 1921–23* (Princeton: Princeton University Press, 1963); Gilbert Badia, *Le Spartakisme* (Paris: L'Arche, 1967); Siegfried Bahne, *Die KPD und das Ende von Weimar* (Frankfurt: Campus-Verlag, 1976); Richard Bessel and E. J. Feuchtwanger, eds., *Social Change and Political Development in Weimar Germany* (London: Sage Publications, 1981); Gerhard Braunthal, *Socialist Labour Politics in Weimar Germany* (New York: Anchor Books, 1973); Richard Breitman, *German Socialism and Weimar Democracy* (Chapel Hill: University of North Carolina Press, 1981); F. L. Carsten, *Revolution in Central Europe, 1918–19* (Berkeley: University of California Press, 1972); Richard Comfort, *Revolutionary Hamburg* (Stanford: Stanford University Press, 1966); J. S. Drabkin, *Die November Revolution 1918 in Deutschland* (Berlin: Deutscher Verlag der Wissenschaften, 1980); Dick Geary, *European Labour Protest 1848–1939* (London: Croom Helm, 1981); Richard Hunt, *German Social Democracy 1918–1933* (Chicago: Quadrangle Books, 1970); Martin Jay, *The Dialectical Imagination* (Boston: Little, Brown, 1973); Max Kele, *Nazis and Workers* (Chapel Hill: University of North Carolina Press, 1972); Reinhard Kühnl, *Der deutsche Faschismus in Quellen und Dokumenten* (Cologne: Paul-Rugenstein, 1975); Kühnl, *Die nationalsozialistische Linke 1925–1930* (Meisenheim: Hain, 1966); Richard Lowenthal, *The Bolshevisation of the Spartacus League* (London: Chatto and Windus, 1960); Timothy Mason, *Arbeiterklasse und Volksgemeinschaft* (Opladen: Westdeutscher Verlag, 1975); David Morgan, *The Socialist Left and the German Revolution* (Ithaca: Cornell University Press, 1975); A. J. Ryder, *The German Revolution of 1918* (Cambridge: Cambridge University Press, 1967); Eric Waldman, *The Spartacist Rising of 1919* (Milwaukee: Marquette University Press, 1958); Ruth Fischer, *Stalin and German Communism* (Cambridge: Harvard University Press, 1948); Ossip K. Flechtheim, *Die KPD in der Weimarer Republik* (Frankfurt: Europäische Verlagsanstalt, 1966); David Schoenbaum, *Hitler's Social Revolution* (New York: Doubleday, 1966); Isidor Wallimann and Michael Dobkowski, eds., *Genocide and the Modern Age: Etiology and Case Studies of Mass Death* (Westport CT.: Greenwood Press, 1987); Istvan Deak, *Weimar Germany's Left-Wing Intellectuals* (Berkeley: University of California Press, 1968); Tim Mason, "National Socialism and the Working Class, 1925–May 1933," *New German Critique* 11 (Spring 1977): 49–93; and Mason, "The Workers' Opposition in Nazi Germany," *History Workshop Journal* 11 (Spring 1981), pp. 120–37.

For a discussion of the political influence and fate of Jews, Catholics, and women in the Weimar Republic, see S. Adler-Rudel and Leo Baeck, *Ostjuden in Deutschland 1880–1940* (Tubingen: Mohr, 1959); Steven Aschheim, *Brothers and Strangers: The East European Jew in German and German Jewish Consciousness* (Madison: University of Wisconsin Press, 1982); Renate Bridenthal and Claudia Koonz, eds., *Becoming Visible: Women in European History* (Boston: Houghton Mifflin, 1977); Richard Evans, *The Feminist Movement in Germany, 1894–1933* (London: Sage Publications, 1976); Max Horkheimer and Theodor W. Adorno, *Dialectic of Enlightenment* (New York: Herder and Herder, 1972); Marion Kaplan, *The Jewish Feminist Movement in Germany* (Westport, CT: Greenwood Press, 1979); Richard S. Levy, *The Downfall of the Anti-Semitic Political Parties in Imperial Germany* (New Haven: Yale University Press, 1975); Guenter Levy, *The Catholic Church and Nazi Germany* (London: Weidenfeld and Nicolson, 1964); Werner Mosse and Arnold Paucker, eds., *Deutsches Judentum in Krieg und Revolution 1916–1923* (Tübingen: Mohr, 1971); Werner Mosse, ed., *Entscheidungsjahr 1932: Zur Judenfrage in der Endphase der*

Weimarer Republik (Tubingen: Mohr, 1960); Donald Niewyle, *The Jews in Weimar Germany* (Manchester: Manchester University Press, 1980); Niewyle, *Socialist, Anti-Semite and Jew* (Baton Rouge: Louisiana State University Press, 1971); Stephen Poppel, *Zionism in Germany, 1897–1933* (Phildadelphia: Jewish Publication Society, 1977); Jill Stephenson, *The Nazi Organization of Women* (London: Croom Helm, 1980); Seymour Drescher, David Sabean, and Allan Sharlin, eds., *Political Symbolism in Modern Europe* (New Brunswick NJ: Transaction, 1982); and Claudia Koonz, *Mothers in the Fatherland* (New York: St. Martin's, 1987).

Notes on the Contributors

David Abraham is author of *The Collapse of the Weimar Republic: Political Economy and Crisis*.

Tony Barta, senior lecturer in history at La Trobe University in Australia, is working on a study of social and political history of Dachau.

Jane Caplan is assistant professor of history at Bryn Mawr College. She has published several articles and chapters on the Weimar and Nazi periods.

Michael N. Dobkowski, professor of religious studies at Hobart and William Smith Colleges, is co-editor, with Isidor Wallimann, of *Towards the Holocaust: The Social and Economic Collapse of the Weimar Republic* and *Genocide and the Modern Age: Etiology and Case Studies of Mass Death*.

Geoff Eley, associate professor history at the University of Michigan, has published widely in the field of nineteenth and twentieth-century German history. His books include *From Unification to Nazism: Reinterpreting the German Past* and *The Peculiarities of German History*.

Ben Fowkes, senior lecturer in history at the Polytechnic of North London, is author of *Communism in Germany Under the Weimar Republic*, a study of the German Communist party.

Kurt Gossweiler is a member emeritus of the Academy of Sciences in

Berlin. He has published four books on the Nazi period including *Aufsätze zum Faschismus*.

Reinhard Kühnl is professor of political science at Phillipps-University in Marburg, West Germany. He is the author of several books on German Fascism and the Weimar period including *Die Weimarer Republik*.

Derek S. Linton is assistant professor of history at Hobart and William Smith Colleges. He has published articles on Wilhelmine Germany.

John D. Nagle is professor of political science and director of foreign and comparative studies of the Maxwell School at Syracuse University. He is the author of, among other books, *System and Succession: The Social Bases of Political Elite Recruitment*.

Kurt Pätzold is professor of German history at Humboldt University in Berlin. He is the author of a number of studies on German fascism.

Brian Peterson is a professor of history at Florida International University. He has published a number of articles on the working-class movement and organizations in Germany.

Gunter W. Remmling, who did undergraduate and graduate degrees in Berlin, is professor of sociology at Syracuse University. His books include *Road to Suspicion, Basic Sociology,* and *Towards the Sociology of Knowledge*.

Isidor Wallimann, lecturer in sociology at the School of Social Work in Basel, and at the Institute of Sociology, University of Bern, Switzerland, is co-editor, with Michael Dobkowski, of *Towards the Holocaust: The Social and Economic Collapse of the Weimar Republic* and *Genocide and the Modern Age: Etiology and Case Studies of Mass Death*. He is the author of *Estrangement: Marx's Conception of Human Nature and the Division of Labor*.

Index

Abraham, David, 12, 88, 89, 204
Adler, Max, 255
Adorno, Theodor W., 16
Agricultural policies: in Nazi Germany, 176; in Weimar Germany, 174, 175–76
Agricultural workers, 175, 176, 178
Agriculture, 31–32, 35, 48, 57; and industry, 31–32, 35, 54, 56
Anti-Fascist Action Committee (AFA), 297–99, 301, 307–9, 312
Anti-semitism, 13, 85, 176, 215, 222–23, 242; and nationalism, 240, 241–42; and Nazis, 183, 202, 270
Anticlericalism, 180–81
Anticommunism, 158–59, 160, 221–25, 241, 244, 268, 271, 273, 274–75, 277, 278–79
Antidemocratic movements, 71, 72, 77, 92, 196–97, 200, 202–3
Antifascism, 236, 242–43, 244, 245, 267–68, 274, 277, 298; and communism, 15, 103–4, 289–90; in Federal Germany, 16, 297–301, 304–6, 308–9, 311–13
Arbeitsgemeinschaft, 48, 153, 155, 166
Aristocracy, 32, 172, 179, 180, 183, 185
Armed forces, 107, 108, 117, 121, 257–58, 268
Arrow Cross, 83, 85
Althusser, Louis, 128
Aufhauser, Siegfried, 253
Auschwitz, 219–20, 279, 283

Austria, 89, 91
Authoritarianism, 71, 72, 87, 89
Autonomy: of fascist state, 108, 116, 132, 134, 141–42, 144; in Weimar Republic, 22, 24–25, 113

Baglieri, Joseph, 91
Bauer, Otto, 104–5, 108, 119–23
Bavaria, 174, 179–84, 187, 292, 294, 300, 304–5, 307
Bavarian Communist Party, 306
Bavarian Peasant Association (BBB), 180
Bavarian People's Party (BVP), 158, 180–82, 225–26, 243, 297, 304–5
Bavarian Volksbund, 304–5, 307
Bebel, August, 217
Beerhall Putsch, 175, 182
Bismarck, Otto von, 154
Blucher Association, 184
Bolshevists, 89, 278–79
Bonapartism, 45, 123, 131; and fascism, 105, 109–10, 116–17, 119; and rise of Hitler, 104, 105, 117–18, 123; and rise of Louis Napoleon, 105–8, 111
Borchardt, Knut, 27, 29
Bormann, Martin, 137
Bourgeois democracy, 75; and fascism, 103, 111, 115, 120; in 19th c. France, 105–8, 111; in Weimar Germany, 36, 38, 50, 51–52, 54, 112, 113, 115–16, 155, 158, 160, 162, 247–48, 249, 253, 261, 302

327